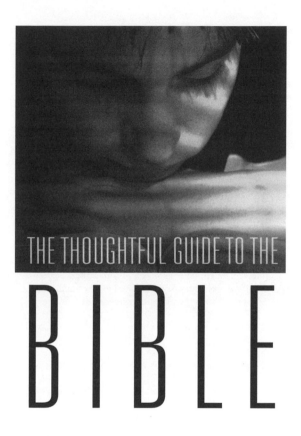

THE THOUGHTFUL GUIDE TO THE

BIBLE

ROY ROBINSON

BOOKS

Copyright © 2004 O Books
46A West Street, Alresford, Hants SO24 9AU, U.K.
Tel: +44 (0) 1962 736880 Fax: +44 (0) 1962 736881
E-mail: office@johnhunt-publishing.com
www.johnhunt-publishing.com
www.O-books.net

U.S. office:
240 West 35th Street, Suite 500
New York, NY10001
E-mail: obooks@aol.com

Text: Roy Robinson © 2004

Text set in Minion by Andrew Milne Design
Cover design: Krave Ltd

ISBN 1 903816 75 0

A CIP catalogue record for this book is available from the British Library.

Printed in USA by Maple-Vail Book Manufacturing Group

Bible quotations are given from the New Revised Standard Version of the Bible
unless otherwise indicated.

Bible versions are indicated by the following abbreviations:

RSV: Revised Standard Version
NRSV: New Revised Standard Version
KJV: King James Version (otherwise known as the AV, Authorized Version)
GNB: Good News Bible (also known as TEV, Today's English Version)
JB: Jerusalem Bible
NJB: New Jerusalem Bible
JBP: J B Phillips' Version
NIV: New International Version
RV: Revised Version

Dedication

I dedicate this book
to those two congregations
in which I have been privileged
to be both member and minister:

Oxted United Reformed Church
in Surrey,
&
Emmanuel Church, Bungay,
(United Reformed and Methodist)
in Suffolk,
both in the United Kingdom

and
In Loving Memory
of my Parents,
Thomas David and
Mary Rebecca
Robinson,
who loved the Bible
and welcomed every insight
into its message.

CONTENTS

Preface   5

APPROACHES TO THE BIBLE

Chapter 1   Two Images of the Holy Bible: A Traditional Approach   8
Chapter 2   Two Images of the Bible: An Inductive Approach   23

THE MAKING OF THE BIBLE

Chapter 3   Of Scribes, Scripts and Scrolls   32
Chapter 4   On Textual Criticism   42
Chapter 5   The Old Testament: History of the Jewish People   58
Chapter 6   The Old Testament: the Torah   73
Chapter 7   The Old Testament: the Prophets of Israel   87
Chapter 8   New Testament "Archaeology"   99
Chapter 9   The Life and Letters of Paul   113
Chapter 10   The Synoptic Gospels   128
Chapter 11   A thumbnail Sketch of the Gospels   142
Chapter 12   Apocrypha Old and New   168

THE INTERPRETATION OF THE BIBLE

Chapter 13   Biblical Interpretation I   176
Chapter 14   Biblical Interpretation II   188
Chapter 15   Many Genres, Many Meanings   203
Chapter 16   A Critique of Fundamentalism   222
Chapter 17   Biblical Criticism: Attack and Defense   242

THE ENGLISH BIBLE

Chapter 18   The Story of the English Bible   258

THE AUTHORITY OF THE BIBLE

Chapter 19   The Bible as Word of God   276
Chapter 20   Protestantism: Bible, Tradition and the Spirit   301
Chapter 21   Authority in Practice: a Case Study of Two Churches 314

POSTSCRIPT

Chapter 22   The Horizons of Our Vision   340

Appendix/Acknowledgements/Biblography   353

PREFACE

This book began life as an evening course offered at the Oxted Christian Center in the mid 1980s, with an ecumenical audience, entitled "Reading the Bible with New Eyes." It was intended, as this book is intended, for those thoughtful people, committed Christians of many professional skills, who sit in our church pews and who have never been helped to know how to read the Bible with understanding. They are aware of how, in every field of human endeavor, whether in astrophysics or in molecular biology, revolutions of knowledge have taken place that affect almost every aspect of our daily living. But they are not so aware of the revolution in our understanding of the Bible, which has been achieved over the last 200 years. This revolution enables us to read the Bible with "new eyes."

I would hope that the book might be particularly helpful to those Christians training to be lay preachers or auxiliary ministers, even perhaps for those considering reading theology at university or training for the ministry. It is intended also for those many splendid people outside of our churches, some of whom have said wistfully to me: "I would like to read the Bible but hardly know where to begin." I hope that this book might bring enlightenment and pleasure to them.

It is not intended as a guidebook to the whole Bible. There are many excellent handbooks that cover that need. Whilst it contains a great deal of hopefully accurate information, its method is to engage the reader to do his or her own thinking and come to his or her own conclusions. My own recollection of studying theology 50 years ago (an occupation that has never ceased) is that whilst many books conveyed the results of excellent scholarship, few dealt with method or obliged me, as a student, to do my own research and so come to my own conclusions. This book therefore contains some element of DIY and the more the reader can engage with this the more he or she will profit from it.

Hopefully the reader will benefit from the fact that, during most of my life, I have been a teacher: in a small theological college in Africa, in secondary schools and in churches in the United Kingdom. In the first four chapters especially, I found it difficult to switch from dialog with my audience to the written form of the book.

I recall visiting York Minster many years ago. I had entered the Chapter House and was wandering about vaguely, when one of the official guides approached me offering her services. Initially I resented this intrusion, but she was persistent. She pointed me towards a tiny statuette – at first I couldn't see it – she said "Stoop to your left, now look upwards" and there it was. I had to admit that without her guidance I wouldn't have seen it or half of the treasures in that wonderful building. My aim in this book is to point the reader where to look in the pages of the Bible and to see what he or she had previously missed.

Roy Robinson, 2004

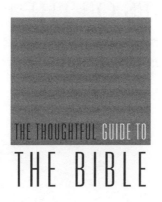

THE THOUGHTFUL GUIDE TO

THE BIBLE

APPROACHES TO
THE BIBLE

CHAPTER 1:
TWO IMAGES OF THE BIBLE

I: The Holy Bible: a traditional approach

Oh, No, it has to be a Holy Bible

Please take a good look at this cartoon by Taffy Davies.[1] Here is a woman wanting to buy a Bible. Let's call her Aunt Sally. If she is confused, why do you think this is? Did you have any similar problem when you last bought a Bible? For Aunt Sally, none of these new version Bibles looks right. She's not interested in Revised or New or Standard or International or Good News as titles for the Bible. She has a particular image in mind of what a real Bible should be like. She wants a Holy Bible.

When Aunt Sally asks for a "Holy Bible," what do you think she has in mind? You might begin by asking what the words "Holy Bible" mean to you? Depending on your age, you might come up with a description of what the first Bible ever given you by your parents or Sunday school teacher looked like. Just recall its cover, the blackness of it, the crinkly surface, the gold lettering, the feel and the smell of it. Whilst, 50 years ago, you would have taken for granted that that's what a Bible looks like, how do you feel now about its traditional image? What does its appearance suggest as to what sort of book it is? Does this attract or repel? Does its appearance give any kind of indication as to what its content might be like? You might then compare it with the appearance of some of the newer versions. How do you feel about them?

---

[1] Cartoon by Taffy Davies, from *THE BIBLE: the Story of the Book*, p 23, by Terence Copley, published by the Bible Society, 1990 © Terence Copley

What does the word "Holy" in the title imply? To most people it indicates "different," i.e. a book different from the kind of books we might take out from the public library. It means "special," "to do with or belonging to God." What kind of image of God or of the Christian religion does the traditional format suggest? We might also ponder what Aunt Sally finds attractive in this image. Does her attitude have anything to do with her age? The fact is that more Bibles bearing the title "Holy Bible" are sold in US and British bookshops than all those having other titles put together. This surely tells us much about the general public's perception of the Bible in particular and of religion in general.

THE

HOLY BIBLE

CONTAINING THE

OLD AND NEW TESTAMENTS

TRANSLATED OUT OF THE ORIGINAL TONGUES
AND WITH THE FORMER TRANSLATIONS
DILIGENTLY COMPARED AND REVISED BY
HIS MAJESTY'S SPECIAL COMMAND

AUTHORIZED KING JAMES VERSION

Appointed to be read in churches

CUM PRIVILEGIO

OXFORD

PRINTED AT THE UNIVERSITY PRESS

OXFORD UNIVERSITY PRESS

LONDON   NEW YORK   TORONTO

New Emerald Refs.

BOOK OF MOSES, CALLED

ENESIS

Now let's open this Holy Bible. Let me lodge a disclaimer. I have no intention of disparaging the Authorized Version (which our typical Holy Bible will most likely be), the version used and loved by our forbears over the past three and a half centuries and which has nourished the spiritual life of millions. I am simply concerned here with the problem of image and of that in today's world. What do you make of the title page and its references to "His Majesty's special command," to the fact that it is "appointed to be read in churches" and that it has been printed "cum privilegio?" What reactions do you feel to these ponderous phrases?

Let me respond to these questions. They remind us that the King James Bible was the product of a particular political as much as religious situation (with which I will deal more fully in Chapter 18 on the English Bible). King James I, recently come to the English throne (he was already James VI of Scotland), wanted to stem the tide of reforming fervor in the land but without alienating the Puritans. His decision to command a fresh translation of the English Bible was a sop to the latter, yet one designed to counter what he perceived as the pernicious influence of the Geneva Bible. He detested this not so much for its translation but for the anti-monarchical sentiments expressed in its marginal notes. His version, published in 1611, has been commonly known as the Authorized Version, but this is a misnomer. Authorization would have required an Act of Parliament, which it never received. The King James Version is therefore a more accurate title. It was "appointed to be read" in all Parish Churches by royal decree (and other versions thereafter suppressed). And, as a matter of tight State control, it could be printed only by the King's printer, Robert Barker, which is indicated by the "cum privilegio" (meaning that he alone had the privilege of printing it).

Let's dip into the first book, Genesis. The title is, "The First Book of Moses, called Genesis." What does the reference to Moses imply? That he wrote it or that it is about him? And what does the word "Genesis" mean? I will answer such questions further on. Now let's look at the text. What are your immediate impressions? In what way is this book set out differently from the books you took out from the library last week? Small print, double columns, each verse numbered and starting new line; all these factors convey the impression that this is unlike any modern book. What does this suggest? That it is or isn't a book to be read continuously as, for example, we would read a novel? Of course, older people brought up within the life of the Christian Church will have no difficulty with this image of the Bible, but can we put ourselves into the shoes of the people who weren't brought up with the Bible and don't normally attend church? Is this a book, thus presented, that they would be able to read with any understanding? The evidence is that many of them want to be able to read the Bible and are looking for help to be able to do so.

•••

BC and AD: it's more PC (politically correct) in these days to divide time between BCE (Before the Common Era) and CE (the Common Era). We can understand that it would be uncomfortable for an orthodox Jew or a Muslim to refer to "Before Christ" and "In the Year of our Lord" as "Anno Domini" means. But since this book will likely be read mainly by people of Christian culture, it seems preferable to stick with the familiar terminology of BC and AD. In any case, the Common Era also begins from the Birth of Christ.

•••

Assumptions we make

The Holy Bible, as traditionally understood and presented, carries with it a whole baggage of assumptions. Taken for granted for many centuries, many of these, on examination, are shown to be questionable if not quite erroneous. It is ironic that those most attached to a traditional understanding of the Bible are usually the least aware of how far the Bible in our hands today has been shaped and framed by a thousand and one stages of editing that were not present when its constituent books first saw the light of day. It was this process of editing that creates many of the problems that modern readers confront, because it was responsible for so many of the assumptions that obscure rather than illuminate.

Let us test ourselves on the assumptions we make about the Bible. You might like to answer these questions (with apologies for those that will insult your intelligence):

---

1. *Do you assume that the Bible is a book rather than a collection of separate books now bound together in one volume?*
2. *Do you assume that the titles of the various books within the Bible are original to them?*
3. *Do you assume that the titles which contain names indicate reliably who wrote those books?*
4. *Do you assume that the Bible was always divided into the chapter and verse divisions that are given in our modern versions?*
5. *Do you assume that the Bible was originally written in English?*
6. *Do you assume that the books of the Bible are arranged in the chronological order of their writing or in that of the history they recount?*
7. *Do you assume that the Bible was meant to be read straight through as we would read a novel?*
8. *Do you assume that the Old and New Testaments were always bound together as one book?*

9. *Do you assume that God is the true Author of the Bible, who used human writers as scribes to write at His dictation?*
10. *Do you assume that the Bible therefore conveys one true doctrine, one infallible message, one trustworthy viewpoint on every matter, because it is the utterance of God's Spirit?*

May I suggest that you note your answers to these questions, put them aside and then come back to them at the end of this chapter (and perhaps yet again at the end of the book). You might then like to compare whether, during the course of reading it, you have changed your mind on any of them.

Assumptions that become dubious

Let's look at them briefly, in the light of the scholarly work that has been taking place over the last 200 years.

1. Do you assume that the Bible is a book rather than a collection of separate books now bound together in one volume?

Many a modern reader surely scans the contents page of a Bible and sees the separate headings as akin to chapter headings rather than as constituting separate books. But no Christian could ever have thought of it as A Book until the fourth century AD at the earliest, because it had never existed as such until that time. The Jews, including Jesus and all the first generation of Christians, only knew the Bible as a collection of separate scrolls housed in the Ark[2] within the synagogue. The first Christian writings were also on scrolls of papyrus or parchment, but as time went by, and churches were making collections of, say, all the letters of Paul, or of all four gospels, the scroll became increasingly unwieldy, so they came up with a new form, that of the Codex. It was possibly a Christian invention. In time, probably early fourth century, the entire Bible, Old and New Testaments, could be produced between the covers of a Codex[3]. For the first time, the books could look like A Book. But, in the Greek language, even that was called TA BIBLIA, The Books, and never TO BIBLION, The Book.

---

[2] The Ark in every Jewish synagogue is a special cupboard containing the holy scrolls of Scripture.
[3] Codex: this was the earliest form of book in distinction from the scroll. There is further explanation in Chapter 3.

2. Do you assume that the titles of the various books within the Bible are original to them?

Hebrew books didn't have any titles at all. They were referred to simply by the first words of their text. Thus the Hebrew text of the first book of the Bible starts, "Bereshith," meaning, "In the Beginning," of which the title known to us, Genesis, is the Greek translation. All of the book titles known to us stem from the Greek translation known as the Septuagint (the Version of the Seventy), undertaken in about the third century BC. Some translate the first word or words of the Hebrew, as with Genesis; but others rather summarize the content of the book. The second book is, in Hebrew, "Shemoth," Names, but the Greek title is "Exodus," meaning "The Way Out," which effectively summarizes the story of how Israel was led out of Egypt by Moses. The fifth book, Debarim, meaning Words or Things, became in the Greek version, "Deuteronomy," The Second Law, since it tells of Moses re-presentation of God's Law for the Israelites as they were about to enter the Promised Land.

The titles of the New Testament books were not on the original manuscripts (so we believe) but were supplied for them early in the second century AD. They are therefore part of the editorial process, part of early Church tradition.

3. Do you assume that the titles which contain names indicate reliably who wrote those books?

Starting with Genesis, we usually assume the full title "The First Book of Moses called Genesis" to mean that Moses was its author and that he wrote all the five books attributed to him. That was the traditional view of the Jewish people. Jesus himself, referring to the books of the Pentateuch (as the five scrolls came to be called), regularly referred to them with some such expression as *"as Moses said ... "* Of course, this may have been simply the most commonly used designation rather than an endorsement of their authorship.

But the attribution was not original to these books. The Hebrew Bible doesn't contain it. Within the Pentateuch, there are references to Moses writing down the laws given him by God at Sinai, but never, within the text, is there any claim to the effect that he wrote the entirety of the Five Scrolls. That is traditional belief. And that is largely the case throughout most of the Bible. Most of the writings that comprise it were anonymous or written by those whose names have long since been lost. For example, we can rightly assume that the books of the prophets contain the messages they declared on behalf of God, but they didn't write them down. In the case of Jeremiah, we know who did: his faithful disciple and scribe Baruch.

But for the great majority, we can have no idea who recorded their teachings.

When we come to Paul, we can have no doubt, for his signature as author is writ large, not on title pages, but within the letters he wrote. But even in his case, mistakes were made. The King James Version lists Hebrews as written by Paul. That is certainly mistaken. Read it for yourself and you will realize it cannot have been written by the same man as wrote all the other letters attributed to him. The gospels are a different matter. They are anonymous, although there are a few clues within the text. Luke's individuality, both in gospel and Acts, can be glimpsed through his opening addresses to Theophilus. Matthew's description of the scribe who brings out treasures new and old provides a sort of identikit picture of Matthew as possibly a converted scribe. And what we call John's Gospel has mysterious hints about the role in its composition of "the beloved disciple." But none provide names. So the gospel titles, naming names, are not an original part of their text. They were provided by the Church of the second century. They were part of the Church's tradition.

---

4. Do you assume that the Bible was always divided into the chapter and verse divisions that are given in our modern versions?

There were various ways of indicating divisions of the text in the Hebrew Bible and in the Greek translations of it, but none of these correspond with those we have in our modern Bibles. They were never standardized, so that it wouldn't have been possible to refer from one version of the Bible to another. The modern chapter divisions for the entire Bible are usually attributed to Stephen Langton whilst a lecturer in Paris (he later became Archbishop of Canterbury) and to Hugo of St Cher in the 13th century; and these are now standard in all versions. But many of their chapter divisions are distinctly unhelpful. The book of Genesis begins with a poetic account of creation which clearly ends in the middle of the fourth verse of chapter two. How much more helpful it would have been had that marked the end of chapter one. And in Mark's Gospel, what we read as the first verse of chapter nine clearly concludes all that Jesus said to his disciples at Caesarea Philippi. It would have been considerably clearer had that verse been assigned to chapter eight.

Verse divisions, to facilitate easy cross-referencing didn't appear until the 16th century AD. These were first printed in Robert Etienne's (Stephanus) Greek New Testament of 1551. An apocryphal account had it that his father marked in the verse divisions whilst riding horseback between Paris and Lyons, jotting in a verse division for every jolt of the ride. This could account for the oddity of some of these divisions! Whilst facilitating exact references, the verse divisions have had an unfortunate consequence. They have encouraged the notion that each verse is meaningful regardless of its context, as if it had a life of its own (thereby encouraging a literalism of the text).

---

5. Do you assume that the Bible was originally written in English?

The question may appear absurd, but some people speak as if it were the case, even though the lady's defense of the Authorized Version on the grounds that "what was good enough for St Paul is good enough for me" is hardly credible. The books of the Old Testament were written in Hebrew, with a few sections of some late writings in Aramaic (of which Hebrew was a localized dialect). From the fifth century BC onwards, when the Jews had become part of the Persian Empire, they increasingly spoke Aramaic as the most widely used lingua franca, such that Hebrew became confined largely to the synagogues.
Jesus himself spoke Aramaic and a few Aramaic expressions surface in the New Testament. But the manuscripts that contain these expressions were all written in Greek, at a time when the epicenter of the new Christian faith had moved out of Palestine into the wider Graeco-Roman world. By means of the Greek language, the Gospel could be disseminated throughout the then civilized world.

These facts make the matter of translation of crucial importance. It is bizarre that some Christian groups have so exalted the Authorized Version of 1611 as if that were THE inspired Word of God, as if the English text (and that of the early 17th century) were the original text of the Bible. No translation is perfect. We always need to check any translation against the Hebrew or Greek text that lies behind it. The advantage of our modern translations is that they are based on knowledge of the texts, languages and culture of the ancient world far surpassing that of all previous generations.

---

6. Do you assume that the books of the Bible are arranged in the chronological order of their writing or in that of the history they recount?

Neither of these are correct assumptions. In the ancient world, books were arranged in libraries on principles quite different from those we adopt. A set of books of similar genre were usually arranged in order of their length, i.e. from the longest to the shortest. In the Old Testament, the books of the Prophets are so ordered, from Isaiah, the longest, down to Malachi, the shortest. This has nothing to do with the chronology of their origins and considerably obscures a proper historical understanding of the prophets.

The same is the case with the Letters of Paul. They too are arranged from longest to shortest without regard to the chronology of their writing. It would be unfortunate for a reader, wanting to get to grips with the mind of the apostle, to start with the Letter to the Romans, for it is Paul's "theological blockbuster." Far better to start with the minuscule Letter to Philemon to get a glimpse of Paul in miniature, then perhaps to look at 1 Corinthians and to come last of all to Romans. A consequence of the traditional ordering is to obscure important features of the apostle's message. For example, in the earliest letter, 1 Thessalonians, the imminent expectation of Jesus' return in glory is the dominant theme. Whilst Paul never abandoned the belief, it is evident from the letters studied in chronological order that the expectation faded and ceased to be quite so prominent in his teaching. It is therefore somewhat disquieting that almost all modern translations still retain the ancient ordering of the books. There have been some re-ordered Bibles published, but they have never succeeded in supplanting the traditional ordering.

Some of the most significant advances in biblical scholarship came about when scholars, having abandoned the traditional dating of books, suggested quite other explanations of their origins. For instance, Wellhausen's Four Documentary Hypothesis came about as a result of him realizing that Old Testament history made much better sense on the supposition that the Law of Moses had been largely written *later than* the time of the Kings and the Prophets rather than as, in the traditional account, *before* them. This will be explained in Chapter 6.

---

7. Do you assume that the Bible was meant to be read straight through as we would read a novel?

Many a reader naturally assumes that the Bible is to be read in continuous sequence, as one would any other book of history or work of literature. It is true that there is a story-line, but it is frequently obscured, like a river that disappears underground. For example, the story of Moses leading the Hebrew slaves out of Egypt is clear enough until Exodus chapter 19, but thereafter it disappears, only emerging again at Numbers chapter 11. Obstructing (for so it seems) its flow are considerable bodies of legal material, commandments, rules and regulations devised over many centuries, but because all was ascribed to Moses, inserted in the story at that point.

So we have to sympathize with those who laudably set out to read the Bible from cover to cover, but who give up half way through the laws pertaining to sacrifices in Leviticus or get lost in the Wilderness with the Children of Israel. It would be helpful for readers to realize that the Bible contains a wide variety of types of literature, each appropriate in particular circumstances. If you were a priest about to do your turn of duty in the Temple, you would need to consult Leviticus to make sure that you offered the sacrifices in the correct manner. But if you were a simple worshiper going up to the Temple at Passover, you would rather turn to those Psalms termed "Songs of Ascent." These were the songs you would sing approaching the Temple gates. And at Passover, you would certainly be reminded of the whole story of the first Passover, recorded within the Book of Exodus. If you were a peasant, seeking to establish your rights to land threatened by a rapacious landlord, you might consult those seemingly interminable genealogies to be found at various points in order to demonstrate that you were a true Israelite entitled to your bit of the land parceled out by Joshua when your ancestors entered Canaan. The main point is to realize that the Bible is a library. When you become aware of its wide variety of literature, you know to which section to turn, just as you know your way about the shelves of your local library.

---

8. Do you assume that the Old and New Testaments were always bound together as one book?

They were not. The Jewish Bible to this day comprises only what Christians call "the Old Testament." To the Jewish peoples, their covenant relationship with God is not old but still the basis of their way of life. Only Christians regard Jesus as having brought a new revelation of God, thereby establishing a new covenant between God and all those who come to Christ. This newness of Christian faith rendered "old" what had gone before it. But it didn't thereby render it totally invalid, as if obsolescent. The Christian Bible comprises Old and New Testaments, to which the Roman Catholic and Orthodox Churches add a further collection of books termed the Apocrypha.

The relative authority of each of the Old and New Testaments and the Apocrypha remains a matter of some confusion. It was already in the earliest days of the Church, issuing in a number of fierce debates. Were Christians to be bound by the whole Law of Moses? Were male converts to be circumcised? Since Christians abandoned the entire system of animal sacrifices (even though commanded by God), are they still bound by the moral regulations of the Old Testament? Such matters are still disputed. One thing is clear: that for Christians, Jesus' example and teaching has to be the yardstick by which we determine what is right for Christians.

---

9. Do you assume that God is the true Author of the Bible, who used human writers merely as scribes who wrote at His dictation?

This has been the traditional assumption and is still asserted today. In a recent Roman Catholic publication of considerable importance, *The Interpretation of the Bible in the Church*, the preface written by Cardinal Ratzinger refers to God as "the genuine Author." In the sense that God is the source of everything that exists, this is understandable. But if directly applied to the Bible, it poses more difficulties than it solves. The consequences of assuming God to be the author are dire:

❖ One, we should have to hold Him responsible for the errors, contradictions, discrepancies and repetitions that are undoubtedly present in the pages of the Bible, let alone some of the morally repugnant behavior which the biblical authors assumed were approved or sanctioned by Him. If we attribute these rather to human authors, then God's perfection is not compromised.

❖ Two, if God is held to be the Author, then we can hardly make any rational criticism of what He has written. There was a long period within Old Testament history when God's holiness was conceived of as fearfully dangerous. To approach Him too closely, or any object partaking of His holiness, was to be struck dumb or dead. Thus was Uzzah struck dead because of his accidentally touching the Ark (2 Samuel 6.6-7). For all too long, people regarded the Bible with a similar superstitious awe. To question any part of it was to invite the wrath of God.

❖ Three, God's authorship precludes a proper appreciation of the very human qualities which the authors of the various books brought to the task.

❖ Four, the supposed authorship of God is dubiously claimed even with the pages of the Bible. At several points within the Books of Exodus and Deuteronomy it is stated that God wrote the Ten Commandments on the two tablets of stone (e.g. Exodus 34.1 & 34.28). This is not easily reconciled with the assertion that these were written down, at God's command, by Moses (Exodus 24.4 & 34.27). Was that not most likely a hyperbolic way of asserting that the core of the Torah was given by God? Apart from some references in the Psalms to passages having been written under the direct influence of the Holy Spirit, there is very little claim made or impression given throughout the length and breadth of the Bible that affirms divine authorship. Once that assumption is questioned, then the human authorship becomes the more apparent (as will be demonstrated throughout this book), i.e. by writers who understood themselves to be in the service of God and who were open to His Spirit but who nevertheless remained human and thereby fallible.

---

10. Do you assume that the Bible therefore conveys one true doctrine, one infallible message, one trustworthy viewpoint on every matter, because it is the utterance of God's Spirit?

Traditionally, most Christians have believed this. For which reason, all churches have spoken of the Bible as "The Word of God." In my Chapter 19 I will examine what this expression means. It cannot imply that every word within its pages is reported as a transcript of what God has said. Take almost any single episode and we will recognize that we are hearing many voices. For example, within the story of Adam and Eve in the Garden of Eden, don't we hear the voices of the narrator of the story, of Adam, of Eve, of the serpent and of God? It would be absurd to suppose that every word uttered was God's word, as if God were playing the ventriloquist.

It is better to regard the Bible as the transcript of a dialog between God and a human cast of thousands. These latter convey all the ignorance, confusion and wickedness, but also the passion, faith and courage that characterize human behavior, but within the mayhem we can discern the voice of God. Even the Word of God is not expressed in one monolithic fashion. The most obvious example is that it required not one but four Gospels to convey the fullness of Jesus' life-story. Within them, there are some discrepancies, even contradictions, but overall they provide a convincing picture of Jesus as the incarnate Son of God. Within the early Church, there was fierce debate on several issues, such as the inclusion of the Gentiles in the Church. The people of the Bible were not unlike us. They didn't all see eye to eye. So, within its pages, we hear both sides (or more) of many debates in which Jews and Christians were trying to discern the Will of God. So, to this day, the solution to many a contentious subject cannot be resolved by the mere quotation of particular verses of the Bible. The Word of God for our day sometimes feels more like a precious metal that has to be mined at some depth below the surface, requiring much effort and persistence as we grapple with the Bible's message.

These 10 questions and tentative answers will be more fully pursued as we proceed further into this book. If you are from a distinctly "evangelical" background, you may have found some of them, particularly questions nine and ten, disturbing, perhaps contrary to your most cherished beliefs. May I counsel patience, and if you persist to the end of the book, you may possibly see both the questions and answers in a different light. At the end of the day, you have to make up your own mind and so provide the answers that satisfy both your intellect and your faith.

Assumptions that obscure

The trouble with assumptions is that they are mostly unexamined. We take them for granted. They lie hidden in the deep recesses of our minds. But they have the effect of blinding us, like cataracts in the eye, to the evidence that lies before us. They remain unexamined until such time as some personal or social crisis forces us to examine them. This can happen when somebody undergoes a crisis of faith. It typically happens within fundamentalist groups when somebody taught to revere every word of the Bible suddenly realizes that he or she can no longer believe what the group teaches. This happened in European society from the time of the Renaissance when an intellectual elite began questioning the dogmatic assumptions that had dominated the Middle Ages. Descartes was typical of the new spirit, when he established the principle of doubting everything that he could not verify for himself. The Reformation followed later by the Enlightenment only quickened the process. It was the spirit that led to the birth of modern science, which has revolutionized our world. It led also to a new approach to the understanding of history. Once its principles were applied to the study of the Bible, then another revolution was set in motion. Sadly, this biblical revolution is not nearly well enough known amongst Christian people.

Our image of Bible and our image of God

In all of this, I have been making the point that with the Bible as traditionally presented, especially in the kind of "Holy Bible" that most of us knew from childhood, there is a whole baggage of assumptions that, on examination, are shown to be dubious, mostly wrong. And my suspicion is that there are a considerable number of people "out there," who don't attend churches, who assume this image of the Bible to be the only one available. This would go a long way to explain why the Bible may still be the world's best-seller but is probably the least read and understood of all best sellers.

My suspicion is that, if this characterization of the Holy Bible is still prevalent, it suggests that the Bible is regarded by most as an ancient relic, to be revered in an essentially superstitious fashion, part of our history but irrelevant for today. And, if the assumption is that this is "the book of which God is the Author" as it is frequently called, I would have to ask, if that is the popular image of the Bible, then whatever is the popular image of God? Of a God who is also ancient, remote, and irrelevant, locked up in an ancient book rather than a living reality? If that's the case, then God too has an image problem and needs a new public relations consultant. I think it is the case that image of Bible and image of God go hand in hand.

There's a further consequence. If God is its author, a God who is understood as Holy in the sense of awesome and frightening, his book largely a set of rules and regulations designed to keep us in order, then the Bible is a book about which we shouldn't ask awkward questions, but rather believe and obey, because it is God's Word. I am reminded how until about two hundred years ago, nobody living in the Alps dared to climb the peaks. They were supposedly the abode of gods, spirits and demons who resented any intrusion into their spheres. It took a few mad dogs of Englishmen to demonstrate that you could climb the mountains with impunity. However dangerous they were, it wasn't because of the gods! It required a similar sort of daring, from the Enlightenment onwards, to begin asking critical questions about the Bible.

Of course, the Bible doesn't need to be like that. Most of us are long familiar with Bibles that look quite different and have quite a different feel to them. But is there any suspicion, as in that cartoon, that they are not quite the real thing? And if that is the case, is it because the most powerful images of religion that people have are those derived from the years of childhood, and in childhood, this was the kind of Bible we knew. In society at large, don't we constantly find people of middle age and upwards who haven't been to church for years and who assume it is exactly as they knew it 40 or 50 years ago. And if they have a Bible at home, isn't it as likely as not to be a King James Version?

There are Christians to whom this image (as I have presented it) is still quite acceptable. I notice with interest and some ironic amusement that, whilst most modern Christians gladly accept and use the many modern and attractively produced versions of the Bible (whilst still treasuring the incomparable English of the King James Version), the more extreme fundamentalists cling to the Authorized Version as alone the infallible Word of God (ignoring the fact that it is just one translation amongst many). They cling to this image of the Bible, to this notion of God and it has become for them an idol.

"May I show you a better way," as Paul wrote to his friends at Corinth. In the second chapter, we will attempt to outline a quite different way of approaching the Bible, so as to be able to see it as if with "new eyes."

FINDING YOUR WAY AROUND THE BIBLE

It is advisable to acquaint yourself with the table of contents in the opening pages of your Bible, so as to become familiar with all the books of Old and New Testaments. As you do so, you should note the abbreviation by which they are indicated for purposes of reference. It is mostly commonsensical. A specific passage is indicated firstly by giving the book, secondly the chapter number, thirdly the verse number. For instance, Gen.1.26 indicates the book of Genesis, the first chapter and the 26th verse. Frequently, it will be suggested that you read several verses, e.g. Dt.26.1-11 indicates that you should read verses 1 to 11 in Deuteronomy chapter 26. Occasionally we need to distinguish between two or more parts of a verse. In this case, to the verse number will be added a, b, or c. For example, the so-called second creation account is usually held to begin at Genesis 2.4b.

THE NAMES AND ORDER OF THE BOOKS OF THE BIBLE

With the abbreviations usually used for them

THE OLD TESTAMENT

Genesis	Gen.	2 Chronicles	2 Chr.	Daniel	Dan.
Exodus	Ex.	Ezra	Ezra	Hosea	Hos.
Leviticus	Lev.	Nehemiah	Neh.	Joel	Jl.
Numbers	Num.	Esther	Est.	Amos	Am.
Deuteronomy	Dt.	Job	Job	Obadiah	Ob.
Joshua	Josh.	Psalms	Ps.	Jonah	Jon.
Judges	Jg.	Proverbs	Pr.	Micah	Mic.
Ruth	Ru.	Ecclesiastes	Ec.	Nahum	Nah.
1 Samuel	1 Sam.	Song of Songs	S. of S.	Habakkuk	Hab.
2 Samuel	2 Sam.	Isaiah	Is.	Zephaniah	Zeph.
1 Kings	1 Kg.	Jeremiah	Jer.	Haggai	Hag.
2 Kings	2 Kg.	Lamentations	Lam.	Zechariah	Zech.
1 Chronicles	1 Chr.	Ezekiel	Ezek.	Malachi	Mal.

THE NEW TESTAMENT

Matthew	Mt.	Ephesians	Eph.	Hebrews	Heb.
Mark	Mk.	Philippians	Phil.	James	Jas.
Luke	Lk.	Colossians	Col.	1 Peter	1 Pet.
John	Jn.	1 Thessalonians	1 Th.	2 Peter	2 Pet.
The Acts	Acts	2 Thessalonians	2 Th.	1 John	1 Jn.
Romans	Rom.	1 Timothy	1 Tim.	2 John	2 Jn.
1 Corinthians	1 Cor.	2 Timothy	2 Tim.	3 John	3 Jn.
2 Corinthians	2 Cor.	Titus	Titus	Jude	Jude
Galatians	Gal.	Philemon	Philem.	Revelation	Rev.

CHAPTER 2:
TWO IMAGES OF THE BIBLE

II. The Bible: an inductive approach

Let's begin with another Taffy Davies cartoon.

Yipeee!! A letter from Peter – just discovered!!

What is depicted in this cartoon can encapsulate a whole new approach to the Bible, and yet, as the cartoon itself suggests, perhaps it isn't really so new. After all, for the early Christians, there were occasions of startling discovery, as for instance, when a congregation first received a copy of Mark's newly written Gospel or when Paul's latest letter arrived in Corinth or, as in the cartoon, some Christians were presented with a newly-minted letter from Peter. Some of the most amazing discoveries were made last century in Egyptian rubbish dumps! Never having seen or heard of these writings before, they must have examined and read them with "new eyes" and open minds. This, we suggest, is possible for us as we approach the Bible, once we learn to set aside some of the traditional assumptions.

The Dead Sea Scrolls

The most astonishing discovery of manuscripts last century was that of the Dead Sea Scrolls. I will recount the main outlines of the story (about which there are a number of competing accounts).

DISCOVERY
In the spring of 1947, some Arab shepherds had moved their flocks up the rocky slopes at the north-western end of the Dead Sea, where spring rains had yielded fresh vegetation. One of the goats wandered up a steep cliff-face and into a cave. A shepherd boy, Muhammad edh-Dhib (Muhammad the Wolf) hurled a stone into the cave so as to chase the goat out and was startled to hear the sound of breaking pottery. He returned the next morning with his cousin and together they climbed the cliff and entered the cave. They were surprised to see a number of sealed earthenware jars and, hopeful of treasure, broke the seals. Their disappointment must have been great to discover inside nothing but tattered documents. Pulling them out, those made of papyrus just disintegrated in their hands but some were of tougher material, parchment. So the first of the Dead Sea Scrolls were discovered.

Some months later, a Bethlehem merchant called Faidi Salahi (or possibly a man known as Kando) heard that the Bedouin were holding some scrolls. One or both of these made contact with them and they agreed to bring some of the scrolls to market. They bought some of them, themselves having no idea of their value. Kando used the mediation of George Isaiah, a member of the Syrian Orthodox Church, to take some of the scrolls to St Mark's Monastery in Jerusalem, thinking that his friends there would be interested in them, but they too were quite unable to evaluate them. Eventually, their presence came to the attention of Professor Sukenik at the Hebrew University and of John Trever, an American expert in biblical manuscripts. Trever examined them and immediately recognized them as being considerably older than any Hebrew scrolls he had ever seen. Other scholars were alerted. At that period, the situation in Palestine was tense, with the first Arab-Israeli War about to break out and the subsequent establishment of the State of Israel. Trever and Millar Burrows, his senior, persuaded the monastery authorities to fly the scrolls out to the USA for laboratory examination, most fortunately, since the monastery was badly damaged in the fighting. The war and the subsequent redrawing of boundaries meant that the site of the caves was now in the State of Jordan, making the caves difficult to access from the Israeli side.

ARCHAEOLOGICAL INVESTIGATION
Once access was possible, archaeologists led by a team from the famous Ecole Biblique of Jerusalem began systematic examination of the caves. They found

that serious damage had been done by the Arab fortune-seekers. They subsequently found other caves, containing yet more scrolls at some distance from the first finds. But chief attention was given to the remains of buildings quite close to the caves in which the first discoveries were made. The site was known as Khirbet Qumran (Khirbet meaning "Ruin"). It had been previously assumed that the remains were of a Roman fortress. The excavation revealed that it had been a religious community, a kind of monastery, before being occupied by the Romans. Moreover, it had been a community in which the copying and production of scrolls had been of prime importance. There was a room that had clearly been a scriptorium and water tanks in which, it was assumed, the members had taken daily ritual baths. They most probably belonged to a Jewish religious sect known as the Essenes (a minority of scholars deny this identification). There were also signs of severe destruction by fire, and amidst the ruins, arrow-heads distinctive of the Roman 10th legion. Now the pieces of the jigsaw could be fitted together. It was known that the 10th Legion had been stationed at Jericho during the first Jewish War that culminated in the sacking of Jerusalem in AD 70. They must have advanced on Qumran as a center of Jewish resistance in AD 68; but, even as they were coming, the community must have hidden its precious scrolls in the nearby caves. The Essenes thereafter simply disappeared from the pages of history. How extraordinary that their library remained (mostly) undiscovered for nineteen hundred years!

WHY SO IMPORTANT?

Why was this discovery so important? Prior to it, the oldest known manuscripts of the Hebrew Bible were from the 10th century AD, namely, the Ben Asher Codex in St Petersburg and the Aleppo Codex. In the caves, there were found copies or fragments of copies of every book of the Old Testament (except that of Esther), besides commentaries on the Bible, other religious writings and documents to do with the life of the community. Since most of these manuscripts have been dated to the last two centuries BC and the first half of the first century AD, we have here the Old Testament as it was known in Jesus' time, a thousand years older than our previously known evidence for it.

But, for the present, it is a quite other matter that we want to stress. Put yourself in the position of those scholars, such as Burrows, Trever and Sukenik, who first examined the scrolls. Out of this exercise I am suggesting a quite different way of approaching the Bible. You have before you some scraps of papyrus or complete parchment scrolls of which you have no previous knowledge as to their authorship, provenance or importance. You have to start asking absolutely basic questions about them. In what language is the writing? In what kind of script? How old is the document lying before you? Can you tell just from the script or from references within it? Who wrote it (if no author can be identified, what sort of background does it suggest)? For whom was it written? What is its content? What was the purpose of its writing? How does this content relate to other knowledge we possess? Now, of course, the biblical archaeologists and palaeographers[4] immediately recognized the great majority of the scrolls to be portions of the Bible, or being writings akin to the Bible; nevertheless, because of their antiquity, they had to approach them without presuppositions. All very hypothetical, you may think. But if we contrast this with the kind of stereotypical approach generally assumed with the concept of "Holy Bible," carrying its heavy load of assumptions, you will notice a remarkable difference.

Let's suppose!

Now let's make an enormous leap of the imagination. Suppose the entire Bible had disappeared soon after the completion of its writing and then was as dramatically rediscovered as were the Dead Sea Scrolls, such that we had to approach its investigation as if without any prior knowledge, setting aside the kind of assumptions people usually bring to the reading of the Bible. It is admittedly impossible not to carry with us some presuppositions as part of the mental lumber we carry in our heads. Nevertheless we may try to set these aside and ask of it those same basic questions. This is the alternative approach I am suggesting. It is the approach of modern scholarship over the past three hundred years with just about everything to do with the past. It is largely since the Enlightenment of the early 18th century that scholars, especially in Western Europe, began to ask such basic questions. They were following the example of Descartes, who determined to set aside all preconceived notions, to doubt all received wisdom and to establish for himself what to think and believe. (It is a method that could hardly be adopted by most of us in our daily life, since we have to assume that what our schoolteachers taught us was true, until such time as we discover otherwise!) It is also the method of *induction* rather than of *deduction*.

Deduction and induction[5]

By the late Middle Ages, humankind had accumulated a considerable amount of knowledge and wisdom, of which Church and University (essentially under the supervision of the Church) reckoned themselves to be the guardians. The study method was that of *deduction*. You started out from certain set principles and

---

[4] i.e. Those who study very old writings (from Greek "palaeo," ancient; and from "graphein," to write)
[5] It is the case that in everyday English we commonly use the verb "deduce" to cover the senses of both deduction and induction, often in cases where we should more properly use "induce". This can cause some confusion. But here we are using the terms as they are used in logic and in the sciences.

theories accepted as "gospel truth," the basis of which was antiquity, authority and tradition rather than evidence. You deduced from those principles what you could know and practice. The Church accepted the divine inspiration of the Bible as a given "fact" without enquiry. On all scientific matters, it had elevated the writings of the Greek philosopher Aristotle to the status of quasi-revealed truth. The trouble was that some of Aristotle's teachings were plainly wrong, for example, that the Earth was the center of the universe. Anybody who questioned such assumptions was suspected of heresy, harshly treated, even burned at the stake.

But in the 16th century, scientists such as Galileo began applying a quite different method, that of *induction*. With his improved telescope, he observed the four moons of Jupiter, showing that some objects didn't orbit the Earth but another planet. He observed that the surface of the Moon was uneven and pock-marked with craters, so induced that the heavenly bodies were not perfect spheres as had been assumed. He observed sun-spots and that they moved, proving that the Sun was itself in motion. For him, this demonstrated that Copernicus had been right, when on purely theoretical grounds, he had concluded that the Earth orbits the Sun and that everything is in movement. In Galileo's case, this was an example of the collection of data and the application of reasoning, eventually producing a new theory of the Solar System. The immediate reactions in Catholic Italy were ambivalent. "Famous philosophers (whom we would call scientists), including some of Galileo's former colleagues at Pisa, refused to look through any telescope at the purported contents of Aristotle's immutable cosmos[6]." But at the Collegio Romano in Rome, its Jesuit astronomers had already "obtained telescopes of their own and now as a group corroborated all of Galileo's observations." Whilst they could not deny the evidence of their own eyes, the Church hierarchy was not ready to accept the theoretical consequences to be induced from the data because these threatened their presuppositions, i.e. of the inerrancy of the Bible and of Aristotle's philosophy. So the Inquisition forced Galileo to recant his heresies, imprisoned him for years and made his life a misery. But Galileo was right and the Church was wrong! It took three and a half centuries for the Church to apologize and admit its mistake.

Deduction, as a method of logical thinking, begins with general principles (or assumptions) and deduces conclusions from them. It follows that, if those initial assumptions are sound, then the conclusions deduced from them are likely to be justified. But we have already learned that many of the basic assumptions that used to be made about the Bible are not sound and therefore lead to

[6] Quotations from Dava Sobel, *Galileo's Daughter*, pp 40 & 42, Fourth Estate limited, London, 1999

erroneous and sometimes harmful consequences. Induction is the logical opposite, beginning with particular facts; it then infers general principles from them. To give a simplistic illustration, we might compare the respective investigative methods of Inspector Lestrange with those of Sherlock Holmes[7]. Lestrange uses the deductive method, assuming from the start that the crime was committed by the butler in the pantry with the carving knife and then sets out to find the facts to prove it. He does so, and as a result the wrong person would have hanged, were it not for Holmes' timely intervention. Holmes on the other hand operates by induction. He makes no immediate assumptions. To him, everybody in the house is a potential suspect. He searches painstakingly for clues, assembles the evidence and from it induces the identity of the murderer. As we know, Holmes was a master of acute observation. A scuff on the elbow, mud on the boots, every minute observation built up a picture, which leads him to the arrest of the guilty party.

• •

It goes without saying that all the discoveries of modern science are based on the inductive principle; although it is also the case that at times supposedly scientifically-achieved knowledge about the universe turns out to be erroneous. But it is only by the steady accumulation of data that a fashionable theory (treated as if dogma) can be overturned, having been demonstrated to be false. A hundred years ago, Einstein assumed the universe to be static and at first refused to believe the increasing body of evidence that showed it to be expanding. But he had the humility to admit to his error and embrace the theory of the Expanding Universe.

• •

The Biblical revolution

If there was a Copernican revolution, so there was also a Biblical revolution. It was a daring leap when Biblical scholars decided that they had to approach the Bible as they would any piece of ancient literature. They had initially to set aside the assumptions that it was a book so holy, so God-inspired, that to raise critical questions about it was irreverent and dangerous. What came to be called *Higher Criticism*[8] frequently scared many devout Christians because some of the early critics used the new tools as weapons with which to attack the Church and to ridicule Christian faith. But after the initial shock, more and more devoutly

---

[7] In the detective stories of A Conan Doyle (1859-1930). Although it has to be admitted that even Holmes asks Dr Watson, "What do you deduce from these facts?" when induce would have been more correct.

[8] *Lower Criticism* concerns matters such as the text and language in which a document had been written; *Higher Criticism* applied itself to the content of the document, ie to its history and theology.

Christian scholars realized that they too had to employ the tools of literary and historical criticism. Many did so at great personal cost. William Robertson Smith (1846-94) was hounded from his chair as Professor of Old Testament at the Free Church College in Aberdeen because he was teaching a properly historical approach to the Bible. In time, such scholars were able to convince the main-stream churches that their researches were not destructive of Christian faith, but greatly illuminated it. In consequence, Christian scholarship, abandoning the traditionalist assumptions, has been enabled to build up for our benefit a far more comprehensive and convincing picture of the origins and development of the Bible and hence of Christian faith. The result is that we, who largely take the fruits of their labors for granted, can have a greater degree of assured knowledge of the historical roots of Christianity than has been available to any generation since that of the first Christians.

But, in reality, there is nothing intrinsically new about this approach, since this was the situation of the early Christian Church regarding all the written documents that came eventually to constitute the New Testament. They had adopted the Old Testament quite uncritically (the first generation of Christians themselves being Jews) as their Bible. But when new specifically Christian writings, such as the letters of the apostle Paul, began to appear, they had at first to evaluate them without any preconceptions. They didn't bear a label marked "Holy Scripture" or carry any kind of divine "imprimatur."[9] They didn't at first exude any kind of palpable authority other than that of the immediate impact of what Paul had written. It was only over the course of probably several decades that they began to be considered as of such value as to be readily copied and circulated amongst the churches, eventually being read at Sunday worship following the Old Testament readings. In course of time they themselves were treated as in some sense "scriptural," as is evident from a chance remark in 2 Peter 3. 15-16. To the early Christians, the new writings were quite as much "out of the blue," new discoveries, as were the Dead Sea Scrolls to the 20th-century archaeologists. Hence the sense of excitement encapsulated in Taffy Davies' cartoon.

Recapitulation

In these two chapters, I have been making a contrast between two images of the Bible: the first that of the Bible as Holy Book, different from all others, sanctioned by Church authority and, in previous ages, by Royal authority; and the second that of the Bible as a set of scrolls, which we are invited to investigate for ourselves with as few presuppositions as possible other than that of seeking to know the truth.

---

[9] Imprimatur: this Latin word meaning "let it be printed" is used in the Roman Catholic Church to indicate a book that has been officially approved by the Church authorities.

The first, as handed down to us, was a product of an ancient mind-set. The method being that of deduction: you began from the assumption that the Bible is God's book, penned at His dictation, such that every word of it is divinely inspired and therefore infallible. It followed that it had to be treated as if wholly different from any other book such that you shouldn't apply to it the same criteria of literary criticism as to any other book; that it was written by venerable figures such as Moses or David or John the beloved Disciple; that you must therefore treat it reverentially and not ask critical questions about it; that if you find apparent contradictions within it, then you should assume that they are apparent only, that the problem must be in your perception rather than in God's word. You read it then as literal fact, thereby assuming, for instance, that the world was created in exactly six days and that the sun literally stood still at Joshua's command, etc.

You thus totally ignore the fact that the Jewish people (who made up the great majority of Bible writers) expressed themselves in a multi-faceted fashion: such that metaphor, parable, allegory, riddle, legend and myth came to them quite as readily as historical record and narrative. They were not themselves literalists. By contrast, the literalism or positivism of our present-day fundamentalists is quite a modern, rationalistic phenomenon, alien to the world of the Bible. This is just one illustration of the way in which literalism distorts and obfuscates any true understanding of the Bible. It is a modern heresy.

Finally, a word of disclaimer. I would never want gratuitously to disturb anybody firmly wed to the old, traditionalist view of the Bible (with which most of us were brought up) provided that s/he is not aware of any contradictions or difficulties in that approach and so is quite happy with it. But if you are so aware, then I want to suggest another way, which is for me a better way. I prefer to start with the scrolls in the earthenware jars, because I recognize in them *"treasure in earthen vessels."* If we examine them, finding out who wrote them, when and why, and what is their significance, we then have to ask how and why did the Church, the Christians of from 1900 to 1600 years ago, recognize them as "sacred" and add them to the list of scripture? So, if we begin with the scrolls, we may end up, not perhaps with a tattered copy of a "Holy Bible", but with something like this, whether a GNB or an REB or an NRSV, and discover that in their new gloss covers, they may still convey God's Word to us in the 21st century as, in other garb, the "Holy Bible" did to our forbears in centuries past. For, seen from a different perspective, the library of books which is the Bible can still remain an inspiring source of authority for our Christian life and faith today. In the rest of this book, I will attempt to demonstrate how that can be.

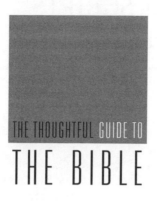

THE THOUGHTFUL GUIDE TO
THE BIBLE

THE MAKING
OF THE BIBLE

CHAPTER 3:
OF SCRIBES, SCRIPTS
AND SCROLLS

The earliest writing

Whatever else the Bible may be, it is certainly "writing." In the New Testament, the most common way of referring to what we call the Old Testament is as "hai graphai," "the writings" (meaning usually the sacred scriptures). Writing is traceable amongst the peoples of the Middle East from around 3000 BC. At first it consisted of simple pictorial figures, which gradually became stylized, most spectacularly in the "hieroglyphics" of Egypt. Since it involved engraving on stone, its uses were limited. As the name implies, it was the preserve of the priests (Greek "hieros," priest; "glyphics," a variant of "graphics" from the verb "graphein," to write). It meant then "priestly writing." In the rest of the Middle East, it was as "cuneiform," a word meaning wedge-shaped. The scribe employed a wedge-shaped stylus to prick the letters into tablets of wet clay, which were then left to dry in the sun. Whilst we can say that none of the Bible was written by either of these methods (except possibly for the two tablets of the Law written by or given to Moses on Mt Sinai), much of the ancient folklore of the Middle East, traces of which were to appear later within the Bible, certainly was.

The Epic of Gilgamesh

To give but one illustration. Henry Layard was British Consul in Iraq in the middle years of the 19th century. His real interest and passion was for archaeology. Every bit of his spare time was spent in investigating those strange mounds, called by the Arabs "tells," in the desert. They were the sites of ancient cities. In the 1840s he had the remarkable fortune to begin uncovering the great Palace of Nineveh, capital of ancient Assyria, and even more remarkably, to discover within it the library of the great King Ashurbanipal (reigned 668-627 BC). This King had collected several thousands of clay tablets written in cuneiform script and now they were rediscovered. At about the same time in Persia, a British army officer called Henry Rawlinson was learning to decipher cuneiform. Layard dispatched many of these tablets to the British Museum, others went to the Louvre in Paris. It was in the British Museum some years later that George Smith, assistant to Rawlinson, began translating the tablets, and one day, to his surprise, he found himself reading this:[10]

• •

Utnapishti spake unto him, unto Gilgamesh: "Gilgamesh, I will reveal unto thee a hidden thing and a secret of the gods will I tell thee. Shuruppak, a city that thou knowest and which now lies [in ruins on the bank] of the Euphrates, when that city was old and there were yet gods within it, the great gods decided to bring on a deluge ... But Nin-igi-ku, even Ea, sat (invisibly) with them, and repeated their words to the reed brick-bond (of the Council room), saying: 'Brick-bond, brick-bond, wall, wall! Brick-bond hearken, wall remember! (Echo this message unto Utnapishti): Lord of Shuruppak, son of Ubar-Tutu, destroy thy house and build a vessel! Abandoning riches, do thou seek out living-kind: despising possessions, preserve what has life: thus load in the vessel the seed of all creatures ...

'"When something of morning had dawned, I commanded that the land be assembled ... (For four days were gathered the parts of the vessel) – the boys fetching pitch, while the stronger brought (timber-)materials ...

So the vessel was finished. "All that I had I now loaded aboard her. All I had of silver I loaded aboard her, all I had of gold did I load aboard her; yea, of the species of all living creatures, all that I had did I load aboard her. I made enter the vessel all my family and kindred; beasts wild and domestic and all of the craftsmen I made enter the vessel ...

"Came the set time appointed: who was sending the bane, on the previous evening did pour down the rain. I gazed up at the look of the weather; it was fearful to behold, and I entered the vessel and did close down my doorway ...

"When something of morning had dawned, there arose a black cloud from the horizon. While Adad (the Storm-god) was thundering within it, there went on ahead (the gods) Shullat and Hanish, went forth (his) lieutenants across mountain and plain ... But as the Horror-(cloud) of Adad passed over the heavens, it turned aught that had light into uttermost darkness ... Swift blew the storm, it passed over the land like a battle. No man could make out his brother, nor could people be seen from the heavens. Even the gods were afeared at the deluge, took to flight and went up to the heaven of Anu, cowered they like dogs and crouched down at the outer defenses.

---

[10] Extract from the Epic of Gilgamesh reproduced in *Documents from Old Testament Times*, edited by D Winton Thomas, Harper Torchbooks, 1958. The Penguin Classics edition of the Epic is readily available and is well worth reading.

"For six days and [seven] nights the wind blew, and the flood and the storm swept the land. But the seventh day arriving did the rainstorm subside and the flood which had heaved like a woman in travail; there quieted the sea, and the storm-wind stood still, the flood stayed her flowing. I opened a vent and the fresh air moved over my cheek-bones. And I looked at the sea; there was silence, the tide-way lay flat as a roof-top but the whole of mankind had returned unto clay. I bowed low: I sat and I wept: o'er my cheek-bones my tears kept on running.

"When I looked out again in the directions, across the expanse of the sea, mountain ranges had emerged in twelve places and on Mount Nisir the vessel had grounded. Mount Nisir held the vessel fast nor allowed any movement. For a first day and a second, fast Mount Nisir held the vessel nor allowed of any movement.

"On the seventh day's arriving, I freed a dove and did release him. Forth went the dove but came back to me: there was not yet a resting-place and he came returning. Then I set free a swallow and did release him. Forth went the swallow but came back to me: there was not yet a resting-place and he came returning. So I set free a raven and did release him. Forth went the raven and he saw again the natural flowing of the waters, and he ate and he flew about and he croaked, and came not returning. So all set I free to the four winds of heaven, and I poured a libation, and scattered a food-offering, on the height of the mountain. Seven and seven did I lay the vessels, heaped into their incense-basins sweet-cane, cedarwood and myrtle. And the gods smelled the savor, the gods smelled the sweet savor, the gods gathered like flies about the priest of the offering."

••

What was George Smith reading? It is clearly the story of the Flood, in a rather more literary version than that in the Bible, one written down many centuries before the Bible version of it. We know today that versions of the story were common to all the peoples of the Middle East, each in variant forms. It is most unlikely that any of the Bible authors had read the Epic of Gilgamesh. The story was simply part of the common folklore. To the people of Victorian England, it introduced the singular (perhaps shocking) notion that the Bible was not an isolated phenomenon, but was closely related to the cultural background of the Middle East. They had assumed the biblical account of the Flood to be totally unique. Once that assumption is dropped, the Bible story becomes much more intelligible as we are able to relate it to its social, cultural, political and religious background.

An alphabetic script

A great King like Ashurbanipal could collect a library of many thousands of cuneiform clay tablets. But clay tablets were hardly a convenient material for everyday use because of their weight, nor was cuneiform a "user-friendly" form of script. The scribe had to learn more than 300 characters. A breakthrough came sometime in the middle of the second millennium BC. In southern Lebanon there gradually emerged a simpler type of cuneiform, using only 30 characters and this so-called Ugaritic Script is the basis of not only the Hebrew and Greek scripts, but even of our English alphabet. It is called "Ugaritic" script because it was the excavation of the city of Ugarit (also known as Ras Shamra) on the Mediterranean coast of Lebanon, with its great library, which first revealed it. This script was syllabic, i.e. each character indicated the sound of a syllable rather than a picture. At first recognizably still a form of cuneiform, it gradually evolved into the more familiar letters that we recognize and use today. It represented a remarkable breakthrough, without which literacy could never have become a common human capacity rather than the privileged possession of the few.[11]

For our purposes, the important point is that when the Jewish people began the writing of the Bible, it was this script that they adopted. More than that, Hebrew itself was not their original language. The ancestors of the Jews were Arameans, speaking Aramaic, as a verse in Deuteronomy 26.5 makes clear. When the Israelite went to the Temple with his harvest gift, he was to make this solemn declaration: "A wandering Aramean was my ancestor; he went down into Egypt and lived there as an alien, few in number, and there he became a great nation, mighty and populous." The "wandering Aramean" probably indicated Jacob. When his descendents settled in Canaan, they adopted the local language from which developed their particular dialect of it, Hebrew. They wrote it in the Ugaritic script, which was eventually adopted by all the newly literate peoples, including, eventually, ourselves. Thus we have …
in Hebrew: Aleph, Beth, Gimel, Daleth …
in Greek: Alpha, Beta, Gamma, Delta…
in English: A, B, C, D …

This was not the only contribution of the people of Lebanon. The city of Gebal, south of Ugarit, was a busy seaport, trading with Egypt where the papyrus reed grew in profusion along the banks of the Nile. The citizens of Gebal imported vast quantities of this papyrus from which they manufactured a high quality

---

[11] Concerning which, F F Bruce wrote: "Believers in the Providence of God may well conclude that it was by that providence that, when the Bible first began to be written, there lay to hand for the purpose a form of writing, recently invented, the understanding of which was not restricted to specially trained readers, but lay within the capacity of Everyman." *The Bible and the Parchments*, Pickering and Inglis, 4th Edition 1984.

writing material. Because of this renown it became known as "Byblos," Book Town (from the Greek, "Biblion," a book). You cannot have failed to spot the origin of our words for paper, and, of course, Bible.

Papyrus

As compared with stone plinths or clay tablets, the advantages of papyrus were enormous: cheap, easily available, providing a smooth writing surface. The down side was of course its fragility. Which largely explains why none of the original manuscripts of the Bible have survived. Humidity is the greatest enemy of papyrus. How were papyrus scrolls produced? The papyrus reed grows profusely along the river Nile. Its stem is triangular in shape and can be the thickness of a man's wrist. Cut into sections about a foot long (the section was called in Greek a "canon" and this was sometimes used as a ruler for measuring). This was then sliced lengthwise. Pieces were laid down vertically, then others placed horizontally above them. The two layers were then hammered till the sap stuck them together. Dried in the sun, the upper surface was then rubbed with a pummice-stone to produce a smooth writing surface. The scribe wrote on this with a quill pen using an ink made by mixing soot with a resinous glue. For the purpose of writing longer scripts, any number of papyrus sheets were glued together. The resultant scroll could be up to 35 feet long.

It is worth noting that, quite frequently, some disjunction in the text of the Bible can be most easily explained on the supposition that originally joined up sheets of papyrus had become unstuck and re-arranged in the wrong order. It is highly likely that the last sheet (perhaps sheets) of Mark's Gospel became detached and lost forever. It is possible that St John's account of all that occurred on the last evening of Jesus' life (the Last Supper discourse) was originally in at least two sections, for it is odd to read at the conclusion of John 14.31 the words of Jesus, "Come, let us go" since there follows three further chapters of what Jesus continued to say on that occasion. It would be readily explicable if 14.31 marked the bottom line of a sheet of papyrus that had somehow become detached from another containing chapters 15 to 17. It is possible that the various sections of the Book of Leviticus, each starting with "And the Lord said to Moses," which frequently repeat what has been written in a previous section, were originally separate sheets of papyrus, which have at the last stage of editing simply been glued together without any attempt to tidy up the consequent repetitions.

Parchment

The other much-used writing material was parchment, a more durable but more expensive material. "Parchment" derives from Pergamum, a city in Asia

Minor. A legend tells how the King of Pergamum had the ambition of building up a library to exceed that of King Ptolemy of Egypt, but, to spite him, Ptolemy ordered an embargo on papyrus exports to Pergamum. In frustration, his scribes came up with the preparation of animal skins. The skin of young calves produced the best surface, hence the term "vellum," from veal. As might be expected, the best biblical manuscripts are on parchment.

Let us now presume that the books of the Bible had been written and that we are concerned simply with the processes by which they were copied and so handed on down to us. We will concentrate largely on the books of the New Testament.

The professional work of the scribe[12]

Throughout the ancient world, writing was largely a professional task. Amongst the Jews, it was left to scribes; amongst the Gentiles, to slaves. We should imagine the majority of the population as illiterate. But even a man as highly literate as Paul normally used a scribe. So we can envisage his letters to the churches as being written by dictation. Of course, his amanuensis was always (one supposes) a fellow Christian and he usually adds his personal greeting to the recipients (see Romans 16.22). We may picture the apostle seizing the quill and adding his personal word, if for no other reason than that the letter should be seen to be genuine (and not a forgery). See I Corinthians 16.21, 2 Thessalonians 3.17, and Philemon 19.

So throughout the early centuries, we should visualize the books of the Bible being copied by professional scribes. Not always competently. Bishop Augustine of Hippo complained about incompetent scribes translating badly and copying inaccurately. There must have been many a Christian congregation too poor to employ a professional, so making its own, perhaps inferior, copies. There must have been many a faulty copy lying around. In scribal businesses, the copying was mostly done from dictation. The copyists either stood at a desk or sat on a low stool or bench, laying the scroll across their knees. First they ruled margins left and right, divided the sheet into columns about 3.5 inches wide, then filled in transverse lines. Sometimes the sheet was pin-pricked to determine where the lines were to be drawn. When it came to writing, the letters were not inscribed on the lines, but rather, hanging from them. But most interestingly from our viewpoint is that they left no spaces at all between words and even sentences. Where does one word end and the next begin, or one sentence and the next? Imagine the room for confusion for later readers. For example, supposing we

---

[12] I am entirely indebted in this section, and throughout this chapter, to B M Metzger's classic account, *The Text of the New Testament*, Clarendon Press, Oxford, 1964.

had this in English: GODISNOWHERE. How would you read it? As "God is nowhere" or as "God is now here"? Nor was there much if any punctuation, so it isn't always possible to distinguish between a statement and a question. There were sectional divisions, but these varied considerably between different manuscripts so were of no use for cross-referencing.

The writing of long scrolls was arduous and many a scribe added his personal comments at the conclusion of his work. One wrote: "Writing bows one's back, thrusts the ribs into one's stomach, and fosters a general debility of the body." Quite frequently, these words occur: "As travelers rejoice to see their home country, so also is the end of a book to those who toil in writing!" Others close with, "The end of the book; thanks be to God!"[13] It's good for us, who take the printed Bible for granted, to remember with gratitude the immense debt we owe to those who, for a thousand years and more, copied every word of it by hand!

Types of script

In the Greek world, three types of script were used: *"Cursive"* was a kind of running script used for less important documents such as personal letters, invoices, etc. We should probably imagine Paul's letters being written in this form. But for more important documents the script was *"Uncial,"* to us, Capitals. The word means literally "the 12th part of," presumably because each letter took up about a 12th of the line. It follows that the most important biblical manuscripts are uncials and they are designated by a letter of the Greek or Hebrew alphabets followed by a number. Thus, Codex Sinaiticus is א01[14] ; C Alexandrinus is A 02 ; C Vaticanus is B 03, etc. Then towards the eighth century AD, the *"Minuscule"* script was adopted. This was a cursive script, with letters joined up, about half the size of uncials, and therefore faster, less costly and easier to reproduce. Its adoption made manuscripts both cheaper and more readily available, with the result that extant minuscule scripts of Bible books outnumber uncial scripts by ten to one. But they are mostly of later date and inferior quality than the best of the uncials.

The Masoretes

The Jews were meticulous in the preservation of their scriptures, which they learned to recite by heart. This was the more necessary as a majority of Jews lived far away from their homeland and were not so conversant with Hebrew. The Hebrew script had been of consonants only and was not intended as more than an aide-memoire. There was a danger that it might be misread and

---

[13] All these examples are from Metzger, op cit, pp 17-18.
[14] א is Aleph, the first letter of the Hebrew alphabet.

misunderstood. Accordingly, in the early centuries of the Christian era, a group of scholars who became known as the Masoretes (from "masorah," Tradition) standardized the text of the Old Testament. Evidence from the Dead Sea Scrolls shows that before the time of Jesus the Old Testament text was still variable. For example, one version of the prophet Jeremiah from Qumran is a third briefer than other Jeremiah scrolls in their collection. But before the destruction of their monastery, the text had become standardized (more or less to that which

GENESIS. בְּרֵאשִׁית

1 בְּרֵאשִׁית בָּרָא אֱלֹהִים אֵת הַשָּׁמַיִם וְאֵת הָאָרֶץ׃ וְהָאָרֶץ הָיְתָה תֹהוּ וָבֹהוּ וְחֹשֶׁךְ עַל־פְּנֵי תְהוֹם וְרוּחַ אֱלֹהִים מְרַחֶפֶת עַל־פְּנֵי הַמָּיִם׃ וַיֹּאמֶר אֱלֹהִים יְהִי אוֹר וַיְהִי־אוֹר׃ וַיַּרְא אֱלֹהִים אֶת־הָאוֹר כִּי־טוֹב וַיַּבְדֵּל אֱלֹהִים בֵּין הָאוֹר וּבֵין הַחֹשֶׁךְ׃ וַיִּקְרָא אֱלֹהִים לָאוֹר יוֹם וְלַחֹשֶׁךְ קָרָא לָיְלָה וַיְהִי־עֶרֶב וַיְהִי־בֹקֶר יוֹם אֶחָד׃

וַיֹּאמֶר אֱלֹהִים יְהִי רָקִיעַ בְּתוֹךְ הַמָּיִם וִיהִי מַבְדִּיל בֵּין מַיִם לָמָיִם׃ וַיַּעַשׂ אֱלֹהִים אֶת־הָרָקִיעַ וַיַּבְדֵּל בֵּין הַמַּיִם אֲשֶׁר מִתַּחַת לָרָקִיעַ וּבֵין הַמַּיִם אֲשֶׁר מֵעַל לָרָקִיעַ וַיְהִי־כֵן׃ וַיִּקְרָא אֱלֹהִים לָרָקִיעַ שָׁמָיִם וַיְהִי־עֶרֶב וַיְהִי־בֹקֶר יוֹם שֵׁנִי׃

וַיֹּאמֶר אֱלֹהִים יִקָּווּ הַמַּיִם מִתַּחַת הַשָּׁמַיִם אֶל־מָקוֹם אֶחָד וְתֵרָאֶה הַיַּבָּשָׁה וַיְהִי־כֵן׃ וַיִּקְרָא אֱלֹהִים לַיַּבָּשָׁה אֶרֶץ וּלְמִקְוֵה הַמַּיִם קָרָא יַמִּים וַיַּרְא אֱלֹהִים כִּי־טוֹב׃ וַיֹּאמֶר אֱלֹהִים תַּדְשֵׁא הָאָרֶץ דֶּשֶׁא עֵשֶׂב מַזְרִיעַ זֶרַע עֵץ פְּרִי עֹשֶׂה פְּרִי לְמִינוֹ אֲשֶׁר זַרְעוֹ־בוֹ עַל־הָאָרֶץ וַיְהִי־כֵן׃ וַתּוֹצֵא הָאָרֶץ דֶּשֶׁא עֵשֶׂב מַזְרִיעַ זֶרַע לְמִינֵהוּ וְעֵץ עֹשֶׂה פְּרִי אֲשֶׁר זַרְעוֹ־בוֹ לְמִינֵהוּ וַיַּרְא אֱלֹהִים כִּי־טוֹב׃ וַיְהִי־עֶרֶב וַיְהִי־בֹקֶר יוֹם שְׁלִישִׁי׃

וַיֹּאמֶר אֱלֹהִים יְהִי מְאֹרֹת בִּרְקִיעַ הַשָּׁמַיִם לְהַבְדִּיל בֵּין הַיּוֹם וּבֵין הַלָּיְלָה וְהָיוּ לְאֹתֹת וּלְמוֹעֲדִים וּלְיָמִים וְשָׁנִים׃ וְהָיוּ לִמְאוֹרֹת בִּרְקִיעַ הַשָּׁמַיִם לְהָאִיר עַל־הָאָרֶץ וַיְהִי־כֵן׃ וַיַּעַשׂ אֱלֹהִים אֶת־שְׁנֵי הַמְּאֹרֹת הַגְּדֹלִים אֶת־הַמָּאוֹר הַגָּדֹל לְמֶמְשֶׁלֶת הַיּוֹם וְאֶת־הַמָּאוֹר הַקָּטֹן לְמֶמְשֶׁלֶת הַלַּיְלָה וְאֵת הַכּוֹכָבִים׃ וַיִּתֵּן אֹתָם אֱלֹהִים בִּרְקִיעַ הַשָּׁמַיִם לְהָאִיר עַל־הָאָרֶץ׃ וְלִמְשֹׁל בַּיּוֹם וּבַלַּיְלָה וּלֲהַבְדִּיל בֵּין הָאוֹר וּבֵין הַחֹשֶׁךְ

Cp 1, 1 ᵃ mlt MSS ב maj; Orig Βρησθ vel Βαρησθ, —σεθ; Samar *Barašit* | 10 ᵃ Var^{Ka} | 11 ᵃ ᵃ = 6⊍ | 14 ᵃ 6 | דְּשָׁא עֵשֶׂב 15 ᵃᵃ 6⊍ | הַשָּׁמָיִם 15 | 16 ᵃ 6 εἰς ἀρχὰς, I 𝔐.

Cp 1, 1 ᵃ prps א בְּרָא | 6 ᵃ ins וַיְהִי־כֵן ex 7; cf 6 et 9. 11. 15. 24. 30 | 7 ᵃ dl יְהִי־כֵן ex 7; cf 6 et 6 ad 8 | 9 ᵃ ˡ prb מִקְוֵה = 6 συναγωγήν et ins וַיַּרְא אֱלֹהִים כִּי־טוֹב; cf 4. 10. 12 etc et 6 ad 8 | 9 ᵃ ˡ prb מִקְוֵה = 6 συναγωγήν (cf 10) מקוה המם | 6 ᵇ ˡ הַיַּבָּשָׁה וְתֵרָא אֶל־מָקוֹם מִתַּחַת הַשָּׁמַיִם הַמָּיִם וִיקָּווּ + ; cf v 12 et 3MSS ᴍᴀᴧ6⊍ᴊᴧⱱ | 16 ᵃ dl ᵃ

I

we have in Hebrew Bibles today). The Masoretes also added vowel sounds above and beneath the consonants (because the text itself was inviolable and so could not be altered) and some punctuation marks, so as to aid more accurate public reading. For them, accuracy of copying was a sacred duty, to which they devoted their whole lives.

It is probably from them that there grew that extraordinary reverence for the scrolls that is still characteristic of Orthodox Jews, such that to mistreat them, or to miscopy, was the gravest of sins. An imperfect copy had to be destroyed. One worn out by long usage accompanied a rabbi to his grave (or was walled up in a special cupboard known as a "genizah"). The text of the Hebrew Bible was always safe in the hands of the Masoretes. The consequence is that Christian translators of modern times invariably turn to the masoretic text (abbreviated as MT in Bible footnotes) as the basis for their translation. Christians have always been absolutely indebted to Jewish scholars for the accuracy of the Old Testament text.

The Christian adoption of Greek

A word of explanation may be helpful as to why Christian scribes were invariably copying from Greek rather than from Hebrew. As we know, the first Christians were all Jews, even though some were Greek-speaking (e.g. the Hellenists mentioned at Acts 6.1). But by the end of the first century, the Gentiles far outnumbered Jews in the Church. By then, cordial relations between Christians and Jews had totally broken down. This had been provoked by the sort of confrontational episodes which are recorded in the Acts and in Paul's letters. The situation was exacerbated by the events surrounding the Roman sacking of Jerusalem in 70 AD. Prior to the siege, the Christian community there had taken flight across the Jordan. To Jews, their action must have seemed traitorous. In about AD 85 the rabbis in council at Jamnia excommunicated all followers of the Nazarene (as Jesus was called by them) from their synagogues. They were thenceforth ritually cursed on every Sabbath. This marked a final breaking-point. Christianity and Judaism were henceforth two distinct religions. And yet, the Church still regarded the Jewish scriptures as its holy book. But it was invariably read in Greek and not in Hebrew. It had adopted the translation known as the "Septuagint" as its own.

The Septuagint (LXX)

This version had been prepared, beginning in the third century BC, for the use of the large Jewish population living in Egypt, especially around Alexandria. A legend accounts for its name. The ruling Ptolemy had requested the High Priest in Jerusalem to send him the six finest scholars from each of the 12 tribes of Israel to translate the Books of Moses into Greek. Two of them appear to have gone missing en route! Seated in separate cells, they worked on their translation for 70 days, at the end of which they all shouted "Amen!" Comparison showed 70 identical scripts. Such is the legend! The reality was quite different, displaying considerable differences in the quality of translation. Nevertheless, the LXX gained a vastly wider influence in the Graeco-Roman world than ever the Hebrew Bible could have done and it became THE Christian version, to the extent that the Jews repudiated it and opposed to it other translations by Aquila, Theodotion and Symmachus. A sad consequence was that knowledge of the Hebrew Bible became virtually lost within the Church (and was not recovered until after the Reformation). A scholar such as Jerome, in the fourth century, was an exception. He went to live in Bethlehem, where he learned Hebrew from a rabbi in order to be able the better to translate the Old Testament into Latin. The Septuagint Bible is frequently referred to by the abbreviation "LXX."

Titles of Bible Books

In Chapter 1 I referred to the fact that the titles of the books in any English Bible are derived from the Septuagint. Every time we read the words Genesis, Exodus or Deuteronomy, we are reading Greek.

Christian Adoption of the Codex

In time, another difference distinguished Christians from Jews. The Jews always maintained the form of the scroll for their scriptures, whereas the Christians early on adopted that of the *Codex*. This involved folding the sheets of papyrus or parchment so that they could be inscribed on both sides, then stitching the sheets together along the spine, i.e. it was virtually the form of book that has lasted till our times. It was then placed within covers, originally made of tree bark. From the word "caudex," bark, derives codex; in the plural, codices. There is some evidence to suggest that the codex was, if not a Christian invention, certainly popularized by its Christian usage. Recent evidence suggests that the codex form was widely adopted because it facilitated all four gospels or the entire corpus of Paul's letters to appear between two covers. Eventually it was able to contain the entire Christian Bible. The codex was vastly easier to use than the scroll. The abbreviation "C" is used to denote a codex, as in C Sinaiticus.

CHAPTER 4:
ON TEXTUAL CRITICISM

I doubt whether many of us pay much attention, when we pick up a new translation of the Bible, to all the processes that went into its preparation. Our inattention may be rather like being invited to dinner with neighbors and sitting down to a splendid meal without a thought for all that went into the choice of menu, the recipe to be followed, the buying and preparing of the ingredients, and the actual process of cooking. Probably the cook alone knows all the time, effort and thought that made that meal possible.

The first decision translators have to make concerns the text they are to use: which Hebrew text for the Old Testament, which Greek text for the New Testament. Here, by "text" we mean the entire document, in its original language (and not the preacher's opening words: "Today's text is from Mark's Gospel, chapter six and verse 13" on which s/he is going to preach). As we have seen already, we don't possess the original of any of them, but only copies. So what are the choices? At first sight, they are bewildering. Let's take just the New Testament. On the last figures available (1989)[15], we have 5,488 manuscripts of parts of the Greek New Testament, comprising 96 papyri, 299 uncials, and 2,812 minuscules, the rest being Church lectionaries. Fifty-nine manuscripts contain the entire New Testament; 1,500 contain the entire gospels. In practice, the situation isn't quite so bewildering since scholars have been sifting and evaluating these manuscripts during the past 200 years.

The purpose of textual criticism

The purpose of textual criticism is to establish a text as close as possible to that originally written. You might think that impossible and to some extent it is. No decision about what is the true text can ever be absolutely certain, but it can be based on the evidence available. By minute comparison between manuscripts, it is usually possible to detect where errors or alterations have crept in.

••

Criticism: in scholarly usage, criticism has a quite different meaning from that in everyday speech. It doesn't mean making pejorative, insulting or destructive comments about a person or a product. It means rather using our critical faculties so as to make proper judgments, weighing up the pros

---

[15] Given in the *Oxford Companion to the Bible*, pp 486 f, Oxford 1993.

and cons about the matter in hand. The word derives from the Greek verb, "krinein," to decide, make a judgment. It will be realized that there could be no intellectual work of any usefulness without the proper exercise of criticism. That's part of "loving the Lord your God with ...all your mind".

• •

Let's set up a hypothetical situation (as illustrated in the diagram overleaf). Here we have an original document which we will call the *Original Script*. Suppose that three scribes, A, B and C made copies of it and we award them percentages for accuracy of copying. Suppose then, that in the next generation, A's work is copied by two scribes, B's by just one, and C's by perhaps 4 scribes working in a scriptorium. Again, we award marks for accuracy. You will note that some scrolls weren't copied by anybody, so the important ones are those within the chain of tradition. Then let's suppose that the only manuscripts extant today are those I have colored dark grey, such that we have 1 descendant of A, one of B and perhaps five of C. Now, let me ask you: which of these extant manuscripts is the most accurate, giving us a text closest to the original? Is it a matter of numbers? Is it a matter of age? You will see that it isn't either of these. The worst errors might have crept in at an early stage and then been multiplied. We will agree, I think, that in this hypothetical situation, the manuscript descending from Scribe A is the most accurate.

Families of manuscripts

This is the sort of process the textual critics apply to thousands of manuscripts. What is done initially is to sort them out into "families." If we think of "families" not so much as groups of copyists but rather as various centers of early Christianity, we are on the right tracks. Let us invent another hypothetical situation. Suppose we have before us the Gospel of Mark, the original of which has only just been completed, let's say, in Alexandria in Egypt. Its fame spreads, such that various Christian congregations want to have a copy of it. Each sends a representative to Alexandria who makes his own copy of the Gospel. Suppose the copyist from Antioch makes some significant alteration (perhaps misses an entire paragraph or page) or spells the name of Bethsaida differently (there are three different spellings of this Galilean town in the manuscripts), takes his copy back home and there multiple copies are made of it. They will probably all contain those initial mistakes. So, in time, the manuscripts emanating from Antioch will differ more or less markedly from those produced at Caesarea or in Ephesus. In time, the copies emerging from each of these three centers will have their own "family likeness."

❖ **The Alexandrian:** Alexandria was a city of high culture, renowned for its great library and its learning. It became a major center of Christianity, with Origen (third century AD) the first great Christian biblical scholar. So we

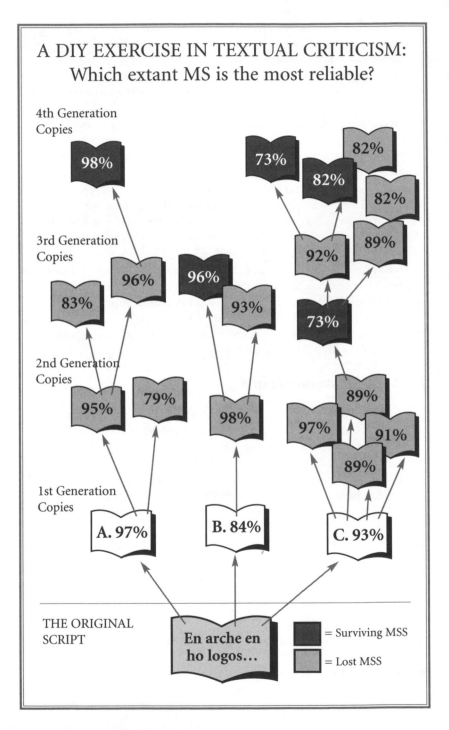

A DIY EXERCISE IN TEXTUAL CRITICISM:
Which extant MS is the most reliable?

4th Generation
Copies

98%

73%

82%

82%

82%

3rd Generation
Copies

89%

92%

83%

96%

96%

93%

73%

2nd Generation
Copies

95%

79%

98%

89%

97%

91%

89%

73%

1st Generation
Copies

A. 97%

B. 84%

C. 93%

THE ORIGINAL
SCRIPT

En arche en
ho logos...

= Surviving MSS

= Lost MSS

would expect Alexandria to be foremost in safeguarding the text of the NT, and so, we have reason to believe, it did. It is well represented in the early papyri such as P45, and by the great uncial manuscripts Vaticanus and Sinaiticus. All of these are classified as Alexandrian.

❖ **The Caesarean:** this Roman seaport, gateway to Palestine, also became a center of Christian learning. It is conjectured that Origen brought manuscripts of the Alexandrian family to Caesarea, where it became mingled with those of "Western" type, such that Caesarean manuscripts tend to display this mix. It was from this area that Jerome, the great translator of the Bible into Latin, worked.

❖ **The Western Text:** this is a text-type in which copyists were evidently at their freest in making alterations to the text. An interesting example is that of Codex Bezae, named after Theodore Beza (John Calvin's successor at Geneva) and presented to Cambridge University. For example, in Luke 6, between vv 4 & 6 in our versions, Codex Bezae has this verse: "On the same day, seeing one working on the Sabbath day, he (Jesus) said to him, "Man, if you know what you doing, you are blessed; but if you do not know, you are accursed and a transgressor of the law." This verse is not to be found in any other manuscripts, so will invariably be omitted in any modern translation. Bezae's version of Acts is almost a 10th longer than the versions otherwise known. Whilst Codex Bezae's additions are of interest to scholars, it will generally be reckoned an inaccurate manuscript.

❖ **The Koine or Byzantine Type:** this is the type of text represented by the great majority of manuscripts, but it is probably the least reliable. It was termed "Koine" a word descriptive of the everyday speech of Greeks (as opposed to the Classical Greek of the great poets and dramatists) and "Byzantine" because Byzantium, once named Constantinople, remained the chief center of Christian Greek culture long after the Western Church had become chiefly Latin-speaking and negligent of its Greek roots. The Byzantine Church, under the direct rule of the Emperor, was for centuries the chief producer of Greek manuscripts but they were not always the most accurate.

Some famous manuscripts

Let's look briefly at some of the most important manuscripts, beginning with the papyri. The New Testament papyri are discoveries of the last century (almost as remarkable as the Dead Sea Scrolls). Papyrus cannot survive a damp climate, but it can in the dry heat of Egypt such that the excavation of Egyptian rubbish dumps has yielded remarkable finds from the earliest years of Christian faith. Amongst them have been several fragments of the New Testament. Textual scholars designate the papyri by a capital P followed by a number.

P52 is a scrap measuring no more than two by three inches containing a few verses of John's Gospel. It has been dated to within the first half of the second century AD. Since this gospel was probably not written until the very end of the first century, the fragment represents a copy from perhaps within 30 or 40 years of the original. It is thereby probably the oldest surviving fragment of the New Testament. Metzger's comment is memorable: "Although the extent of the verses preserved is so slight, in one respect this tiny scrap of papyrus possesses quite as much evidential value as would the complete codex. Just as Robinson Crusoe, seeing but a single footprint in the sand, concluded that another human being, with two feet, was present on the island with him, so P52 proves the existence and use of the fourth gospel during the first half of the second century in a provincial town along the Nile, far removed from its traditional place of composition (Ephesus in Asia Minor)." (Metzger: *Text of the New Testament*, OUP. p.39)

P64 consists of tiny fragments of Matthew's Gospel, the first of which contains parts of Matthew 26.7-8 on one side and Matthew 26.31 on the other. A German scholar, Peter Carsten Thiede, has recently caused a scholarly "storm in a teacup" when he claimed that these fragments housed in Magdalen College, Oxford, were to be dated from about AD 50, i.e. to within 20 or so years from the crucifixion of Jesus. This was sufficient to grab headlines in the Sunday papers since most New Testament scholars suppose Matthew's Gospel not to have been produced until the 80s or 90s AD. If Thiede were correct, then the entire modern consensus as to the dating of all the gospels would have to be turned on its head. But Thiede has convinced few other scholars. The episode demonstrates that the dating of manuscripts is not an exact science and can be controversial. (See G Stanton *Gospel Truth*, pp 11-9 for a rebuttal of Thiede's claim.)

Let's look at some of the uncials. **Codex Vaticanus**, dating from the early fourth century, is recognized today as one of the best and most accurate. It is housed in the Vatican library, but nobody knows how it got there.

Codex Sinaiticus makes for a much better story. Count Von Tischendorf, a German aristocrat, worked in the service of the Russian Tsar in the middle years of the 19th century. His passion was for seeking Bible manuscripts. To that end he visited the Monastery of St Catherine, at the foot of Mt Sinai, in 1844. One day, he saw a monk collecting what looked like antique sheets of parchment. Tischendorf asked what he was going to do with them. "Light the fire" was the answer. He pleaded with the monk not to do so, learned that many had already been burnt but managed to take possession of 43 leaves. He recognized them as being older than any biblical manuscripts he had ever seen, being sheets of a Septuagint Bible. His enquiries as to whether the monastery had more of the same met with a stony silence.

Tischendorf returned to the monastery in 1853, but discovered nothing of significance. He was there again in 1859, and was on the point of abandoning his search, when, on the last evening of his stay, he was invited to coffee with the steward. He presented him with a facsimile copy of the 43 sheets that he had previously rescued and that he had had published in Germany. The steward then announced that he too had a copy of the Septuagint. He produced a manuscript wrapped in red cloth from a closet. "There before the astonished scholar's eyes lay the treasure which he had been longing to see ..." writes Metzger. "This was an almost complete Septuagint Bible." Tischendorf asked if he could borrow it for the night and sat up all night examining it and transcribing parts of it. Returned to Cairo, he began negotiations as to how he could get possession of it. Eventually he persuaded the monks to present their Bible to the Russian Tsar as patron of their monastery, which they did. (I gathered quite recently that the story told at the monastery today is that Tischendorf cheated them out of it!) So it arrived in Russia and was named Codex Sinaiticus. Ascribed to the early fourth century AD, it is thus the earliest complete (bar a few missing bits of the Old Testament) Septuagint Bible known. The New Testament section of it contains two books, the Shepherd of Hermas and the Epistle of Barnabas, which did not eventually obtain recognition as scriptural books. This demonstrates that, at the time of its writing, the contents of the New Testament had not yet been fixed. After the Russian revolution, it was sold to the British Museum for £100,000 and there it can be seen today. Codex Sinaiticus is coded with the Hebrew letter א (Aleph) **01**.

The Textus Receptus

The art of textual criticism is not entirely modern, since Origen in the third century was aware of textual variants and went to the immense effort of compiling a version in which the Hebrew and Greek texts (in four different translations) were arranged in parallel columns for easy comparison. But textual criticism as a scientific discipline dates from the last two centuries. Before then, there had been no scientific evaluation of manuscripts and many of the best manuscripts were not yet available. There had therefore grown up during the Middle Ages a text largely determined by the Koine or Byzantine type which came to be known as the "Textus Receptus" (the Received Text). With the new invention of printing available from 1492, the great humanist scholar Desiderius Erasmus was largely responsible for its widespread diffusion. Anxious to print the text of the Greek New Testament (to forestall likely publication by others) he took the few Greek manuscripts available to him, edited them as best he could and had the resultant text published. It was his second edition of 1521 on which Luther based his German Bible translation and Tyndale the first translation into English. Later, Robert Etienne (Stephanus), the Paris printer, published further editions. That of 1551 included, for the first time, the verse divisions that are still in use today. The apocryphal tale is that Stephanus' father added them whilst riding horseback from Paris to Lyons and this is held to account for their unevenness. More likely, he added them at the wayside inns on his route. Theodore Beza[16] continued this tradition, as did the Elzevir brothers, prominent Dutch publishers and printers. These latter, in a 1633 edition, claimed, "The reader has the text which is now received by all, in which we give nothing changed or corrupted." Hence it was called the "Textus Receptus," (abbreviated as TR), the text on which all the major Protestant translations were based, including that of the King James Version. On which, Bruce Metzger, the doyen of textual critics, makes this judgment: "So superstitious has been the reverence accorded the TR that in some cases attempts to criticize or emend it have been regarded as akin to sacrilege. Yet its textual basis is essentially a handful of late and haphazardly collected minuscule manuscripts, and in a dozen passages its reading is supported by no known Greek witness."[17] It is only in the light of modern knowledge that we realize how faulty and inadequate the TR was. Needless to say, this is a major justification of the necessity of modern translations.

It is therefore a strange anomaly that Christian fundamentalists should be so fiercely attached to the King James Version. If they really believe in the verbal inerrancy of the Bible, that inerrancy cannot reside in any English version, since these all differ. It must reside in the original Hebrew and Greek manuscripts. They should therefore be the more devoted than most to the recovery of the original texts and be foremost in recognizing the inadequacy of the Textus Receptus.

Establishing the text

So how do today's translators proceed? They will use the best available text, of the Hebrew and the Greek, now available as a result of the painstaking effort of the textual critics of the past two centuries. It isn't that today's scholars are any cleverer than those of previous centuries. It is rather that the ever increasingly sophisticated tools of modern scholarship were not available in past ages; and what we have learned to call "Information Technology" disseminates knowledge almost at the speed of light. In Erasmus' time, there was excuse for ignorance; today there is no such excuse. "All the world's our oyster," including the world of Bible scholarship.

Let's suppose we are translating the gospels. The translator will likely have a text like this in front of him, the Synopsis Quattuor Evangeliorum (Synopsis of the

---

[16] Beza was a great biblical scholar, who succeeded Calvin in leadership of the Genevan Reformation.
[17] Metzger, p 106.

THE GREEK TEXT OF THE NEW TESTAMENT

Extract from "SYNOPSIS QUATTUOR EVANGELIORUM", edited by Kurt Aland, published by Wurttembergische Bibelanstalt, 1964 Stuttgart,

Four Gospels). Overleaf you will see the Greek text of Luke's Gospel at 1.57-80, the text which the editors believe to be the closest possible to what was originally written by Luke. In the sidelines there is space to include anything parallel to be found in the other Gospels, but there is nothing comparable to this section. Underneath are the textual variants. Via the superscriptions in the text, the editors indicate what differences are to be found in other manuscripts. Where there is a difference of wording or spelling, all the manuscripts containing that difference are listed, as are the manuscripts that support the text that the editors have selected.

Then, at the bottom of the page, verse by verse, references are given to other Bible passages that may throw light on the word or phrase used in the text. For example, what Zacharias said is full of echoes of the Old Testament. So, if you followed up these references, you would have a clear picture of the background to what he said.

And in the English Bible?

Now, does any of this appear in our English Bibles? If you look in a Good News Bible (also known as Today's English Version), you will find that some of these references are given, those the editors have thought would be most useful to you in understanding the passage. They refer you to Leviticus 12.3, to Malachi 3.1 and to Isaiah 9.2. The Revised English Bible doesn't give any such references, but it does give any really important textual variants. (See further concerning the Magnificat.)

The student without any Greek or Hebrew is advised to buy a Bible with the Oxford Annotated Notes. It's called an Oxford Study Bible (there's also a Cambridge equivalent).This gives the minimal amount of essential information to be able to read the text with understanding; with sectional summaries, any important textual variations, explanation of difficult words and essential references to other Bible passages. I would strongly recommend it to any serious student of the Bible such as lay preachers and teachers.

For those deeply attached to the KJV (whose literary merits are enormous), it should be realized that its chief defect has nothing to do with the translation but everything to do with the fact that it was based on a text known today to be defective. The translators were therefore wholly blameless. They could only work with the knowledge available to them at that time. Today, our knowledge of the underlying text is vastly greater, as is our understanding of the Hebrew language and this is the chief justification of our modern translations.
An interesting example of the application of recently discovered knowledge concerns some text in 1 Samuel. All previous English versions have begun

chapter 11 with the rather abrupt introduction of "Nahash the Ammonite." The text as it stood gave no explanation for who he was or for his cruel treatment of the Israelite inhabitants of Jabesh Gilead. But scholars had been long familiar with the fact that the Greek Septuagint had, at this point, some verses which did not appear in the Masoretic Text and yet provided information that shed vital illumination on the passage. They were never printed in any English translation. But, they are now, thanks to a Hebrew manuscript found amongst the Dead Sea Scrolls which gives the text which must have been used by the Septuagint translators. These extra verses are appended to chapter 10 in the New Revised Standard Version. They don't yet feature in either REB or GNB. Incidentally, this demonstrates that the MT is not always accurate. Careful attention to the footnotes in our Bibles will show how frequently translators have turned to the Greek or Syriac or other early translations to elucidate where the Hebrew is obscure.

Most readers of the Bible today will remain blissfully unaware of the achievements of textual criticism, based on meticulous study almost as arduous as that of copying the Bible by hand in the days before printing. Yet these scholars deserve our recognition and thanks. They are the true "backroom boys," who accomplish an immense labor before the translator can even begin his work.

SOME IMPORTANT ABBREVIATIONS:

It is also as well to become familiar with the commonly used abbreviations used by Bible students, such as:

KJV	=	King James Version (also known as the AV, Authorized Version)
GNB	=	Good News Bible (also known as TEV, Today's English Version)
RSV	=	Revised Standard Version
NRSV	=	New Revised Standard Version
REB	=	Revised English Bible
JB	=	Jerusalem Bible

NT	=	New Testament
OT	=	Old Testament
BC	=	Before Christ
AD	=	Anno Domini, "in the Year of our Lord," ie after Christ.
MS	=	manuscript; MSS = manuscripts
DSS	=	Dead Sea Scrolls
MT	=	Masoretic Text
TC	=	Textual Criticism

The footnotes in your Bible

Footnotes are usually ignored. Their presence will depend on which modern version Bible you are using. A "Study Bible" should contain all the more important ones. The GNB, REB and NRSV give all the most important ones and their presence is of some importance. For they indicate where the textual critics are not absolutely certain of the underlying Hebrew or Greek text. To omit them is to give a spurious spur to the notion of their infallibility.

Let us take just one page of the Old Testament, that of 1 Samuel chapter 10, as it is given in the NRSV (on page 353 in the Oxford Study Bible) and have a look at the footnotes. Here are some extracts: "22: Then Samuel took Saul and his servant-boy and brought them into the hall, and gave them a place at the head of those who had been invited, of whom there were about thirty. 23: And Samuel said to the cook, 'Bring the portion I gave you, the one I asked you to put aside.' 24: The cook took up the thigh and *what went with it*[d] and set them before Saul. Samuel said, 'See, what was kept is set before you. Eat; for *it is set before you*[e] at the appointed time, so that you might *eat with the guests*.'[f] So Saul ate with Samuel that day."

Beneath the text above is a small area of footnotes, given in the box below:

> *d* Meaning of Heb uncertain   *e* Q Ms Gk: MT *it was kept*   *f* Cn: Heb *it was kept for you, saying, I have invited the people*   *g* Gk: Heb *and he spoke with Saul*   *h* Gk: Heb lacks *and he lay down to sleep*   *i* Gk: Heb *and they arose early and at break of dawn*   *j* Gk: Heb lacks *over his people Israel. You shall . . . anointed you ruler*   *k* Or *the Hill of God there*   *m* Or *the hill*

Each superimposed letter marks where there is a footnote in the printed version. The first, d, says: "Meaning of Heb uncertain." Honest translators! They admit they are not sure. The KJV said at this point *"and that which was upon it."* The second, e, says: e. Q MS Gk: MT *"it was kept."* What does this indicate? MT stands for "Masoretic Text" i.e. the Hebrew version edited by the Masoretes. This is what the KJV translators followed: hence *"for unto this time hath it been kept for thee."* The NRSV translators have followed the sense of a Greek manuscript found at Qumran (hence Q MS) and so report Samuel as saying: "Eat; for *it is set before you ...*" The third footnote (f) says: Cn. Heb *"it was kept for you, saying, I have invited the people."* Cn. indicates a correction. It is important to know what is meant by a correction. Clearly the translators believed that there was some mistake in what the Hebrew text conveys (admittedly exceedingly minor). The foreword to the NRSV defines a correction as follows: "Correction: made where the text has suffered in transmission and the versions provide no satisfactory restoration but where the Standard Bible Committee agrees with the judgment of competent scholars as to the most probable reconstruction of the original text." (NRSV Study Bible, p xxviii)

Some examples of textual criticism

1. WAS BARABBAS ALSO CALLED JESUS?

It is only in more modern translations that we find, perhaps to our surprise, the suggestion that Barabbas may also have been called Jesus.

The text concerned is to be found at Matthew 27. 15-17: This is what we read in the **KJV:** "Now at that feast the governor was wont to release unto the people a prisoner whom they would. And they had then a notable prisoner called Barabbas. Therefore when they were gathered together, Pilate said unto them, Whom will ye that I release unto you? Barabbas, or Jesus which is called Christ?" There appears here to have been a straight choice: Barabbas or Jesus? But in some modern translations we have this:

GNB: "At every Passover Festival the Roman governor was in the habit of setting free any one prisoner the crowd asked for. At that time there was a well-known prisoner named **Jesus** Barabbas. So when the crowd gathered, Pilate asked them, "Which one do you want me to set free for you? **Jesus** Barabbas or Jesus called the Messiah?"

In the **REB,** we read this: "There was then in custody a man of some notoriety, called **Jesus** Barabbas. When the people assembled Pilate said to them, 'Which would you like me to release to you – **Jesus** Barabbas, or Jesus called Messiah?'"

Likewise in the **NRSV:** "At that time they had a notorious prisoner, called **Jesus** Barabbas. So after they had gathered, Pilate said to them, 'Whom do you want me to release for you, **Jesus** Barabbas or Jesus who is called the Messiah?'"

The Greek Text: What do we find in the Greek text? (As printed in the Synopsis Quattuor Evangeliorum,1964). In transliterated script we read this: "Eichon de tote desmion episemon legomenon *Barabban ... tina thelete apoluso humin: *Barabban e Iesoun ton legomenon Christon?" This translates as: "They had then a prisoner called Barabbas ... which one do you wish me to release to you, Barabbas or Jesus who is called Christ?"

At the places marked with an asterisk, some manuscripts have inserted here the word *"Iesoun," i.e.* Jesus, in both. Which manuscripts add the word Jesus? They are Θ, λ pc, sy (s, pal), Or (pt):

Θ = Uncial 038, of the ninth century, in Tbilissi, Georgia
λ pc = a few minuscule manuscripts (mostly late)
sy s pal = some Syriac and Palestinian manuscripts from St Catherine's Monastery.
Or Pt = some writings of the Alexandrian theologian Origen

In the second instance above, the textual apparatus indicates that "Iesoun" is omitted in all manuscripts other than Uncial 038. This is weak textual evidence. So why do most modern versions include it? It may be for the obvious reason that because the name Jesus was held especially sacred in Christian circles, no scribe would likely attribute it to anybody else, especially to somebody as notorious as Barabbas. But has sufficient notice been taken of the fact that this name is not to be found in Mark's narrative, on which Matthew's account is based, and that Matthew frequently dramatizes material for greater effect. Since "Iesous" is the Greek form of the Old Testament "Joshua" (meaning "The Lord saves"), the dramatic effect was enormous of presenting Barabbas and Jesus as equal claimants to being the saviors of their people. For Matthew, of course, any claim by Barabbas was obviously false. Something of such a claim could have been implicit even without naming him Jesus, since the name "Barabbas" means "Son of the Father." The inclusion of "Jesus" demonstrates Matthew as a dramatist, not as a historian. The historical case for Barabbas being called Jesus has to remain extremely dubious.

2. WHATEVER HAPPENED TO THE ENDING OF MARK'S GOSPEL?

Those well acquainted with this Gospel in the KJV will know that its last chapter contains 20 verses. They may then be surprised to find that in most modern versions only eight verses are printed. In the GNB, after verse eight you will find this superscription "An Old Ending to the Gospel," containing 12 verses, and, further on, "Another Old Ending" with just two verses. What is the problem?

The "Textus Receptus" contained all 20 verses, but you will recall that it was based on poor manuscript evidence. The decisive point for modern translators is that the oldest codices **B** (Vaticanus) and ℵ (Sinaiticus) conclude at verse eight, that many of the early translations into oriental languages lack verses 9-20; that the Church fathers Clement, Origen and Eusebius show no knowledge of them; whilst Jerome (translator of the Vulgate) wrote "almost all the Greek copies do not have this concluding portion." [18]

It is the case that the overwhelming number of manuscripts contain these extra verses; hence their inclusion in the Textus Receptus and hence the KJV. But the fact that none of these are as early as the codices B and ℵ mentioned above,

---

[18] Metzger, p 226.

that some also include an alternative Shorter Ending (as in the GNB as alternative verses nine and ten), and that codex W (Washingtoniensis) gives yet a further expansion of verse 14, all points to uncertainty as to what the original ending of Mark's Gospel was. So the question has to be asked: Is the section Mark 16.1-8 the original conclusion to the gospel? Is that how Mark intended to conclude it, or was he interrupted so as to be unable to complete it? It can readily be imagined that he might have been arrested quill pen in hand and thrown into a Roman prison. Or, was it possible that he had completed it, but that his conclusion was irretrievably lost? A sheet of papyrus could easily have been torn off and lost.

On the face of it, it would seem strange that a book intended to convey "Good News" should have intentionally concluded with women running away from Jesus' tomb in a state of terror! This would have left the gospel's readers with the Resurrection announced but in no way experienced. Some scholars argue for this ending as being intentional. But the fact that early copyists added a number of alternative endings would indicate that they didn't believe the gospel to be properly concluded at verse eight.

We can be sure that the additional verses were not penned by Mark himself. The Longer Ending contains no fewer than 17 words that are never used by Mark in the rest of his gospel. A fairly cursory reading of these verses (even in English) demonstrates them to be in content and in style quite unlike the work of Mark. Furthermore, the fact that their substance reads like an abbreviation of resurrection episodes reported in the gospels of Matthew, Luke and John, shows that their author was acquainted with these other gospels (all written later than that of Mark by between 20 and 40 or so years). Hence the addition is that of an anonymous Christian scribe who supposed that Mark's Gospel without his appendix was incomplete.

Of course, such a conclusion does not render these additional verses valueless (even though we may consider some of its content as verging on the apocryphal, e.g. verse 18). It was undoubtedly the complete gospel, including these verses, which was "canonized" by the Church; and is therefore part of what we might call the "authorized" New Testament. Personally, I consider the additional verses as so derivative as to be of little historical value (except as evidence of apocryphal accretions to the text).

3. THE COMMA JOHANNEUM
In Greek grammar, the "comma" is not our familiar punctuation mark, but a brief unit of text. The text in question is to be found at 1 John 5.7, which you will find in the KJV but not in any reliable modern translation. It reads thus: "For there are three that bear record in heaven, the Father, the Word, and the

Holy Ghost: and these three are one." What is its history? Needless to say, this verse was part of the Textus Receptus, was in the Latin Vulgate and was widely held throughout the Middle Ages to be a key "proof-text" for the doctrine of the Trinity. Therefore to question its authenticity was to make oneself suspect of heresy! But when Desiderius Erasmus, the greatest humanist scholar of the early 16th century, set out to publish a reliable text of the Greek New Testament, he knew that this verse was not to be found in any good Greek manuscript. Its omission from his first edition was greeted with hostility. Erasmus unwisely offered that he would include it if anybody could produce a Greek manuscript that included it and such a manuscript ("made to measure" so we may suspect) was duly produced. Erasmus was as good as his word, but he printed it with a footnote to the effect that it was against his better judgment. Today's textual critics would certainly uphold Erasmus' judgment. This notorious verse is not present in any of the earliest manuscripts and first appears in the quotation of a Spanish manuscript, then appeared in the Vulgate from circa AD 800 and so came into the Textus Receptus. What explains its insertion? It is most likely a theological gloss on the preceding verse, written as an annotation into the margin of a script – such glosses were commonplace. It would have been natural for a scholarly monk to read the references in verse six to the "three witnesses, the Spirit, the water and the blood" as figuratively having to do with the doctrine of God as Holy Trinity and to write his comment into the margin so that less astute readers might see the point. It only required one copyist to assume this to be part of the text and so to insert it. Once others had copied that manuscript, it came to be assumed to be an original part of what John had written. But overwhelming scholarly consensus sees it as the gloss that it was. It is therefore omitted from all respectable modern versions.

The original text

A major finding from more recent research in the Dead Sea Scrolls is that by the time of Jesus the text of the Old Testament scriptures had not yet been firmly fixed. Where several copies of one and the same Old Testament book, dating from the last two centuries BC, were discovered, they show many variations of text. This is especially the case with the books of the Prophets. This even suggests that, in some cases, the search for THE original text may be quite illusory, because no one original text ever existed. On the other hand, later copies dating from the middle of the first century AD demonstrate a more uniform text. It looks as if, during the centuries spanning the period BC to AD, there was a significant development towards the standardization of the text, a process which was brought to completion by the Masoretes.

The chief impression from the Dead Sea Scrolls, giving us a Hebrew text older by a thousand years than any previously known, is of the astonishing accuracy of the work of copyists across that yawning time-gap. Whilst modern translations incorporate many minor alterations thanks to the evidence of the scrolls, the main text of the Hebrew Bible is very little different from that of the famous Aleppo and Ben Asher codices of the 10th century. Whether Jews or Christians, we are indebted to the Masorites.[19]

---

[19] See Hershel Shanks, one of the chief authorities on the Dead Sea Scrolls, in *The Mystery and Meaning of the Dead Sea Scrolls*, Random House, New York © 1998 Biblical Archaeology Society.

CHAPTER 5:
THE OLD TESTAMENT

PART I – A bird's eye view of Jewish history

It is necessary to have some idea of this before we consider how the various books of the Old Testament came to be written. To some extent this is putting the cart before the horse, because it is only as a result of the application of literary and historical methods to the study of these books that a plausible account of the history emerges. And yet the place of these books can only be understood within the history. It's a "Which comes first, the chicken or the egg?" kind of situation. I propose here to give the history with a few remarks about literary aspects of it; with the process reversed in the next chapter when we will look at the literature with some comments about the history it relates.

The Bible tells a story; it is essentially a story book. But to translate the story into credible history (as this is understood in today's world) is by no means simple. Many different genres of literature are employed in the telling of it, each bearing its own kind of meaning. We cannot possibly treat mythology or legend as if they were straight-forward historical reporting. I will deal with these different genres in chapter 15. Nor should we forget that most of the Bible story was told by word of mouth (what we call oral tradition) over many centuries; such that the writing down of it is quite belated. We have to allow for the elaboration of it as part of the story-teller's art, as well as the "spinning" (to use a contemporary and hotly debated subject) applied to the story, often in the interest of some centuries-later ideology or theology. Each genre of story, as each section of the written record, has to be carefully evaluated by trying to diagnose (sometimes guess at) its origins and development through the centuries. In the next chapter I will seek to give some explication of what processes were at work.

THE PERIOD OF THE PATRIARCHS (C 17TH-12TH CENTURIES BC)

From out of the mist of the myths and legends of pre-historical times (depicted in the first eleven chapters of Genesis) Abraham is the first recognizably historical character to emerge (although some scholars would doubt this). He is the first of the Patriarchs, the founding fathers of the Jewish nation. With him the story of the Jewish people begins. Yet we cannot assign him even to a particular century, only remark that he and his descendants fit the milieu (well understood now thanks to archaeological discoveries) of the early to mid-second millennium BC. Even to describe Abraham, at this stage, as a Jew is anachronistic. He is recorded as being a descendent of Shem (one of the three sons of Noah), hence a "Semite." At some stage his descendents became called Hebrews, a designation that probably derives from the word "Habiru" which shows up frequently in ancient inscriptions and documents from the Middle East. It is evident in these that the Habiru did not comprise an ethnic group, but were rather a social class. They were wanderers, vagabonds, often trouble-makers (the city dweller's prejudice) living on the fringes of civilization, ready to hire themselves out as day-laborers or mercenaries.

Genesis 11.31 informs us that Abraham's Father, Terah, set out on a journey from the city of Ur. This places the family background within the first great civilization of Mesopotamia, that of Sumeria, later to be replaced by Babylonia. Even though Abraham and his descendants are invariably depicted as nomadic wanderers (rather than city-dwellers), they were influenced by the civilization they had left behind them. This was even more so when, at least a thousand years later, the leaders of the Jews were exiled to Babylonia.

Abraham is depicted as the first man with whom God enters into a personal relationship and whose attitude is portrayed as that of "faith," i.e. of total trust in the promises of God. The promise of a son seemed fragile, yet in the end, beyond all expectation, Isaac was born to his wife Sarah. From Isaac descended Jacob, who was renamed Israel, through whom came those twelve sons who become the eponymous founders of the Twelve Tribes of Israel. Some scholars suppose the accounts of the Patriarchs to be descriptive of tribal events rather than of historically recognizable individuals. It is probably Jacob who was alluded to as "a wandering Aramean" in the creedal statement we find in Deuteronomy 26.5. This would place his family origins in the vicinity of Haran, to the north-east of Palestine.

A major consideration has to be of the fact that nomadic shepherds and tribal peoples did not keep written records. Their histories were passed on by word of mouth over many centuries, were doubtless shaped in the process with some exaggeration of those features most important to story-tellers. Any attentive reader will note how they had special interest in the origins of names of people, places (especially sacred places) and customs. Such accounts are technically known as "aetiological," from the Greek, "aetios," a reason or cause. The processes of what occurs in oral tradition are the special province of those critics who practice what is called "Form Criticism," since those involved in traditional story-telling tend to follow a detectable pattern.

During Jacob's time, a severe crisis struck, that of famine. By providence, the youngest son bar one, Joseph, had been treacherously sold into slavery in Egypt, had there risen to high power and had taken steps to withstand the famine. In consequence, his father and brothers were at first forced to come to Egypt for food and later invited to settle there. Although Joseph's story is clearly a legendary tale, there are clues that suggest a historical foundation which is plausible. For a period Egypt was ruled by the Hyksos (their kings formed the 15th dynasty from circa1630–1521 BC), a Semitic people kin to the descendants of Abraham. Only under them does it seem credible that Joseph could have risen to the post of chief minister. And yet within a generation or so, the Hyksos were expelled and a native Egyptian dynasty restored to power. Thus Exodus 1.8: "Now a new King arose over Egypt who did not know Joseph ..." likely alludes to a new dynasty of Egyptian rulers, the 19th, under Seti I (1308-1290 BC) and Rameses II (1290-1224 BC), the likely Pharoah of the Exodus. We are thus moving onto firmer historical ground, even though the biblical accounts of these events were not written until centuries later.

So the descendants of the Patriarchs were enslaved in Egypt and remained there, supposedly for 430 years (thus Exodus 12.40); or, more credibly, for four generations. There is some circumstantial evidence to suggest that many of the Hebrew ancestors had never in fact left Canaan, did not participate in the Exodus, and only joined up, by covenant agreement, with those who had, once these latter settled in Canaan. It was at that stage, that all the tribes united in a common religious faith in Yahweh as their God.

THE PERIOD OF THE EXODUS (13TH CENTURY BC)

After a long period of oppression under the Pharaohs, the slaves were at last led out of Egypt by Moses. He is the formative figure in Jewish religion, for it was under his inspirational leadership that a rabble of slaves were welded into a people unified under a new religious allegiance. This was to a God who announced his name to be Yahweh (usually rendered as "The Lord" in English translations). At some stage, the people learned to associate Yahweh with the God El formerly worshiped by the Patriarchs. Thus their story was welded together with that of Moses. The Bible tells how Yahweh manifested himself to Moses at the Burning Bush, ordered him to confront Pharaoh with the demand that the slaves be set free, punished the Egyptians by means of terrifying plagues, led them through the desert to the foot of Mt Sinai, where he delivered the covenant under which he undertook to be their God and they vowed to be His People. The Ten Commandments encapsulated the obligations they undertook to observe.

We have to note that, as with the Patriarchs, so with the Exodus, the accounts within the Bible are the result of centuries of oral transmission of the story, such that we cannot be certain of anything more than a blurred outline of what occurred.[20] It is odd that there are no corroborative records at all from the

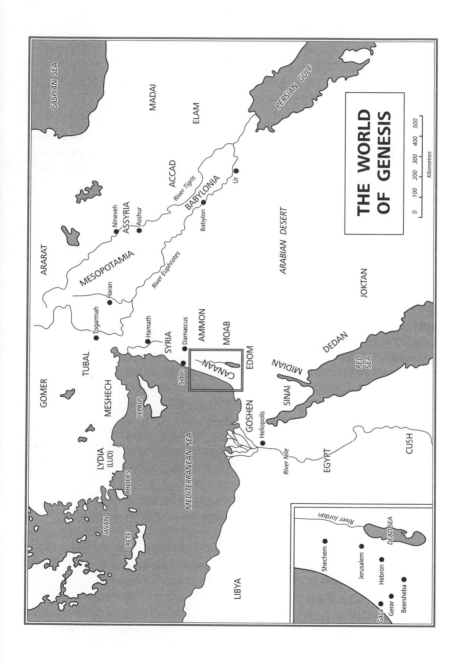

Egyptian side of the matter. On several points, the biblical record is undoubtedly exaggerated. Over the centuries, the miraculous crossing of the Sea of Reeds (that's how the Hebrew, "Yam Suf" should be translated), doubtless one of the fresh water lakes near Suez, had been erroneously mistaken for a crossing of the Red Sea. The numbers of Hebrews trekking through and living off the desert is impossibly high (as Werner Keller observed in *The Bible as History*). So what we have in the books of Exodus and Numbers is an account written retrospectively. Since the Jewish people relived these dramatic events every year at the Passover feast, as if they had been personally present, the numbers probably represent a census of those who, centuries later, remembered and celebrated the event. Moses led the people, through innumerable trials, to the edge of the Promised Land of Canaan, where he died, having handed over leadership to Joshua.

THE CONQUEST AND OCCUPATION OF CANAAN (12TH CENTURY BC)

Entering the Promised Land, the Hebrews encountered stiff resistance. The Canaanites represented a confederation of city-states living behind high-walled cities and of a high but effete civilization. The Hebrews burst upon them with all the passion of desperation and new burning faith (as the Arab Muslims would do centuries later) and slowly subdued them city by city. Indeed it was a sort of "jihad" or "holy war" the Hebrews believing that God had commanded them to effect the wholesale slaughter of the inhabitants. The books of Joshua and Judges represent a horrific picture of "ethnic cleansing" (which must appear morally repugnant to Christians).

The accounts are nevertheless inconsistent. The wholesale destruction of everything Canaanite in origin simply didn't happen (as some supposed that it should). The fact is that the Hebrews largely adopted the Canaanite way of life, became city-dwellers, took up agriculture, learned to speak the local language (for the Hebrew language is in origin Canaanite) and eventually to write using the Ugaritic script. When they built a Temple to Yahweh, it was wholly Canaanite in style (its design and materials being supplied by King Hiram of Tyre). When King David stormed Jerusalem and made it his capital, it is clear that its Jebusite population remained and even the priesthood descended from

---

[20] It is notable that a number of modern historians-cum-journalists are keen to prove the historicity of many Biblical events, including the events of the Exodus. Graham Phillips, in *Act of God*, claims to link them with dateable events in Egyptian history. His account is considerably dependent on being able to convince us that the Exodus occurred at least 150 years earlier than has so far been the consensus in the scholarly community; for he argues that the Ten Plagues of Egypt, and the drowning of the Egyptian army in the "Red Sea" were the results of the massive eruption of Mt Thera in c 1390 BC. His account is enthralling, but is the case proven? I think not yet.

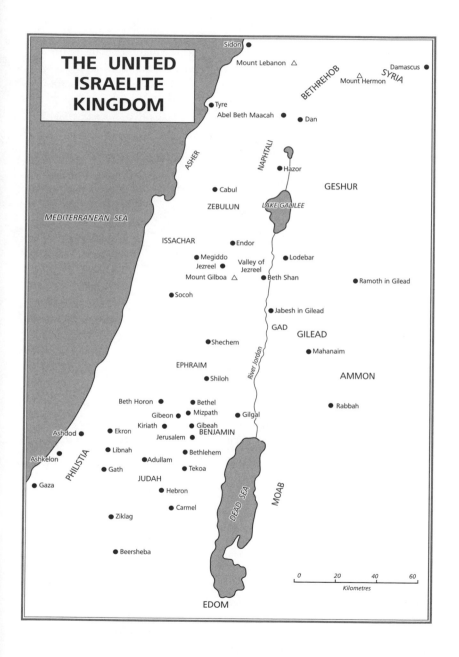

THE UNITED
ISRAELITE
KINGDOM

Sidon

Mount Lebanon △

BETHREHOB

Damascus

SYRIA

Mount Hermon △

Tyre

Abel Beth Maacah

Dan

ASHER

NAPHTALI

Hazor

GESHUR

Cabul

ZEBULUN

LAKE GALILEE

MEDITERRANEAN SEA

ISSACHAR

Endor

Megiddo

Lodebar

Jezreel

Valley of
Jezreel

Mount Gilboa △

Beth Shan

Ramoth in Gilead

Socoh

Jabesh in Gilead

GAD

GILEAD

Shechem

Mahanaim

EPHRAIM

AMMON

Shiloh

Beth Horon

Bethel

River Jordan

Gibeon

Mizpath

Gilgal

Rabbah

Kiriath

Gibeah

Ashdod

Ekron

Jerusalem

BENJAMIN

Ashkelon

Libnah

Bethlehem

PHILISTIA

Adullam

Tekoa

Gaza

Gath

JUDAH

DEAD SEA

MOAB

Hebron

Carmel

Ziklag

Beersheba

0   20   40   60
Kilometres

EDOM

Melchizedek remained in place. Amongst David's warriors, many were of non-Hebrew origin.

The persisting Canaanite influence was insidious for the pure religion of Yahweh brought in from the desert. There is evidence that very many Hebrews virtually adopted the local pagan religion. This can be seen in the names they bore, e.g. Jerubaal, better known to us as Gideon. The "Baals" were the gods of Canaan, the name meaning "owner," that is, of the land. It can be readily understood how the assumption would have been made that, since the Baal owned the land, it would yield crops and feed cattle only if the appropriate sacrifices were made to the "Owner." Each Baal had his "Ishtar," goddess, and she too demanded devotion. A common find even in Israelite cities is of figurines of such goddesses. Much Canaanite religion was of a blatantly sexual nature. Fertility depended on the copulation of the gods and goddesses and this was to be imitated by their human devotees. Even Temples therefore had their attendant prostitutes, both male and female. There seemed to be the distinct possibility that the religion of Moses would be totally submerged in this new environment. It might well have been were it not for the Prophets of Israel. These were the champions of Yahweh. Of whom more anon.

THE PERIOD OF THE UNITED KINGDOM (10TH CENTURY BC)

The Hebrews were not the only peoples on the move and seeking a new patrimony. The Philistines originated in Cyprus (before that most likely from Greece) and attempted to land in the Nile Delta. Repulsed by the Egyptians in a great sea battle (well recorded on a massive frieze by the Egyptians) that took place circa 1165 BC, they settled instead on the southern coastline of Palestine (a name deriving from their occupation of it) at much the same time as the Hebrews were entering from the eastern desert. The two cultures were bound to clash.

At first, the Philistines had a big technological advantage. They possessed the secret of smelting iron, giving their armies a huge advantage over their bronze-wielding enemies. This largely explains the numerous Israelite disasters recorded in 1 Samuel. But the crisis of Philistine domination forced the cohesion of the otherwise disparate Israelite tribes. United by little more than a common faith (however diluted) and some memory of common origins as descendants of Jacob, they were forced into political change. Only allegiance to a king could unite them. Within 1 Samuel, opposing viewpoints to this proposal are evident. Samuel, both Judge and Prophet, regarded the choosing of a human King as implying rejection of Yahweh as Divine King. The religious allegiance should have been enough. He warned the people of the consequences of kingly rule, which they would live to regret. The other viewpoint has Samuel grudgingly realizing that a king was necessary and as seeking out and anointing (a sign of God's choosing and blessing) Saul as the first king of Israel. He soon fell out with Saul, because the latter usurped the religious leadership of the divinely appointed prophet. Perhaps this is the first example of that age-old conflict between secular and religious power, to be played out through the centuries as between emperors and popes, kings and bishops, parliament and priests.

FOR YOUR READING:

1 Samuel 4.1-22: A terrible battle and its consequences
1 Samuel 8.4-10.27: The demand for a King and the choice of Saul (be prepared to detect two sources present here, portraying different attitudes towards the kingship)

Recognizing in Saul a failure, Samuel proceeded, at God's urging, to anoint a new king in secret. This was David, the son of Jesse. David was hugely successful in battle against the Philistines, but his successes aroused such jealously in Saul that he was forced into exile, during which he acted as a mercenary for his erstwhile foes and lived by brigandage. But, on Saul's death, David was recognized as King by the southern tribes of Judah and Benjamin, and shortly after, by the northern tribes. He captured Jerusalem and established it as capital of a united Israel, conveniently for our memory, in 1000 BC. Under him, the borders of Israel were greatly extended (so as to occupy the territory promised by God to Abraham and his descendants) and a powerful government established. So was created the powerful myth of Davidic rule, buttressed by the prophecy of Nathan that David's dynasty should never lack for a successor (a myth that is apparent throughout the Old Testament, underlines much of the New Testament presentation of Jesus as Messiah and is still a potent image in present-day Israel). For the first time in history, Israel was a force to be reckoned with in Middle Eastern politics.

There were important repercussions for the writing of the Old Testament. David established a government organized on Egyptian lines, with an important post, that of secretary. For the first time, there would be the official keeping of records of state. So Israel (at the highest level) became a literate community, in which the scribe played an important role. If all of the history recorded in the Bible until this time has been an Oral History, much marked by the arts of story-telling, of legendary accretion and of folk memory over centuries, from this point onwards we begin to have contemporary recording of events. Not forgetting that the mass of its population would have remained illiterate. This is the raw material of history proper. Not only are there court records, but also more specifically religious writings emanating from Temple priests and the circles of the prophets. Within the next century, the first production of a continuous history of Israel from the time of Abraham would be made.

David's old age was marred by various acts of folly, arising mostly out of the family feuds between the offspring of his many wives. And his final wish to build a Temple of Yahweh was thwarted by divine interdiction. This was, of course, the author's theory: why didn't David, Israel's superstar, build the Temple? It was by God's Will, not David's neglect. So it was Solomon who built the Temple, but at enormous cost. The forced labor gangs employed to build it were indistinguishable from slaves. Whilst Israel prospered, with Solomon's reputation for wisdom achieving international fame, inwardly the kingdom was seething with unrest. This broke out into open revolt under his son and successor, Rehoboam. This split wide open the ever-present sense of grievance between the northern and the southern tribes. So, in the year 922 BC the united kingdom divided as between Israel in the north under the rebel leader, Jeroboam and Judah in the south under the successors of Solomon. It is from this Southern Kingdom that we designate its descendants as Jews (i.e. the people of Judah).

YEARS OF RIVALRY & THE GREAT PROPHETS (9TH TO 6TH CENTURIES BC)

There followed centuries of "sibling" rivalry, sometimes involving bitter conflict, very occasionally co-operation between Israel and Judah. This is depicted in the Books of the Kings, themselves based on official records of both kingdoms. So we typically read, "The rest of the acts of King X, Y or Z, are written in the book of the Chronicles of Israel … or of Judah." This is moralizing history, for each king is judged according to his obedience to or rebellion against the lordship of Yahweh. We detect in it the strong influence of the prophets.

The prophets came to prominence because these were years of great danger for the religion we call Yahwism. Canaanite influence was pervasive (as I have outlined on p. 62). When Kings arose who actively promoted pagan religions, such as Ahab of Israel under the instigation of his evil wife, Jezebel, Yahwism was in danger. As always, the danger produced its hero of the hour. The first was **Elijah**, whose very name breathed defiance: Eli-jah, "*Yahweh is my God.*" The second Book of Kings describes his moments of despair and of triumph, leading to the rout of the prophets of Baal on Mt Carmel. He was succeeded by Elisha, Micaiah and others, whose main characteristic was outright opposition to every vestige of Canaanite paganism. They recalled Israel and Judah to allegiance to Yahweh alone. The depictions of these prophets are legendary in character, so we need to recall that, although historical records were being kept (but only in royal circles), the oral tradition was still active.

This distinguishes these early prophets from those we describe as *Writing Prophets*. Not, most likely, that the prophets themselves wrote much, but rather that they gathered disciples about them who memorized and eventually wrote down their masters' forthright messages. Isaiah, as a courtier, certainly could write. He is depicted as writing the names of his children on tablets (Isaiah 8.1-4), but others were probably illiterate. Jeremiah was usually accompanied by his faithful scribe, Baruch, who wrote as the prophet dictated. About some of them we know very little biographically, but only what they declaimed as "*the word of the Lord*".

There is one over-riding reason why the messages of the prophets were written down so as to become, in time, parts of the Bible. There had been continuous conflict between true prophets and lying prophets. Those we count as "true" were so considered because what they prophesied, especially regarding the impending fate of Israel, and later of Judah, came to fulfillment. It was as if documents long held in secret were suddenly produced as if to say: "If only you had heeded the words of the prophet X, then these dire calamities would not have overtaken you. This is the written record of their testimony and of your folly." For in 722 BC, the city of Samaria, capital of Israel, was sacked and the northern tribes dispersed to all parts of the Assyrian Empire. Thus Israel had ceased to exist. From hence arose the stark theological question: "Had God's covenant promise to Israel thus been rendered null and void?" It is considerably grappled with in the Book of Deuteronomy, in which it is made plain that the maintenance of the covenant is dependant on Israel's obedience to God. For some time, hopes of restoration were placed on the remaining Kingdom of Judah. But its people were no more faithful than those of Israel, about which Jeremiah agonized. Attacked by the Babylonians in 597 BC and again 10 years later, it too was destroyed, Jerusalem sacked, the Temple burned to the ground and its leading citizens marched into exile in Babylonia. This was probably the lowest point of Jewish history, an experience as agonizing to Jews then as was the Holocaust two millennia later. It looked as if Jewish history had come to a dead end and God's covenant with His people been nullified.

THE EXILE (587-537 BC)
This was the most painful and yet the most formative period for the Jewish people. Their capital in ruins, the Temple desecrated, it was as if their God had deserted them. "*By the waters of Babylon, there we sat down and wept ...*" (Psalm 137), so felt their leaders in exile. And yet it was out of this enforced absence in a foreign land that the seeds were sown of a new religious understanding. They came to understand that their God was not confined to the Temple precincts or even to the territory of Judah, that He was Lord of the whole earth. It seems likely that it was this experience of exile which promoted the process by which the religious documents of the past were brought together and given an

editorial framework that reflected the total experience of the Jewish people. What was produced was the Torah, a definitive record of the laws of God as revealed at first to Moses and accumulated over many centuries. The Jews had become the people of a Book. If one name is attachable to this process, it is that of **Ezra**, nicknamed the Scribe. With it came the realization that the Study of the Law of God in meeting places that came to be called "*synagogues*" was an adequate substitute for the offering of sacrifices in the Temple. A distinctively new religion to be known as *Judaism* was in the throes of being born.

Some 50 years after the calamitous destruction of Jerusalem, the Babylonians were themselves conquered by King Cyrus of Persia. He was a remarkable King of international and tolerant outlook and he ordered that the Jews and other captive peoples should be permitted to return to their homes. These moments of high drama were captured by the anonymous prophet whom we call the Second Isaiah, who announced the Good News of Yahweh's personal leading of His People back to their homeland. His writings, contained in Isaiah chapters 40-55, comprise the spiritual high-point of Jewish religion and seem to prefigure the spirit of Jesus' proclamation of the Gospel.

THE RESTORATION OF JEWISH LIFE (537-320 BC)

Amongst those who returned were two outstanding leaders, Nehemiah and Ezra. The dates of their return are difficult to determine. But, under the first, the walls of Jerusalem and the foundations of a new Temple were built; under the second, a religious revival was put into effect, centered on the study and application of the Torah. Bit by bit, Jewish national life was restored, but there occurred also unfortunate side effects in the shape of a fierce sense of national exclusiveness bordering on the xenophobic. This was instanced in particular by action taken against those who had contracted marriages with foreign women. Strict observance of the Sabbath was also a hall-mark.

For almost two centuries, the Jews enjoyed a relatively peaceful existence under the mostly benign rule of the Persians. This came to an abrupt end around the year 321 BC. Alexander the Great won a stunning victory over the Persians at the river Oxus and the whole of the Middle East lay at his feet.

THE PERIOD OF GREEK RULE (320-63 BC)

The Jews fell under the rule of the Greeks. After Alexander's early death, their territory was disputed between the dynasties established by Alexander's generals, the Ptolemies who had seized Egypt, and the Seleucids who established themselves in Syria. Over the entire region, the Greek culture known as Hellenism became the all-pervasive influence. Everywhere, the educated learned to speak Greek and adopt the Greek way of life. Even in Jerusalem, an amphitheatre was constructed, featuring public baths and Olympic-style athletics were contested in the nude.

These practices were deeply inimical to devout Jews. The tensions were exacerbated by the determination of King Antiochus IV "Epiphanies"[21] to wipe out the Jewish religion. In 186 BC, his troops stormed the Jerusalem Temple, desecrated the holy place by sacrificing swine on the altar and ordered all Jews to desist from practicing circumcision and other rituals. This was too much for Matthias and his seven sons, who became known as the Maccabees (the "Hammerers"). They slew a party of Greek officials come to enforce the new rules and thus sparked off the Maccabean Revolt. At first, the Jewish zealots were successful and managed to restore the sacrifices in a purified Temple. The account of their victorious entry to Jerusalem was remembered in Jesus' day, for the story of his entry on Palm Sunday carries echoes of that earlier event.

Amongst them, at least three groups emerged. First were the **Hasidim**, who practiced extreme devotion to the Torah, even to the extent of being martyred rather than to take up arms on the Sabbath. Second were the **Pharisees**, who first emerge during this period as those equally desirous of living by Torah without going to the extremes of the Hasidim. Third were the **Hasmoneans**, who were less scrupulous as regards religion and were eager to exploit the situation for their own political ends. They established a dynasty of rulers, who constantly squabbled. From out of the Hasidim we can just recognize those purists who, disgusted with the political compromises of the Hasmoneans, withdrew completely from public life and withdrew to the desert to establish a religious community beside the Dead Sea. The story of this tumultuous period is recounted in the three Books of the Maccabees, to be found in the Apocrypha.[22]

THE PERIOD OF ROMAN OCCUPATION (63 BC-AD 5)

During the first century BC, the power of Rome waxed as that of Greece waned. A period of civil war amongst the Romans culminated in a battle in 63 BC in which General Pompey defeated Mark Anthony to take control of the Eastern Mediterranean. Pompey entered Jerusalem, demanded entrance to the Holy of Holies (which was reserved for the High Priest alone) and could hardly believe his eyes that it was empty of statuary. Where was the god? The Romans had no desire to rule directly, but gladly handed this over to their puppet, Antipater. He and his family, better known as the Herodeans, were Idumeans (Edomites in Old Testament language) but had adopted the Jewish religion out of convenience. They had remarkable agility at backing the "winning side" in all the perturbations of Roman politics. So it came about that Antipater's son

---

[21] "Epiphanies" means literally "revelation of God," indicating that this mad king supposed himself to be a divine being. The word reappears in the liturgical calendar in the season of Epiphany, ie the manifestation of God in Jesus that was recognized by the Three Wise Men.
[22] An explanation of the Apocrypha can be found in Chapter 12.

Herod was appointed King of the Jews in 40 BC and fought his way into Jerusalem three years later. Thus was set in place the situation into which Jesus was to be born in 6 or 5 BC.

DIAGRAM: HISTORY OF THE JEWISH PEOPLE

The diagram opposite is intended to give you some visual idea of the history of the Jewish people. It pictures Jewish history as a succession of high points and low points, with mountains, valleys and plateaus at various levels in between. The highest peak consists of the covenant God gave to Israel through the mediation of Moses on Mt Sinai. The lowest abyss into which Israel fell occurred in 721, when its capital Samaria fell to the Assyrian invaders and its people were deported; a little over a century later a similar fate befell Judah. With Jerusalem destroyed and the people's leaders sent into exile in Babylon, it looked as if Israel's story had come to an abrupt end. But there was to take place a "resurrection" – when King Cyrus permitted the Jews to return home. The history is complicated, but if you can hold this image in mind, you will the more easily be able to place events into their proper sequence within the story.

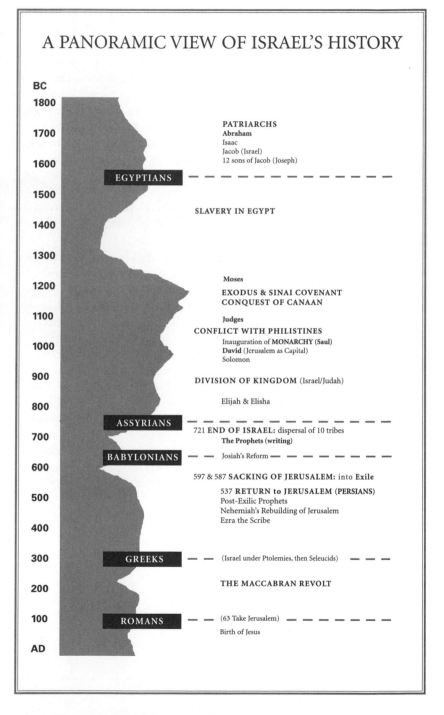

A PANORAMIC VIEW OF ISRAEL'S HISTORY

BC

1800

1700 — PATRIARCHS
Abraham
Isaac
Jacob (Israel)

1600 — 12 sons of Jacob (Joseph)

EGYPTIANS

1500

1400 — SLAVERY IN EGYPT

1300

1200 — Moses
EXODUS & SINAI COVENANT
CONQUEST OF CANAAN

1100 — Judges
CONFLICT WITH PHILISTINES

1000 — Inauguration of **MONARCHY** (Saul)
David (Jerusalem as Capital)
Solomon

900 — DIVISION OF KINGDOM (Israel/Judah)

800 — Elijah & Elisha

ASSYRIANS

700 — 721 **END OF ISRAEL:** dispersal of 10 tribes
The Prophets (writing)

BABYLONIANS — Josiah's Reform

600

— 597 & 587 **SACKING OF JERUSALEM:** into **Exile**

500 — 537 **RETURN to JERUSALEM (PERSIANS)**
Post-Exilic Prophets
Nehemiah's Rebuilding of Jerusalem
Ezra the Scribe

400

300 GREEKS — (Israel under Ptolemies, then Seleucids)

200 — THE MACCABRAN REVOLT

100 ROMANS — (63 Take Jerusalem)
Birth of Jesus

AD

71

The Christian calendar[23]

During Jesus' time, the calendar in use counted the years since the accession to power of Julius Caesar in Rome. It was known as the Julian Calendar. By the sixth century AD it seemed more appropriate to Christians that the years should be counted from the birth of Jesus Christ. The task of computing the new calendar was given to a Roman monk named Exiguus Dionysus. The fixed date to determine Jesus' birth was that it occurred during the reign of Herod, shortly before his death. Unfortunately, Dionysus made a mistake of some five or six years, because subsequent evidence fixes Herod's death at 4 BC. We have therefore to assign Jesus' birth, oddly, to 5 or 6 BC.

THE JEWISH SCRIPTURES

Within these tumultuous years of Jewish history, marked more by disaster than by peace or prosperity, and involving both military occupation by foreign powers and rule by puppet kings, what had happened to Jewish religious belief and hopes? In spite of the assimilation of some, at first to Persian and then to Greek ways, there was always a sizeable number of Jews who clung to their traditional religious practice. Amongst these, the authority of certain written documents emerged and became a pre-eminent feature of their religion. It is likely that the process began in the days of the monarchy, accelerated during the exile and gained momentum on return to the Holy Land. By the time of Jesus, the Jews had become the People of a Book, acknowledging the Mosaic Torah as the chief authority for their religious beliefs and practices, the Prophets as the commentary that explained the chief events of their history in terms of their people's obedience or disobedience to God, and the Writings as a collection of scriptures that inspired and enlightened them in every sphere of life.

---

[23] See Norman Davies, Anno Domini, in *Europe, A History*, p 267.

CHAPTER 6:
THE OLD TESTAMENT

PART 2 – The Mosaic Torah

JEWISH BIBLE, CHRISTIAN BIBLE

The Christian Bible is divided into two main sections, Old Testament and New Testament. The word "Testament" can cause us problems because its meaning has changed since it was first used by the early English translators for the Greek word "diatheke." This denotes a binding agreement between two parties, i.e. a treaty or covenant. Our use of "testament" in the legal term "Last Will and Testament" still retains that original sense. The word could be used in a purely secular sense, whether in making a business deal or in concluding a treaty between two nations. Within the Bible the over-riding sense is that of an accord between God and the people whom He has adopted. This is not an accord between equals, but rather one in which God takes the initiative and offers the agreement out of sheer grace. The most favored term is therefore covenant, so that the two sections of our Bible would be better renamed "The Books of the Old Covenant" and "The Books of the New Covenant." This usefully reminds us that the books themselves don't constitute a covenant, or testament, but that the covenant is the unifying theme of their contents. Nor should we forget that, for Jews, the covenant that God made with Israel through the mediation of Moses on Mt Sinai remains valid to this day and will remain so till the coming of the Messiah. It is not "old" to them. The Christian belief is that, at the Last Supper, Jesus instituted a "new covenant" by which God offered to every follower of Jesus a new relationship with Him on a different basis than that of the "old." But then, for them, Jesus was the Messiah.

EXERCISE

You might look up the following examples of "covenants" within the pages of the book of Genesis. Note carefully the covenants that are agreements between equals and those which imply a relationship of superiority-inferiority. In the Jeremiah passage, reflect on how and why Christians understood them as prophesying the giving of a "new" covenant.

Genesis 9.8-17; 17.1-8; 21.25-34; 31.43-50. And elsewhere: compare **Exodus 24.3-8** with **Mark 14.17-25**, having perused **Jeremiah 31.31-34** en route.

THE ORDERING OF THE JEWISH BIBLE

There is some importance for us to give consideration to the ordering of the books of the Jewish Bible, for the Old Testament in Christian Bibles marks a strongly edited version of it. This is neatly summarized for us in Taffy Davies' cartoon comparison. In the shelving on which the books of the Jewish Bible are ranged, we will immediately note the following:

1. Of the three great sections of it, the order is that of the **TORAH** (Teaching), the **NEVIIM** (Prophets) divided into "Former" and "Latter," and finally, the **KETUVIM** (Writings). By contrast, the Christian Old Testament has the ordering: Law (Torah), Writings and Prophets. This Christian re-ordering was deliberately undertaken so that the words of the prophets should be seen to be fulfilled in the events recorded in the New Testament. It is indeed striking to move directly from the prophecies of Malachi, the last book of the Old Testament in the Christian version, into the opening pages of Matthew's Gospel. This was not quite as miraculous as a pious acquaintance supposed. He assumed that it was thus divinely arranged. It was rather a Christian editorial decision to make the prophecy-fulfillment theme crystal clear.)

2. That there are fewer books here, because the books of Samuel, Kings and Chronicles have each been subdivided in two within the Christian Bible; and the Minor Prophets (one volume in Hebrew) have become 12 separate books in the latter. Hence the Jewish Bible contains 24 scrolls but the Christian Old Testament is made up of 39 books.

3. The Jewish ordering is of particular usefulness in so far as it indicates most clearly which Old Testament books were the latest to be written, i.e. those ranged on the two bottom shelves. A quick comparison between the Jewish and the Christian ordering can yield some illuminating results. For example, the case of the **Book of Ruth**. In the Christian ordering, it is to be found nestling between the books of Judges and 1 Samuel, thus fitting well within the historical situation disclosed at the end of the period of the Judges. But finding it amongst the Writings in the Jewish Bible is a clue to its origins, as a historical novel, set in the time of the Judges, yet reflecting the religious interests of a much later period. Or take the **Book of Daniel**. Ranged as it is in the Christian ordering immediately after the books of the great prophets, Isaiah, Jeremiah and Ezekiel, we might readily assume Daniel to be one amongst the great prophets of Israel. Yet close attention to the text of Daniel demonstrates that this scroll belongs to a quite different milieu. Its late fitting in the Jewish order illuminates its late origins. Although the story is set in the time of the Babylonian Exile of the sixth century BC, its writing occurred in the second century BC and is a reaction to the Seleucid assault on Jewish faith (see page 68) that sparked off the Maccabaean revolt.

THE JEWISH BIBLE & THE CHRISTIAN OLD TESTAMENT

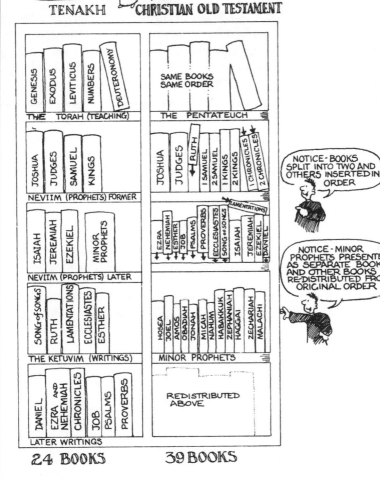

Cartoon by Taffy Davies, from THE BIBLE, The Story of the Book, by Terence Copley, Bible Society, 1990 © Terence Copley.

FOR YOUR READING

Read the book of Ruth and decide for yourself what was the chief purpose in writing it. Do you consider it a straight piece of history or perhaps a historical novel carrying a moral or theological purpose? The clue to its interpretation is contained in the closing verses, with their genealogical list. It will help to remember a) that Ruth was a Moabitess, i.e. a foreigner; and b) that David was the greatest folk hero of Jewish history. It would be also helpful to have some historical background as to how the Moabites were regarded by the Jews (you could look up a Bible dictionary). You might look up these passages: Deuteronomy 23.3-6 and the episode referred to there i.e. in Numbers 22.1-6 & 25.1-5. You may need to contrast these bits of evidence with the kind of situation described in Ezra 10, which may have occurred not so long before Ruth was written. Finally, do you see any relevance of these events to a Christian understanding of race relations today?

With an outline of the history in mind, we turn now to ask how and why the books of the Old Testament, Law, Prophets and Writings came to be written. In this chapter I will attend to the first section of the Jewish Bible, the Torah, always the most important and authoritative part of it.

THE TORAH

In the Greek translation called the Septuagint it was termed the Pentateuch (from "penta," five, "teuchoi," containers, i.e. of scrolls) and this is what they are most commonly called by scholars. In English they have been traditionally called "the Five Books of Moses" which indicates the traditional notion that they were written by Moses. The text itself indicates that Moses wrote at least some part of it, e.g. at Exodus 24.4: "Moses wrote down all the words of the Lord ..." (also Deuteronomy 31:9).

In New Testament times, the Torah could be referred to by Jesus and by his interlocutors by the expression "Moses said ..."; for example, Jesus told the cured leper to "offer the gift that Moses commanded" (Matthew 22.24); he could refer to the Torah's provision for a man to divorce his wife as "commanded by Moses;" and in Mark 12.19 "what Moses wrote for us" concerning a man who had died childless.

Torah has usually been translated into English as "Law," but somewhat misleadingly. The Hebrew means "divine instruction." To Jews, Torah was the revelation of God's will for His people, how they should live and how they should worship Him. The study of Torah was the devout Jew's chief delight, as is evident in Psalm 119.

We should probably not conclude from these references that Jesus had any particular insight into the authorship of the Pentateuch, but rather that he was using the commonly used ascription. The tradition that Moses wrote all of it stood throughout Christian history until the late 17th century, when it was questioned by two Frenchmen, Jean Astruc, a Physician and Richard Simon, a priest.

ONE HAND OR MANY?
Following their lead, the following observations have been made:

1. Moses could hardly have written the account of his own death (in Deuteronomy 34)! The objection had already been met by the assertion that that chapter and the succeeding books had been added by Moses' successor, Joshua. But we note that the style is that of all the preceding chapters.

2. There are considerable differences of style of writing within the five books which suggest, more plausibly, different authors. The reader can easily test this by comparing the style found throughout the book of Deuteronomy with almost anywhere else in the Pentateuch. Or s/he may read a familiar story like that of the Flood and ask whether this reads more naturally as the product of one writer or as that of two or more.

3. Passages of different style correspond with differences of terminology when referring to God. In Genesis, we find passages referring to God by the Hebrew name *Yahweh* ("the Lord" in English versions) in some passages, *Elohim* ("God") in others, *Yahweh Elohim* ("the Lord God") in yet others. This can be visually depicted by using different highlighter coloring of the Yahweh, Elohim and Yahweh Elohim passages. This demonstrates how they lie almost like different strata in rocks.

4. These differences in the names of God correspond with theological differences, as I will spell out further on in this chapter.

5. There is a large amount of repetition, even contradiction, inexplicable if all is the work of one author. For example, at Exodus 6.3 God reveals his name to

Moses in the Sinai Desert as YHWH (Yahweh), declaring that He has not previously been known by that name. Yet, the name Yahweh had been used from Genesis 2.4 onwards as Yahweh Elohim and from Genesis 4.4 onwards as Yahweh alone. It is assumed in these sections that the Patriarchs had worshiped God as Yahweh from the beginning. Both repetitions and contradictions are readily explicable if we have to do with accounts written by different authors.

6. The considerable amount of legal material contained in the Torah contains a large amount of repetition, suggesting the presence of several codes of law, each reflecting different historical and social circumstances, most of it dealing with matters which would have been totally unforeseeable by Moses.

FOR YOUR READING

Read the Story of the Flood in Genesis 6.5-9.19 and ask yourself these questions: 1.Does it read as one unified narrative or do you detect here the work of more than one hand? 2. If your answer to the latter is "Yes," how would you distinguish their authors? Try to account for any repetitions or discrepancies that you have noted. Do these coincide with the names used of God? Don't be too concerned if you cannot positively identify where one account ends and another begins. There are bound to be some fuzzy edges. Your study would be assisted by noting in parallel columns those items in the story which differ, so as to have a comparative survey. Then you might consider what the story meant to those who wrote it bearing in mind especially the differences between the Flood Story contained in the Epic of Gilgamesh and its presentation in the book of Genesis.

WELLHAUSEN'S RESOLUTION

Modern critical research addressed these issues from the early 19th century onwards. They were largely resolved by Julius Wellhausen in his *History of Israel*, its English version being published in 1878. He observed that the kings and prophets of Israel had little or no knowledge of the Mosaic laws, a fact inexplicable on the assumption that Moses had promulgated them all during his lifetime. This observation was reinforced by the account of the reformation that took place under King Josiah in the year 621 BC. It was sparked off by the discovery of "a book of the law" during refurbishment of the Temple in Jerusalem. Its prescriptions gave rise to a radical reformation in which all the pagan shrines still surviving were ruthlessly destroyed. The account of it, in 2 Kings 22.1–23.25 climaxes with a celebration of the Passover, about which we read in 23.22: "No such Passover had been kept since the days of the judges who judged Israel, even during all the days of the kings of Israel and of the kings of

Judah ..." This clearly implies that the Mosaic laws for the Passover, given initially in Exodus 12, were unknown in Israel until 621 BC, i.e. some six centuries later.

The complete Torah, Wellhausen concluded, could not have been issued by Moses in the 12th century BC but more likely by Ezra the Scribe in the fourth century. The Torah was therefore the result of a long historical process that probably began with Moses as mediator of the Sinai Covenant, which included some rudimentary but fundamental laws (perhaps "the Ten Words," as the Ten Commandments were known in Hebrew), and was subject to a continuous process of expansion, revision and editing over many centuries. He identified four main written sources which came to be designated by the letters J, E, D and P.

The four sources

I. The earliest source is **J**, the work of **the Yahwist**. There was some ambiguity as to whether the first letter was pronounced as J or Y, recalling that God had been called Jehovah in the early English versions. Writing in the 10th or ninth century, the Yahwist was Israel's first historian. He was probably a Judean (from the tribe of Judah) reflecting the viewpoint of the southern tribes. He assumed that God had made himself known as Yahweh from the beginning, hence it is his hand evident from Genesis 4.4 onwards. His view of God is strikingly "anthropomorphic" (describing God as if a magnified human: see, e.g. Genesis 3.8; 3.21; 7.16).

••

A God called Jehovah: the translation of God's name as Jehovah was an easily made mistake. The Hebrew Bible used consonants only, until, in the early centuries of Christianity, the scholars known as Masoretes added a system of vowels in order to enable the public reading of scripture by those who no longer spoke Hebrew in daily life. Because the Hebrew text was sacred, it could not be tampered with. So the vowels had to be added either above or beneath the consonants. The consonants of the Divine name (known as the "tetragrammaton," i.e. the four letters) were YHWH in Hebrew. This name was never read aloud (for fear of taking the Name in vain). In place of it, the rabbis substituted an alternative, less sacred word, ADONAI, usually translated "Lord". So what vowels were the Masoretes to supply for the Tetragrammaton? They supplied the vowels actually read, i.e. those for ADONAI, to the consonants of YHWH; but no Jew was so foolish as to suppose that this should be read as JEHOVAH. The early English translators were not to know this.

••

II. The second source was **E**, the work of **the Elohist**. He names God as Elohim throughout Genesis, assuming that God didn't reveal the name Yahweh to Moses until the moment described in Exodus 6.2-9. He was probably of the tribe of Ephraim (one of the northern tribes) indicating that there are distinctive regional viewpoints expressed in these early sources. To him, God was rather more distant than as conceived by the Yahwist. In E, God appears in dreams or communicates by angelic visitors, e.g. in the stories about Joseph. E may be dated to the ninth or eighth century BC.

III. The third source is **D, the Deuteronomist**. This is the only source that can be dated with confidence. As we have seen, a "book of the law" was discovered in the Temple during renovations (see 2 Kings 22. 8 f) in consequence of which King Josiah commanded a radical reformation of religious practices. So precisely did his instructions accord with what was prescribed in Deuteronomy that we can only suppose it was that, or the core of it, that was discovered. Deuteronomy is clearly a "revamping" of the earlier laws of Moses for a new age and situation. The Greek title, indicating "the second law" also summarizes its intention. Whilst Deuteronomy includes some quite ancient material (including some prescribing the barbarous slaughter of entire communities of Canaanites (Deuteronomy 7.1-2), it also reflects the spiritual and ethical teaching of the great prophets of Israel. This is evident in its majestic concept of God as the Lord of the whole earth and its special concern for marginalized members of society such as aliens, widows, orphans and slaves. There is a strongly humanitarian edge to much of the Deuteronomist's teaching.

IV. The fourth source is designated **P**, standing for **the Priestly writers**. These are moreover the editors and eventually the publishers of the entire work. They stamp an impression of unity on all these disparate sources, wishing to inculcate that the whole Torah stemmed from God's law given originally to Moses. They collected the earlier writings of J and E, incorporated them within their own writing, weaving them into one continuous narrative. We may wonder why they didn't make a more complete job of removing inconsistencies, contradictions and repetitions, but we can only guess that they dared not tamper with sources already regarded as "sacred" writings. It follows that much of the Pentateuch appears like a patchwork quilt. But they left Deuteronomy largely as it was.

THE HAND OF THE PRIESTS

The hand of the Priests is readily visible throughout the Pentateuch. They were the keepers of chronological and genealogical lists; they made strong distinctions between "clean" and "unclean" (what is "kosher"); were vitally concerned with everything to do with sacrifice, the duties of priests, the proper keeping of the Sabbath and the ritual of the Temple. We may wonder whether their God had become rather remote, concerned with cult rather than with conduct; and yet, it was they who incorporated the entire content of Deuteronomy with its transcendent theology and more humanitarian considerations into their finished work.

You really need to test out the Four Document hypothesis for yourself since "the proof of the pudding is in the eating." The Wellhausen theory will only convince if it enables you to read hitherto obscure passages with more understanding.

FOR YOUR READING

Genesis 1.1-2 4a As the final editors and publishers of the Torah, the Priestly writers contributed a fitting opening to their narrative, their account of creation. It could be compared and contrasted with the Yahwist's account of the same, beginning at 2.4b. Note carefully the structure of the P account: what does the refrain at the end of each paragraph suggest? (That it is a poem or song with a chorus-like refrain?) It would be helpful to draw a plan of P's concept of the universe (the features of which appear to be based on Babylonian cosmology). This is not surprising if, as we suspect, the account was written during or after the period of exile in Babylonia. Note the concept of the "firmament," like an enormous dome overarching the Earth, separating the waters above from those below. Clearly what we call space was thought of by them as liquid. Note how they conceived sun, moon and stars to be. You may ponder the question: what was the length of a day prior to the creation of the sun on the fourth day? What, according to this account, is the relation of humankind to the rest of the animal creation? Do you think we are meant to consider this a scientific account of creation, to be compared with modern theories of cosmology or is its purpose entirely different?

If so, what is its purpose? One clue is to suppose that, as with much story-telling, the "punch-line" comes at the end (i.e. is it chiefly a song about the sabbath, which had become a vital aspect of the Priestly religion?) Ponder the suggestion that this song was the text of a great annual New Year festival in the Temple in which the goodness of creation was re-enacted and the Sabbath celebrated. Most importantly of all, what does this passage reveal about God (especially the P writers' concept of God) and His relationship with humanity? Note the P characteristics: creation was effected by God's Word ("Let there be... and it was...",) creation was by "separation" of one element from another, the goodness of everything made, the repudiation of pagan beliefs (e.g. of any notion that sun, moon and stars were themselves deities to be worshiped), humanity as made in God's image (which comprises male and female together) as the high point of God's purpose, to have charge over all creatures as God's stewards. Finally, God's achievement is celebrated in the Sabbath rest.

MOSES AS THE ORIGINATOR OF TORAH

How does this modern understanding of the Pentateuch affect our appreciation of Moses' role in it? The theory immediately removes many of the inconsistencies that were glaring in the traditional attribution of it all to Moses. Yet we need to understand why it was so attributed to him. Moses was the founding figure of the distinctive faith of the Old Testament. Although we can know little about him as a historical person, for our sources have all passed through centuries of oral tradition such that much of the account is distinctively legendary, yet he towers over the scene. Without him, the distinctive faith of Israel is inexplicable. He welded a rabble of slaves into a people by the force of his apprehension of Yahweh as the God who had rescued his people, bound them to Himself in covenant and led them to the land of His Promise. And he gave them a structure of fundamental Law. It was not surprising therefore that as the Israelites, settling in Canaan, encountered new situations that required new legal rulings, that these a) were built on the foundation of the Ten Commandments and b) that they were considered still to be "Laws of Moses." His spirit (we might rather say the Spirit of God that was in him) still guided them. There is a parallel in English legal history. King Alfred was the first great English law-giver. For centuries after him, every new law enacted was still thought of as law promulgated by Alfred. So Moses remained the foundational influence within the Torah, even though it took centuries and a thousand and one accumulations and revisions made by priests, judges and prophets, all working "in the spirit of Moses," to arrive at the whole "Book of the Law" (identical with our Pentateuch) which Ezra the Scribe read to the people of Jerusalem in the fourth century BC.

FOR YOUR READING

Ezra 7.1-13 for the circumstances in which Ezra was permitted to return to Jerusalem; and **Nehemiah 8. 1-18** for his role in introducing the Book of the Law (Torah) to the people. Note carefully any indication that what the people heard in the public reading of the Torah was new to their ears. Does this, in your view, support the hypothesis that what Ezra read out was the completed Torah?

The Oral Tradition

Since Wellhausen's day, there has been considerable debate, a fair consensus in accepting his hypothesis, some totally rejecting it and many others refining it. Some find evidence for more than four sources. Probably the greatest revision of the theory has come from those questioning how early the reduction of Israel's story to written form took place. These emphasize the role of oral tradition, whereby stories would have been passed on by word-of-mouth for centuries before they were ever written down. This must have been the case with the stories about the Patriarchs, living as they did in the midst of the second millennium BC; with the Exodus from Egypt and the entry into Canaan. People who were migratory for centuries would hardly carry written records with them except perhaps for something like the Ten Commandments in their portable Temple, the Ark of the Covenant.) Writing comes only with settlement in towns and the adoption of a sedentary way of life, which hardly occurred for Israel before the year 1000 BC. Even then, this was only for a small elite who lived in or around the king's court. The tendency nowadays, as a result of more intensive archaeological excavation of sites in the Holy Land, is to postpone by centuries any picture of the Israelites as a settled city-dwelling (and thereby a literary) people.

It follows then that the earlier sources, notably of J and E, probably represent what were originally oral traditions; hence the legendary character of much of their portrayal of the Patriarchs, of Moses and the Exodus, of the settlement in Canaan, of the Judges who had periodically to save Israel from their enemies and of those Prophets such as Elijah and Elisha who championed allegiance to Yahweh alone against all temptations to revert to paganism. It is possible to discern within the Old Testament some accurate remembrance of the days when all was oral and nothing yet written, especially in little snatches of poetry (since these were most easily remembered), such as we find in Numbers 6.24–26; or Numbers 10.35-36; Numbers 21.14–15, 17-18 & 27–30; or, the longer poem in Judges 5. Even Deuteronomy, whose promulgation we can mostly assign to the seventh century BC, contains passages that are likely of extremely ancient origin, such as Deuteronomy 26.5–11 and 27.11-26. But, at some stage, these oral traditions were committed to writing. This likely took place in various regional centers of special religious significance in Israel in the centuries before everything was centralized in Jerusalem, places like Bethel, Gilgal, Hebron, Shechem, Shiloh and others. We should imagine stories of particular local significance being collected, for example, at Hebron concerning Abraham and Isaac; or further north, at Bethel, stories about Jacob. It is also highly likely that it was in such centers that the customary laws governing the local community were gathered and written. The regional character of many laws would account for the originally separate legal codes that lie side-by-side in the Torah.

At some point the written "histories" dubbed J and E, were set down and treasured in the areas of their production. Some have championed the view that the Yahwist was the world's first historian, possibly earlier even than Homer (the author of the Iliad and the Odyssey, usually dated to the ninth or eighth BC).

THE IMPACT OF TWIN DISASTERS (721 & 597 BC)

It would seem likely that no attempt was made to bring together a national history and to codify a national legal code until two cataclysmic events had occurred. In 721 BC the capital of Israel, Samaria, was ransacked by the Assyrians and its people dispersed, this marking the end of the state of Israel. This enabled the southern Kingdom of Judah, centered on Jerusalem, to adopt the mantle of all that was meant by Israel and to attempt to continue the national traditions. One result of this is that henceforth the Judean viewpoint predominates, making for a revisionist history in which the city of Jerusalem, the Davidic dynasty of Kings, the Temple and its priesthood take center stage. But Judah's independence was not to last long. Prophets warned that it was because of disobedience to Yahweh that Israel had been punished, and that a like fate would befall Judah if its people did not repent and return to the Lord. Under King Josiah, some attempt was made at radical reformation, with the destruction of heathen shrines (including many that had previously been held sacred in Israel) and centering all worship in the one Temple in Jerusalem. But it was all too late. The Babylonians stormed and ransacked Jerusalem, including its Temple, in 597 BC and returned 10 years later to send most of the leading Jews into captivity. For 50 years these remained in exile. The last King of the Davidic line died in captivity. It appeared that all of God's promises to Abraham and his successors had come to naught.

IN EXILE (587-537 BC)

But the harsh experience of captivity in fact led to a much deeper and longer lasting reformation in the religious thinking of those Jews in exile. In fact, the conditions of their exile were not harsh. The evidence is that the Jewish community in exile flourished. When 50 years later, from circa 537 BC, King Cyrus of the Persians, the new overlord of Babylonia, permitted the Jews to return to their homeland, it would seem that many chose to remain in Babylonia, which became, in centuries to come, a major center of Jewish culture and religion. A major recension of the Talmud, representing the peak of Jewish religion and practice, would be produced many centuries later within this community. It becomes apparent that the experience of exile was the catalyst from which emerged a religious revolution. Jews in exile realized that their god Yahweh was not confined to the Jerusalem Temple, that he was the Lord of the Universe and God of all peoples. It seems likely that it was in exile that the process began of drawing together the various records, oral and written, of Israel's past; and producing one continuous account, all edited from a predominantly priestly view-point. The final content and shape of the Torah was undoubtedly determined by those we call the Priestly writers.

This entire process was accelerated by the return to Jerusalem of those Jews who accompanied Nehemiah and Ezra. Much occupied with the re-building of the city walls and of the Temple, they were equally determined to rebuild a community of people wholly consecrated to God's Service. Hence the predominant interest in the Torah of, on the one hand, the stories of the Patriarchs, of Moses and the Exodus, depicting Israel as God's chosen people; and, on the other, in all the laws pertaining to the furnishing of the Temple, the duties of the priests and the detail of the sacrifices by which the community's relationship with God would be regulated. If we wish to single out the precise point at which the Torah emerges, it would be in the record of Ezra's promulgation of the Torah, described in Nehemiah chapter 8. It is likely that the "book of the law" displayed before the assembled people was virtually identical with the Five Books of Moses to be found in our Bibles. These books of the law were ascribed to Moses' authorship. We could summarize the matter by saying that what Moses had begun, had been handed on orally over many centuries, then written down, was finally completed by Ezra the Scribe. The entire process had taken some nine centuries.

The traditional view ascribed the completed Pentateuch to God's inspiration as channeled through just one person, Moses. The newer consensus of scholarship need not imply any rejection of the notion of inspiration, but rather to see it as being diffuse, as being transferred to the whole community of the People of God over countless generations and through many centuries. If we need chapter and verse to support this, we might cite the episode recounted in Numbers 11. Moses, overburdened by the demands of his people was commanded to choose out 70 elders to share the burden. Some of the Spirit that was in him was transferred to them. To attribute all inspiration to Moses uniquely is not justifiable. To suppose that the Pentateuch was written by many pairs of hands rather than by one need not affect how we regard the Old Testament as sacred scripture.

COMPLETION OF THE JEWISH SCRIPTURES

By means of the process I have described, all the writings ascribed to Moses were collected and edited into the form of five large scrolls known as the Torah, the "divine instruction," or the Five Books of Moses (in Greek, the Pentateuch), which has ever since been the corner stone of the religious system known as Judaism. We might say that the Torah is to Jews what the Gospel is to Christians. By the time of Jesus, the scrolls of the Prophets and the Writings had been added to the Torah; thus making up the completed Jewish scriptures known as the TANACH. This acronym is made of up of "TA," from Torah; "NA," from Neviim (the plural of "nabi," prophet) and "CH," from Chetuvim (or Ketuvim), writings.

ENDNOTE:

Had I read Walter Brueggemann's excellent *"An Introduction to the Old Testament"*, with the subtitle *"The Canon and Christian Imagination"* before writing these chapters rather than after, I would have altered my account slightly on two counts. First, I would have explained more explicitly than I do how a great deal of Israel's retelling of its past is in order to shed light on the situation current at the time of its recording. Brueggemann demonstrates convincingly that the Torah's account of the Exodus and of Israel's subsequent forty years wandering in the Wilderness is considerably colored by its probable composition in Exile in Babylon. The Jews then were experiencing their own hope of Exodus and home-coming. Both the Priestly writers and the Deuteronomists selected and highlighted those elements of the ancient stories that would facilitate their re-entry into the Promised Land. They were not interested in history as mere facts, but only as yielding guidance for a community under Yahweh their God.

Second, I would have given a little more credence to the 'canonical' stage of the scrolls. Whilst not ignoring the constitutive segments (J, E, and continuing oral traditions) that go to make up the completed whole, the Torah, it was this final stage that became authoritative for the Jewish people and ultimately for Christians.

CHAPTER 7:
THE OLD TESTAMENT

Part 3 – THE PROPHETS OF ISRAEL

The writings of the prophets form the second section of the Hebrew Bible and these are divided into two sub-divisions:

A. THE FORMER PROPHETS:

These are what we would think of as historical books, those of Joshua, Judges, Samuel and Kings. In the Hebrew Bible, the latter two form just one book each, whereas in the Christian Bible they were subdivided into two. But why are they classified as "prophets?" Because they contain history written from the prophetic point of view. There is no such thing as neutral, objective history. The prophets were the great spiritual teachers of Israel, who taught their people to see their history as one of God's constant inter-action with them, as a dialog in which God is faithful, Israel sadly unfaithful, and from their disobedience flowed a series of disasters. So prophetic history was written to put over the spiritual truth, to rub home the moral lesson. From which it was hoped that those who read it and those who heard it would draw the proper conclusions, amend their lives and live by God's laws. This moralistic history is particularly apparent in the Book of Kings. The king who is faithful to God brings blessing and peace to his people; the king who is unfaithful ("who did evil in the sight of the Lord") brings calamity. Some kings, such as Omri, of great importance historically, received hardly more than a mention, simply because they didn't attract either prophetic approval or disapproval. Others, of far less importance historically, received much attention, because some spiritual lesson was to be learned from their example.

B. THE LATTER PROPHETS

These are the books of the prophets proper since they contain the collected oracles of prophets such as Isaiah, Jeremiah, Ezekiel, together with those termed "Minor Prophets," such as Amos, Hosea, Joel, etc. The term "minor" does them a disservice, suggesting their inferiority by comparison with those first named. The term relates solely to the length of their writings. All 12 of them could be contained within one scroll. For the importance of their teaching they were in no way inferior. In some cases, they are both more comprehensible and quite as powerful as those which have a scroll to themselves.

These two sections comprise what in the Hebrew Bible is termed the **NEVIIM**, the plural form of the word "nabi" meaning "prophet." Just as with the case of the Pentateuch, the assembling of the writings of the prophets was a slow process, over a long period of time, reaching its completion in the centuries immediately before Christ such that Jesus himself referred to his people's scriptures as "the Law and the Prophets." By his day, the latter had obviously achieved recognition alongside the Torah as a part of the spiritual heritage of the Jewish people, although the more conservative minded, such as the Sadducees, regarded the Torah alone as authoritative. But in the synagogues, selections of the Prophets were read each Sabbath after the readings from Torah. Recall the episode at Nazareth in which Jesus was handed the scroll of Isaiah, from which he read (Luke 4.16-20). It isn't clear whether he read a passage set by the authorities or himself chose which passage he would read.

It is possible to imagine Torah and Prophets as being in some respect in opposition to each other. Certainly they represent two strands of influence (to be found in most religions) as between the "institutional" and the "charismatic." The chief influence in forming the Torah was that of the priests, who controlled the Temple, the ritual and the legal systems – these were naturally conservative, the guardians of the past. The prophets, by contrast, were more inspirational, radicals, looking to find God and His Will in the here and now. Frequently they clashed as they still do in church circles. But the opposition can be exaggerated. Sometimes the tendencies converge. Moses was undoubtedly the great legislator (or so he was perceived in the tradition) but he was also regarded as the greatest of all the Prophets. As Deuteronomy 34.10 puts it: "There never has yet arisen in Israel a prophet like Moses, whom the Lord knew face to face." But prophets too could become institutionalized, mere pawns subservient to the will of the current monarch. Jeremiah, during the last days of the Davidic monarchy, found himself as much opposed by the prophets as by priests and people. The discernment as between true and false prophecy was always a major issue in Israel.

THE BEGINNINGS OF PROPHECY

These are humble and therefore obscure. It would seem that, as in most human societies, there were always some people endowed with a "sixth sense," people with telepathic powers, who dreamt dreams and saw visions, which they then interpreted to those without such powers. In some societies, these were called shamans or medicine men.

In 1 Samuel 9, we hear about a man called Kish who had lost some donkeys. He dispatched his son Saul, with a manservant, to find them. The servant suggests that they consult a Man of God called Samuel. At verse nine there is the interpretative comment: "When someone wished to consult God, he would say, Let us go to the seer. What is nowadays called a prophet used to be called a seer." A seer, a man with a "sixth sense," a clairvoyant. As the story develops, Samuel anoints Saul, in secret, to be King of Israel. And Saul is told that his election as King will be confirmed when, going homewards, he will meet with a band of prophets, playing lute and drum and fife, with whom he will fall into a prophetic ecstasy. When this happened, the people exclaimed, "Is Saul also amongst the prophets?" Evidently, such charismatic behavior (sounding like manifestations of the Toronto Blessing) was expected of bands of prophets. To Saul, it was confirmation that his anointing with oil (representing God's choice and blessing of him) was for real. Bands of prophets evidently displayed "weird" behavior, as we may suspect, in part self-induced by dancing and drumming, producing a trance-like ecstasy. Interestingly, those who came to be regarded as the great prophets of the Bible, although displaying some "psychic" powers, largely distanced themselves from such behavior. They were characterized by depth of spiritual insight and moral judgment rather than by bizarre behavior. And they tended to be "loners" rather than members of bands. These latter come to be representative rather of false prophecy.

THE CHAMPIONS OF YAHWEH

From out of such obscure origins, there arose prophets who were major figures in the life of Israel. They arose to give combat to those pagan influences that threatened to destroy the distinctive faith of Israel. Such were Elijah and Elisha. Their very names bear witness to their allegiance: "Eli-jah," My God is Yahweh; and "Eli-sha," My God saves. They became the champions of Yahweh as the sole God of Israel, which put them in immediate confrontation with a king such as Ahab, whose wife Jezebel had most blatantly imported her foreign gods with her. The graphic accounts of their confrontation are to be found in 1 Kings 17-2 Kings 13. The markedly legendary character of these accounts will readily be observed, which is best explained on the assumption that their deeds were recounted by popular story-tellers over several generations and grew in the telling. This is not to question their undoubted importance in rescuing Israel from the surrounding paganism. The story of Ahab's vineyard demonstrates how cheaply paganism valued a poor man's life and how Elijah's action procured the rights of the common man, rights only secured in obedience to God. It also shows beyond any doubt that, for the prophets, there could be no division between religion on the one hand and matters of politics, economics and social life on the other. The outcome of this series of events is a coup d'etat sanctioned, and to some extent instigated, by Elisha. Another prophet of similar ilk was Micaiah. The story of his disputation with a band of prophetic "yes men," recounted in I Kings 22, is particularly instructive.

The Writing Prophets

What distinguishes the prophets whose books are to be found in the Old Testament from those considered above is that, with them, we have written records of their messages. It is not that these prophets themselves wrote any of the books named after them, but that their disciples and associates recorded many of their speeches.

THE PROPHET AMOS

We will illustrate the most important considerations to make when reading the prophets with one example only, that of the prophet Amos. If we are to understand his message, or that of any of the prophets, we need a certain amount of prior information. Here the prefaces given in many modern translations, such as the GNB, are most helpful. We need to know when the prophet lived and in what political-cum-social-cum-religious circumstances he prophesied. In the case of Amos, the first verse gives us invaluable information: "The words of Amos, who was among the shepherds of Tekoa, which he saw concerning Israel in the days of King Uzziah of Judah and in the days of King Jeroboam son of Joash of Israel, two years before the earthquake." (Amos 1:1). The references to Uzziah of Judah and to Jeroboam of Israel are easily checked out. Most modern Bibles will have a chronological chart appended, such as that in the GNB. Here we learn that Uzziah reigned in Jerusalem from 781–740 BC and Jeroboam II in Samaria from 783-743 BC. From any standard history of Israel, we would learn that because the great empires of Egypt and Assyria were comparatively quiescent at this time, it had allowed the Israelites to experience a previously unheard of prosperity. A careful reading of the book of Amos will reveal the kind of abuses, social, economic and religious that had arisen in Israel in consequence of this prosperity. The earthquake mentioned must have been high on the Richter scale for it is referred to also in Zechariah 14.5.

BIOGRAPHICAL INFORMATION

One passage only within Amos yields important biographical information. Even this is more than we have for some of the prophets. This is in chapter 7, vv 10–17: "Then Amaziah, the priest of Bethel, sent to King Jeroboam of Israel, saying, Amos has conspired against you in the very center of the house of Israel; the land is not able to bear all his words. For thus Amos has said, Jeroboam shall die by the sword, and Israel must go into exile away from his land. And Amaziah said to Amos, O seer, go, flee away to the land of Judah, earn your bread there, and prophesy there; but never again prophesy at Bethel, for it is the king's sanctuary, and it is a Temple of the kingdom. Then Amos answered Amaziah, I am no prophet, nor a prophet's son; but I am a herdsman, and a dresser of sycamore trees, and the Lord took me from following the flock, and the Lord said to me, Go, prophesy to my people Israel."

Amos was a man of Tekoa, a village some 12 miles south of Jerusalem, within the territory of Judah. But he had traveled north into Israel in order to prophesy at Bethel, the royal sanctuary, as he believed God had commanded him. Since his message pronounced doom on King Jeroboam, it was hardly surprising that his message aroused the ire of Amaziah, the priest of Bethel. The priest first of all insults the prophet (or so we may assume his addressing him as "seer" to imply), then adjures him to return to his own land and prophesy there. In his response, Amos appeals to his divine calling. At first sight, his words "I am no prophet nor a prophet's son" appears to disown the appellation "prophet." But he is distancing himself from the bands of prophets to be found at such sanctuaries, regarding them as false prophets. Then he describes his vocation. It was whilst he was herding the sheep and tending the fig trees that the Lord "took him" and commanded him to prophesy to the people of Israel.

THE SOURCE OF THE PROPHET'S INSPIRATION

How did such a prophet, who prefaced his words with "Thus says the Lord," receive his divine messages? The very first verse of Amos speaks of "*The words ... which he saw concerning Israel.*" The REB translates: "He received these words in **visions** about Israel ..." In chapter 7, we are given examples of such visions: we have that of a swarm of locusts devouring the crops (vv 1-2); of a forest fire sweeping over the land (vv 4-6); and of Yahweh himself standing, like a master builder, with plumb-line in hand, checking the rectitude of a wall (vv 7-9). In 8.1 the Lord shows him a basket of ripe fruit. In what follows, we have punning on the Hebrew for fruit (qayits) and for the end (qets). We may guess that the fruits were over-ripe, near their end; from which simile God declares that Israel is about to come to its end. At 9.1 the prophet sees the Lord standing beside the altar (presumably of the Temple in Jerusalem). But the most telling information is to be found at 3.7-8: "Surely the Lord God does nothing, without revealing his secret to his servants the prophets. The lion has roared; who will not fear? The Lord God has spoken; who can but prophesy?" Another insight (from another prophet) is given in Isaiah 50.4-5: "The Lord God has given me the tongue of a teacher, that I may know how to sustain the weary with a word. Morning by morning he wakens, wakens my ear to listen as those who are taught. The Lord God has opened my ear ..." In this case, the message was audible rather than visionary. By whatever means, whether in visions, voices or dreams, God reveals his purpose to those He himself has called to be his spokesmen. The heart of the matter is put most clearly in Jeremiah 23.18: "For who has stood in the council of the Lord so as to see and to hear his word? Who has given heed to his word so as to proclaim it?" The metaphor is that of a King surrounded by his most favored servants. He divulges his secret purposes to those whose sole duty is to put them into effect. The response to this rhetorical question is clear: only those truly called of God in contrast to those who speak lies and vanity. For the issues at stake, see Jeremiah 23.16-22.

HOW WAS THE PROPHET'S MESSAGE CONVEYED?

There was a long tradition amongst pre-literate peoples to count amongst them inspired spokesmen who uttered their thoughts in rhyming verses. It would seem that this was the case with the prophets; a fact which is much more easily recognized in all the modern versions which set out their speeches as poetry. The chief characteristic of Hebrew poetry is that of parallelism, which can be appreciated from almost any page of the prophetic writings: e.g. at Amos 8.4-8:

> "Hear this, you that trample on the needy,
>   and bring to ruin the poor of the land, saying,
> "When will the new moon be over so that we may sell grain;
>   and the sabbath, so that we may offer wheat for sale?
> We will make the ephah small and the shekel great,
>   and practice deceit with false balances,
> buying the poor for silver and the needy for a pair of sandals,
>   and selling the sweepings of the wheat."

You will notice that the inset lines reflect those preceding them. Each is a simple variant on the line before it. Although it adds very little to the thought of the preceding line, it is a powerful rhetorical device, by which the essential message is rammed home into the hearers' minds. There is surely no doubt that such rhythmical speeches would have been the more easily remembered than any shapeless prose. We can detect the refrain "yet you did not return to me," in 4.6-12, indicating one formula that the prophet used. It is likely that part of the prophet's equipment was this ability to versify and, equally, the sacred duty of his disciples that they should commit the messages to memory. At a later stage, they rendered them in writing.

THE KEY FEATURES OF AMOS' MESSAGE

When Amos journeyed into Israel, he saw much that disturbed him deeply: behavior in market place and law court, in royal palace and Temple that was totally alien to the manner in which God's People should be conducting themselves.

❖ Amos perceived himself as God's spokesman. What he proclaimed was not any personal opinion, but the message entrusted to him by God. A majority of all the prophecies are concluded with the ringing declaration: "Thus says the Lord." Therefore he was in no way silenced by the anger of Amaziah at Bethel's Temple, but rather provoked into making a yet harsher prophecy (7.16-17) as to the fate awaiting King Jeroboam and Israel.

❖ Amos' vision was fed by a profound understanding of the greatness and majesty of God (perhaps the fruit of long hours of meditation whilst guarding the sheep). At 4.13, 5.8-9 and 9.5-6 we have creed-like verses that celebrate the glory of God in creation and in human affairs – they possibly derive from Temple worship.

❖ Amos' prophecy was international in scope. He knew that Yahweh, the God who had created Israel out of the rabble that had emerged from slavery in

Egypt, was the God of the whole earth. His prophecies were not therefore confined to Israel and Judah but to all the surrounding nations. In chapters one and two, we read of his denunciation of the conduct of the peoples of Damascus, Gaza, Tyre, Edom, Ammon, and Moab before then turning the spotlight onto Judah and finally on Israel; pronouncing the punishment to fall on each of them. This was doubtless a clever strategy, for in dealing first with Israel's enemies, he would likely have won the keen attention of his audience only then to "blast" their eardrums with the fierce judgment of God against them.

❖ Had any of his audience supposed that Israel alone had been favored with God's guidance to their Promised Land, they would have been surprised to hear Amos' assertion that Ethiopians, Philistines and Syrians had equally been led by God to the place of His appointing (9.7-8). How would his Israelite audience have reacted to the statement that the Ethiopians were as valuable to God as the Israelites? Here is already a sharp riposte to the exclusivism that had become typical of Israel.

❖ If any then had asked what advantage there was in being God's specially chosen people, (a matter to which Paul had to address himself many centuries later, in Romans 9-11) Amos' reply was startling. He represents God as declaring: "Hear this word that the Lord has spoken against you, O people of Israel, against the whole family that I brought up out of the land of Egypt: You only have I known of all the families of the earth; therefore I will punish you for all your iniquities." (3.1-2) We might paraphrase this as meaning: "The more God has favored you, the more He has the right to expect from you. And in so far as you fail Him, the more will you be punished." How terrible to be God's chosen people!

❖ Amos' fiercest attack was on those who exploited and cheated the poor and destitute. The unheard of prosperity experienced during Jeroboam's reign had evidently made the rich richer and the poor poorer. So throughout the book we read example after example of both the ostentatious wealth of some and the utter destitution of others; and that such blatant discrimination was aided and abetted by the very institutions that should have been the guardians of the God-given rights of the whole people. For an example of the oppression of the poorest, see the following passage: "For three transgressions of Israel, and for four, I will not revoke the punishment; because they sell the righteous for silver, and the needy for a pair of sandals. They who trample the head of the poor into the dust of the earth, and push the afflicted out of the way…" (2.6-7). When an Israelite became so poor that he could not meet his obligations, the only recourse was to sell himself into slavery. He could evidently be bought for a few pieces of silver, or even at the cost of a pair of sandals. Or, see 8.4-6, with its depiction of the greed of the rich merchants who long for the end of their religious festivals, so that they can pursue their fraudulent sales in exploitation of the poor, to whom the refuse of the wheat was sold, and even then, using false balances.

❖ Most damnable of all was what took place in the royal Temple at Bethel, for in the place in which God's holiness should be evident and His commandments obeyed, they were the most blatantly flouted. It is clear in 2.6-8 that sacred prostitution was practiced there (as was commonplace in the Temples of Baal); that landowners lounged about with garments taken as security against loans (against the clear teaching of Deuteronomy 24.1-12); and that wine from a man's vineyard given in payment of fines was being openly drunk in the Temple. That drunkenness was a problem is evident from 4.1.

❖ So corrupt had the Temple become that Amos could mock those who attended its rituals: "Come to Bethel – and transgress; to Gilgal – and multiply transgression; bring your sacrifices every morning, your tithes every three days; bring a thank-offering of leavened bread, and proclaim freewill-offerings, publish them; for so you love to do, O people of Israel! says the Lord God."(4.4-5) "A lot of good may it do you!" we can imagine him adding. And at 5. 21-24, he launches the most devastating attack on a religion which sought to bribe God into turning a blind-eye upon their offences: "I hate, I despise your festivals, and I take no delight in your solemn assemblies. Even though you offer me your burnt-offerings and grain-offerings, I will not accept them; and the offerings of well-being of your fatted animals I will not look upon. Take away from me the noise of your songs; I will not listen to the melody of your harps." God cannot abide hypocritical religion. He can accept the worship only of those who practice justice in their dealings. In several magnificent verses, Amos expressed the only kind of religion that was acceptable to God. The above quoted passage concludes with this: "Let justice roll down like waters, and righteousness like an ever-flowing stream." (5.24) In the same chapter we have: "Thus says the Lord to the house of Israel: Seek me and live; but do not seek Bethel, and do not enter into Gilgal …" (5.4-5); and: "Seek good and not evil, that you may live; and so the Lord, the God of hosts, will be with you, just as you have said. Hate evil and love good, and establish justice in the gate; it may be that the Lord, the God of hosts, will be gracious to the remnant of Joseph." (5.14-15). In Israelite townships, the only public area for either trade or the administration of justice was just inside the city gate. It was there that the elders met to conduct their business.

❖ The height of Israel's folly was in its people's facile assumption that "the day of the Lord" would see the destruction of their enemies and the triumph of Israel. Amos' riposte was devastating to their pride: "Alas for you who desire the day of the Lord! Why do you want the day of the Lord? It is darkness, not light; as if someone fled from a lion, and was met by a bear; or went into the house and rested a hand against the wall, and was bitten by a snake. Is not the day of the Lord darkness, not light, and gloom with no brightness in it?" (5.18-20)

❖ What was the nature of the punishment that would fall on this disobedient people? They were to be numerous: blight and mildew on their crops, drought and famine of bread, but worse, a famine "of hearing the words of the Lord" (8.11-12) such that those desirous of seeking the word of the Lord would not find it. It would be as if God had turned his back on them. Then there would be foreign invasion, with terrible slaughter amongst the people, for God would use other nations as His instruments of punishment. Punishment would fall most heavily on the King and his counselors, who had lead Israel astray; and finally, the people be led away into captivity (5.27, 6.14).

❖ Amos saw beyond the apparent tranquility of Israel's situation vis-à-vis the great empires of the Middle East. He knew that the Assyrians, after a long period of weakness, were now beginning to "flex their muscles" and would shortly threaten all of these small kingdoms. The passage 6.1-3 indicates that the Assyrian invasion was already under way, such that neighboring cities already lay in ruins. How right he was, for in 721 BC the Assyrians laid siege to Samaria, and, under King Sargon II, captured the city and dispersed its most important citizens. This marked the end of Israel as an independent nation.

❖ We do not know whether Amos lived to see the destruction of Israel in 721 BC; probably not. And yet there are passages here that imply that what he had prophesied has indeed occurred. For instance: "Hear this word that I take up over you in lamentation, O house of Israel: Fallen, no more to rise, is maiden Israel; forsaken on her land, with no one to raise her up." (5.1-2) Unless it were the case that he foresaw the event so vividly that it were to him as if it had occurred. However, it is highly likely that the very preservation of Amos' speeches was because of what happened in 721 BC. The fall of Samaria was the final vindication of the prophets' message. Those who had memorized his teaching must have felt, when the blow fell, that such things would not have happened had Israel heeded Amos' message. These terrible events proved beyond all doubt that he was a true prophet who had declaimed the Word of God.

Our canonical book of Amos ends on a note of optimism, for the passage 9.11-15 prophesies the restoration of Israel. It has to be questioned whether these were indeed prophecies of Amos? It has to be said that such notes of optimism are not to be found elsewhere in his book. It would seem likely that they were added some two centuries after Amos' day, by those who had experienced the Babylonian exile and who had returned to Jerusalem, believing that God was indeed about to restore Israel (note that the expectation of it was still being asked in the early days of the Christian Church, for see the question posed by his disciples to Jesus, reported in Acts 1.6). It was not unknown for editors to bring even a sacred writing up-to-date, even to the point of misrepresenting the prophet's message.

EVOLUTION OF OLD TESTAMENT SCRIPTURES

1800	THE ORAL TRADITION
	Myths and Folk-tales about beginnings of
1700	the world and humankind.
	●●●●●
1600 PATRIARCHS	Legendary Stories about the Patriarchs:
	Abraham, Isaac, Jacob, & Joseph.
1500	●●●●●
SLAVERY IN EGYPT	Stories explaining origins of names of
1400	people, places and customs.
	●●●●●
1300	Stories about Moses and the Exodus – the
	Sinai Covenant and wanderings in the
EXODUS (Moses)	wilderness – and the entry into Canaan.
1200	●●●●●
JUDGES	Clusters of stories & early laws collected in
1100	religious sanctuaries such as Shechem,
	Bethel, Gilgal, Shiloh, etc.
1000 MONARCHY Saul, David, Solomon	
900 DIVISION OF KINGDOM	
PROPHETS	Book of Jashar
800	Book of the Wars of Yahweh
	First historical recording in royal courts
700	The J History of Israel
END OF ISRAEL(721)	The E History of Israel
600 Josiah 's Reform	
FALL OF JERUSALEM	The D (Deuteronomists') History of Israel
THE EXILE	
500 RETURN (Ezra, Nehemiah)	
400	The P (Priestly) History of Israel collating J, E & D — CONTINUING ORAL TRADITION
300	
THE GREEKS	
200	The written records of the Prophets
MACCABEAN REVOLT	The Writings: Psalms, Proverbs, etc.
100	
ROMAN OCCUPATION	
AD Birth of Jesus	The Tanach (complete Hebrew Bible) comprising Law, Prophets and Writings

DIAGRAM: THE ORIGINS AND DEVELOPMENT OF THE OLD TESTAMENT SCRIPTURES

The diagram opposite is a visualization of the processes by which the writings of the Old Testament came to be written, edited and finally published, set against the background of Israelite history.

FROM ACTUALITY TO PUBLICATION

It is likely that the book of Amos took centuries of editorial reflection to take the form in which we have it in our Bibles. The evidence suggests that it was only in the last two centuries BC that all the prophetic books were assembled together, considered to be scriptural and regularly read in the synagogues as commentary on the Torah. This is evident within the New Testament. Recall how Jesus, present in the synagogue at Capernaum, was handed the scroll of the prophet Isaiah and how he read from chapter 61, "The Spirit of the Lord is upon me…" Evidently Jesus found his spiritual sustenance in the prophets; and this he passed on to his disciples. There are numerous references in the gospels to "the law and the prophets" (at Matthew 7.12, 11.13, 22.40: Luke 16.16) indicating that a twofold division of the Jewish scriptures was accepted in Jesus' day.

THE WRITINGS

A third section of the Jewish scriptures, "the Writings", was gradually accrued and added to "the Law" and "the Prophets." These included a collection of the psalms sung in the Temple, the proverbs and other scrolls containing moral and religious advice known collectively as "Wisdom." One of these, Ecclesiastes, displays a spirit of world-weary skepticism, declaring that "there's nothing new under the sun" and that "all is vanity." Another was an inspired poem, Job, which questioned the common assumption that all suffering was punishment for sin. It also included much more recent writing that commented on quite recent historical events. The book of Daniel, written in reaction to the Seleucid onslaught on Jewish faith to which the Maccabees reacted (in the early second century BC), was deliberately written as if describing events of some centuries before. It was thus a secretly coded call to resistance. This latter book undoubtedly influenced either Jesus himself or the gospel writers in the so-called Apocalyptic passages (Mark13 etc.)

CANON OF THE OLD TESTAMENT

By Jesus' time, we cannot assume that a definitive Old Testament Canon had been established. Evidence from the Dead Sea Scrolls indicates that around the first centuries BC and AD, there was still some blurring between books that would be included and those that would not. It used to be supposed that, in the aftermath of the First Jewish War, after the destruction of the Second Temple, the surviving rabbis met at Jamnia in the 70s AD and, amongst other decisions, drew up a list of agreed scripture that has stood ever since as the Canon of their scriptures. The evidence for so formal an authorization of the Canon is now disputed, but it seems that from about that time, the Jewish Bible consisted of the three sections which comprise the **TANACH**. This acronym, commonly used by Jews to describe their completed Bible, is made up from TA for Torah, the Law; NA for Neviim the Prophets and CH for Ketuvim (it can equally be spelled Chetuvim) for the Writings.

However it had been formulated, Christians simply adopted the Hebrew scriptures wholesale as their Old Testament; differing only on the status of those books which had been written in Greek and which in time came to be designated as the Old Testament Apocrypha.

FORTHTELLERS NOT FORETELLERS

It will be apparent from all that we have heard of Amos's speeches, that they are wholly addressed to the situations which immediately confronted the people of Israel in his own day and age. He read the situation and declared God's judgment on it, which he perceived to be already in process of occurring. It was not untypical of the prophets to foreshorten the period within which God was going to act. In this case, the complete fulfillment of what Amos prophesied did not occur until the year 721 with the Assyrian sacking of Samaria (which we assume to be several years later than his encounter with the priest at Bethel). In view of age-old misconceptions of the prophet's role, he was definitely not a crystal-ball gazer, pretending to forecast the events of centuries ahead (like some ancient Nostradamus, the 16th-century French astrologer). Therefore it is a misuse of the Bible to attempt to find within it direct predictions of what is happening in the world today. What is undeniable is that because human behavior remains as it always has been, and God's judgment on it is consistent, we may discern patterns of events in history that appear to be repetitions of what has occurred before. In this sense, the writings of the prophets may still speak powerfully to the problems of our own time. To summarize, the prophets were *forthtellers* of God's Word rather than *foretellers* of the future.

CHAPTER 8:
NEW TESTAMENT
"ARCHAEOLOGY"

Were you ever shown a SIRDS? The letters stand for Single Image Random Dot Stereogram. I was first shown one in a weekend magazine. I stared and stared at this colorful but apparently meaningless pattern and could make nothing of it. Then I was shown a book called the *Magic Eye*; and by much application, eventually I saw IT and was duly amazed. Here you have an apparently two-dimensional picture; but when you see through it, the picture becomes astonishingly 3D. It has a dimension of depth. The surface appearance may be of a tank-full of fish all equidistant from your eyes. But see it in stereogram, then the picture has depth so that the fish appear to be swimming at different distances from you.

An archaeological dig

I would like, if it's possible, to help you see the New Testament in 3D so that the words on the page take on a dimension of depth. But may we change the metaphor? Pictures of archaeological excavations in progress are commonplace on TV and in magazines. On most sites in the Middle East, the ruins of ancient cities stand up above the flood plain as a great mound of earth. In Arabic these are called "tells." They are as they are because, when cities whose buildings had been constructed out of the local mud brick were destroyed by earthquake or military assault, their new occupants simply leveled the rubble and built anew on it. Over many centuries, a city could grow to several hundred feet above the level of its very first occupation. In Israel in 1999, I was privileged to stand on the tells of a number of famous sites, such as Megiddo and Jericho, where archaeologists are still at work. Their method, refined over the past hundred years, is first of all to dig a shaft, and as it is being dug, to try to identify the separate strata, each of which constitutes a distinct period of occupation of that city. It follows that the further down they dig, the further back in time they are going, even to the first construction of the city. The lowest stratum at Jericho takes us back to about 7,000 years before Christ!

In some tells, as many as 20 or more periods of occupation are uncovered. Having built up an overall idea of the antiquity of the city, the archaeologists then begin a more painstaking uncovering of a small area, layer by layer. What especially interests them is what artifacts are discovered at each level:

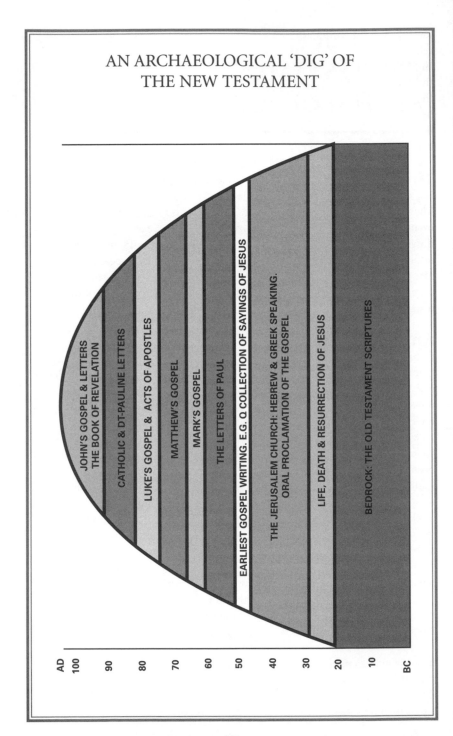

AN ARCHAEOLOGICAL 'DIG' OF
THE NEW TESTAMENT

JOHN'S GOSPEL & LETTERS
THE BOOK OF REVELATION

CATHOLIC & DT-PAULINE LETTERS

LUKE'S GOSPEL & ACTS OF APOSTLES

MATTHEW'S GOSPEL

MARK'S GOSPEL

THE LETTERS OF PAUL

EARLIEST GOSPEL WRITING. E.G. Q COLLECTION OF SAYINGS OF JESUS

THE JERUSALEM CHURCH: HEBREW & GREEK SPEAKING.
ORAL PROCLAMATION OF THE GOSPEL

LIFE, DEATH & RESURRECTION OF JESUS

BEDROCK: THE OLD TESTAMENT SCRIPTURES

AD
100

90

80

70

60

50

40

30

20

10

BC

identifiable parts of buildings, household utensils or clothing, tools or weapons, religious objects such as images or documents. Most abundant is pottery, and since fashions of pottery have evolved over many centuries, it is chiefly from these that the dates of occupation of each stratum can be identified. Remember, the deeper down you go, the further you are regressing in time. But, it may also be the case that some artifacts are much older than the stratum in which they lie, such as objects that survived the earthquake or were saved as precious heirlooms that were taken into the newly built city.

The New Testament as a "tell"

My suggestion is that we think of the New Testament as a "tell" which we are invited to excavate. Here are 27 books, a collection of sacred writings formed by the early Christian Church over a period of rather less than 100 years. In order to distinguish them from the books of the Hebrew Bible, they were called the New Testament. As scrolls in the hand, we might imagine them to have been written and published at more or less the same time. In reality, nothing could be further from the truth. Each of the 27 books had its own origin in time and place. Recall our second Taffy Davies cartoon: the little Christian waving a scroll in his hand and calling to his friends: "Yippee, a letter from Peter?" Every one of these scrolls would have come as a novelty to those who first received them. A great deal of modern New Testament scholarship has been trying to reach back into the origins of each scroll and to ask who wrote it, using what sources, when, for what particular need, to whom was it addressed and how was it received? This search could only be carried out by setting aside many of the assumptions previously made about its origins, many of them of hallowed Church tradition.

As we look back into early Christian history, can we discern the distinctive strata out of which the New Testament scrolls might have emerged? I am thinking of that early history as the "tell" and of the writings as the "artifacts" which belong to each stratum. Let's look at the general picture first. And I will build it up from the bottom (which is of course nonsense in archaeological terms!).

STRATUM 1: THE LIFE, DEATH AND RESURRECTION OF JESUS

What is the bedrock on which the Christian Church was built up? It has to be the life, death and resurrection of Jesus; let's call this Stratum 1. Immediately, we have to recognize the stark fact that Jesus never wrote a book, nor were his immediate disciples in any hurry to do so. There's some evidence to suggest that, even after his death, when the truth of the resurrection had dawned, they expected his imminent coming again (see Acts 3.19-21). But, although there were no cine cameras or tape recorders to record his deeds and his words, these were so memorable in form and content as to be likely to endure for long in the memory of his disciples. We can assume that very many of these came to be recorded in the Gospels (but even that assumption will have to be tested). Another factor of great importance is that clearly Jesus and his followers set great store by the Hebrew scriptures. He understood his own mission in relation to them. We may count these as the prime artifacts from this period. But the fact is that from this Stratum 1 we have no tangible artifacts to put on display. The tangible records of the Jesus Story have to be assigned to other strata.

STRATUM 2: THE JERUSALEM CHURCH

Stratum 2 is that of the early Church in Jerusalem which can be dated from circa 30 (the probable date of Jesus' crucifixion) to AD 68, when the remaining Christian community took flight across the Jordan before the Roman siege sealed off the city for destruction. We owe knowledge of this community chiefly to Luke in the Acts of the Apostles, being the sequel to his Gospel. It is the case that these volumes are usually assigned to a quite late stratum, i.e. to AD 80-90. But Luke was a careful historian, who used whatever sources were available, as he explains in the prologue to the Gospel (Luke 1.1-4). These are detectable in some of the earliest preaching of the apostles as reported in chapters 1-9 in Acts: for they are characterized by some constructions strange in Greek (of which Luke was a master) that are termed "Semitisms," i.e. they indicate sources that were originally in Aramaic or Hebrew. They also include a theological understanding of Jesus' life (the technical term for which is "Christology") which is markedly different from that which became eventually the "orthodox" understanding. Peter's speech at Pentecost in Acts 2.22-36 or again at 3.12-26 are good examples of this. Whilst we cannot assume that these are verbatim speeches of Peter (for authors in the ancient world regularly invented the speeches their heroes were likely to have pronounced) yet there are pointers here to authentic reporting.

We can be sure that the Jerusalem Church was the crucible within which much of the Jesus story was originally minted; for in the apostles' teaching and fellowship (Acts 2.42) to which the emergent Christian community eagerly attended, what else was recounted other than the words and works of Jesus? And out of it the primitive doctrine of Christianity was forged. But at this early stage, communication was all by word of mouth. There was no immediate thought of writing anything down.

Hebraic and Greek

The Jerusalem Church was not uniform. Although all were Jews, there was some division as between the Hebraic-speaking members and those Greek-speaking. At one point, this threatened the unity of the Church (Acts 6), in consequence of which seven "deacons" were chosen to administer the charitable funds. They all bear Greek names. In time, the division between the two groups became wider. So we have here to distinguish between two strata, naming that of the Hebrew-speakers as Stratum 2a and of the Greek speakers Stratum 2b. The "Hebrews," under the leadership of James the Lord's brother, adhered to strict observance of the whole Torah of Moses, including the circumcision of converts. Whereas the "Greeks" supposed much of the Torah to have been in practice revoked by Jesus and therefore urged the acceptance of Gentiles into the Church without submission to circumcision. This dispute lead to the first great council of the Church, which is reported in Acts 15, in which the more liberal view prevailed. The "Hebrews" became increasingly marginalized. Some of their more extreme elements continued to dog the footsteps of the apostle Paul (if they are identical with the "Judaizers" who appear in several of his letters) but they virtually disappear from the pages of history when they fled across the Jordan in AD 68. They are probably still identifiable as those termed "Ebionites" (the "poor ones") in some early Christian writings.

The Greek speakers were at first led by Stephen, whose arrest and early martyrdom are recounted in Acts 6 and 7. They were the first group to encounter severe persecution (8.1) which necessitated most of their number to leave Jerusalem (whilst the Hebraic Christians appear to have been left unmolested) with the effect that they carried the gospel out of its Jewish matrix. It would seem that Paul, at first the bitterest persecutor of the "Greeks," became the outstanding exponent of their viewpoint, i.e. of the incoming of the Gentiles as the fulfillment of God's plan.

STRATUM 3: THE LETTERS OF PAUL

These undoubtedly comprise the first tangible artifacts that we find on our site, handwritten documents that form the earliest Christian literature. Not, of course, that any of their originals remain, but sufficient copies of them do to be assured that they are authentic. Paul was converted on the Damascus Road in circa AD 36. After a lengthy stay in Arabia (Galatians 1.17) , he went up to Jerusalem to confer with those called "the pillars of the Church," i.e. Peter, James and others. Although, in Galatians, Paul plays down the significance of this visit (asserting that his version of the gospel was received directly from God rather than from any human source), we may assume that through such contacts he learned the traditions of the Jerusalem Church (which became so important to him). It was therefore with the backing of the "pillars" that he launched his great mission to the Gentiles, of which we have some record in Acts chapters 13 onwards. It was in the course of these missionary journeys that he both founded churches and kept in close touch with them by letter. We can be sure that he had no thought of writing "scripture" that would one day rank beside that of the Old Testament. They were occasional pieces, dashed off to meet some pressing need of rebuke or encouragement for his converts. We can be sure that some of his letters did not survive. We know for sure that he wrote a letter to the Laodiceans (Colossians 4.16) and a third one to the Corinthians. But some were so treasured as to be shared between different congregations and eventually to be received as "scripture" on a par with the scrolls of the Old Testament. I will say more about the dating of his letters in the next chapter.

There is one factor in Paul's letters that may appear surprising, that is, that he makes so little mention of Jesus' life and teaching. Paul's great theme is that of his Death and Resurrection as the events by which God saves His people. It is likely that he assumes his readers' knowledge of Jesus' story as having been taught to converts and as being rehearsed whenever Christians met together for worship and instruction. Otherwise, it is of significance that Paul stresses the Tradition, both that he himself had received from the earlier apostles and which he had passed on to his converts. Note this carefully in his account of the Last Supper in 1 Corinthians 11.23-26: "For I received from the Lord what I also handed on to you ..." He used very similar terminology when he presented the essence of his "creed" in 1 Corinthians 15.1-9, noting especially vv 1 and 3. These passages illustrate how the gospel faith was passed on from generation to generation of Christians (or, in terms of our metaphor, from stratum to stratum).

STRATUM 4: THE BEGINNINGS OF WRITTEN "GOSPELS"

We cannot tell how early it was that some Christian teachers set out to make a written record of the stories in circulation about Jesus' words and deeds. It may have preceded Paul's ministry or perhaps it was contiguous with it. It is alluded to by Luke in his prologue: "... many have undertaken to set down an orderly account of the events that have been fulfilled among us ..." (Luke 1.1). The continuation is important: "... just as they were handed on to us by those who from the beginning were eye-witnesses and servants of the word..." Here again we have this significant word "handed on" (in Greek from the root of the word "tradition").

❖ Luke alludes here to the period during which the gospel was proclaimed by word of mouth, firstly by those apostles who had been eye-witnesses of all that Jesus had done and said, then by "the servants of the word", i.e. the preachers of the gospel. This likely covered at least the first generation of Christians, possibly the first two generations. Does his wording about an "orderly account" imply that others had been "disorderly" (in the sense of badly organized)?

❖ It is highly likely that early on, sayings of Jesus or episodes in his life were jotted down on odd scraps of papyrus or on potsherds (pieces of broken pottery). There are episodes and sayings in the early chapters of Mark's Gospel which are so "shorthand" in their brevity and lack of detail as to suggest they might have been such jottings that Mark simply strung together like beads on a string, as one scholar put it.

❖ The next stage would have been to group together sayings on a particular theme (e.g. that of salt, e.g. the three sayings about salt in Mark 9.49-50); then perhaps sequences of parables, such as we find in Mark chapter four.

❖ There are some clues to suggest that the first sequence of events to have been "welded" together to form a continuous narrative was that of Jesus' last week in Jerusalem, from his entry on Palm Sunday to his death and burial. In some such ways we may imagine the raw material being collected together that would one day be "fleshed out" as a written gospel.

However, before that was to happen, somebody did bring together a collection of the sayings of Jesus together with those of John the Baptizer. No such scroll has ever been found, but, when we come to examine the gospels of both Matthew and Luke, it becomes clear that they both had access to a written source, which they both freely used; but which had not been used by Mark. This hypothetical document was early dubbed "Q" (from the German word "quelle," which means "source").

STRATUM 5: MARK'S GOSPEL

It is the almost unanimous consensus of scholars that Mark's was the first complete gospel to be written, thus overturning the traditional supposition that Matthew's was the first and that Mark's was a mere shadow of it. You will only be convinced of the reasoning by yourself working through a synopsis[24] which enables you to compare some of the many episodes in which Matthew, Mark and Luke recount what is clearly an identical story; and ask of yourself what is the most likely explanation both of their points of agreement and disagreement? The consequence of this recognition is considerable, i.e. that Mark takes us closest to the very humanity of Jesus (which later became obscured by the desire to portray rather his divinity). This recognition is probably the greatest discovery of modern New Testament scholarship. It has rescued Mark from some 18 centuries of neglect to become the corner-stone of our understanding of Jesus.

But when was Mark's Gospel written? There can be no certainty, but a date round about AD 65-70 seems likely. A traditional but dubious hypothesis (from the second century) is that the author had been Simon Peter's interpreter; that the gospel comprises much of Peter's eye-witness testimony; and that it was written shortly after Peter's martyrdom in Rome during the savage persecution at the hands of the crazed Emperor Nero, i.e. in AD 64. Added to this is the generally accepted supposition that, by 65 or thereabouts, the entire generation of the apostles and other eye-witnesses had died; that there then dawned the recognition that their testimony might equally die unless it was committed to

---

[24] You will learn what a synopsis is in Chapter 10.

written form. Some scholars believe that some content of chapter 13 (the apocalyptic passage) betrays an actual knowledge of events that occurred during the Roman siege of Jerusalem in 70, such as to presume a post AD-70 date.

STRATUM 6: THE GOSPEL OF MATTHEW

We need to take note that all of the gospels are anonymous. It was Church tradition in the second century that ascribed their authorship to apostles of Jesus in the case of Matthew and John; and to close associates of apostles in that of Mark and Luke. Modern study has made these attributions extremely dubious. However, we will continue to refer to them by their traditional titles. Modern gospel study has established beyond reasonable doubt that the gospel attributed to Matthew used as its core structure that already written by Mark, to which were added sayings of Jesus (and of John) from the Q collection; also a number of traditions known only to the author. But "Matthew" subjected all his sources to his own powerful interpretation of the Jesus story. For example, he wove sayings of Jesus derived from Mark and Q and his own source into an orderly structure of teaching, which he then inserted in five major blocks of teaching into the Marcan framework. The first, what we call the Sermon on the Mount (chapters 5-7), demonstrates his genius; for he took sayings which, in Luke, are scattered somewhat randomly throughout the narrative and skillfully arranged them as one continuous "sermon". There is little doubt that he was deliberately representing Jesus as a new Moses, giving a new Christian Torah on the mountain-top; hence the five blocks of teaching reminding us of the five books of the Pentateuch. We may consider the author then as a pastor and teacher of new converts. From analysis of the gospel, we can deduce that he was addressing a Christian community, rooted in the Old Testament, but whose relations with the synagogue had already reached breaking-point or would soon do so, i.e. circa AD 85 when Jewish Christians were excommunicated from the synagogues. This was a second or more likely third generation Christianity, whose weaker members ("these little ones") needed careful shepherding if they were to be kept within the fold. Although the most distinctly Jewish of all the gospel writers, since Matthew portrayed Jesus as the rightful Messiah and put much emphasis on his fulfillment of Old Testament prophecies, yet he was equally open to the influx of Gentiles into church.

STRATUM 7: LUKE'S GOSPEL AND ITS SEQUEL, THE ACTS OF THE APOSTLES

Like Matthew, Luke also used Mark's narrative as the basic framework of his own gospel (although there is some evidence that there may have been a so-called "proto-Luke," to which Mark's account was later added) and the Q collection of Jesus' sayings. To these he added much material of his own, including such loved parables as those of the Prodigal Son and of the Good Samaritan. This should remind us that even towards the end of the first century, stories were still being handed on through the oral tradition that had not yet been committed to writing. In his preface, Luke has told us of his careful research and use of earlier sources. If Matthew were the most Jewish of the gospel writers, then Luke was certainly the most Greek. Greek by birth, he had a fluent command of his native tongue. Tradition identified him with Luke the physician and traveling companion of Paul.

Luke's Gospel is clearly designed to make its appeal to the enquiring intelligentsia of the Graeco-Roman world. It is dedicated to a certain Theophilus, whose title "Most Excellent" may indicate him to have been a high Roman official. So he sets the gospel story within the time-frame of Roman history, citing a decree by the Emperor Augustus as the occasion of Mary and Joseph's journey to Bethlehem. The second volume of his narrative sets the story yet more firmly within the Roman world, in which Roman governors and Greek cities feature prominently, the narrative concluding with Paul resident in Rome, awaiting trial by Caesar. In the Acts of the Apostles, Luke was keen to demonstrate that what Jesus was enabled to do in Palestine, his disciples were empowered by the Holy Spirit to continue to do throughout the empire.

STRATUM 8: THE GOSPEL AND LETTERS OF JOHN

The origins and development of the gospel attributed to John are shrouded in mystery. For although it features the story of Jesus up to his Passion and Resurrection, it does so from a remarkably different perspective from that of the Synoptic Gospels. Whereas Mark set Jesus' entire ministry within the space of little more than one year, culminating in a unique journey up to Jerusalem, the Jesus of John's Gospel is frequently in the holy city, attending it at several festivals. Whereas for the Synoptics, Jesus' confrontation with the money-changers and sellers of sacrificial animals occurs at the end of his ministry (and is the action which provokes his arrest), John places it at the very start. Whereas in Mark, Jesus eats the Passover meal with his disciples in the upper room, in John the meal occurs on the eve of the Passover; such that Jesus dies as the Passover lambs are being sacrificed in the Temple. What is yet more remarkable is that the Jesus of John's Gospel speaks in a wholly different manner from how he is represented as speaking in the Synoptics; sometimes in lengthy, somewhat tortuous debates with "the Jews;" and sometimes in long meditative discourses with his disciples. Whereas in the Synoptics, Jesus makes little claim for himself except as the spokesman for God (his messiahship is largely hidden), in John he doesn't hesitate to proclaim his unique relationship with God. There is no parallel in the Synoptics to the seven great "I am" sayings that we find so prominently in John.

The problems this raises of apparently irreconcilable differences were recognized at least by the early second century. One noted scholar, Clement of Alexandria, termed John's "the Spiritual Gospel." Was he implying that John sat somewhat loose to historical detail and wished to bring out the deeply theological significance of Jesus' ministry? There is some general consensus today that whilst this gospel contains authentic remembrance of some aspects of Jesus (e.g. that he was frequently in Jerusalem), the gospel is best understood as a series of profound meditations on Jesus' life, written probably late in the first century or even in the early years of the second century such that we should see "John" as an early theologian comparable to Paul.

The three letters ascribed to John do not relate easily to the gospel of that name. But as with each of the gospels, we should probably consider them as emerging from a Christian community living in a particular place and holding a distinctive theology. We may then think of these letters, as well as the gospel, as stemming from what scholars call "the Johannine community."

STRATUM 9: THE LETTER TO THE HEBREWS

This stratum may well be misplaced. What is undeniable is that few scholars today would attribute this letter to Paul (as it still is in the KJV). The language and the theology is quite different. We cannot with any assurance date it. Some argue that it is likely earlier than AD 70. Since its entire argument is to demonstrate how much greater is the once-for-ever sacrifice of Jesus Christ over the multitudinous sacrifice of animals in the Temple, it would have given the author an unanswerable "knock-out strike" to be able to write: "See, the Temple lies in ruins – so all your bloody sacrifices have been rendered obsolescent."

STRATUM 10: THE DEUTERO-PAULINE LETTERS

In some writings traditionally attributed to Paul there are many signs pointing to their origin in circumstances later than that of his lifetime. This is the case particularly with the two Letters to Timothy and one to Titus. The socio-religious background within them has been described as that of emerging "Catholicism," one in which the Church as a hierarchical structure, imposing discipline and facing hostility, is very apparent. Since much of the content sounds "Pauline," we should probably consider them to be the products of people who looked to Paul as their "father in God" and who didn't hesitate to use excerpts from his writings to be the foundation of their pastoral letters.

The same is probably the case with the Letter to the Ephesians. Much of it is distinctively Pauline, and yet, there are also words and concepts that are not to be found in any of his undoubtedly authentic letters. It may then be attributed to a close disciple of Paul.

STRATUM 11: THE "CATHOLIC" EPISTLES AND REVELATION

None of these are easy to place. They include the two letters ascribed to Peter and those of James and of Jude. James may well be quite early. The book of Revelation is an apocalyptic work, akin to shorter apocalypses we find within the gospels, such as in Mark 13; and to much of the book of Daniel in the Old Testament. The word "apocalypse" means literally "uncovering" or "revelation," i.e. they purport to be revelations of things to come, given in dream or vision, to an inspired man of God. The Eastern Orthodox Church was always wary of Revelation and was slow to admit it into their canon of the New Testament. Even today, it does not feature in their lectionary readings. It prevailed in the Western Church, but we may note that Martin Luther didn't consider that Christians were bound for ever by the decisions of the early Church regarding the Canon. He judged each book as to whether it promoted what to him was the key note of the gospel, i.e. that we are saved by the Grace of God which we receive in faith. On that ground, he rejected the Letter of James as "a right strawy epistle," relegating it together with the second Letter of Peter, Jude and Revelation to the end of his edition of the New Testament, a decision which Tyndale adopted in his translation.

What conclusions may we draw from this outline?

Probably the most important yet controversial finding of modern scholarship concerns the gospels. Understood traditionally as almost contemporary, eye-witness accounts of Jesus as seen and heard by his closest disciples, the revisionist view sees them quite differently – rather as how Jesus' life-story was perceived in different Christian communities of two or three generations later. Of course, such communities had absorbed the stories told about Jesus and his sayings from the earliest times onwards – there had to have been eye-witnesses at their very first telling – for they certainly weren't simply inventions. As we have noted, Luke's preface gives the clue to this. Although the traditional attributions to apostles, or apostles' associates, now appear unwarranted, the named apostle may have been somewhere present near the source from which the gospel emerged. Possibly Matthew was the first collector of stories about Jesus, whose witness was taken up and developed by an anonymous teacher in the Church. In all probability, such a teacher was a powerful communicator, for the editing of such disparate material into so convincing a portrait of the master demanded a high skill. But we shouldn't think of such an author as working in isolation. Each author undoubtedly worked within a particular Christian congregation, which, according to its place and circumstances, had developed a particular perspective on Jesus' life-story. This is what makes each gospel, named after Matthew, Mark, Luke and John unique and distinctive, each in its own way. They serve as four distinct witnesses, giving their response to the question: "Who was and is Jesus?"

Overall, what is most positive about this newer understanding? The answer is not dissimilar to that we derived from the new understanding of the Torah. Rather than attributing every word to Moses, what the Torah really conveys is the tradition of a whole community of the People of God over many centuries. It is not so different with the New Testament and the gospels in particular. They too constitute an accumulation of reports, over a period of decades rather than centuries, about the words and works of Jesus, as these had been collected and sifted and edited before they attained the written form by which we know them.

In both Old and New Testaments, instead of the somewhat static approach of the traditional understanding, we have in its place a picture which is dynamic, of communities of living people, not unlike ourselves, neither more nor less inspired by the Holy Spirit than we are, yet who, having witnessed those events by which God had rescued them from futility and failure, struggled to give their new faith articulation. We may see them as part of a living stream that flows originally from "the City of God" (employing the language of Psalm 46.4), which, in Old and New Testaments, carved out a particular course within human history, which refreshed and rendered fertile a hitherto barren land. The exciting thing is that we, the Christians of today, still live by and are refreshed from this same river, only at some two thousand years further down-stream. Our task today is to do much as they did, and, inspired by their story, work out for ourselves how we may still live by the Torah and the Gospel in today's world.

Some examples from Matthew's Gospel

What effect does this approach have on our reading and understanding of the books of the New Testament? It radically affects the assumptions that we bring to our reading. Let us consider three examples, all taken from Matthew's Gospel.

EXAMPLE 1

If we can no longer assume Matthew's Gospel to be an eye-witness account of Jesus' story, but rather an account of how a specific Christian community (possibly inland from Antioch in Syria) looked back on Jesus' story some 50 to 60 years after his crucifixion, then our perspective reading it has perforce to be different. For instance, Matthew's chapter 13 is a compendium of parables (based on that of Mark's chapter 4). In vv 3-8 we have the original parable of the sower. From vv 10-7, we have an extended discussion of the meaning of the parables, centered on the interpretation of Isaiah 6.9-10. And from vv 18-23, we have an allegorical interpretation of it. The seed is evidently "the word of the kingdom" and various causes are given for the failure of the seed sown in the ground, such as "tribulation or persecution, the cares of the world or delight in riches." It is highly unlikely that in Jesus' day any explanation would have had to be given of such parables. A parable that needed explanation would have been like the joke that has to be explained, i.e. a poor joke! There is evidence that the point of Jesus' parables was immediately perceived by those for whom it was intended; see for instance Mark 12.12; Matthew 21.45.

It is far more likely that it was in the different cultural setting, that of the Graeco-Roman world, that the Jewish usage of parables was not so well understood; in which parables that usually had one main point (like the punch-line of a joke) were turned into allegories. Reading between the lines, we may be over-hearing a keen debate within Christian circles, centering on the Isaiah 6. 9-10 passage, why was it that so many had heard Jesus' preaching (or that of early Church preaching) and yet had not come to faith? Hence much of Mt's chapter 13 is the record of early Christian debate about the reception given to Jesus' proclamation of God's Word.

EXAMPLE 2

The above point can be seen yet more clearly in Mattthew's chapter 18. Embedded in it (Matthew 18.10-14) is the parable of the lost sheep. In Luke's version of this parable, the lost sheep clearly stands for "the tax collectors and sinners" who had come to listen to Jesus and the harsh criticism of the scribes and Pharisees against such fraternization with excommunicates from the synagogue. Here the parable discloses God's special love for the outcast, which he demonstrates in his own welcome towards them. Matthew gives a quite different setting to the parable. The context is talk about the place of "children" and "little ones" (vv 3, 6, 10); and the dark reality that there are those who cause such to sin, to undergo beguiling temptations, those who despise others, a brother who sins against brother, who pushes the limits of forgiveness almost to breaking point. It is likely that these "little ones" are not necessarily the physically young, but rather new converts to the faith who are all too easily lost. Here then we have a picture of the Church of the late first century having to cope with matters of discipline, of loyalty and apostasy. In Matthew 16.18 and 18.17 we have the only usage of the word "church" (in Greek "ecclesia") in the gospels. We have to wonder whether the final rejection of the sinner in the words "let him be to you as a Gentile and a tax collector" (18.17) does not mark a sad denial of Jesus' gospel. We cannot imagine the Lord who consorted with tax collectors and sinners using such dismissive language.

EXAMPLE 3

In Matthew 23.1-36 there is a large collection of sayings attributed to Jesus in devastating criticism of the scribes and Pharisees. Although there are episodes in the gospels depicting the Pharisees in hostile confrontation with Jesus, there is nothing comparable to the scathing attack contained in this chapter (except for some sayings within John's Gospel, e.g. John 8.44), although we cannot be sure to whom Jesus' words were spoken. Pharisees are said to be present in verse 13, but towards the end of the chapter they are referred to simply as "the Jews" [25]). If Jesus loved everybody, how can we explain his extreme anger against the Pharisees, who, from all historical evidence, were mostly high-minded men who sought to live in strict adherence to the Torah? We should not forget that the fair-minded Gamaliel was a Pharisee, as was Nicodemus, and that Paul was proud to claim his Pharisaic allegiance during his trial before the Sanhedrin (Acts 23. 6-10). The question has therefore been raised as to whether Matthew's chapter 23 accurately reflects a situation within Jesus' lifetime, or rather that pertaining from about AD 85 when Christians had been excommunicated from the synagogues following a decree issued by a council of Rabbis at Jamnia? It would seem that, from that date, relations between Christians and Jews became exceedingly bitter. Within the text, it seems probable that what appears to be predicted in verse 34 (with its references to "killing and crucifying, scourging and persecuting") was written in view of what was already occurring.

Jesus' life and teaching in retrospect

All these examples are taken from just one gospel. We could cite other examples throughout the New Testament. The conclusion then is that if we are aware of this "History of Traditions" approach, then we will be the more aware of the flux and flow of early Christian thought and behavior. In the gospels, we can discern something of what was happening in and around Jesus during his brief ministry of AD 29-30; but we are reading it from the perspective of second or third generation Christians. Referring back to the opening metaphor of this chapter, you may begin to enjoy seeing the New Testament in "3D", as a "SIRDS," no longer as a flat non-historical record, but as one dynamic with dimensions of depth, as Christians struggled to find in Jesus' life-story words and deeds that illuminated their attempts to walk the Christian Way in ever new situations.

---

[25] The hostile designation "the Jews" has been the subject of much concerned debate, since it appears to underpin an attitude of virulent anti-Semitism. It appears usually to indicate "the Jewish leadership" such as that of the High Priest and his acolytes rather than the Jewish race. After all, Jesus himself and all of his disciples were themselves Jews.

CHAPTER 9:
THE NEW TESTAMENT

The life and letters of Paul

It is easy to imagine somebody opening the pages of the New Testament for the first time, taking it for granted that she should start at the gospel of Matthew, work her way through all four of the gospels, read the Acts of the Apostles and then launch into Paul's Letter to the Romans and so on, reading from beginning to end. Of course, there's nothing to prevent anybody from doing just that. It would be in accordance with the final editing of the books of the New Testament (which occurred not earlier than the third century AD) but not at all with the order in which the books were written.

The traditional route

Let us follow that route and see what image it yields. Starting with the gospels, you may immediately wonder why there have to be four of them, the first three of which show many similarities. They are therefore called the Synoptic Gospels because they are best "seen together." Then in the Acts of the Apostles you read the story of the early Church, with the preaching of the Christian message beginning from Jerusalem until it has reached as far as Rome. (We could entitle Acts as "How they brought the Good News from Jerusalem to Rome"). In it, you find two heroic figures, those of Simon Peter in the first half, of the apostle Paul in the second. Their stories are recounted deliberately in parallel as being respectively the Apostle to the Jews and the Apostle to the Gentiles. In this latter part, we are introduced to Paul, pick up some details of his life-story, in which we find his conversion story so prominent as to be repeated three times, read of his heroic missionary journeys, his establishment of churches in Asia Minor and in Greece, and finally, of his journey up to Jerusalem, there to face the beginning of his passion (again told so as to be to some degree parallel with that of Jesus) but with the difference that he is not to die in Jerusalem, but as a Christian martyr in Rome.

Here we sense a dramatic denouement, portrayed with great skill, which shows how the Christian Way, beginning in a provincial backwater, has within 30 years moved center stage, for Rome was the seat of Imperial Power. It is as if Christ has come to challenge Caesar in his own lair. Just as Jesus had stood powerless before the High Priest, so now Paul would stand in chains before Caesar, representing a power totally subversive of worldly power.

An alternative route

But modern scholarship suggests a wholly different route, realizing that the gospels and, in the case of Luke, the gospel together with its appendage, the Acts, are comparatively late-comers on the scene. It is undoubted that the very earliest of Christian writings are the letters of Paul and that this is where we should commence our journey.

We can already appreciate the importance of Paul. Paul is the man who beyond all others transforms the Christian faith from being just one of a number of small Jewish sects (most of which vanish without trace, as did the Essenes, the Sadducees and the Ebionites) so to become a world-wide religion. This much the Acts of the Apostles conveys. But it is less successful in conveying either the personality or the message of the apostle. It reports some speeches given by Paul on important occasions, such as that in the Forum at Athens (Acts 17.16-34) or on trial before the Sanhedrin (Acts 23) in Jerusalem. But to a large extent we suspect that Luke, its author, did as all Greek historians did, wrote speeches which they placed on the lips of their heroes (of course based on whatever evidence they possessed as well as on what they supposed the hero would have said). We cannot pursue here the question of the historical accuracy of the Acts, a matter that has been hotly debated, especially as regards its portrayal of Paul. The fact is that the Lucan speeches do not reflect the major emphases of Paul's own writings. The case is probably like that with the gospels: although some reliable historical sources (oral rather than written) lie behind them, they are literary creations in the service of the gospel.

The critical principle is this: *always trust the primary sources* (i.e. what Paul himself wrote) *rather than secondary sources* (i.e. what others, in this case Luke, wrote about him).

How may we approach Paul's writings?

1. It is remarkable that the writings attributed to Paul comprise almost half the content of the New Testament, i.e. 13 out of 27 documents.

2. How many of these did Paul himself write? The very question may appear bizarre; but it is not. Recall my earlier comments about Church traditions of the second century, some of which we know now to be dubious.

3. In time, even the Letter to the Hebrews came to be attributed to Paul; and he was so credited with its authorship in the KJV as it was still in the Revised Version of 1881. This attribution apparently derived from Jerome and came thence into the enormously influential Vulgate Bible. It has been wholly abandoned in

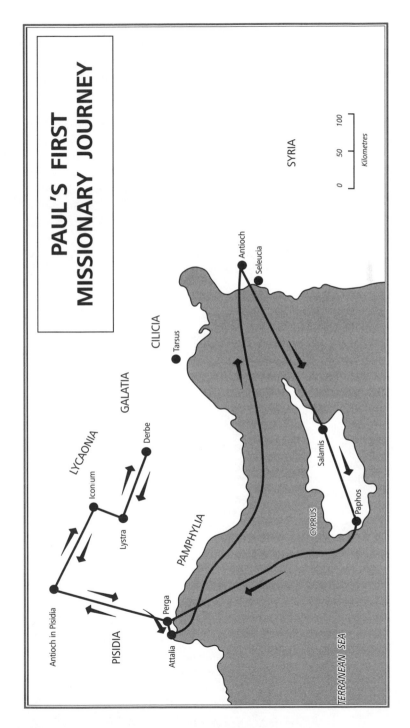

PAUL'S FIRST MISSIONARY JOURNEY

SYRIA

0   50   100
Kilometres

CILICIA

● Tarsus

GALATIA

LYCAONIA

Iconium

● Derbe

Lystra

Antioch in Pisidia

PISIDIA

PAMPHYLIA

Perga

Attalia

Antioch

Seleucia

Salamis

CYPRUS

Paphos

MEDITERRANEAN SEA

modern times. Even a slight acquaintance with the language and content of Hebrews demonstrates without any doubt that it cannot have been penned by Paul. Nowadays an author's vocabulary, grammatical constructions, and leading ideas can be analyzed by the computer. Paul's output has been thus analyzed by numerous scholars, so we can have little doubt as to what was genuinely Pauline.

4. Paul always announced his authorship in the opening lines of each letter. This was standard practice in the Graeco-Roman world. Here is a typical Pauline opening, from the Letter to the Romans: "Paul, a servant of Jesus Christ, called to be an apostle, set apart for the gospel of God, the gospel concerning his Son …" See also the opening verses of 1 Corinthians, 2 Corinthians, Galations, Philippians, Colossians, 1 Thessalonians, and 2 Thessalonians; but note in how many of these he wrote in conjunction with one or more of his co-workers: Sosthenes, Silvanus, Tertius or Timothy. We may wonder how far, if at all, these others contributed to their content; even if it were negligible, it yet shows how Paul understood himself to be working in partnership with other Christian workers.

5. He also added his own signature at the end of his letters. It is important to recognize that even so highly literate a man as Paul nevertheless still used an amanuensis. In Romans 16. 22 the scribe is named as Tertius. In 1 Corinthians 16.21-24, Paul adds his own poignant last word: "Why the personal signature?" Paul's world experienced as much fraudulent practice as does ours. He wanted the Corinthians to know for sure that this was his letter. The point is made yet more clearly at 2 Thessalonians 2.1-2: "As to the coming of our Lord Jesus Christ…we beg you, brothers and sisters, not to be quickly shaken in mind or alarmed, either by spirit or by word *or by letter, as though from us,* to the effect that the day of the Lord is already here." The REB translates here: "or any letter purporting to come from us."

The termination of the Letter to the Galatians may have a further meaning: "See what large letters I make when I am writing in my own hand!"(Galatians 6.11) It should not be assumed to imply that he had personally penned the entire letter. But does his postscript indicate that he suffered from poor eyesight? It has been conjectured that a painful eye-affliction was his "thorn in the flesh," about which he wrote so movingly in 2 Corinthians 12.7.

6. It may seem shocking to today's readers to hear that some of what we had supposed to be letters of Paul may not have been his at all. We live in a world in which copyright laws are fiercely maintained and in which plagiarism is deemed a criminal offence. It was not so in the ancient world. In the world of the Old Testament, we have already seen that there was a long tradition of working "in the spirit of Moses." We have seen that with Moses and the process by which the

Pentateuch was compiled over many centuries. It would have been much the same with the followers of Paul. For long after his death, the likes of Timothy and Silvanus would have deemed it their duty to continue to propagate their master's understanding of the gospel. When we come to the Pastoral Epistles (those of 1 & 2 Timothy and Titus), there are indications that they address a situation both in the Church and the world later by some decades than those during which the apostle lived and worked. And yet, reading them, there is a great deal that reads as authentically Pauline. Is it not understandable that his disciples would have used a considerable clutch of genuine writings of the apostle to address the new situation faced by his converts. In the world of the time, there would have been nothing deemed dishonest were they to have dispatched these letters as if from Paul himself.

7. There is nothing certain about the dating of Paul's letters, or which were issued by the apostle himself (rather than by his disciples), but those genuinely Pauline have to be ascribed to the period between 50 and 64 (the year in which Paul most likely met his death). Here is one such classification:

I. The early letters (circa AD 50):1 & 2 Thessalonians.
II. The great letters (in the mid 50s): Romans, 1 & 2 Corinthians, Galatians & Philippians.
III: The Captivity Letters (in the early 60s): Philemon, Colossians (possibly also Philippians and 2 Thessalonians).
IV: Post-Pauline: Ephesians, 1 & 2 Timothy, Titus.

8. We should note that the majority of these letters were addressed to a particular congregation, mostly to those founded by Paul himself, the exception being that sent to the Church in Rome. The nature of the latter, the most weighty theological work that Paul was to write, was probably intended to win the support of the Roman congregation before his arrival amongst them, especially in view of the hostility he faced in some Jewish Christian quarters. It follows that the issues on which Paul wrote were usually issues specific to that congregation. If there was a problem at Corinth about the excessive valuation of the charismatic gift of "speaking in tongues," there is no evidence to suggest that there was any problem about it in any other congregations. We should not assume that what Paul addressed to a specific congregation on a specific topic would have applied generally. And yet, the fact that his letters were speedily collected and treasured by countless churches implies that these found in them teaching that was relevant to them also.

9. The order in which Paul's letters are arranged in our Bibles tells us nothing about their origins. As in most ancient libraries, they are arranged according to length, i.e. with Romans first and Philemon last. This can be misleading to the

uninitiated. We can imagine somebody wishing to "tackle" St Paul, beginning at the Letter to the Romans. Since this is by far the most deeply theological of his writings, it is the worst place at which to start. Start rather at the little missive to Philemon, comprising just one chapter in the New Testament, a charming letter dealing with one highly personal matter to do with Philemon's run-away slave, Onesimus, who has come to Paul in prison, seeking his advice. Then go to Philippians, perhaps then to 1 Corinthians. We would advise too to use a modern translation, since the KJV is at its most incomprehensible in its translation of Paul. Probably the most "user-friendly" version (especially for a first reading) is that by J B Phillips, published under the title "Letters to Young Churches." By paraphrase rather than word-for-word, it brilliantly transposes Paul's thinking into our modern world.

10. We have to accept the entirely fortuitous origin of Paul's letters. Never for one minute did the apostle suppose he was writing scripture (on a par with that of the Old Testament). He wrote as occasion demanded. Having a deep commitment to those new communities of Christians which he had founded, he retained a strong affection for them, responded to their questions, and, when needed, rebuked them for their failings. This required him to be in constant communication with them, which he did, chiefly through personal contact. He and his co-workers were constantly "on the road." Keep a look out in the letters for every reference to the comings and goings of his close associates. They kept him in touch; but whenever he could not personally visit the churches, he wrote to them. Here are some references to look up: Romans 15.22–29 for Paul's travel plan to visit Rome en route to Spain; in 1 Corinthians 16.1-12 the apostle further reveals his travel plans, also those of Timothy and Apollos.

The First Letter to the Corinthians was evidently occasioned by the arrival of Chloe's people, about whom we know nothing. They were probably members of Chloe's family, possibly household slaves. They evidently reported to Paul the fact of quarrelling amongst the Corinthian congregation. The later remark that "it is actually reported that there is immorality among you…" (5.1) probably came to him from the same source. In 4.17, we learn that Paul has already sent Timothy to Corinth and in verse 19 that he himself expects to come to them soon. In 5.9 we learn also that he had already sent them a letter of strong advice (which no longer exists, unless parts of it are quoted in 2 Corinthians) not to associate with Christians whose behavior was scandalous. This reference reminds us that Paul wrote letters (probably many of them) which did not survive. It is therefore right to regard those in the New Testament as the survivors of a much larger correspondence. Another such letter no longer extant was addressed to the church at Laodicea, as is evident from Colossians 4.16: "And when this letter has been read among you, have it read also in the church of the Laodiceans; and see that you read also the letter from Laodicea." Here is the first evidence of a letter addressed to one church being made use of in another, a practice which escalated greatly, such that some of the earliest codices are complete editions of Paul's letters.

The letters become "Scriptural"

Since such letters were doubtless read aloud in Christian assemblies for worship, probably following readings from the Old Testament (possibly also from the earliest forms of the gospels), it was not surprising that they came to be understood as in some sense scriptural. This is clear in the Second Letter of Peter (probably one of the latest writings of the New Testament, i.e. circa AD 100): "So also our beloved brother Paul wrote to you according to the wisdom given to him, speaking of this as he does in all his letters. There are some things in them hard to understand, which the ignorant and unstable twist to their own destruction, as they do the other scriptures." (2 Peter 3.15) Here, an unknown writer (the attribution to Peter is certainly incorrect) of the turn of the first century can appeal to the name of Paul as well-known amongst the recipients of his letter; can refer to "all his letters" as if belonging to a collection of them, which, however "hard to understand," are already thought of as scriptural.

It is likely that some of the letters were designed to be received as circulars, i.e. to be disseminated amongst several churches. One such is the Letter to the Ephesians. The preface to it in the *Oxford Annotated Bible* version (p1415) states: "Because the earliest manuscripts and patristic quotations make no reference to Ephesus in 1.1 and because the letter contains no local allusions or personal greetings, most scholars regard it as an encyclical or "circular letter" of which copies were distributed by Tychicus (6.21-22) to several churches in Asia Minor. When Paul's correspondence was collected into a corpus, a copy of this letter was probably secured from Ephesus, the capital of the Roman province of Asia, and the present title was then affixed."[26]

An important consequence of the above is to realize that no New Testament writings appeared with an obvious divine "imprimatur."[27] If we ascribe them to divine inspiration, this wasn't by any means obvious, at least not immediately. It was only gradually, as Christian preachers, teachers and the congregations in which they ministered, came to value them that their inherent authority was recognized. The truth of the Christian revelation is not imposed on believers by any divine "diktat" voiced by an infallible Bible; it is something that dawns on humble Christian believers by its inherent value.

---

[26] Oxford Annotated Bible, the RSV version, p 1415.
[27] From Latin, an official permission to publish a writing, mostly used for documents issued within the Roman Catholic Church.

What degree of authority should be attributed to Paul's letters?

Paul was often (we are tempted to write usually) controversial. The letters themselves disclose him as frequently in fierce verbal combat with those who opposed both his claim to be an apostle (since not one of the 12 disciples) and his understanding of the gospel. There were many who queried his authority. The debate continues to this day, especially as regards some of his ethical teaching. This affects, to give but one example, the place of women in the Church; for it is in Paul that we read that "women should keep silence in Church." See I Corinthians 14.33–35.

It is important to note that Paul himself recognized an authority greater than his own. In his teaching regarding the relationship between the sexes, in 1 Corinthians 7, he makes a distinction between the Lord's teaching and his own: "To the married I give this command – not I but the Lord – that the wife should not separate from her husband." Further on, in verses 25-26 concerning unmarried people, he declares: "Now concerning virgins, I have no command of the Lord, but I give my opinion as one who by the Lord's mercy is trustworthy. I think that, in view of the impending crisis, it is well for you to remain as you are." Paul's personal opinion clearly has lower status than does the direct word of the Lord. Nevertheless, Paul's own authority remains considerable. He ends the chapter with this: "I think I have the Spirit of God." (7.40). Elsewhere, he claims for Christians exercising judgment together that "We have the mind of Christ" (1 Corinthians 2.16).

He claimed to be an apostle by the direct calling of God. The biblical meaning of the Greek "apostolos" probably derives from the Hebrew concept of the "shaliarch," one who was the personal representative of a great ruler whose authority was that of the one he represented. Paul claimed to be the specially chosen apostle of God and therefore to speak with the delegated authority of God. But did that make him infallible? Surely not!

Paul and Jesus

Another factor that may surprise us in these letters is as to how little Paul refers to events in the life of Jesus or to the sayings of Jesus. Did he not know them or was he indifferent to them? He employed a phrase that might appear to suggest the latter. In 2 Corinthians 5.16 he wrote: "From now on, therefore, we regard no one from a human point of view; even though we once knew Christ from a human point of view, we know him no longer in that way." Previous to these words, Paul had been writing about the effects of Jesus' sacrificial life and death as transforming the human situation. In view of this, he says, we regard Christians as having been raised to life beyond death; therefore, we no longer regard them from a human point of view. Then he adds the notion that this applies also to our thinking about Jesus Christ. The very manner of Paul's conversion experience, when Christ revealed himself in visionary form to him on the Damascus road, would have rendered his attitude towards him different from that of the other apostles. They had known Jesus in the flesh, having shared in his ministry from Galilee to Jerusalem. Paul had not personally known him during his lifetime, but only as the Risen Lord in glory. Therefore it is likely that his converts were taught to think of Jesus in the same way. This is evident throughout his letters. Jesus is the one who has carried us through death into life eternal; he is the one who intercedes for us; he is the one who lives within us. There was no need to hark back to the details of his earthly life.

But, we should not imagine Paul to have been indifferent to Jesus' human life-story. Since he himself had founded the churches to which he later wrote, he must surely have conveyed to his new converts at least an outline of the story of Jesus. After all, this was part of the early Church's proclamation, as this is recorded in the Acts of the Apostles. It is possible that Galatians 3.1 refers to this: "You foolish Galatians! Who has bewitched you? It was before your eyes that Jesus Christ was publicly exhibited as crucified!" Paul's expression that Jesus Christ had been publicly exhibited as crucified "before your eyes" is incomprehensible unless it implies that he had given them so graphic an account of the crucifixion that *it was as if* they had themselves witnessed it.

Paul had no need to refer in his letters to what their recipients already knew. The fact that he rarely if ever quotes any gospel sayings is readily explicable. The gospels as written documents did not as yet exist, although their accounts of Jesus' words and works must have been part of the early Church's oral preaching and teaching.

Yet Paul was not ignorant of the tradition. On two occasions (of crucial importance) in his Letter to the Corinthians, he refers to the Christian tradition, which he had passed on to the Corinthian Christians.

Paul, hero or villain?

The last paragraph is of importance if we are face up to a constant accusation leveled at Paul, i.e. that he was the real founder of Christianity as a universal religion. The thesis goes that Jesus had no intention of founding the Church; that he worked for the renewal of Israel alone and had little interest in the Gentile world; whose message was of the coming Kingdom of God. Paul turned all this into a message about Jesus, in whose life story he took no interest, turning him into a Divine Redeemer and Savior akin to those worshiped in the Mystery Religions[28] then rife in the lands of the eastern Mediterranean.

But the thesis does not fit the facts:

❖ If Paul's attention was chiefly on the Death and Resurrection of Jesus rather than on his earthly life, so was that of the Early Church as we discern it in the speeches of Simon Peter as reported by Luke in the Acts of the Apostles (what is termed the "Kerygma," meaning "proclamation," a public announcement like that of a town-crier).

Although Paul claimed vociferously that "his gospel" was received by divine revelation, he did go up to Jerusalem some three years after his conversion on the Damascus road, conferred with "the pillars of the Church," including Peter and James, the Lord's brother. Fourteen years later, he was again in Jerusalem, where, he says: "I laid before them … the gospel that I proclaim among the Gentiles, in order to make sure that I was not running, or had not run, in vain." (Galatians 2.2) Although the meeting was occasionally fractious, it concluded with the Jerusalem leadership approving Paul's version of the gospel: "When James and Cephas and John, who were acknowledged pillars, recognized the grace that had been given to me, they gave to Barnabas and me the right hand of fellowship, agreeing that we should go to the Gentiles and they to the circumcised."(Galatians 2.9)

❖ Paul never turned his back on the churches of Judea, including that in Jerusalem (as he surely would have done had he disowned the Judean churches' understanding of Christian faith). "The pillars of the Church" had demanded that he remember the poor of their community. A considerable section of his letters to the Church in Corinth (1 Corinthians 16.1-4 & 2 Corinthians 8 & 9) concerns the practicalities of the collection that he was to carry personally to Jerusalem. These chapters read like the first ever campaign of Christian Aid!

❖ In two chapters of supreme importance for the understanding of Paul's faith, he put considerable emphasis on the Tradition which he had received. The first concerns his account of the origins of the Lord's Supper. The matter arises quite fortuitously. It seems that the Corinthian Christians' observance of this had become quite scandalous, for what should have been a sharing of bread and wine had become rather the cause of deep division. The wealthy were bringing sufficient food and drink (so much as to make themselves drunk!), whilst the poor had nothing to eat or drink! Addressing himself to the problem, Paul had cause to remind them of the institution of the Supper. "For I received from the Lord what I also handed on to you, that the Lord Jesus on the night when he was betrayed took a loaf of bread, and when he had given thanks, he broke it

---

[28] The Mystery Religions: these were mostly of middle Eastern origins, some of which had penetrated the Roman Empire, even Rome itself. They were so-called because they held secret teachings and rituals, divulged only to those initiated into their cult. One such was Mithraism which became popular amongst Roman soldiers. Its initiates were baptized in the blood of a bull.

and said, 'This is my body that is for you. Do this in remembrance of me.' In the same way he took the cup also, after supper, saying, 'This cup is the new covenant in my blood. Do this, as often as you drink it, in remembrance of me.' For as often as you eat this bread and drink the cup, you proclaim the Lord's death until he comes."(1 Corinthians 11. 23-26)

❖ You will recognize an account of the climactic moments of the Last Supper similar to that of the gospels, being especially close to that of Luke 22.17-20.

The word "tradere" (Latin) means "to hand over," "surrender," even "betray", from which we derive the word Tradition. The imagery is that of the handing on of the baton in the relay race. Paul is absolutely clear that what he passed on to the Christians of Corinth was what he had "received from the Lord." This can hardly imply that Paul had himself been present at the Last Supper. Nothing in all his letters claims that he had ever met Jesus in the flesh. It must mean that he had received a precise account of what occurred on the last evening of Jesus' life from those who had been present at the Supper table, i.e. from those apostles with whom he had conversed in Jerusalem. It was that account that he had passed on to new believers in Corinth.

❖ The second usage of the concept of Tradition occurs in 1 Corinthians 15. Here Paul appeals to the very heart of his understanding of the gospel, which is evidently misunderstood by some in the Corinthian congregation. Here is what he wrote: "Now I should remind you, brothers and sisters, of the good news *that I proclaimed* to you, *which you* in turn *received*, in which also you stand, through which also you are being saved, if you hold firmly to the message that I proclaimed to you – unless you have come to believe in vain. For *I handed on to you* as of first importance *what I* in turn had *received*:
- that Christ died for our sins in accordance with the scriptures,
- and that he was buried,
- and that he was raised on the third day in accordance with the scriptures,
- and that he appeared to Cephas, then to the twelve. Then he appeared to more than five hundred brothers and sisters at one time, most of whom are still alive, though some have died. Then he appeared to James, then to all the apostles. Last of all, as to someone untimely born, he appeared also to me." Here then is the heart of Paul's understanding of the gospel. Not something invented by him, but something which he had received from those Christians before him (when he was still a Pharisee intent on the destruction of the new faith) and which he had passed on to his converts in Corinth. We see in these words the embryonic beginning of a distinctively Christian creed, that proclaims Christ as the One who had died (by crucifixion), who was buried and was raised by God from the dead, appearing ultimately to Paul just as he already appeared to Cephas (Peter) and many others.

❖ In these two illustrations, we perceive that far from inventing a new religion (that hadn't existed before), Paul was utterly loyal to the essentials of the faith handed on to him from the first apostles of Jesus.

❖ There are other passages of Paul which reflect his acquaintance with words of Jesus. In Acts 20.35 he is reported as saying to the elders of the Church at Ephesus: "I have given you an example that by such work we must support the weak, remembering the words of the Lord Jesus, for he himself said, 'It is more blessed to give than to receive.'" None of the gospels report this saying (not even Luke's, who must have written these words). It makes one wonder how many other words of Jesus may not have survived.

❖ We may also reflect on Romans 12.9-21 and how much of its content reflects the spirit and sometimes the wording of the Sermon on the Mount; just as I Corinthians 13, Paul's paean in praise of Love, has rightly been described as his portrait of the character of Jesus. Could anybody doubt that without much apparent knowledge of Jesus' lifetime, he could yet be very close to the Spirit of the Lord?

The letter to Philemon

Let us make this our study text. It has the huge advantage of comprising no more than half a page of our Bibles. It is unique in being the only one of Paul's letters addressed to a named individual; although others are named together with Philemon and behind them is the church that meets in his house. We are at a stage of Christian development when "church" quite definitely denotes a congregation of people rather than a building.

I suggest that first you read the letter right through to get a general impression of its contents. Then we may pursue these questions:
1. What is the structure of the letter? It follows closely the customary format of letter-writing common in Graeco-Roman society. So we have:

a. The Salutation, 1.1-2: The writer discloses his name, Paul, and something of his present circumstances, i.e. that he is in a Roman prison; that Timothy accompanies him; and he then addresses those to whom the letter is sent, i.e. Philemon, named as friend and colleague, together with Apphia (possibly his wife) and Archippus (a Christian worker also mentioned in 1 Corinthians 4.17) and the congregation that meets in his house.

b. The Greeting, v 3: "Grace to you and Peace from God our Father and the Lord Jesus Christ." This greeting, almost standard in Paul's letters, interestingly combines the Greek and the Hebrew forms of daily greeting, "Charis" (grace) and "Eirene" (peace), the latter doubtless translating the Hebrew "Shalom."

c. The Thanksgiving, vv 4-7: Paul always warmly commends the faith of those to whom he is writing (even when there are matters on which he may further on have to rebuke them). He is a man of prayer, his Christian friends always close to his heart and mind.

d. The Main Theme, vv 8-20: This concerns a certain Onesimus, evidently a slave in Philemon's household, who has run away from his master, has sought out Paul even in prison, and, by his influence has become a Christian (see verse 10: "Whose father I have become in this prison") and has served Paul admirably. Now Paul is sending the run-away home to his master, evidently carrying this letter with him. The purpose of the letter is to persuade Philemon to receive his slave home in a generously Christian manner.

There are a number of points that will be helpful to note:
i. That the name Onesimus means "useful" and was a name much used for slaves. Hence the play on words in verse 11: has he been useful or useless?
ii. Although we are not told in so many words that Onesimus had run away from Philemon's household, it is implied in the terms Paul uses, such as "sending him back" (12), or "receive him back" (15). Had he also stolen something of his master's? Was that the wrong he had possibly committed (verse 18), or was Paul offering to make pecuniary recompense for the labor lost during his absence?
iii. Notice the manner in which Paul seeks to persuade Philemon. He would be entitled, as Christ's apostle, to impose his will by diktat; but he prefers to appeal to Philemon's better nature or rather, to his Christian conscience. He would rather win Philemon's free consent rather than enforce a decision by compulsion (14). How does he do this? He refers to the run-away as "my child" (10), whom Paul has "fathered" into Christian faith (10). We may conjecture that Onesimus had met with the apostle on an earlier occasion, presumably in Philemon's home, and that he had made so favorable an impression for the slave to seek him out, even in goal. There he has served Paul admirably, so much so that Paul would have liked to have him remain with him (13). So strong has the bond between them become that, in sending him back, Paul is as if sending "his very own heart" (12). He appeals to Philemon to welcome this slave as he would have welcomed the apostle himself. Finally, he reminds Philemon, that on returning, Onesimus will be no longer just a slave, but a fellow Christian believer, "a dear brother" (16).
iv. We may note that the conditions of Paul's imprisonment were not, at this stage, over-harsh. It would seem likely that he was not as yet in prison on any capital charge; such that fellow Christians such as Onesimus and Epaphras (23) were able to attend him; and that he was able to write from his cell. The same is evident even when he was in Rome, waiting to be tried before Caesar, as we

realize in Acts 28. 16-31. It was more a matter of "house-arrest."

e. Conclusions consequent on the theme (21-22) Paul concludes in the confident expectation that Philemon will meet his wishes; that he will "do more than I ask." And there is finally a homely touch: "Please have a room ready for the apostle whenever he is released from prison" (22). Sadly, we have no idea whether Paul's hope was fulfilled.

f. Closing Greetings and Benediction (23-25): Here we learn of a fellow prisoner, Epaphras (who was Paul's chief co-worker in the founding of the Church at Colossae, himself a native of that city). See Colossians 1.7 & 4.12. Also mentioned amongst Paul's entourage are Mark, Aristarchus, Demas and Luke (23). It is tempting here to imagine two of our gospel writers being present in Paul's company, but, the names Mark and Luke were common enough in the Graeco-Roman world. We could only succumb to the temptation if it were possible to detect anything within the gospels under their names that could be considered evidence of their presence with Paul at this point. There is none.

Further matters for reflection

1. What was it about this brief, highly personal letter (so different from the weighty epistles dispatched to Rome or Corinth) that persuaded Christians of the early Christian centuries to value it as "scripture" and eventually incorporate it into the New Testament? How would you justify its inclusion in the Christian Bible?

2. What does the theme of this letter contribute to any debate about slavery? As we know, slavery was extremely widespread in the Graeco-Roman world (less so in Jewish society). Jesus' message (Luke 4.16-19), derived from Isaiah 61, included the proclamation of "release for prisoners" and the letting "broken victims to go free." Yet neither Jesus nor Paul instituted any open campaign against slavery. Should they have done so? Would such a campaign have been practicable? For Paul's thinking on the matter, see also his teaching addressed to the Corinthians in 1 Corinthians 7. Although most of the chapter concerns sexual relationships, the principles he applies covers equally the status of slaves (see especially 7.21-24). You might ask yourself the question: Does Paul's perspective given in this chapter apply to all times and circumstances? Or was it

---

[29] By interim ethic is meant an ethic, or code of behavior, applicable for a strictly limited period of time. The question is much debated whether Jesus' teaching in the Sermon on the Mount was intended as a pattern of behavior which he expected his disciples to follow for all times, or was it applicable only during the brief period expected between Jesus' pronouncements and the incoming Kingdom of God on earth.

what some have called "an interim ethic")[29] Did Paul think and advise as he did because he supposed that the Age in which he was living was about to be wound up (see 1 Corinthians 7.29-31), with Jesus returning in glory to establish the Kingdom of God on earth? Once the Church had come to recognize that a long stretch of history lay ahead of it, did it simply abandon Paul's teaching on this matter? Why was it that 1800 years had to go by before William Wilberforce and others set out to abolish the slave trade, and later, the very institution of slavery?

3. For your consideration: in view of the above discussion, how authoritative do you believe Paul's teaching to be on the matter of the status of women in Church and Society and on sexual relationships in general? Are his pronouncements on these matters binding for ever on Christians, or should they rather be seen as his personal attempts to settle matters of some controversy in the first century, which are no longer relevant in the considerably changed circumstances of life in the 21st? If the latter is your conclusion, then what are the criteria for making truly Christian judgments for our own time? What are our sources of Authority? I will try to deal with this huge issue in Chapters 19 to 21.

CHAPTER 10:
THE SYNOPTIC GOSPELS

A quite casual acquaintance with the gospels readily perceives that the gospels of Matthew, Mark and Luke display a marked likeness in many respects and that John's Gospel, by contrast, is markedly different.

The authorship of the gospels

We might assume that this was cut and dried. Surely the four gospels were written respectively by Matthew, Mark, Luke and John? So Church tradition tells us, but these attributions were not original to the first manuscripts. The gospels, unlike for example Paul's letters, contain no signatures – they are anonymous. We cannot even be sure when the traditional titles were first added to them, but it was not before the second century. Nor can we know for sure by what authority these particular names were appended. However, for present purposes, we will refer to them by their traditional names, although further on we will have to note how modern scholarship has questioned these.

Some information about their authorship, but of an ambiguous nature, can be gleaned from second century Christian writings, but these are not wholly consistent nor are they easy to interpret. But the emerging tradition was clear enough, i.e. that Matthew and John were apostles of Jesus, that Mark was the traveling companion and "interpreter" of Simon Peter, and that Luke was a close companion of Paul. Thus all four of them were considered to be "apostolic," having been written either by apostles or by confidants of apostles, and were thus reliable witnesses to the story of Jesus. It was this that gave the four the stamp of authenticity (especially as compared with those other gospels[30] that were rejected as apocryphal even though these also had names of apostles attached to them). And so the Tradition was handed on through Christian history and has only been subjected to serious criticism in modern times.[31] It had one serious consequence. Since Matthew's Gospel was supposedly written by the apostle Matthew (the tax collector, also known as Levi), and since its

---

[30] We will say something about these apocryphal gospels in Chapter 12.
[31] There were great Biblical scholars (such as Origen and Jerome) in the early centuries who did address some of the discrepancies and difficulties inherent in supposing all four gospels to be products of apostolic witness. For instance, they were aware of some of the stark differences between the first three Gospels and that attributed to John. Biblical criticism did not commence only in modern times; but it was only in modern times that it could be pursued systematically and with all the tools provided by information technology.

contents include almost the entire subject matter to be found in Mark, it was assumed that Mark's Gospel was an abbreviation, a mere shadow of Matthew's. In consequence, Mark's Gospel was almost universally neglected, its importance only being rediscovered in the 19th century. Nor could the true relationship between the gospels be appreciated until the tools of literary and historical criticism could be applied to them.

The Synopsis

Modern gospel research began in earnest in 1776 with J J Griesbach who proposed a wholly new way of looking at the first three gospels, i.e. by printing them side-by-side, in parallel columns, wherever their subject matter converges, so that they can be studied together. The result was the SYNOPSIS (from the Greek for "seen together"). The three have subsequently been termed "the Synoptic Gospels." The results of their systematic study together have been dramatic. All modern study of the gospels starts here. It obliged a completely new approach to the matter of their authorship. If you could establish a) that Mark's Gospel was the first to be written, and b) that Matthew had used Mark's Gospel as the basis of his own, could the traditional notion be valid? Since it was never claimed that Mark was either an apostle or eyewitness of Jesus, would Matthew, one of the Twelve, have based his testimony on that of one less qualified than himself? We may add to this that Matthew also used another written source, which has been called Q (from the German "quelle," meaning "source") besides other material known only to himself. Add to this the impression, via detailed study of the text, that this gospel (as we know it) was the product of second or third generation Christianity, somewhat removed in time and venue from its origins, it becomes increasingly dubious to suppose it to be the work of an apostle.

A somewhat similar argument can be applied to consideration of Luke's and John's Gospels. Both, although very differently, look like the products of a lengthy process of reflection and editing, like the slow maturing of good wine, over several decades. The main consensus of critical scholarship today would doubt that any of our gospels, in their finished state (i.e. as we know them) are written by apostles. It may still be claimed that they are in some respect "apostolic."

It follows that we have to re-examine the notion of authorship. We cannot apply any modern notions of this to the Bible. We have to abandon any idea of Matthew or John sitting at a desk, quill and ink to hand, reference books close by, to write a gospel as a modern author might tackle a biography at his keyboard. Indeed, it would be safer to imagine not so much an individual person as an entire Christian community engaged in the process of recording its experience.

A hypothetical reconstruction of Gospel Origins

WE WOULD ENVISAGE A PROCESS
SOMETHING LIKE THIS

At the First Stage: Imagine a Christian community, almost wholly Jewish but with a few Gentile converts, living at some distance from Jerusalem perhaps fifteen years after the Crucifixion, i.e. in about AD 45. They meet together every Sunday before daybreak for worship, prayer and breaking of bread together. In this way they remember Jesus. From time to time, they are visited by one of the apostles, or one of their close associates, an evangelist, prophet or teacher, who recounts to them one or more episodes about Jesus. Let us suppose that their most reputed visitor was Matthew, the apostle who had been a tax-collector before he was called by Jesus. So his version of events was that most familiar to them, which could explain how it was that the gospel that emerged decades later within this community came to bear his name.[32] It is possible that he was also a collector of Old Testament prophecies that appeared to foretell key events of Jesus' life-story and of some of the Lord's sayings.

At the Second Stage: We can next suppose that the anonymous leader of this congregation began writing down some of the sayings of Jesus, on potsherds or scraps of papyrus, just as he had heard them from the lips of Matthew and others.

At the Third Stage: Imagine this community some 30 years later. There have taken place some momentous events since we last visited it. After a calamitous civil war (that largely passed them by), the Temple in Jerusalem has been sacked and the city itself ruined (in AD 70). This confirms these Christian villagers in their allegiance to Jesus, for he had prophesied the destruction of the Temple. But in order to avoid the troubles, the villagers have been forced to migrate northwards into the hinterland behind Antioch in Syria, where they have rebuilt their village. In the meanwhile, terrible news had come from Rome, of the persecution of Christians, with many martyrs, amongst them Simon Peter and the apostle Paul. Let us surmise that their own mentor Matthew had long since perished of fever whilst traveling into Arabia. This made them cling all the more to their memories of all that he had taught them. Their new teacher was busily collecting together all the information that he could. He had come into the possession of a scroll, telling the story of Jesus' ministry in Galilee and his death

---

[32] This is taking seriously what Papias, Bishop of Smyrna (in Asia Minor) wrote in c. 130 AD, namely, that "*Matthew compiled the 'logia' in the Hebrew language and each one interpreted it as he could.*" We cannot know for sure what is meant by "logia," but it could mean "sayings." The Hebrew language more likely means Aramaic, which was the living dialect used in those times. However, there's no evidence to suggest any part of Matthew's Gospel had been first written in Aramaic. But the Jesus' story must have been recounted originally in Aramaic, since that was the language of Jesus and his disciples.

in Jerusalem, written by a certain John Mark, about whom little was known at the time. The teacher had procured another scroll, containing sayings of Jesus and of John the Baptizer. Nobody knew who had compiled this, but it was a useful supplement to what they already knew. Meanwhile, in their new community, relations with the local synagogue had worsened. Jews were hardening their hearts against the Christians. Some Christians had gone back to the synagogue. In spite of which, there had taken place a considerable influx of Gentile converts.

At the Fourth Stage: The situation described above has deepened. The Christian community is now wholly separate from that of the synagogue. Gentiles considerably outnumbered the Jews in it. The teacher has become a highly reputed leader of the Christians, known throughout the province. His ability as a teacher of new converts is highly regarded. As such, he feels the need for a more complete account of Jesus' life and teachings than Mark had managed. So he sets to work to produce a new documentation of the story. He admires the clear outline that Mark's account had given, so he adopts that as the basic outline for his own work. He polishes up Mark's sometimes barbarous Greek, abbreviates where little is lost by so doing and occasionally amends the picture given. He rather winces at the all too realistic (and human) portrayal of Jesus' emotions, preferring to leave them out (after all, his community worships Jesus as Son of God in glory), also the passages less than flattering to the apostles. It doesn't do (so he supposes) to show the founder members of the church to have been such numb-skulls! Our teacher also uses that Collection of Sayings (that we call Q). With his passion for orderliness, he tidies them up under thematic headings, and with his fine poetic sense produces the masterpiece we call the Beatitudes. Of course, Jesus was the inspired origin of these sublime sayings, but it was the Teacher who presented them in the form we know. The Lord's Prayer too was in that "Q" collection, but the Teacher included in his gospel account that slightly fuller and more polished version that was being prayed daily in his congregation's Worship. To that he added all the stories and memoirs that Matthew had recounted, undoubtedly with that "spin," that eye for heightened dramatic effect that had characterized his telling of them.

The gospel that eventually emerged out of this long process, which came to be called "Matthew's Gospel," arose out of a particular community and at a particular time, and was the outcome of a lengthy process extending over several decades. The account given above is to some extent fictitious, but it accounts for some of the distinctive features of the gospel called Matthew's.

A method of synoptic study

At this stage it is of vital importance that you do your own critical study of one or more episodes as these are set out in a Synopsis of the Gospels, since you will only be fully convinced of the modern theories if you have tested them for yourself.

We have in Matthew 19. 13-15 and its parallels a well-loved episode in which parents bring their children to Jesus, seeking his blessing on them, as it is told in each of the Synoptic Gospels. We have set them out in three parallel columns so as to facilitate an easy comparison of the three accounts. I suggest that you use this simple method for which you will need some colored crayons and a ruler. (You may wonder whether you are being asked to undertake some theological mathematics? You will see the point of the exercise only when you have done it.)

1. Underline in red all the words that are identical within the three columns. Where an identical word is used, but in a different person or tense, use a broken line. What amount of identity of wording do we have across all three versions? How many words are identical or nearly so? Does it convince you that we have here three versions of one and the same episode?

2. Next, we underline in blue identical wording as between Matthew and Mark but that differs in Luke's version. How many words are identical between Matthew and Mark to add to those already underlined in red ?

3. We next underline agreement as between Mark and Luke (but which differs in Matthew) in green. How many words are identical between Mark and Luke to add to those already underlined in red?

4. Carrying out a careful comparison of the three accounts, answer these questions:

a) Do you suppose they are reporting the same episode?
b) How do you account for their marked similarity? Is it accounted for because all three gospel writers were present at this episode and it happens they used the same language to describe it? Or, is it more likely that one of these accounts is the original, and that the others copied from it? If so, which is the original?
c) In what are they most in agreement?
d) How do you account for their differences?
e) Can you discern any theological differences between the three?
f) Can we draw any conclusions as to the authorship of these three gospels?

The word count additions can give us only an approximate idea of the degree of identity as between the gospels, remembering that to be completely valid the exercise has to be carried out in the Greek text. For it is in Greek that the question of the literary relationship arises. In the Greek text[33], there are 24 words identical or very nearly so across all three versions; a further three words

THE BLESSING OF LITTLE CHILDREN:
A SYNOPTIC COMPARISON

Matthew 19:13 - 15	Mark 10:13-16	Luke 18:15 - 17
13 Then little children were being brought to him in order that he might lay his hands on them and pray.	*13 People were bringing little children to him in order that he might touch them;*	*15 People were bringing even infants to him that he might touch them;*
The disciples spoke sternly to those who brought them;	*and the disciples spoke sternly to them.*	*and when the disciples saw it, they sternly ordered them not to do it.*
*14 **but Jesus** said,*	*14 **But** when **Jesus** saw this, he was indignant and said to them,*	*16 **But Jesus** called for them and said,*
*"**Let the little children come to me, and do not stop them;for it is to such as these that the kingdom** of heaven **belongs**."*	*"**Let the little children come to me; do not stop them; for it is to such as these that the kingdom** of God **belongs**.*	*"**Let the little children come to me, and do not stop them; for it is to such as these that the kingdom** of God **belongs**.*
	*15 **Truly I tell you whoever does not receive the kingdom of God as a little child will never enter it**."*	*17 **Truly I tell you, whoever does not receive the kingdom of God as a little child will never enter it**."*
*15 **And he** laid **his hands** on them and went on his way.*	*16 **And he** took them up in his arms, **laid his hands on them**, and blessed them.*	

identical as between Matthew & Mark (but a further 14 if Matthew 18. 3 is considered parallel to Mark 10.15 and Lk.18.17); and there are 25 words identical as between Mark and Luke.

What are the results of our comparison?

1. We will note that the greatest degree of identity is in the actual words Jesus spoke to the people present, "Let the little children come to me ..." Were we to pursue such comparisons throughout the gospels, we would discover that this is usually the case; demonstrating that what the early Christians considered of the greatest importance was to remember what Jesus had actually said. But, there are some exceptions to this rule: Matthew in particular had no hesitation in altering what Jesus was reported as having said where he found it ambiguous or unacceptable (for whatever reason – I will give some examples further on).

2. The comparison between Matthew and Mark does not amount to a great deal. We will note the agreement on "little children" (whereas Luke has "babes"); that the disciples "spoke sternly" to their parents; and at the end of the account, that Jesus "laid his hands on them." This latter phrase may possibly convey the idea that Jesus' action was a ritual action akin to the "laying on of hands" in Christian healing and in commissioning disciples (e.g. in Acts 8.18; 1 Timothy 4.14; 2 Timothy 1.6; and Hebrews 6.2). This would be more significant for Matthew than for Mark, since Matthew's Gospel has a far greater interest in specifically "churchy" matters.

3. Comparison between Mark and Luke reveals a greater degree of verbal identity than between Matthew and Mark; which is normally the case. We should note as of importance their designation in common of "the Kingdom of God," whereas Matthew has "kingdom of heaven." Matthew's variant shows "Matthew" as a devout Jew, who, in order not to transgress the fourth commandment, will not speak the name of God in public, but rather substitutes for it "heaven."

4. Matthew alone adds to the words "that he might lay his hands on them...and pray." Matthew presumably intends to demonstrate that the laying on of hands was always accompanied by prayer.

5. Mark and Luke quote Jesus' words about the Kingdom as being open only to the childlike in heart. Matthew also is aware of this text, but has already used it in slightly different context elsewhere in his gospel, in 18.3 and so leaves it out here.
6. Possibly the most surprising feature of this episode is that Mark alone

---

[33] In *Synopsis Quattuor Evangeliorum*, ed By Kurt Aland, Wurtemburg Bible Society, Stuttgart, © 1964 on page 337.

indicates Jesus' anger at the attitude of his own disciples, who had evidently attempted to turn away these villagers bringing their children; and which occasioned his saying, "Let the let children come to me ..." Whilst retaining the saying, neither Matthew nor Luke mention what lay behind it, i.e. that Jesus was angered by their attitude. This is significant, because this is one of several episodes in which Mark alone alludes to Jesus' human emotions (such as anger, compassion, grief, etc) or to some failure of the disciples, which receive no mention at all in the other gospels. It is as if these, written within communities that worshiped Jesus as Lord and regarded the disciples with awe, were in danger of forgetting the reality of his human life and the fallibility of his followers.

Wherever there is difference of interpretation as between the gospels we can only seek the solution that makes best sense. For instance, in the example given above, consider the two options:
i. Did the original version of the story (as reported by Matthew and Luke) make no mention of Jesus' anger at his disciples' attitude and Mark alone add this to his depiction of the event? Or ...
ii. Did the original version (that of Mark) contain the reference to Jesus' anger and Matthew and Luke omit it for some doctrinal reason? When we add the further examples of their omission of other references to the Lord's human emotions, no ii appears the correct inference. Matthew and Luke both had some unease about depicting Jesus in too human a light.
We might tabulate the results of our comparisons of this episode as follows:

THE BLESSING OF LITTLE CHILDREN (AGREEMENTS AND DIFFERENCES)

	Matthew 19. 13-15	Mark 10.13-16	Luke 18.15-17
1	Little children	Little children	... babes
2	... lay his hands on..	... touch them	... touch them
3	... and pray		
4		Jesus was moved with indignation	
5	the Kingdom of heaven	the Kingdom of God	the Kingdom of God
6		Not to receive the Kingdom as a child is to debar oneself from it	Not to receive the Kingdom as a child is to debar oneself from it
7	He laid his hands on them ... and departed.	He blessed them, laying on hands	

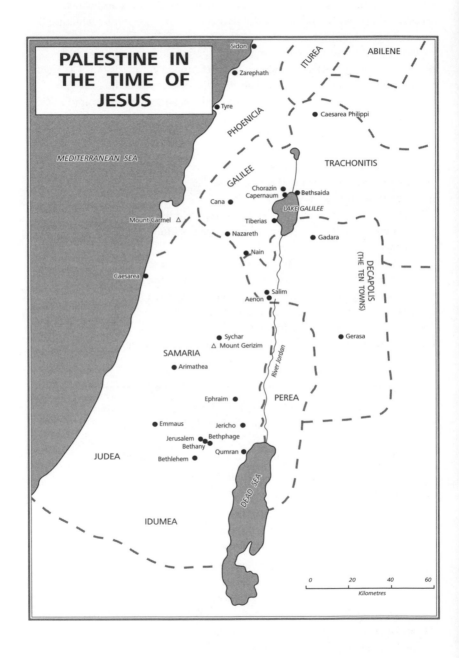

PALESTINE IN THE TIME OF JESUS

Sidon

Zarephath

Tyre

PHOENICIA

ITUREA

ABILENE

Caesarea Philippi

MEDITERRANEAN SEA

GALILEE

TRACHONITIS

Chorazin
Capernaum
Bethsaida

Cana

LAKE GALILEE

Mount Carmel △

Tiberias

Nazareth

Gadara

DECAPOLIS
(THE TEN TOWNS)

Nain

Caesarea

Salim
Aenon

Sychar
△ Mount Gerizim

Gerasa

SAMARIA

River Jordan

Arimathea

Ephraim

PEREA

Emmaus

Jericho

Jerusalem Bethphage
Bethany

Bethlehem

Qumran

JUDEA

DEAD SEA

IDUMEA

| 0 | 20 | 40 | 60 |

Kilometres

Finally, what conclusions may we draw as to the literary relationship between these three accounts and what effect does it have on the matter of their authorship?

Examination of the entirety of the gospels yields these results:

a. The content of 80%[34] of Mark's Gospel is reproduced (with alterations) within Matthew's Gospel. Put in another way, 51% of Matthew's Gospel reproduces content to be found in Mark.

b. The content of 65% of Mark's Gospel is reproduced (with alterations) within Luke's Gospel. 53% of Luke's Gospel reproduces content to be found in Mark.

c. In a considerable majority of cases, the *wording* of Mark's Gospel is in a majority by comparison with Matthew and Luke, i.e. where Matthew and Mark agree, Luke may disagree; where Luke and Mark agree, Matthew may disagree.

d. The same is to be observed in *the order* in which events occur. Where Matthew and Mark agree on the order, Luke may not; but where Luke and Mark agree, Matthew may differ. Mark is nearly always in the majority.

e. Similar evidence pointing to Mark's priority becomes apparent when considering the reasons for either Matthew or Luke diverging from Mark on matters of theological sensitivity.

A further example will make this plain. Where Mark and Luke report Jesus' baptism at the hands of John in similar terms, Matthew alone makes a fundamental alteration. All three gospels present Jesus as himself asking John for baptism, but Matthew alone adds this dialog: "John would have prevented him, saying, 'I need to be baptized by you, and do you come to me?' But Jesus answered him, 'Let it be so now; for it is proper for us in this way to fulfill all righteousness.' Then he consented." (Matthew 3.14-15) What accounts for this striking addition? Is it not most likely that Matthew, believing Jesus to have been sinless (as eventually became the orthodox Christian dogma), had to explain why Jesus should have sought a baptism that was specifically for sinners? His addition gives us to understand that Jesus didn't need baptism for the reason others did, i.e. that they were sinners, but rather to realize a requirement from God "to fulfill all righteousness" (which presumably means something like, "fulfill all that was necessary for the salvation of the world.")

---

[34] Figures reproduced from V Taylor, *The Gospels, a Short Introduction*, Epworth Press, London, 1960, p 44.

For a further example, you might compare Mark 10.18 and Luke 18.9 with Matthew's variation of this episode concerning "A question about inheriting Eternal Life" in Matthew 19.17. How do you account for Matthew's variation?

The Priority of Mark

A considerable consensus amongst scholars is that the above factors are only explicable on the assumption that Mark's was the first gospel to be written; and that both Matthew and Luke used copies of it when they penned their gospels. This assumption is referred to as The Priority of Mark.

Thus Mark's Gospel has become the corner-stone of all modern study of the gospels, so overturning the traditional view (held since St Augustine in the early fifth century) that it was an abbreviation of Matthew. Synoptic comparison reveals that, far from being an abbreviation of Matthew, it is rather Matthew's account which foreshortens Mark's narrative as well as adding much more material from other sources. The recognition of Mark's priority enables us to read it as the gospel that takes us closest to the earliest witness to the reality of Jesus' life and ministry.

The consequence is to recognize that both Matthew and Luke had a copy of Mark before them at some stage in the writing of their gospels. They accepted the basic outline of Mark's Gospel, i.e. that Jesus' primary mission took place in Galilee, after which he journeyed up to Jerusalem where he was to suffer and die. However, both used the Marcan outline in quite different ways. Matthew distributes Marcan material quite evenly throughout his gospel; whereas Luke uses it chiefly in two large blocks. Neither follows Mark slavishly, but alters the text for reasons of better style or differences of theological emphasis. The alterations they make can be very revealing of their priorities in recounting the story (which is the matter of a fruitful method of study called Redaction Criticism; "redaction" having to do with the final stages of editing).

The Source named Q

It appears that Matthew and Luke used another source in common. For there are a substantial number of passages in which Matthew and Luke have almost identical text which is not derived from Mark. Here is an example, from the preaching of John the Baptist, as it is presented in these two gospels:

What observations can we make here?

1. This section, which could be entitled "The Appearance and Preaching of John the Baptist," begins quite differently in Matthew and Luke. In Matthew, it comes immediately after the story of Jesus' birth, concluding with his family's

THE PREACHING OF JOHN THE BAPTIST:
A SYNOPTIC COMPARISON

MATTHEW 3: 1 – 10	LUKE 3: 1 - 10
3.1: In those days John the Baptist appeared in the wilderness of Judea, proclaiming, *2: 'Repent, for the kingdom of heaven has come near.'*	*3.1: In the fifteenth year of the reign of Emperor Tiberius… the word of God came to John son of Zechariah in the wilderness.* *3: He went into all the region around the Jordan, proclaiming a baptism of repentance for the forgiveness of sins,*
3: This is the one of whom **the prophet Isaiah** *spoke when he said, `The voice of one crying out in the wilderness: "Prepare the way of the Lord, make his paths straight."**	*4: as it is written in the book of the words of the* **prophet Isaiah,** **`The voice of one crying out in the wilderness: "Prepare the way of the Lord, make his paths straight.**
4: Now John wore clothing of camel's hair with a leather belt around his waist, and his food was locusts and wild honey. 5:Then the people of Jerusalem and all Judea were going out to him, and all the region along the Jordan,	*5: Every valley shall be filled, and every mountain and hill shall be made low, and the crooked shall be made straight, and the rough ways made smooth;* *6: and all flesh shall see the salvation of God." `*
6: and they were baptized by him in the river Jordan, confessing their sins.	*7: John said to the crowds that came out to be baptized by him,*
7:But when he saw many Pharisees and Sadducees coming for baptism, he said to them, **'You brood of vipers! Who warned you to flee from the wrath to come? 8: Bear fruit worthy of repentance. 9: Do not presume to say to yourselves, "We have Abraham as our ancestor"; for I tell you, God is able from these stones to raise up children to Abraham. 10: Even now the axe is lying at the root of the trees; every tree therefore that does not bear good fruit is cut down and thrown into the fire.**	**'You brood of vipers! Who warned you to flee from the wrath to come? 8: Bear fruits worthy of repentance. Do not begin to say to yourselves, "We have Abraham as our ancestor"; for I tell you, God is able from these stones to raise up children to Abraham. 9: Even now the axe is lying at the root of the trees; every tree therefore that does not bear good fruit is cut down and thrown into the fire.'**

settlement in Nazareth. Luke's first verses read like the probable opening of his gospel (before the birth stories were prefaced before them).

2. Both Matthew and Luke copy Isaiah's prophecy (Isaiah 40.3) concerning "the voice in the wilderness" from the third verse of Mark's Gospel. Whilst Matthew continues to follow Mark's lead in giving a description of John the Baptist's dress and food, Luke has continued with the Isaiah quotation (Isaiah 40.4-5).

3. Matthew continues with some precise identification of those who flocked to the Jordan to receive John's baptism, singling out the Pharisees and Sadducees; whereas Luke does not specify them – they are simply "the crowds."

4. But once we come to the specific words of John's preaching, from Matthew 3.7 and Luke 3.7 onwards, we will note that the wording is very nearly identical (the only exception being that Matthew has "presume," Luke "begin"). Such a degree of identity surely points to a common written source. If it is not from Mark, then we are forced to assume the existence of one that no longer exists. This is the hypothetical document Q, so dubbed from the German for a source, "quelle."

So, in addition to Mark, both Matthew and Luke evidently had another document, which comprised chiefly a collection of the sayings of Jesus (and some of John) with a very few narratives. Study of these sayings suggests that the hypothetical document began with the proclamation of John and ended with prophecies concerning the coming of the Son of Man in glory. As with their use of Mark, Matthew and Luke used Q in quite different ways, Matthew combining Q material with his own collection of sayings and parables in five large blocks of teaching material; whereas Luke appears to inject Q sayings, in conjunction with his own material, throughout his gospel.

5. But both Matthew and Luke had other material that was not derived from either Mark or Q and was therefore unique to them. As hinted above, Matthew tends to use this material, that is dubbed "M" for convenience, intertwined with that from Mark and Q. Luke also has his own material, which is dubbed "L." This he tends to interweave with all that he derived from Q. His Marcan material tends to stand on its own.

The question has been raised whether we need to posit the existence of Q, a minority of scholars proposing that Matthew's Gospel was both abbreviated by Mark and employed by Luke. They explain all the so-called Q passages as Luke's borrowings from Matthew. The following factors tell against this revisionist theory:

i. Matthew's and Luke's accounts of Jesus' birth are quite different from each other and are incompatible to a large extent. Could Luke have written his account wholly ignoring that of Matthew, had he known it? Surely not. And vice versa.

ii. Matthew and Luke share a considerable number of sayings of Jesus, with some narrative, which they use in entirely different ways. Matthew has skillfully woven together many of these sayings thematically into the Sermon on the Mount. Luke has some of these sayings in a comparable address, called the Sermon on the Plain, but he has many others of the sayings found in Matthew's Sermon scattered at various locations throughout his gospel. Had Luke had before him a copy of Matthew's Sermon, would he have broken it up and dispersed it widely? Again, surely not.

iii. Matthew's Gospel contains a number of parables unique to it such as those of
- The Wheat and the Tares, Matthew 13.24-30 & 36-43)
- The Hidden Treasure and the Pearl of great price (13.44-46)
- The Laborers in the Vineyard (20.1-16)
- The Ten Virgins (25.1-13)
- The Talents (25.14-30)
- The Sheep and the Goats (25.31-46)
Is it likely, had he known them, that Luke would have left these out of his own gospel?

iv. It is far preferable to suppose that whilst Luke used both Mark's Gospel and the Q document, he had no knowledge whatsoever of Matthew's Gospel. This alone would account for the considerable amount of material unique to Luke alone. I will pay further attention to this in the next chapter.

Some conclusions

The structure of the Synoptic Gospels can be set out as if formulating a
mathematical equation: Matthew = Mark + Q + M
                                                        Luke   = Mark + Q + L
This may be a useful aid-memoire, but it is misleading if it leads us to suppose the production of these gospels was a merely mechanical affair. The gospels were essentially the products of the living, dynamic witness of the early Church, as it reflected, in different locations and situations, on the meaning of Jesus' words and deeds and re-applied them to the changing situations which confronted it.

CHAPTER 11:
A THUMBNAIL SKETCH
OF THE GOSPELS

Mark's Gospel

It is to be highly recommended that you read through the entire gospel in one or two sittings, preferably in a modern translation, for its full impact to "hit" you. Reading little snippets of it in Church never does it justice.

AUTHORSHIP
The gospel is anonymous. The ascription to Mark dates from the second century. Tradition assumed that the author was Mark, also called John Mark, named in the New Testament. According to this, he was a Jerusalemite, the son of the owner of the house in whose upper room the Last Supper was held; was a cousin of Barnabas, became an associate of Paul (with whom he later fell out) and whom later Peter could address as "my son." According to Bishop Papias' testimony (which is neither wholly lucid nor reliable) Mark had traveled with Peter as his "interpreter."

But Mark was a common name in the Roman world. There is little within the gospel to suggest a close association with either Paul or Peter (nor do the above references make any mention of him writing anything). The internal evidence suggests that the author was a Jew but one who probably spoke Greek from birth (for his Greek doesn't read like translation from Aramaic). His gospel was likely written for a mostly Gentile readership, since it contains a number of Aramaic words which are translated into Greek and where there is reference to a Jewish ritual (in 7.3) this is explained for his readers.

The author was not an eye-witness (as Papias informs us) and was likely a second-generation Christian. For his version of the gospel reads like material that had already formed through the processes of oral transmission, i.e. within the preaching and teaching of the early Church.

THE SIGNIFICANCE OF MARK
As the first gospel to be written (of which we have evidence), Mark's Gospel is of unique importance. As the first, it introduced a new form of literature, a gospel, i.e. a written form of what had previously been a spoken message. It is thus neither biography nor history (although having features of both). A gospel is a kind of

crystallization in writing of what had previously been an orally proclaimed message about what God has done through the life, death and resurrection of Jesus.

It is the gospel which takes us the closest we can get to the life-time of Jesus. It reports more of the Aramaic language that Jesus spoke than any other gospel. It portrays him as a human being who experienced the full range of human emotions, sometimes admitted that he didn't know (13.32), was frequently misunderstood and later deserted by his own disciples; and who suffered a terrible death by crucifixion. And yet he spoke with the authority of God and acted out the works of God (the Greek word Mark uses is "dunamis" (from which we derive the English "dynamite"). It is usually translated "deed of power" or "mighty work." At the end, the Roman centurion in charge of his execution confessed that he is "a Son of God."

THE STRUCTURE OF MARK

Mark's Gospel can be regarded as a drama in two acts, with a prologue and an epilogue. The Prologue, 1.1-13 informs his readers (including us) what the people of Jesus' own day could not have known. The opening words, "The beginning of the Gospel of Jesus Christ, the Son of God" may be understood as the title of the book. It then informs us that what occurred, when Jesus sought baptism at the hands of John, had been predicted in Jewish prophecy. And how, coming out of the Jordan River, the Spirit had descended on Jesus and a voice declared him to be "my beloved Son." Thereafter he was driven out into the wilderness (the location of demonic spirits, of wild creatures and of angels – the latter two of which befriended him) to be tempted. None of this would have been known by the people whom he was soon to encounter in the main body of the drama. The prologue is not unlike that of a Shakespearean play, in which, off-stage, the audience is given vital information without which they could not follow the plot that is to come.

Act I: Jesus' Ministry in Galilee: 1.14- 8.26

Jesus blazes into Galilee proclaiming the imminent arrival of the Kingdom of God: "The time is fulfilled, and the kingdom of God has come near; repent, and believe in the good news." (1.15) We soon learn that the Kingdom is not a political concept, nor a specified territory; but rather the breaking in of God's power and authority to transform the human situation. Mark describes what happens in the Kingdom: fishermen abandon their trade to follow the King; sick people are healed, particularly those possessed by demonic spirits; and people recognize a new note of authority in Jesus' words. Whilst the common people marvel, others representing religious and political authority sense danger and so begins a movement of opposition to Jesus – this reaches crisis-point, when, in 3.6 the Pharisees connive with Herod's men to have Jesus killed. Already, there is anticipation as to how the story will end.

Throughout this section, the question is constantly being asked, "Who is this man?" By means of the written account, this same question was being put to the gospel's readers as it had been to the people of Palestine.

Act II: confession of faith and the journey up to Jerusalem: 8.27-16. 8

The opening episode, Peter's confession of faith in Jesus as the Christ, may be considered both the climax of Act I and the commencement of Act II. The question "Who am I?" is posed now by Jesus himself. The popular supposition is that he is John the Baptist come back from the dead, or Elijah (the prophet expected as the herald of the coming Messiah), or one of the prophets. Putting the question directly to the Twelve, Peter blurts out: "You are the Messiah (Christ)." The word derives from the Hebrew verb "mashiah," meaning "to anoint"; and thus means "the anointed one," i.e. as king. Jesus neither confirms it nor denies it, but begins rather to tell of his suffering to come. With increasing specification, this prophecy is repeated, at 8.31, 9.31, and 10.33-34 (like the tolling of a bell, as one scholar put it). Peter's repudiation of such a future for his Master displays his complete incomprehension of what Jesus' task is to be. The disciples' lack of understanding is a major theme of Mark's account. As if to give the divine response to the disciples' bewilderment, there follows the episode of the Transfiguration (9.1-13) shortly after the first prediction of suffering. On the mountain top, Peter, James and John both witness his transfiguration and hear words almost identical to those heard at his baptism: "This is my Son, the Beloved; listen to him!" This is the divine confirmation that there is nothing mistaken in Jesus' accepted destiny.

Thereafter, the narrative reports the journey up to Jerusalem: "They were on the road, going up to Jerusalem, and Jesus was walking ahead of them; they were amazed, and those who followed were afraid." (10.32) And so unfolds the drama of the last week of Jesus' life in Jerusalem, where he comes into headlong collision with both the Jewish authorities and with the imperial power of Rome. It seems evident at this stage that the expectation was that Jesus and his disciples would suffer together, for had the Lord not declared that those who follow him "should have to deny themselves and take up the cross" (8.34)? The repetition of this theme makes it likely that this gospel was written for a Christian community already undergoing persecution (such as that of Rome in AD 64). But when it comes to the crunch, the disciples desert him. So he alone is arrested, tried, condemned and crucified and finally laid in a borrowed tomb. There follows the muted telling of what occurred in the dawn of the first Easter Day.

Epilogue: 16. 9-20 the lost ending?

The best ancient manuscripts terminate at 16.8 with the women fleeing the tomb in terror. So the question has to be asked: Is this where Mark intended to conclude his gospel? It would seem a strange conclusion for a book that was designed to present Good News. The wording of verse six: ... "go, tell his disciples and Peter that he is going ahead of you to Galilee; there you will see him ..." naturally leads the reader to suppose that the author will recount a resurrection episode in Galilee. It seems preferable to suppose either that this was the point beyond which the author was prevented from completing his work. Did he fall ill? Or was he arrested and imprisoned? Or did he complete his gospel, but its original ending was lost? An end sheet of papyrus could easily become detached from its scroll.

Evidently, early copyists assumed that the gospel was unfinished; and at least two of them attempted to supply what was missing. Hence the two alternative endings we have printed in modern Bibles. The most cursory glance will convince most readers that neither was written by Mark, for both the shorter and the longer endings contain vocabulary that was not that of Mark. In the case of the latter, the content is evidently a pastiche compiled from resurrection appearances of Jesus derived from the other gospels, with some sayings unique to this appendix. This alone, implying that all four gospels were known to whomsoever supplied the last 16 verses, indicates a late date, probably well into the second century.

MARK'S DESIGN
It is highly likely that the Passion Narrative was the first sequential narrative to be made out of the originally disparate elements (known in Greek as "pericopae") in the oral tradition. We cannot know whether it was Mark who deserves the credit for bringing them together into a continuous narrative or whether this had already occurred. The former was probably the case with the structure of the whole gospel. As presented by Mark, Jesus' itinerary fell neatly into two periods, that of his ministry in Galilee and that of his journey up to Jerusalem prior to the Passover Festival. As he tells it, the entire sequence could have occurred within the space of less than one full year. The fact that John's gospel has a quite different framework, with Jesus frequently in Jerusalem and over a period covering three different Passovers, that some evidence in Luke supports this alternative version, demonstrates that Mark's framework is a literary device rather than necessarily a fact of history. The Evangelists are more dramatists than historians.

CHARACTERISTICS
Mark's style is notably racy, with the frequent use of the Greek "euthus," immediately or straightway. The impression given within the opening chapters is one of the almost breathless activity of Jesus. No wonder he needed times of quiet rest when he withdrew from the crowds (see 1.35-38). Many of the

episodes are described in an absolute minimum of words, as if they are little more than shorthand jottings. These "pericopae" were described by K L Schmidt as being like pebbles worn down by the action of wind and waves (i.e. within the processes of oral transmission). Or we might call them "impressionistic sketches." Most of the episodes described raised amongst those who had witnessed them the question as to who Jesus was. Since this gospel has no account of any miraculous birth of Jesus (and within it, the behavior of his Mother and brothers towards him doesn't suggest any knowledge of such an event) the question is the more insistent. From whence does this man from Nazareth, known as the village carpenter, get this wisdom (a wisdom quite unlike that of the scribes)? The two characteristic words that keep arising are "exousia," authority and "dunameis," mighty works. His teaching demonstrates the former; his miraculous healings the latter. At the climax of Act 1, Peter declares that he is the Messiah (8.29); at the climax of Act 2, it is the Roman centurion in charge of the execution, who recognizes in him "a Son of God."

FOR WHOM WAS IT WRITTEN, WHEN AND WHERE?

There can be no certainty about this, except that we can identify a Gentile audience. The very fact that this first gospel was written in Greek and not in Aramaic suggests that already the Church was planted outside of Palestine. Although Mark cites a number of Aramaic words, he always translates them for his readers; and he explains the Jewish custom of handwashing before partaking of a meal (7.3). As regards the time of its writing, the chief point at issue is as to whether it was written before or after the cataclysmic events of the years 68-73 which culminated in the destruction of Jerusalem in 70. Parts of "the little apocalypse," as chapter 13 is called, suggest the imminence or possibly the commencement of the tragedy, without explicitly mentioning the siege of Jerusalem, about which Luke, by contrast, seems quite explicit (Luke 21.20 & 24). So a date just prior to 70 seems appropriate.

Another factor that suggests a date earlier rather than later is in noting Mark's "Christology" by comparison with that of Matthew and Luke. Mark doesn't hesitate to attribute to Jesus a full range of human emotions, from anger to compassion with which Matthew and Luke appear to be ill-at-ease, so much so that they appear to be in danger of losing sight of Christ's humanity. We may be thankful that Mark's Gospel became known before a fossilizing orthodoxy of belief had set in. Nor does Mark hesitate to display the frequent incomprehension, ignorance and eventually betrayal of the disciples (see Mark 4.38-40; 6.52; 8. 17-18; 8.33; 9.18-19; 9.32; 10. 13-14; 10. 35-38; 14.50) – which the other Synoptics alter or omit.

Where was this gospel produced? Tradition ascribed it to Alexandria in Egypt, but there is nothing within it to support this. Other factors point to Rome, especially in the strong emphasis on the sufferings to befall those who follow Christ, in the call to self-denial in 8.34-35: "If any want to become my followers, let them deny themselves and take up their cross and follow me. For those who want to save their life will lose it, and those who lose their life for my sake, and for the sake of the gospel, will save it." Since Roman tradition was that the apostles Peter and Paul both perished in the first great persecution to break out, in Rome in AD 64 when the mad Emperor Nero accused the Christians of having lit the flames that destroyed one fifth of the city, it would seem a likely scenario for the writing of Mark's Gospel.

The Gospel according to Matthew

AUTHORSHIP
We cannot know the identity of Matthew for sure. If there is some truth in Papias' reference to him as "compiling the logia in the Hebrew tongue," then it may be that Matthew the tax-collector, used to wielding a quill-pen, was one of the first to collect sayings of Jesus (= logia?) and became thereby the apostolic figure closest to the source from whence this gospel emerged.

But that he was the author of the completed gospel would seem extremely unlikely. The gospel was written in Greek. It is not translation Greek. It was compiled by somebody who had before him a copy of Mark's Gospel, the hypothetical document we term Q, together with other material he himself had gathered. It would be most unlikely that an apostle and eye-witness would have been so dependent on one who was manifestly not an eye-witness. Besides, the internal evidence within the gospel suggests that it achieved its completion not earlier than the 80s or 90s AD. It is therefore, in its finished form, a product of second or third generation Christianity.

STRUCTURE
Matthew's Gospel is considerably longer than that of Mark. Almost the entire content of Mark reappears in Matthew and that distributed quite evenly throughout its length. Thus Matthew accepts Mark's basic structure, i.e. of a brief Galilean ministry followed by the climactic journey up to Jerusalem. But his usage of Mark is illuminating: he abbreviates, improves upon and sometimes quite radically amends what Mark had written. Thus, the study of Matthew's editorial work on Mark (known as Redaction[35] Criticism in the jargon) is extremely illuminating of Matthew's main emphases. The same is probably the case with his use of the document Q.

---

[35] Redaction: indicates the process of editing a text for publication. It is mostly used for the final stages of the editorial process.

CHARACTERISTICS

1. Matthew was demonstrably a most skilled editor. This is particularly evident by comparison with Luke, who also used both Mark and Q. Matthew has grouped together the teachings of Jesus into five main blocks of material (each concluding with the formula "Now when Jesus had finished all these sayings, he …" did so-and-so). The first of these, in chapters five to seven, comprises what we call the Sermon on the Mount. Luke has a much briefer so-called Sermon on the Plain (in 6); beyond which other sayings of Jesus are liberally scattered throughout his gospel, sayings which in Matthew are grouped together within the Sermon. It is an inescapable conclusion that the Sermon is Matthew's brilliant literary construction (for Luke would surely not have broken up what had been a unity in its origin).

2. It is possible that Matthew's five blocks are intended for his readers to perceive them as the new Christian Torah (comparable to the five scrolls of Moses). For he undoubtedly presents Jesus as a new Moses (for who else could amend Mosaic Torah as he represents Jesus as doing in 5. 21-48?). The going up in a mountain to deliver the sermon would immediately remind readers of Moses ascending Sinai. The theme is equally prominent in the birth story of Jesus: as the child Moses was threatened by the Pharaoh, so Jesus was menaced by Herod.

3. Matthew's Gospel is the most distinctively Jewish of the gospels. Whereas all quote the Old Testament scriptures, Matthew does so yet more; frequently using the formula "This occurred in order to fulfill what was written in the prophet Isaiah …" He presents Jesus in thoroughly Jewish terms, particularly as Son of David and Messiah. The genealogy at the commencement of the gospel portrays Jesus as a direct descendent of Abraham, the founding father of the Jews, and of David, the greatest of all Jewish Kings; indeed the threefold division of the genealogy with 14 names to each division, whilst historically dubious, yet symbolically emphasizes the providential ordering of Jewish history so as to culminate in the birth of Jesus. In the Sermon on the Mount, 5.17-20, Matthew's Jesus stresses the continuing validity of the Mosaic Torah for so long as heaven and earth remain (over against those Christian circles which stressed the replacement of Torah by the new covenant). It is highly probable that this gospel first emerged from within a congregation almost wholly Jewish, that worshiped initially in a synagogue until their expulsion, hence the trauma implied at 10.17-23.

4. But if that was its origin, Matthew's Church was now embracing Gentile converts. He alone adds to the Marcan introduction of Jesus' ministry in Galilee the quotation of Isaiah 9.1-2, showing that it was precisely in "Galilee of the Gentiles" that "light had dawned." The highlight of his nativity narrative was in

the coming of Wise Men from the East, i.e. Gentiles, possibly Persian astrologers, to recognize Christ and to worship him. As at the beginning, so at the end: it is Matthew that most clearly declares the Lord's mandate for the Church's mission: "Go therefore and make disciples of all nations …" (28.18). These twin emphases have led to the supposition that Matthew's Gospel possibly originated in the area of Antioch and its hinterland; for it was here that Gentiles first entered the Church in large numbers (as Acts 13 demonstrates).

5. The material unique to Matthew shows us what were his most characteristic beliefs. He demonstrates distinctive Jewish usages: for example in his reluctance to speak the name of God in public; therefore employs periphrases such as "Kingdom of heaven" (rather than "Kingdom of God" which Mark and Luke happily employ); or, to the paralytic man, "your sins are forgiven you," the passive tense here implying but not specifically saying "by God" (9.2).

6. Matthew's special material (i.e. that not derived from either Mark or Q) contains many parables additional to those known to Mark. Amongst them are gems such as those of the Buried Treasure (13.44) and of the Pearl of Great Price (13.45-46). These convey teaching concerning the imminent (so it seemed at the time of writing) ending of this evil age, when Jesus would return as Messiah to preside over the Judgment of the world. These are parables of warning, of a call to repentance, and to endurance till the end. So we have the parables of the Wheat and the Tares, of the Talents and of the Sheep and the Goats. Although Jesus undoubtedly warned of the fate of the wicked, yet it was Matthew who typically concluded such parables with the "weeping and gnashing of teeth" of condemned sinners.

7. In several instances, Matthew appears to have had "double vision." Whereas Mark had just one person involved, Matthew frequently has two. He has two blind men cry out to Jesus as the Son of David (20.30), two demoniacs living in the caves of Gadara, two lepers seeking healing; and even two animals, an ass and a colt (Matthew 21.2) on which to ride into Jerusalem (even though the Zechariah prophecy (Zachariah 9.9) has always been understood to indicate just one animal, described poetically in typical Hebrew parallelism in which a second line repeats the content of the first). This is one of his more bizarre characteristics.

8. Matthew has a dramatist's eye, and tends to exaggerate as a means of indicating the heightened drama and theological significance of a situation. Thus, after the death of Jesus on the cross, with Mark's report of the tearing of the curtain before the Holy Place in the Temple, Matthew adds the occurrence of an earthquake so violent that it opened up the tombs of dead saints, who, after the Lord's resurrection, entered the city and were seen by many. Matthew

continues in this vein, describing what occurred at the Resurrection (which no other gospel writer attempts to do); for, in his account, this too was announced by an earthquake and the appearance of an angel of the Lord who himself rolled away the stone; all in the presence of the guards set over the tomb and of the women mourners to whom he announces the resurrection. This goes far beyond the witness of the other gospels and can be held to demonstrate the first move towards the apocryphal expansion of gospel narratives.

FOR WHOM WAS THIS GOSPEL WRITTEN?

Much of Matthew's teaching material appears to concern the situation of a church community under extreme pressure of persecution. He has a special concern for new as-yet-untested converts to the faith, who are addressed in this gospel as "little ones" – those assumed to be young children in the other gospels are here those young in faith. A parable such as that of the Lost Sheep, which in Luke's Gospel (Luke 15) clearly indicates the Jew who has wandered from the fold that is Israel, becomes in Matthew (18.10-14) the Christian convert who has succumbed to temptation and strayed from the Church. In chapters 16 and 18 are the only three references to the "church" (the Greek is "ekklesia," meaning the "People called out by God") to be found anywhere in the gospels.

It was also initially a community of Jewish Christians, hence the constant references to Old Testament prophecies and to the Jewishness of Jesus (as Messiah and Son of David); but one to which Gentiles had been admitted and were probably outnumbering the Jews by the time of the gospel's completion. Their admission to the Church is anticipated in the story of the Three Wise Men in their recognition of the divine Kingship in the baby born in Bethlehem. And, if Jesus' initial mission had been to "the lost sheep of the house of Israel" (10. 5-6), by the end of the gospel, it had widened to embrace all the peoples of the world (28.19-20).

WHEN AND WHERE WAS IT WRITTEN AND BY WHOM?

As we suggested in our hypothetical reconstruction in chapter 10, it was probably by a process stretching over several decades and in which several hands played their part. The apostle Matthew may have been at its very beginning but it is impossible to consider him as completing it. We have to make allowance for decades of oral transmission of the gospel material, for the production of Q Sayings of Jesus and of Mark's Gospel; to which we should add some time for rumination and the assembling together of Matthew's Gospel as we know it by an anonymous theologian and teacher of genius. This was certainly post-AD 70 and likely into the AD 80s or 90s, by which time cordial relations between Jews and Christians had broken down irreparably.

Reading between the lines, the author of this gospel is clearly one who had both

Teaching and Pastoral responsibility, we guess for a mixed Gentile and Jewish congregation of the late first century. The area in which such congregations were to be found was the Roman Province of Syria, perhaps inland from Antioch where the followers of the Way were first called Christians (Acts 9.2). It has often been surmised that 13.52 could be his own self-portrait: "… every scribe who has been trained for the kingdom of heaven is like the master of a household who brings out of his treasure what is new and what is old." The author of Matthew was certainly one who treasured the old (the Old Testament scriptures) and yet who embraced the new, the gospel with its universal message.

Luke's Gospel

Luke's is the longest of the gospels. Whilst it incorporates about half of the content of Mark's Gospel and shares with Matthew much material derived from Q, it also incorporates a great deal of material from his own sources, whether these were oral or written.

AUTHORSHIP
Luke's is the only gospel to explain the method and aims of its author. In the prologue, we read: "Since many have undertaken to set down an orderly account of the events that have been fulfilled among us, just as they were handed on to us by those who from the beginning were eyewitnesses and servants of the word, I too decided, after investigating everything carefully from the very first, to write an orderly account for you, most excellent Theophilus, so that you may know the truth concerning the things about which you have been instructed." (1.1-4).

This is an incomparable account illuminating the process by which a gospel came to be written. Let us unpack what it reveals, placing the various items of information in their chronological order.

❖ First, there were "the events that have been fulfilled among us," i.e. the events surrounding the life, ministry and death of Jesus. The "us" indicates that these occurred in the public arena, so were witnessed by many.

❖ Secondly, we have mention of "eyewitnesses…" i.e. those who were Jesus' disciples and followers "from the beginning." In Acts 1.22 the beginning of the gospel story is specified as being "from the baptism of John".

❖ At the third stage were the "servants of the word" i.e. those apostles, evangelists and preachers of the gospel (mostly anonymous) but who included such people as Stephen and Philip.

❖ Fourthly, many had undertaken "to set down an orderly account" of what had previously been the preached message, amongst whom we should have to include Mark, the compiler of a collection of Jesus' sayings that we call Q, and presumably others unknown to us.

❖ Fifthly, Luke himself enters the arena. He had investigated everything to do with Jesus from the start (but we can have no idea as to how and when Luke first heard of Jesus). He claims to be a serious historian who has investigated his sources. He believes that he can do rather better than those before him, in setting out "an orderly account".

❖ And lastly, unlike the other gospel authors, his account is addressed to a named individual, Theophilus, meaning "One who loves God" (unless this is a pseudonym, in which case the gospel is addressed to any reader who loves God); with the honorific title indicating that he was likely a high official in the Roman administration. He evidently knew something about the Christian faith, whether personally as a seeker or as an official whose duty it was to investigate a potentially subversive new sect. The words "about which you have been instructed" suggest the former, even that he was being prepared for baptism (since "instructed" translates the Greek "have been catechized").

❖ But, even here, the author does not reveal his own identity. There seems little reason to doubt the Church's tradition (because all the pressure was to name an apostle and it was never claimed that Luke was such) that point to Luke, at Colossians 4.14 identified as "our dear friend Luke the physician," who was also a traveling companion of Paul. See other references at 2 Timothy 4.11 and Philemon 1.24.

❖ Luke was most likely a Gentile (if so, the only Gentile author in the New Testament), possibly one who had converted to Judaism before becoming a Christian. He was thoroughly steeped in the language of the Old Testament in its Septuagint version and wrote the most fluent Greek of any New Testament writer.

LUKE THE HISTORIAN

The question has often been posed as to whether Luke was indeed the scrupulous historian that he claimed to be in his prologue. The so-called "we" passages in the Acts may represent excerpts from a travel-diary that Luke kept when traveling with Paul in Asia Minor and in Palestine. They are notably clustered in chapters 16, 20, 21, 27 and 28 and are all to do with traveling – evidently the diarist endured the terrible storm that ended in shipwreck on Malta. Marking these "we" references with a highlighter makes the point crystal clear: for example, that although the diarist was with Paul and Silas at Philippi, witnessing the conversion of Lydia (see Acts 16), he was evidently not imprisoned with them. Not until ch. 20 does he re-appear at the words "we sailed away from Philippi." (21.6). Thereafter, he was present with the apostle on his last journey to Jerusalem (chapter 21), but did not witness Paul's arrest and self-defense in the Temple nor his various interrogations before Roman and Jewish authorities; but reappears in chapter 27 as one of those who accompanied Paul when he was to be transported by sea to face trial before Caesar. The final quotation from his diary records their arrival in Rome, which is virtually the climactic point of Luke's second volume.

It is an inference beyond the evidence to suppose that it was whilst in Palestine that he collected the Jesus' material that is particular to Luke's Gospel, although that is not impossible. The researches of Sir William Ramsay in the early 20th century demonstrated how accurate was Luke's knowledge of the titles and functions of the varied ranks of Roman officials about whom he writes in the Acts.[36] But it has to be said: However careful a historian he may have wished to be, he certainly committed some errors. There is no evidence to substantiate his claim, in Luke 2, that the Emperor Augustus decreed that "all the world should be taxed"; nor a decree to the effect that "all went to be enrolled, each to his own city." That would have required several millions of people to have been on the move. And whilst Quirinius was indeed Governor of Syria (the Province that included Judea and Galilee) in the years AD 6-8, when he did conduct a census of the population, that is about 10- 12 years later than the likely time of Jesus' birth. There are similar errors of detail in Luke's mention, in Acts 5.35-37, of those who had rebelled against the Romans, namely Theudas and Judas the Galilean. Judas raised a revolt in AD 6. which was speedily quashed; but Theudas revolt was not put down until 44-46, i.e. later than the time of the episode being portrayed in Acts 5. However, although the detail may be wrong, the point Luke represents Gamaliel as making was perfectly sound – the Romans always dealt ruthlessly with those who stirred revolt against them.

STRUCTURE & METHOD

What Luke wrote was a two-volume work, of which the gospel is the first and the Acts of the Apostles its sequel. Some of the ordering of the gospel is in deliberate reference to what will be later written in the Acts. For example, his account of Jesus' trial before Pontius Pilate (with significant differences from the accounts of Matthew and Mark) is later echoed in the trial of Paul before the Roman Governor Festus). Again some of his ordering of events has strong symbolic significance. His gospel both begins and ends in the Temple in Jerusalem; Acts also begins in the Temple, but ends with Paul, the great missionary to the Gentiles, preaching the gospel in Rome (in spite of his imprisonment), the seat of the Roman Imperial Government.

Luke uses both Mark and Q in addition to his own sources. Where Luke follows Mark, he does so more closely than does Matthew. He may improve the Greek, or make an occasional amendment, especially removing anything that might have appeared derogatory to Jesus or to the disciples. But there are two large sections of his gospel, from 6.20–8.3 and from 9.51–18.14 in which there is no Marcan influence whatsoever. This suggested to some scholars that he may have compiled a gospel (known as "Proto-Luke"), based solely on Q and on his own

---

[36] The relevant pages of Neill's *Interpretation of the New Testament*, 1861-1961 are most illuminating on Ramsay's work. See pp 140-146.

considerable sources, before, at a later date, obtaining a copy of Mark and inserting it into his gospel without disturbing what he had already written. His original gospel may well have begun at 3.1 which reads like the typical opening of a Greek historical work.

By contrast, where Luke has used Q, he has thoroughly meshed it in with his own sources (by contrast with Matthew's method of building Q material into large blocks of teaching content). The fact that his Q quotations are scattered throughout the gospel, unlike Matthew's, suggests that he did not have a copy of Matthew's Gospel in front of him when he wrote his own.

A great deal of material is unique to this gospel alone. Its first two chapters, recounting the births of both John and of Jesus, are unique and written in the style of the book of Samuel. These chapters form a "bridge" between the Old and New Testaments, with pious folk such as Zacharia and Elizabeth, Simeon and Anna belonging more to the old than to the new. And only here do we learn that John and Jesus were cousins (which is not alluded to elsewhere in the gospels). The central section of his gospel, from 9.51-9.27, forms what has been called "The Big Interpolation." This describes Jesus journey from Galilee up to Jerusalem and episodes that occurred en route, a section in which the author has abandoned the Marcan framework, for this section comprises material from Q interwoven with Luke's own material. There are numerous episodes in this section unique to Luke: e.g. those concerning Mary and Martha, or Zacchaeus the tax collector; and, at the cross, Jesus' words of forgiveness for those crucifying him and the salvation of the dying thief. Luke alone has some of the best-known and loved parables, such as those of the Prodigal Son and the Good Samaritan.

A major theme of Luke's is that of "journeying." Whereas Mark placed a clear dividing line between the Lord's Ministry in Galilee and the last week of his life in Jerusalem, Luke has the greater section of his gospel from 9.51 to 19.27, with its solemn prologue "When the days drew near for him to be taken up, he set his face to go to Jerusalem," portraying a series of events and teachings occurring "in via," on the road. Just as in Acts we will hear that the Christian movement was termed "The Way" (9.2) and much of its content is taken up with Paul's missionary journeys.

CHARACTERISTICS
Luke has a powerful sense of the Divine Providence within which all human history is set. What he portrays has been termed "Salvation History," of which the first stage, that of Preparation, was set out in the Old Testament (which Luke knew intimately in its Greek version, the Septuagint); the second stage was that of Jesus' Life, Ministry, Death and Resurrection, the story of which he

depicts in his gospel; and the third is that of the continuation of Jesus' Ministry, through the Holy Spirit, in the Church, whose mission is to the ends of the earth. Luke was the first Christian writer to understand that the Church was to have a future, possibly a long one. This broke new ground and opened up endless vistas by contrast with those expectations, apparent especially in Paul to the Thessalonians and in the apocalyptic sections of Mark and Matthew, that the end of the age was imminent, in which Jesus, the Son of Man, would return in glory, the great Judgment would take place and God's Kingdom would be established on earth. Luke's perception was that the gospel had first to be preached "to the ends of the earth". And the Church would need some prolonged period of time to carry out that commission.

❖ Luke, writing for the intelligentsia of the Graeco-Roman world (as represented by a man like Theophilus), sets his gospel within the background of the Roman Empire. It was an Imperial decree that obliged Joseph and Mary to travel to Bethlehem where Jesus was born. The news of his birth by angels to simple shepherds in the fields is couched in the language of the announcement of the birth of a son to Caesar. But the humility of Jesus' birth contrasts with the pomp of a royal birth. The healing of a Centurion's servant points forward to the pronouncement of yet another Centurion, at the cross, that "this man was innocent." Within the judicial processes which condemned Jesus to death, Luke goes far to exonerate Pilate; three times he has him declare Jesus' innocence. Just as in the Acts, he will portray Roman officials as being mostly sympathetic to Paul.

❖ Luke viewed the possession of riches as a major obstacle to true discipleship of Jesus. Whereas Matthew in the Sermon on the Mount has Jesus proclaim eight Beatitudes, the first of which is for "the poor in spirit." Luke has four beatitudes, the first of which is pronounced on "you poor" (6.20) counter-balanced by four "woes," warnings of judgment, the first of which is against "you who are rich" (6.24). Such a note had already been struck in the Magnificat, with its "he has filled the hungry with good things, and sent the rich away empty."(1.53) Amongst the content which is Luke's alone, we have the parable of the Foolish Farmer who went on expanding his barns (12.13-21) with no thought for his soul; that of "Dives and Lazarus" (16.19-31); that of the Dishonest Steward (16.1-13) with its stark final declaration that "You cannot serve God and Mammon" (Mammon being the Aramaic for wealth).

❖ Luke portrays Jesus as having a deep sympathy for the marginalized members of Jewish society. Women, children, lepers, aliens, Samaritans, tax collectors, even prostitutes; all these, either despised socially or ex-communicated from the synagogues as "sinners," were the recipients of Jesus' welcoming attention. To them were addressed some of the best-loved parables, e.g. the sequence of the Lost Sheep (15.1-7), the Lost Coin (15.8-10) and the Prodigal Son which could have been named "The Lost Son" (15.11-15). All are to be interpreted from Luke's preface to them, telling us of the Pharisees' murmuring that "*he receives sinners and eats with them*" (15.1-2). "The Good Samaritan" (10.29-37) told in response to a question as to the meaning of the commandment to love one's neighbor as oneself (10.25-28) would have shocked a Jewish audience, not only because the Samaritan alone acted lovingly, but also because Jesus' reply shifted attention from the neighbor as victim to the neighbor as one who practices compassionate love.

❖ Whilst the main framework of Luke's account of Passion Week is recognizably that of Mark and Matthew, there are also many differences and additions. In Luke's account, at the Last Supper, two cups are served, one before and the other after the meal. Over the second cup, Jesus spoke of the "new covenant in my blood" (as did Paul in 1 Corinthians 11, but over against Mark and Matthew's "This is my blood ...") The NRSV demotes the second cup to a footnote. After the Supper, Jesus gives significant teaching which is absent in the other Synoptics; including the promise to Simon, that though he will deny his master three times, the Lord will pray for him that his faith should not fail (22.31-34)

❖ Only in this gospel does the crucified Lord pray for the forgiveness of those who have crucified him (23.34). Whereas in Mark and Matthew, both criminals crucified beside him rail against him, in Luke, one of them turns in faith to Jesus and is promised "Today you will be with me in paradise" (23.43). In this gospel there is no cry of dereliction from the cross; rather, Jesus dies in the complete confidence of faith: "Father, into thy hands I commit my spirit" (23.46)

❖ Luke's resurrection stories are notably different from the other Synoptics. In these, Jesus' appearances occur in Galilee (even in Mark, this is the implication); but in Luke they occur in Jerusalem and on the first Easter Day. In Luke, women including Joanna (known only in this gospel) go to the tomb, where they are confronted by "two men ... in dazzling apparel" (cf Mark's "young man" and Matthew's "Angel of the Lord"). These enquire, "Why do you seek the living among the dead?" (24.5). The considerable part of chapter 24 concerns the journey of Cleopas and friend to the village of Emmaus but they do not recognize the stranger who walks with them on the road. Only in the village inn, as he breaks bread, are their eyes opened to know who he is. On their return to Jerusalem, they learn that "*the Lord has appeared to Simon*" (24.34), an appearance about which we know nothing (unless that reported in John 20.1-10).

❖ There follows a meeting (presumably in the upper room). To establish his identity as being more than a ghost, Jesus shows his wounded hands and feet and partakes of food with them. There follows teaching from "the Law of Moses and the prophets and the psalms" that "Christ should suffer and on the third day rise from the dead ... and that repentance and forgiveness of sins is to be proclaimed in his name to all nations, beginning from

Jerusalem. You are witnesses of these things. 49: And see, I am sending upon you what my Father promised; so stay here in the city until you have been clothed with power from on high." (24.46-49). Clearly Luke is here anticipating the story that he will continue in the Acts of the Apostles.

❖ The gospel closes with a brief account of what we call the ascension. But note the simplicity of the account: "While he blessed them, he parted from them…" (RSV) The additional words "and was carried up to heaven" are rightly consigned to a footnote since they are not attested by the best MSS. Strangely, the NRSV restores them to the text. Luke expanded his account of this event in the Acts (1.9-11), but, whereas in the gospel the impression is given that everything reported in chapter 24 occurred on the first Easter Day; in the Acts, Luke sets it all within the framework of 40 days between the Lord's resurrection and ascension, with another 10 till the Day of Pentecost. This latter would appear to be a symbolical (rather than strictly historical) device, since by means of it, Luke is demonstrating how everything in Jesus' story fulfilled what the great Jewish Festivals represented. The Lord died at Passover (the great festival of redemption); and the pouring out of his Spirit on the Church at Pentecost (the celebration of the giving of Torah to Moses) now set his Spirit in hearts and minds rather than on tablets of stone.

John's Gospel

A commonly held belief was that since this gospel was written by the disciple "who leaned against Jesus' breast" at the Last Supper table (13.23), it must in consequence be that closest to the heart and mind of Jesus. It was and remains for many Christians the most loved of the gospels. It was also commonly supposed that a would-be biographer of Jesus could take episodes whether from John or from the Synoptics and mingle them together so as to make one continuously flowing narrative of Jesus' life story. That was the case with Dean Farrer's immensely popular *Life of Jesus* from the end of the 19th century. We still see the practice in some children's editions of the Bible on sale today.

The critical research of the past hundred years makes the first thesis above unlikely and the second impossible. For, whilst John's Gospel is undoubtedly proclaiming the same Jesus Christ as is witnessed to in the Synoptic Gospels, there are many considerable differences between them. Matthew, Mark and Luke bear a family likeness; John is clearly from quite different origins. Today we realize that we cannot simply run them together. That would be as absurd as to take four portrait paintings of, say, HM the Queen, and to suppose that we could make one composite out of the four by superimposing each on top of the other. The result would be a most horrible blur! Each gospel, like each portrait, is to be appreciated for its own particular value. Whilst different, John's Gospel bears its own unique witness to Jesus and is to be appreciated for its own virtues.

There is no consensus amongst scholars as to whether the author of John's Gospel knew and/or used any of the Synoptic Gospels (as we have seen how Matthew and Luke used that of Mark). He must have been conversant with the same oral tradition of the words and works of Jesus, a tradition that solidified especially in the events of the last week of the Lord's life. Whilst his framework of Jesus' ministry is unique to his gospel, there is some wording and some sequence of events which suggests probable acquaintance with one of the Synoptics, e.g. the feeding of the five thousand (6.1-14) is followed by Jesus walking on the water (6.15-21) as is the sequence in Mark (6.30-44 & 45-52).

STRUCTURE

The gospel is made up of a Prologue (1.1-18) and Book of Testimony (1.19-51), followed by the main body of narrative which can be subdivided between the Book of Signs (2.1-12.50), consisting of Seven Episodes, and The Book of Glory (13-20), comprising The Farewell Discourses (chapters13-17) and the Passion narrative (18.1-19.42) concluding with the Resurrection narratives (20-21) of which chapter 21 forms an appendix.

The Prologue (1.1-18)

This is quite unlike any other section of the gospel, or indeed any other writing within the New Testament. It should be thought of as a Poem in praise of the Logos, possibly pre-Christian in origins which the author has used and adapted or was written by him as an introduction to the gospel. Its use of the word "Logos" (translated "Word") is highly significant since it was a term much discussed by the Greek philosophers, amongst whom it indicated the perception that behind all observable phenomena in the world was a rational principle, if you like, a Mind, i.e. the mind of God. For the gospel writer to employ this word at the outset of a narrative largely concerning events that occurred amongst the Jewish people, was to claim universal significance for them. It was to make a huge claim for Jesus that what he represented in his own person was a revelation of the Logos-Word within the human scenario. As Augustine was to write three centuries later, whilst he had read in the philosophers much about the Word, what had never been previously declared was that "the Word became flesh and dwelt amongst us …" (John 1.14)

The Prologue declares that the Word was the agent of God's creation of the universe, being existent from the beginning within God. That He was always coming into the world in the forms of Light and Life, yet was neither recognized nor accepted by men (more specifically, by Israel) in spite of the testimony of prophets such as John; and that in the end, he entered the world in person. In spite of such rejection, the Word enabled those who did receive him to become the children of God. So the Prologue both summarized the content of the Old Testament and what would occur through Jesus' life, death and resurrection.

The rest of chapter one has been called "The Book of Testimonies" (1.19-51), since first John the Baptist, then Jesus' first disciples such as Andrew, Simon, Philip and Nathaniel all declare their faith in Jesus as "The Lamb of God" (29 & 36), as "the One who will baptize with the Holy Spirit" (33), as "The Messiah" (41), "the One of whom Moses and the Prophets wrote" (45), as "the Son of God and King of Israel" (49), and as "the Son of Man to whom heaven will be opened" (51). What was only gradually perceived by the disciples in the Synoptic accounts and about which silence was commanded, is here truth revealed in a flash at the very beginning of the gospel and shouted from the rooftops. This constitutes a major difference between John's and the Synoptic Gospels.

ACT I: The Book of Signs (2.1-12.50)

The first major section has been called "The Book of Signs." Within these chapters are seven major episodes: The Wedding Feast at Cana (2.1-12); the Healing of an Official's son (4.46-54); the Healing of the Lame Man at Bethzatha (5.1-47); the Feeding of the Five Thousand (6.1-71); the Healing of the Man Born Blind (9.1- 10.42); the Raising of Lazarus (11.1- 57 and the Meaning of the Cross (12.1-36).

The first of these episodes concludes with the words: "Jesus did this, the first of his signs, in Cana of Galilee, and revealed his glory; and his disciples believed in him" (2.11). Taken together with 4.54: "Now this was the second sign that Jesus did …" (i.e. the healing of the official's son) suggests that John was in possession of a collection of miracle stories. But he never uses the Synoptics' favorite word "dunameis" (mighty works), but always "semeia," (signs). Looking up all the usages of this term in a concordance indicates clearly what was its meaning. "Signs" were indeed miraculous events which led some to belief, because in them they perceived his glory (i.e. his true identity); whilst others, not perceiving, were hardened in unbelief. Chapter 20.30-31 summarizes the intention of the entire gospel: "Now Jesus did many other signs in the presence of his disciples, which are not written in this book. But these are written so that you may come to believe that Jesus is the Messiah, the Son of God, and that through believing you may have life in his name."

CONCORDANCE: THE WORD "SIGN(S)"

John 2.11, 23; 3.2; 4.48; 6.2, 26; 7.31; 9.16; 11.47; 12.37; 20.30.

But the miraculous occurrences do not stand on their own. Between the second and the third signs are major discourses of Jesus, with, firstly, a highly reputed rabbi called Nicodemus (chapter three); and secondly, a Samaritan woman at Jacob's well (chapter four). And all of the signs from the third onwards lead into prolonged discussions within the circle of Jesus' disciples or into heated arguments with the Jews. They focus not on the miraculous deed but on the Person of Jesus. Signs lead those who witnessed them into belief or disbelief.

ACT II: The Book of Glory (Chapters 13-20)

Within this there are three main sections: first, the Farewell Discourses (chapters 13-17); secondly the narrative of the Passion (chapters 18-19) followed by the Resurrection narratives (20-21). In content, this section clearly parallels the Passion narratives of the Synoptic Gospels, but in a markedly different fashion. The opening words of Chapter 13, set the scene: "Now before the festival of the Passover, Jesus knew that his hour had come to depart from this world and go to the Father. Having loved his own who were in the world, he loved them to the end." This leads directly into the scenario of the Last Supper, with Jesus and the Twelve grouped around the table. But in John there is no account of the Institution of the Communion meal (but then, according to John's chronology, this was the day *before* the Passover, not during the Passover as is presupposed in the Synoptic accounts); instead, that of Jesus' washing the disciples' feet. Did John disapprove of the communion meal, foreseeing that it would become a matter of disputation amongst his followers? There is strong eucharistic teaching given in chapter six in consequence of the feeding of the five thousand, but was this a later addition to this gospel? There can be no assured answers to these questions.

Then follow the discourses at the table, Jesus sharing his valedictory thoughts with his disciples in the most intimate manner. There is evidence here of some stitching together of originally separate addresses, for at chapter 14.31, what reads like a conclusion to the first discourse, we have Jesus saying: "Rise, let us go hence." And yet the Lord's speech continues for a further three chapters. In chapter 17, sometimes called "Jesus' Last Will and Testament," he prays not only for his disciples but for all who will come to believe through their witness. He also points forward as to how they should regard his forthcoming death: "After Jesus had spoken these words, he looked up to heaven and said, 'Father, the hour has come; glorify your Son so that the Son may glorify you, since you have given him authority over all people, to give eternal life to all whom you have given him. And this is eternal life, that they may know you, the only true God, and Jesus Christ whom you have sent. I glorified you on earth by finishing the work that you gave me to do. So now, Father, glorify me in your own presence with the glory that I had in your presence before the world existed.'"(John 17.1-

5). His excruciating death will be not only the means by which he will return to the Father, but by which those who know and love him will enter into eternal life. Even the cross will be a token of his glory.

THE PASSION

There follows the account of his arrest, trial, condemnation and crucifixion. The content is mostly familiar from our knowledge of the Synoptics, but the perspective from which it is viewed is wholly different. In all of it, Jesus is shown to be the One in control. He is the Good Shepherd who lays down his life, voluntarily, for the sheep (10.11). The arresting party falls to the ground before him (18.6) as he offers himself to them; he informs Pilate that he has no authority over him other than that given him "from above" (19.12); just before he expires, he declares: "It is finished", i.e. the mission given him by the Father. At the moment of his death, it is remarked that not a bone of his body was broken (it was usual for the executioners to break the legs of their victims so as to hasten their death), but that blood and water flowed from his wounds (19.33-34) – all of symbolic importance to the author of this gospel. It is precisely at this point that the final editors of this gospel make a point about the authority behind their gospel: ("He who saw this has testified so that you also may believe. His testimony is true, and he knows that he tells the truth.") [19.35] The editors of the NRSV obviously consider this to be a late interpolation into the gospel text; hence the brackets.

THE RESURRECTION

Chapter 20 takes us into this gospel's Resurrection narrative. Whilst all the gospels pinpoint the presence of the women followers of Jesus as the first witnesses of his burial place and the mystery of its emptiness, only John highlights the role of Mary Magdalene. Whilst the mysterious "other disciple," followed by Peter, are credited with both witnessing that the tomb is empty and drawing the proper conclusions, it is to Mary that the Risen Lord revealed himself. Only later on that day did he appear to all the disciples (with the exception of Thomas) in the upper room.

The final words of chapter 20, which I quoted under the section on "signs," read very much like the original conclusion to the gospel. We should also note that everything described in this chapter happens within the 24 hours of the first Easter Day, including the Lord's breathing the Holy Spirit upon the disciples and his commissioning them to continue his ministry (20.21-23), i.e. what Luke, in the Acts of the Apostles, has spaced out over a period of 40 days.

THE APPENDIX: 21.1-25

This chapter is evidently an additional ending to the gospel, compiled some time later than the rest of the gospel. The episode of the disciples (21.1-14) having returned to their fishing occupation on Galilee, although recounted as a third resurrection appearance of Jesus, must originally have stood on its own, because in it the disciples display no knowledge of the Lord's resurrection whatsoever. Only when Jesus reveals himself to them do they share a meal of bread and fish on the beach. Note the eucharistic wording of "*took bread* and *gave* it to them*.*"

Thereafter, there are two main subjects exposed. In the first (21.15-19), Jesus gives Simon Peter the chance of being re-instated as the disciples' leader. His threefold avowal of love for the Lord cancels out the previous threefold denial and he is newly commissioned to feed the Lord's sheep. Thereafter Jesus predicts his being bound and led away to a martyr's death, which we may surmise had already occurred (by tradition, in AD 64, under the Emperor Nero's savage persecution of the Church). The second subject (21.20-24) concerns the likely fate of "the disciple whom Jesus loved." Jesus' enigmatic response as to the possibility of this disciple being still alive "until I come" led to the belief within the Christian community that he would never die. Evidently he had died. That, and continuing dispute as to the precise status of Simon Peter in the Church, would explain the motivation for the addition of this chapter as an appendix to the gospel.

DIFFERENCES BETWEEN JOHN AND THE SYNOPTICS

❖ The chief difference setting this gospel apart from the Synoptics is that of the framework of Jesus' ministry. Mark's framework, followed in essence by Matthew and Luke, is of a ministry of healing, teaching and preaching in Galilee, followed by a decision to go up to Jerusalem, at Passover-time, where, within the space of no more than a week, he is arrested, condemned, crucified and buried. All these events could have happened within little more than one year's duration. John's framework is quite different. Jesus moves frequently between Galilee and Judea and is present in Jerusalem during three different Passover festivals. It is this latter testimony that led to the long-held assumption that Jesus' ministry lasted for some three years or more.

❖ There are further differences in the content of what occurs within these different chronologies. In the Synoptics, the Cleansing of the Temple (after Jesus had entered the city on the Palm Sunday) took place at the commencement of the last week of his life; and was the episode that provoked the Jewish priestly authorities to seek his arrest and condemnation (Mark 12.18). But in John, whilst the entry to the city is much as in the Synoptic accounts, the cleansing of the Temple occurs at the very beginning of Jesus' ministry (John 2.13-22). Whilst it clearly prefigures Jesus' eventual death, it is not the episode that sets it in train; in this gospel, it is his raising of Lazarus that has that effect (John 11.45-53) – an episode that is not so much as mentioned in the Synoptics.

❖ In the Synoptics, Jesus is arrested, tried and killed during the Passover (see Mark 14.1-2), in spite of the haste to complete his arrest (see Mark14.1-2) and trial by night before the feast begins. Hence the disputed question as to whether it was the Passover meal that Jesus shared with his disciples on the eve of his arrest. For in John, Jesus' death occurs prior to the start of the Passover, on the Day of Preparation, at the very moment when the Passover lambs were being sacrificed in the Temple (a comparison of enormous symbolic significance).

❖ In the Synoptics, it is only gradually that the real identity of Jesus is discovered. Whilst those demonically possessed knew its secret (Mk.1.24), and his greatness as a healer was applauded by many, nevertheless he always enjoined silence on those whom he had healed (Mark 1.34; 1.44; 3.11-12; 5.43). Only at Caesarea Phillipi, after some length of time together, did the Lord ask his disciples who they thought that he was (8.29); when Simon Peter spoke out, presumably as their spokesman, that "You are the Christ." (8.29). Even then he forbade them to make this known outside their circle. But in John's account, there is no such reticence. From the very start of his ministry, immediately after his baptism (which is mentioned only obliquely, in John 1.32-34), various of his early followers openly declaim who he is: by John the Baptizer as "The Lamb of God" (1.29 & 36); by Andrew as "The Messiah" (which means Christ) 1.41; by Philip as "the one of whom Moses in the Law and also the prophets wrote, Jesus of *Nazareth* ..." (1.45); and by Nathaniel as "*Son of God*" and "*King of Israel*" (1.49). There is no command that they should be silent. Here, Jesus' identity is openly proclaimed from the very beginning.

❖ In the Synoptics, the main theme of Jesus' teaching is of the imminent coming of the Kingdom of God on earth. The term "Kingdom of God" occurs five times in Matthew (to which add Matthew's preferred expression, "the Kingdom of Heaven," 31 times); in Mark 14 times; and in Luke 31 times. In John, the expression occurs twice only, during Jesus discussion with Nicodemus, at 3.3 and 5. By contrast, in John's Gospel, Jesus openly proclaims himself: as "he who descends from heaven, the Son of Man" (3.13); as the one in whom to believe is to "have eternal life" (3.15). The Samaritan woman expresses her people's hope that "the Messiah is coming;" to which Jesus replies: "I who speak to you am he" (4.26). In argument with his Pharisaic opponents, Jesus declares that it is God, his Father, who has sent him (5.36-37); perhaps most extraordinarily, at the end of his disputation with the Jews in chapter eight, he declares: "Before Abraham was, I am." (8.58)! We have to recall that the meaning of the name Yahweh, God of Israel, was "I AM" (see Exodus 3.14). It is a claim to equality with God. Not surprisingly, such sayings raised the accusation of his opponents that he was a blasphemer and thereby deserving of death. The apogee of these sayings may be seen in the seven great "I AM" sayings. In these Jesus declares himself to be " the Bread of Life" (6.35), "The Light of the World" (8.12), "The Door of the Sheep" (10.7), "The Good Shepherd" (10.14), "The Resurrection and the Life" (11.25), "the Way, the Truth and the Life" (14.6) and "The True Vine" (15.1).

We have to take note also of the quite *different styles of speech* attributed to Jesus in the Synoptics by contrast with John. In the Synoptics, Jesus' speech is mostly in the form of short, pithy sayings given in response to questions or to criticism, e.g. "It is not the well who need a doctor but those who are sick."(Mark 2.17). Or, "Render to Caesar the things that belong to Caesar and to God the things that belong to God." (Mark 12.17). The only longer discourses reported are in the form of parables, such as that of the Good Samaritan or in the apocalyptic passages (Mk.13 & parallels). Even passages such as the Sermon on the Mount are made up of brief sayings which Matthew has skillfully strung together. By contrast, in John, we have few if any of such sayings (John 3.3 is such an exception). We have instead long, rather rambling discourses, in which the thread of argument is not easily discerned, mostly in disputation with "the Jews" or the Pharisees; or, quite exceptionally and in an endearing manner, with his own disciples sitting at the supper table.

How may these differences be understood?

Such major differences require explanation. They constitute the main subject matter of all scholarly research into the origins and interpretation of John's Gospel. But from them we can draw some conclusions:

1. John clearly wrote his gospel in total independence of the Synoptics. Since it is the same Jesus about whom he is writing, we can assume that he was well acquainted with the oral traditions of Jesus' story, but doubtfully of any of the other gospels. Some would argue that he knew both Mark and Luke's Gospels (there are a number of interesting comparisons to be made between Luke and John).

2. We should probably think of John as working within a Christian community (scholars speak of "the Johannine community") somewhat removed from those from which the Synoptics emerged and that had developed its own style of life and thought. We might make a number of deductions about this community: *One*, that it was composed of Jewish converts already predisposed to Hellenistic ways of thinking and of Gentiles familiar with Greek philosophical terms such as Logos, "word." *Two*, that it was in bitter confrontation with one or more Jewish synagogues – hence the extreme antagonism in passages such as John 7 & 8. In this gospel, "the Jews" have become the enemy (as if the fact that Jesus and his disciples were all Jews has been forgotten). *Three*, that there had been

some disputation and conflict even within this community. Possibly it was over teaching about the Lord's Supper that caused some to part company with it: "Because of this many of his disciples turned back and no longer went about with him. So Jesus asked the twelve, "Do you also wish to go away?" Simon Peter answered him, `Lord, to whom can we go? You have the words of eternal life. We have come to believe and know that you are the Holy One of God." (6.66-69). If verse 66 represents a serious rift, with many deserting the Church, then verse 69 represents the Church's response.

Such factors point towards a date towards the end of the first century or early years of the second century.[37] The author of the gospel had meditated on the significance of Jesus' life and ministry over a long period of time, and with his powerful imaginative and mystical intellect, had produced a kind of refracted account of the gospel stories. We should think of him as the "preacher-teacher" of his community and the discourses of his gospel as sermons and the Farewell Discourses as meditative retreat addresses. It is not possible to imagine Jesus as literally declaiming such statements as "I am the Way and the Truth and the Life." But that is what this Christian community had come to believe of him. It seems likely that the Preacher took elements well known from the oral tradition and written in the Synoptics, such as the saying about "not pouring new wine into old parched wineskins" (Mark 2.22 & //s) and created a dramatic story conveying the same truth, i.e. of the miraculous provision of good wine at the Wedding Feast at Cana. For here, the meaning is clear. The gospel of Jesus is as new wine which cannot be contained within the crabbed confines of Judaism.[38]

AUTHORSHIP

But we have to ask, who was the author of this gospel? Is it right to think of one person being responsible for its production? By tradition, its authorship was attributed to John, son of Zebedee and brother of James. But the gospel itself makes no such attribution. In its later chapters, a direct claim is made that it was written by "the disciple whom Jesus loved" (21.20 & 24). "This is the disciple who is testifying to these things and has written them, and we know that his testimony is true." (21.24). The expression itself is strange. Nowhere else is there any suggestion of preference for any one particular disciple. Did he not

---

[37] J A T Robinson, the scholarly Bishop who wrote Honest to God, which made such a stir when published in 1963, proposed that John's Gospel was written before the Synoptics – in books called Redating the New Testament, and The Priority of John (1985). The argument didn't convince many, but it demonstrates how hypothetical the dating of the gospels is.
[38] Of course, such an interpretation makes us uneasy, with its apparent derogation of Judaism smacking of anti-Semitism; but we cannot alter the fact that that was probably the intention of the author. How we make use of such thinking is quite a different matter. Post-Holocaust, we have to be much more sensitive how we speak of another religion's beliefs. And, of course, abandoning fundamentalism, it is wholly permissible to criticize the gospel!

love them all? But, it has to be noted that this attribution comes in chapter 21, itself an appendix to the gospel. The very inclusion of this attribution probably indicates that the question of authorship was under dispute.

Can we identify this "disciple whom Jesus loved?" Not with any certainty. The traditional attribution to John the son of Zebedee was based on the rather flimsy notion that since James, followed by John, is frequently mentioned after Simon Peter on those occasions when Jesus calls the three to accompany him (into Jairus' house, onto the mount of Transfiguration, and in the Garden of Gethsemane); and since the first two were known to have been killed [Peter in Rome, circa AD 64; James by Herod Agrippa (Acts 12.2)], only John remained as one specially favored by the Lord. However, if we list all the occasions when, according to the Synoptics, this John was present with Jesus, it is remarkable that none of these occasions are so much as mentioned in John's gospel – surely a fatal blow to the traditional authorship.

We should also note that, behind the gospel, there is a vibrant Christian community; and that it has something to do, perhaps not with the writing of the gospel, but with its final redaction. In the above-mentioned passage, note the "we know that his testimony is true" (21.24). The testimony of this community is heard at other points in the gospel (1.14 &16; 3;11; 4,22; 6.69) – the community for whom the gospel writer was their teacher and for whom this gospel was written.

We are forced to conclude that the Fourth Gospel is, like the others, anonymous. It is for that reason that it is usually referred to in scholarly circles as the Fourth Gospel. Whoever wrote it was a considerable theologian, comparable only to Paul within the pages of the New Testament. He was far more than a simple chronicler of events. He was a profound thinker of a mystical frame of mind. He took basic teachings from the Synoptics, like that of the Lost Sheep and of Jesus looking on the people as being like sheep without a shepherd and transformed them into a profound allegory about Jesus as the Door through whom sheep enter the fold, of Jesus as the Good Shepherd who lays down his life for the sheep and whose intention is to draw into the fold others not yet within it. This meditation does far more than report mere sayings of Jesus; it meditates on their deep significance as God's revelation within the human life, mission, death and resurrection of Jesus.

Such considerations lead to the conclusion that we cannot take isolated sayings from this gospel and use them just as we do those from the Synoptics. If we ask the question: Did Jesus literally call himself "the Door of the Sheepfold," or "the Good Shepherd," or, indeed proclaim himself openly to be the Son of God, the answer, from a strictly historical perspective, is probably not. For, to have done so, would be in headlong collision with the united witness of the Mark, Q, M and L. This was realized quite early in the Church's history, when some questioned its compatibility with the first three gospels. It was for such reasoning that Clement, the founder of the first Christian School of Theology in Alexandria, termed John's "the spiritual Gospel." This wasn't implying that the others were unspiritual, but rather that the others gave a chiefly historical account of Jesus' lifetime with theological overtones, whereas John created a primarily theological account.

THE HISTORICAL WORTH OF JOHN'S GOSPEL

In spite of Clement's testimony, and a one-time tendency to wholly dismiss the historical usefulness of this gospel, a more balanced view is necessary. Whilst having little interest in the straight chronicling of events, John nevertheless had access to reliable sources of information, some of which are of quite as much value as those available to the Synoptic authors. In many instances, John's account yields information that may well be more accurate than some of that in the Synoptics. Not only does he represent Jesus as being frequently in Jerusalem, but he appears to have possessed a detailed and accurate knowledge of the city. Some scholars were skeptical of John's description of the Pool of Bethsaida, but he was completely vindicated when, in the 1930s, Fr Vincent unearthed what had obviously been a pool, within a complex containing five distinct porticoes. The citing of a pavement called Gabbatha (19.13) has also been verified by the archaeologists.

But it is probably the case that the Evangelist was not primarily interested in points of historical detail. Since the very foundation of the gospel is the belief that "the Word became flesh and dwelt among us," i.e. that in Jesus Eternity had invaded historical Time, his one desire was to draw out the significance, the theological truth, of all that had occurred. It is Theology rather than history, drama rather than simple chronicle, all designed to persuade you and I, its readers, "... that you may come to believe that Jesus is the Messiah, the Son of God, and that through believing you may have life in his name."

CHAPTER 12:
APOCRYPHA OLD AND NEW

The word "apocrypha" can be the cause of some confusion because it is used to indicate quite different things. Its root meaning is "something hidden," but the root doesn't disclose whether the object in mind is hidden because valuable, or hidden because worthless or shameful. Both of these meanings are employed on the fringes of the Bible.

Old Testament Apocrypha

The Apocrypha stands for a section of Jewish religious works written in Greek, and for that reason, never fully accepted by the Jewish religious establishment for whom only Hebrew writings were recognized as scriptural. But they were accepted in the Greek versions of the Old Testament, notably in the Septuagint; and via that route, entered the Roman Catholic and Eastern Orthodox versions of Christianity. Largely through the influence of Martin Luther, Protestantism followed the Hebrew viewpoint, i.e. regarded them as at best useful but not authoritative. Luther's objection to the Apocrypha was that it was used in Roman Catholicism in justification of such practices as the saying of prayers for the dead. The Church of England wording (in the 39 Articles) is significant: "The other books (as Hierome[39] saith) the Church doth read for example of life and instruction of manners; but yet doth it not apply them to establish any doctrine …"

The 14 (or 15) books found in the Apocrypha (Bibles can be bought nowadays with or without it) are as follows: Tobit, Judith, Additions to the Book of Esther, Wisdom of Solomon, Ecclesiasticus, Baruch, the Letter of Jeremiah, the Prayer of Azariah & Song of the Three Jews, Susanna, Bel and the Dragon, 1 Maccabees, 2 Maccabees, 1 Esdras, The Prayer of Manasseh, 2 Esdras.

In some traditions, a few other books are added. This is "a mixed bag" of writings, as you will see. Some are of some importance in popular devotions within Judaism, notably the books of Tobit, Judith and Susanna, the latter two lauding Jewish heroines. The books of the Maccabees are of considerable historical importance, since they recount the armed uprising of the persecuted Jews against the Greek King Antiochus IV Epiphanes early in the second century BC, an uprising led by Judas Maccabeus ("the hammer"). At the triumphal procession celebrating a short-lived Jewish victory, the crowds cut

---

[39] ie Jerome (347-420), the translator of the Latin Bible, the Vulgate.

down and waved palm branches (of which there are echoes in the gospel stories that we read on Palm Sunday). Of greatest theological importance is the Wisdom of Solomon. This is Jewish theology engaging with Greek philosophy in a manner that was influential in early Christian thinking, especially in Paul's designation of Jesus Christ as the Wisdom of God and in John's usage of the term Logos.

Some passages from the Apocrypha are quite familiar to most Christians, being heard read especially on Remembrance Day or in All Saints-tide Services; such as "… the souls of the righteous are in the hand of God, and no torment will ever touch them" from the Wisdom of Solomon, 3.1 and "Let us now sing the praises of famous men, our ancestors in their generations" from Ecclesiasticus 44.

New Testament Apocrypha

Gospel writing didn't come to a full-stop with the writing of John's Gospel. Nor was Christianity one solid monolithic structure. Almost from the beginning there were differences of viewpoint, as between Hebrews and Hellenists in the Jerusalem Church, fierce arguments as to whether Gentiles should be admitted to the Church, Judaizers snapping at Paul's heels and Gnostics claiming special access to the knowledge of God. All of these threatened the unity of the Church. In short, by the end of the first Christian century, there were numerous groups claiming to be the heirs of Christ and producing their own versions of the gospel. Around AD 180 Bishop Irenaeus (of Lyons in Southern Gaul) declared that there were four authentic gospels and no more! His argument was bizarre. Just as there were four cardinal points, he argued, so there had to be four gospels. What was behind his bizarre reasoning was the fact that he was doing battle with many heretical sects, some with one foot in Christianity, the other in any one of the many weird "mystery religions" and varieties of Gnostic philosophies on offer throughout the Roman Empire, all of them alternatives to the Church. He wrote several tomes entitled *Against the Heresies.* Many of these sects produced their own version of the gospel. Not much was known about them until quite recently, because our main sources of information were in the writings of Christian Bishops who were hardly likely to give the sectaries a fair press. That we should give even our opponents a fair hearing is a comparatively modern idea.

Nag Hammadi

The situation changed dramatically in 1945, when some Egyptian peasants dug up an ancient rubbish dump outside their village not far from Nag Hammadi, north of Luxor in the Nile valley and thereby uncovered a library of some 40 documents contained within 12 complete codices, one incomplete. These turned out to be the library of a religious community akin to Christianity but of a most unorthodox nature. Amongst them were texts with the following intriguing titles: The Gospel of Thomas, the Gospel of Philip, the Gospel of Truth, the Acts of Peter, the Acts of the Twelve Apostles, the Letter of Peter, two Apocalypses of James, an Apocalypse of Peter, an Apocalypse of Paul.

The word "apocalypse" is Greek, the antonym of "apocrypha," meaning "something uncovered, revealed." It was quite common for the founders of religions, new or old, to claim that they had received a startling revelation from God which authorized them to set out to attract converts. All these were denounced by the increasingly "catholic" Church as being in some way fraudulent, hence they were dubbed "apocryphal gospels." In such usage, the word had come to mean something more sinister than "hidden," much more like "fraudulent, worthless, to be rejected." Within the Church, the canonization of the approved scriptures was largely so that Christians could immediately recognize which gospels bore the stamp of approval and which were to be rejected.

New assessment of Gnostic sectarianism

Within the past 30 or so years, such apocryphal writings have been given a much more generous assessment than by the early Christian Bishops. The thought is that in the earliest stages of Christianity, there were many options open as to how the Christian way would develop. The ambience of the eastern Mediterranean world was in considerable flux, with the Christian gospel just one amongst any number of competing faiths (not unlike our situation today). The official cult was that of the Gods of Rome, practically supplanted by worship of the emperor as a divine being, but the popular religions were those from the East. Mithraism is the best known of these. It was particularly popular amongst Roman soldiers. One of their Temples, built in the third century AD, has been excavated beneath the streets of London. Its adherents were baptized with the blood of a bull, in which they were drenched. We hardly know when Gnosticism became a widely held belief, but suspect it was mostly post-Christian. Deriving from the Greek "gnosis," literally "knowledge" (you will recognize its derivative "agnostic," one who doesn't know); it offered its adherents the possession of secret knowledge. The Gnostic sects, and these proliferated all over the Roman world, supposed that God had revealed to them a secret, esoteric knowledge as to how to achieve salvation. They had a contempt for everything material, including the human body, believing it to be the creation of a lesser god. To demonstrate such contempt, some punished their bodies by practicing an extreme austerity, whilst others went to the opposite extreme by living licentiously. Common to both was the slogan: "Soma sema," meaning, "the body is a tomb," from which gnosticism set out to provide a means of escape into the higher realms of spirituality. A further consequence was that many of them refused to accept that Jesus had truly become a man. He was a Spirit, who had only feigned to be hungry, thirsty and to feel pain. He only appeared to suffer and die on the cross. From the Greek for "appear," these sectaries were also dubbed "Docetists," those who believed that Jesus "appeared" to be a man of flesh and blood but wasn't really. Such views are roundly condemned in the later books of the New Testament, especially in John's Letters. In 1 John 2.19 it is clear that some have deserted the Christian community: "They went out from us, but they did not belong to us … by going out they made it plain that none of them belongs to us. But you have been anointed by the Holy One, and all of you have knowledge". (2.18-20) John is claiming that the Church possesses the true "gnosis." Then he produces what he regards as the bench-mark of true faith: "By this you know the Spirit of God: every spirit that confesses that Jesus Christ has come *in the flesh* is from God, and every spirit that does not confess Jesus is not from God" (1 John 4.2-3).

A variant form of Christian Faith?

Some scholars believe that the apocryphal writings demonstrate a genuine alternative to the kind of Christianity that developed into the "Catholic" Church, with its emphasis on scripture, tradition and a church order managed by increasingly powerful bishops; that Gnosticism might have produced a type of Christianity that would have been much more akin to Buddhism. That's speculation. Others believe that Christianity and Gnosticism were never compatible, the latter representing a string of heresies. Nevertheless, since the Nag Hammadi discoveries, scholars have been able to study and assess these apocryphal writings as never before. There has been a special interest in the Gospel of Thomas, some claiming that this is a source of Jesus' sayings comparable to those known to us from the Q source. The comparability is more apparent than real.

Herewith the first lines of the Gospel of Thomas: "These are the secret words which the living Jesus spake, and Didymus Thomas wrote them down. 1) And he said He who shall find the interpretation of these words shall not taste death. 2) Jesus said: He who seeks, let him not cease seeking until he finds; and when he finds he will be troubled, and if he is troubled he will be amazed, and he will reign over all." We may agree that there is a seeming echo here of words of Jesus reported in the Synoptics. But few will find the final saying (no 114) authentic but rather abhorrent: "Simon Peter said to them: Let Mary go forth from among us, for women are not worthy of the life. Jesus said: Behold, I shall lead her, that I may make her male, in order that she also may become a living spirit like you males. For every woman who makes herself male shall enter into the kingdom of heaven" !!! It would seem that women fared even worse in whatever community engendered the Gospel according to Thomas than in the "catholic" Church.

The popular and fictitious nature of the Apocryphal Gospels

Most of the apocryphal gospels answered to a popular demand for knowledge that would fill the gaps in the Church's gospels' accounts of Jesus' life-story. So there were a string of infancy narratives, fictional accounts of Jesus' childhood. Some attributed to him the most amazing (and wholly immoral) miracles, such as that another child bumped into him. He said, "Go away" and the child dropped dead!   The Arabic Infancy narrative told of all the weird and wonderful things that occurred when Joseph and Mary had taken refuge with Jesus in Egypt. Music-lovers may be interested to know that some of these stories turn up in Hector Berlioz' Oratorio "L'Enfance du Christ" (the Childhood of Christ). The Protevangelium of James (protevangelium meaning "what occurred before the rest of the gospel story"), a wholly fictitious account of both Mary's and Jesus' childhoods was written both to serve public curiosity and even more to promote the virtue of virginity in an increasingly "catholic" form of Christianity. It both records and explains the rise of Mariology, the adulation of Mary as perpetually virgin and as "Mother of God." Other gospels reported private conversations between Jesus and his disciples, gave much expanded accounts of the crucifixion, and yet others purported to reveal what was said between Jesus and his disciples following his resurrection, during the 40 days before his ascension. In general, it is impossible to conclude that these gospels yield any authentic historical information concerning Jesus and the early Church beyond what can be garnered from the Church's four gospels. They yield fascinating insights into how a religion may be affected by the unfettered imagination and thereby transformed into a sectarian mind-set.

The Gospel of Peter

To give a further example, the Gospel of Peter considerably expands on the Synoptic accounts of the Crucifixion. Its pseudonymous author clearly knew the Church's gospels, but adds to them out of popular folklore and his fertile imagination. I will give in italics what are obvious additions to the Church's narrative. At the crucifixion, we have this: "And they brought two malefactors and crucified the Lord in the midst between them. But *he held his peace, as if he felt no pain.*" Further on, we read: "Now it was midday and a darkness covered all Judaea … *And many went about with lamps [and] as they supposed that it was night, they went to bed or stumbled.* And the Lord called out and cried, *My power, O my Power*, thou hast forsaken me." Then on the Sunday early morning, we read how "*the heavens opened* and *two men came down in a great brightness and drew near to the sepulcher." The stone rolled away of its own accord*, and "the young men entered in." Shortly after, the Roman soldiers guarding the tomb, witnessed this: " … *they saw again three men come out from the sepulcher, and two of them sustaining the other, and a cross following them, and the heads of the two reaching to heaven, but that of him who was led by the hand overpassing the heavens."*

In these extracts, we see a number of features typical of the apocryphal gospels. Clearly based on the Church's gospels, they far surpass them in fantastical and mythological accretions. The author has turned a comparatively sober account into a supernatural drama. The statement "as if he felt no pain" accords with the docetic notion that Christ only appeared to be a man of flesh and blood. The notion of the people stumbling about with lamps in the dark is sheer fiction. The Lord's cry, "My Power, O my Power" is not readily explicable, unless this gospel stems from a sect that regularly addressed God in this way. It is given here as a declaration, not as the cry of anguish that it is in Matthew and Mark's accounts. Then the Resurrection, which the gospels make no attempt to explain (although Matthew's version of it borders on the apocryphal) is here set forth. The Church versions gave no explanation as to the identity of the one or two men seen in or at the tomb, but here, they are seen coming down from heaven. The stone rolls away of its own accord. Three men emerge from the tomb, with the cross following behind them. The cross has become a magical creation which itself bears witness to the Lord (this being clearly at the root of the medieval fantasies concerning the Rood and the miracle-working properties of relics of the True Cross). As for the men, they have become giants and the Lord towers above them, his head in the clouds! This is early popular fiction, to which the Church was susceptible, but eventually denounced as "apocryphal," meaning, to be rejected as worthless.

Islam and its knowledge of Jesus

A point of contemporary interest is this: that it was the apocryphal tradition rather than a more orthodox Christian tradition that had penetrated Arabia before the life-time of Mohammed. The result is that a number of the Koran's references to Jesus reflect this fact, for instance that, as a child, Jesus had modelled some clay birds, breathed on them and they came to life and flew away (Koran, The House of Imran, section 40[40]) – this is straight out of the Infancy Story of Thomas (p392-3)[41] . This in part accounts for how it is that Islam has never had any properly historical appreciation of the life and teaching of Jesus. Its denial of Jesus' death on the cross may stem from this source, in the line with the "Docetics" theory that he only appeared to die. The Koran, however, does not follow the Docetists' reasoning, since it vigorously denies that Jesus was the Son of God. He was a prophet, no more.

---

[40] In *The Koran Interpreted*, Arthur J Arberry, p 52, The World's Classics, © Oxford University Press 1964.
[41] In *New Testament Apocrypha*, Vol 1, ed E Hennecke, W Schneemelcher, England. Translation by R McL Wilson, Lutterworth Press, London © 1959. J C B Mohr (Paul Siebeck) Tubingen. English translation © 1963 Lutterworth Press.

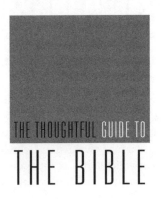

THE THOUGHTFUL GUIDE TO

THE BIBLE

THE INTERPRETATION
OF THE BIBLE

CHAPTER 13:
BIBLICAL INTERPRETATION (I)

Introduction: is any interpretation needed?

That the Bible requires any interpretation at all may surprise some. Isn't it self-explanatory? Not entirely. The very fact that it was written in languages foreign to us immediately poses a problem since every translation is already an interpretation of what was originally written in Hebrew and Greek. This also explains why the question of which of the many translations we choose to read is of such importance, for a faulty translation will necessarily misinterpret. We will sensibly choose a translation that represents the most faithful rendering of the Hebrew and Greek text.

Even when we have a reliable translation, there will still be problems of interpretation, if for no other reason than that the books of the Bible were written over a period of more than a thousand years, and most of these, at a distance of more than two thousand years from our own time. Because the social, cultural, economic, political and religious conditions of those long distant times were so different from ours there is bound to be a great deal of narrative within the Bible that is not immediately comprehensible to us and which requires explanation. Some interpretation will be a simple matter of explanation of words and customs foreign to us.

Interpretation is yet more critical for deeper theological reasons. Since the Bible conveys the story of God's dealings with the people of Israel and later with the early Christian Church and is assumed to be normative for Christian belief and practice, the manner of its interpretation becomes crucial. If we assume its text to be God's Word, divinely inspired and therefore infallible, such that every word is of as immediate relevance to us today as it was when first pronounced, that belief of itself raises huge problems. How do we discriminate between two statements, or themes, which appear to be contradictory? If God commanded the absolute prohibition of what Jews were permitted to do on the Sabbath ascribed to Him in the Torah, how are we to understand Jesus' apparent disregard of it? If the Torah contains a whole code of regulations governing animal sacrifices in the Temple, how do we understand Jesus' evident approval of the prophet Hosea's words, "I desire mercy and not sacrifice" (quoted in Matthew 9.13 & 12.7)?

If we reject the fundamentalist assumptions, there still remain problems of interpretation. What is the relationship between the books of the Old Testament and those of the New? Does the latter wholly supersede the former? If so, why do we retain the Old Testament at all? What is the relationship between the sometimes conflicting viewpoints within both Testaments? If the patriarchs practiced polygamy, took concubines as well as wives, kept slaves in their service, sacrificed animals in worship of God, why should these practices be forbidden to Christians today? These remain live questions in parts of Africa where polygamy, slavery and animal sacrifice have been the norm. If there are conflicting viewpoints in the Old Testament regarding the role of the monarchy in Israel, which should take precedence? There is open divergence on issues of racial purity and, in consequence, about the marriage of Jews with foreign women, as between the policy pursued by Ezra the scribe (in Ezra chapters 9 & 10) and the attitude propounded in the historical fiction which is the book of Ruth (with its reminder that King David's grandmother was a Moabitess).

Since a major theme of this book is that we cannot accept the fundamentalist assumptions, the matter of interpretation is of yet greater consequence. Having abandoned the supposition that God is the author, we have to do instead with a considerable number of human authors (to which we have to add innumerable scribal copyists and editors of texts) most of whom are anonymous. The most common objection to the historical-critical approach is expressed in the question: how then can we know what to believe? It is to address this question that the remainder of this and the following chapters will be concerned.

Guidelines for interpretation

WHAT THEN SHOULD BE OUR METHOD?
We suggest the following approaches:

I. A literary approach.
a. What is the passage to be studied?
b. What is the context within which that passage is set?
c. What can we know as to when, where and why the passage was written?
d. What genre of literature is it?

II. A Historical Approach
a. What kind of evidence does this passage yield? Is it historically reliable enough to descry what actually happened?
b. What are the main themes the author(s) was attempting to explicate and how may they be understood historically?

III. A Hermeneutic[42] approach
a. How is this passage to be understood within the overall structure and message of the Old Testament?

b. In what way does New Testament teaching, especially in the example and teaching of Jesus, affect our understanding of the passage?

c. In what ways has this passage been understood in the past and how has it influenced Christian belief and practice throughout history to the present times?

d. What influence does it have today? Are there any factors inherent in modern knowledge which oblige re-thinking of how it has been traditionally understood?

IV. A psychological-cum-social approach

This approach has been of considerable interest during the last few decades. With what presuppositions or vested interests do we, the readers, approach the passage in question? Does it raise issues that deeply affect us, such that we need to bear in mind all the influences that have contributed to the kind of person each of us is: our birth, our upbringing, the influence of our parents, of church and school, our social and economic status, our political and religious viewpoints, etc. It is hardly surprising that those of us who are WASPS (White, Anglo-Saxon Protestants) will probably see life and the Bible in radically different ways from those who dwell in the shanty towns of Soweto or Sao Paulo or Calcutta. Out of such different backgrounds have arisen distinctive theologies dubbed "Black," "Feminist" or "Liberation."

The above-mentioned factors may not all be deserving of the same attention. Some may be more applicable than others. To consider every one of them may be a counsel of perfection; nevertheless, all should be borne in mind. The proof will be in the application. Rather than approach the considerations theoretically, we have chosen rather to take two concrete examples, one from the Old Testament, one from the New.

Case One: Joshua's conquest of Jericho

Let us begin with the story of Joshua's conquest of the city of Jericho, to be found in Joshua 6.

LITERARY APPROACH:

a. The passage to study is Joshua 6. But to understand this we have to cast the net wider. We need to read the early chapters of the book so as to be familiar with the events leading to the attack on Jericho. And recall the pessimistic report of Joshua's faithless companions that, in Canaan, the men were of "gigantic stature ... besides whom we felt no bigger than grasshoppers" (Numbers 13.32-33). The episode of the spies given shelter by the woman Rahab (Joshua 2) is of obvious importance for its aftermath in chapter 6.22–25 and its repercussions throughout Israelite history (e.g. Rahab[43] as grandmother

---

[42] "Hermeneutic" derives from the Greek verb "to interpret."

of King David. See Ruth 4.21 which names Salmon as father of Boaz but
without naming Rahab as his wife, which Matthew 1.5 does).

❖ We should bear in mind what is the *literary genre* of these passages. Most
scholars regard the book of Joshua as a continuation of the literary sources
found throughout the Pentateuch, considering the Hexateuch (the Six
books) rather than Pentateuch (five books) as the relevant unit. The book of
Joshua depicts the fulfillment of God's promises to Abraham as to the
possession of the land. It is therefore likely that elements of the J, E and P
sources underlie its pages, but it is hardly possible to separate them out. The
J and E sources included stories of great antiquity containing many
legendary elements, we should therefore bear in mind that the stories within
Joshua may be less than strictly historical accounts. If they are recounting
events that should be dated to the 13th century BC or thereabouts, they
were probably not written down until some centuries later. What is
incontestable is that the overall editing of the book is that of the
Deuteronomists (the "revisionists" of the seventh century onwards), those
who brought together the story of Israel within the framework of Yahweh's
covenant with His people. It is likely that the book of Joshua is itself a
revisionist account, i.e. an idealistic looking back over many centuries.

A HISTORICAL APPROACH

❖ We need to set the story within its *context*. For this we should have an
outline picture of Israel's history in our mind's eye, particularly of its
enslavement in Egypt, of its liberation under the leadership of Moses,
ensuing in its escape from Egypt and wanderings through Sinai until its
encampment to the east of the Jordan on the verge of Canaan, regarded as
the land promised by God to Israel; at which point Moses died and Joshua
assumed the leadership of Israel.

❖ We should build up a sketch biography of Joshua. Here one can look up the
references in a concordance, or, better, consult a Bible dictionary (such as
the *Oxford Companion to the Bible*), which will indicate the most important
references. Joshua first appears as a military commander in Israel's battle
with the Amalekites (Exodus 17.8-16). At Exodus 24.13 he is described as
Moses' assistant on the holy mountain, which he had been since boyhood
(Numbers 11.28). Together with Caleb, he had reconnoitered the land of
Canaan, reporting its vulnerability to Israelite attack. When this report was
rejected by their fellow spies, Caleb and Joshua alone were promised entry
into the land. The passage Numbers 27.12-23 describes how Joshua, a man
"strong in spirit" was appointed and commissioned by the laying on of
hands as leader in succession to Moses.

---

[43] Although it has to be said that, historically, this is indeed impossible, since David's birth is
two centuries removed from the likely time of Joshua.

❖ It is helpful to know something of the history of Jericho. It was undoubtedly one of the oldest cities in the world, as was made evident by Kathleen Kenyon's excavations there in the 1930s. Its great tower, whose foundations she uncovered, go back to around the seventh century BC, with human settlement on the site a century earlier. Amongst the debris were several remnants of city walls. The question was whether any of these could be identified with those that had collapsed under Joshua's attack (on which, see further). The opinions of archaeologists have swung from strong affirmation to outright denial (methods of dating are constantly being refined). The latest assessment, from Jerome Murphy O'Connor[44] , being that the devastation (of the walls previously associated with Joshua's attack) took place in the late Bronze Age, "too early to be attributed to Joshua."

❖ In fact, the literary and the historical questions overlap, so that consideration of them cannot wholly follow the logical order of our method.

❖ And so to chapter six. We might ask these questions: is the narrative a unity or are there signs of variant accounts within it? There is certainly much repetition of narrative, e.g. in verses 2-5, Yahweh commands the manner of Jericho's encirclement; in verses 6-7 Joshua repeats the instructions; and in verses 8–14 the instructions are put into effect. But then repetition was a much-used tool of the story-tellers. That there are variant sources is yet clearer if we expand our research throughout the first six chapters. In chapter four especially there is some confusion as to the origin and placement of the 12 stones. At 4.3 Israelites are commanded to take these stones from the middle of the river where the Ark had been held by the priests; in verse eight, they carried them "to the place where they camped;" but, according to verse nine Joshua set them up in the middle of the river. In 4.20 the stones were set up within the camp at Gilgal. The fact that at 4.21-24 there is virtual repetition of the question first posed in 4.6-7 that would be asked by the children of future generations as to the meaning of these stones is strongly suggestive of variant accounts.

❖ Is there any evidence as to when these chapters were written? Not precisely, but, the references to what had been remembered in Israel "to this day" are suggestive of some time gap between the event and the recording of it. Thus at 4.9: "Joshua set up twelve stones in the middle of the Jordan ... and they are there *to this day*" and 5.9: "The Lord said to Joshua, 'Today I have rolled away from you the disgrace of Egypt.' And so that place is called Gilgal *to this day*." That the next section of chapter five reads like the work of the Priestly writers (with its precise dating in verse 10 and its account of a Passover) suggests that the gap is of many centuries, since the Priestly writings are mostly post-Exilic (i.e. from the fifth-fourth centuries BC). To

---

[44] In the Oxford Companion to the Bible, p. 348.

which we will add the reference to "the treasury of the Lord's house" presupposing that the Temple (whether the first or the second) was standing in Jerusalem.

❖ Are there any elements requiring explanation? We would certainly need some explanation of the "Ark of the Covenant." Again, a Bible dictionary or commentary would help here. It was evidently a portable wooden chest, containing the tablets of the Torah, which came to represent God's presence amongst his people. In the wanderings through the Sinai desert, it preceded the people and, at each stopping point, was housed in the Tabernacle, a portable Temple. Then there is mention of the "solemn ban" in verse 17. The explanatory note is then appended: "everything within it belongs to the Lord." This was part of the rules governing the conduct of Holy War. Because the war was being waged at Yahweh's command (such was the belief), all spoils of war belonged by right to Him alone (explicated in verses 17-19), involving the total slaughter of all captured people and animals in sacrifice.

❖ Are there any signs of anachronism in the account? There are indeed, especially in the reference to placing the spoils "in the treasury" (verse 19) and more explicitly in verse 24's reference to "the treasury of the Lord's house." This could refer to a chest kept in The Tabernacle, but much more likely to that in the Temple (not built until almost three centuries after Joshua). This surely suggests a period of writing many centuries after the event. The references to "the book of the Law" (i.e. the Torah) at 1.8, 8.31, 34, 23.6 and 24.26 are also anachronistic. These are passages which most clearly reveal the hand of the Deuteronomistic editors. The complete Torah did not exist until the seventh century at the earliest, more likely the fifth or fourth centuries; but since the Deuteronomists and the priestly writers wanted to attribute it all to Moses, so they "wrote it in" to their accounts of earlier times. This was undoubtedly a fiction. But this is not to deny that there may have been what we might call "early editions" of Torah, since it is reasonable to attribute at least the Ten Commandments in a much simplified form to Moses. The tablets of the Law may well have been a part of Israel's nomadic baggage.

What are the major themes of the Joshua story?

Admitting that the accounts are considerably legendary in nature, written centuries after the events described, written probably as "what should have happened" rather than what actually did, having been shaped into the mould of Deuteronomistic and Priestly versions of Israel's story as the People of God, what are the main themes being propounded?

1. The first is that of Joshua as the true successor of Moses. There are many details in the story illustrative of this theme: apart from the direct statements,

such as 1.5-9 and 1.17-18; there are episodes clearly parallel to those in Moses' lifetime. As Moses was confronted by Yahweh at the Burning Bush, so Joshua came face to face with "the captain of the Lord's armies" (the event occurring immediately prior to the attack on Jericho). The encounter concludes with words almost identical with those addressed to Moses: "The commander of the army of the Lord said to Joshua, 'Remove the sandals from your feet, for the place where you stand is holy.'" (5.15), cp Exodus 3.5. Then the crossing of a miraculously dried up Jordan river-bed is clearly parallel to that of Moses leading Israel across the Sea of Reeds.

2. The second is the assertion that it is their God, Yahweh, who leads Israel in battle. "The Captain of the Lord's armies" is probably to be thought of as a personification of Yahweh in human guise. Every step taken in the crossing of the Jordan and in the attack on Jericho is undertaken in obedience to the divine command. The very taking of Jericho was not effected by military strategy, but rather by a massive display of religious symbolism. The sevenfold procession around the walls, with the Ark at its center, reads more like a great procession in the Jerusalem Temple than a military maneuver. It is notable that the citizenry of Jericho makes no appearance at all in this account (except to be slaughtered!). Not a rock or spear is hurled nor any word of defiance uttered. The author wants us to understand that it was the overwhelming display of Yahweh's power that demolished the defenses of Jericho.

3. The third theme is that of the Unity of Israel. There is suspicion that this first incursion into Canaan was that of some tribes only.[45] For when, in Joshua 24, Joshua renews the covenant at Shechem, there has been no account of how that area had been conquered. It was probably occupied by tribes that had played no part in the Exodus from Egypt nor in the conquest of Canaan. But the story written centuries later seeks to portray all 12 tribes as having taken part in the conquest; hence the considerable emphasis in chapter four on the setting up of the 12 stones as a perpetual reminder of their unity.

4. The fourth theme is that of the incorporation of other peoples into Israel. This is illustrated by the story of Rahab, the prostitute who, occupying rooms built within the walls of Jericho, was in a position both to hide the Israelite spies and to enable their escape over the wall. There is no moral judgment of Rahab as a prostitute. Her distinction is to have recognized the awesome power of Yahweh, having heard of his terrifying deeds from Egypt to the border of Canaan and therefore of the uselessness of defense. In 2.11, this pagan woman declares her credo that "Yahweh your God is he who is God in heaven and on earth". Her faith is rewarded by the promise that she and her household will be

---

[45] See the judicious comments of J Bright, *History of Israel*, pages 123-127.

saved from massacre (from 6.22-25 evidently a large household). This bucks the trend that all Canaanites were to be slaughtered; for here we have a concrete example of a social group which embraced the faith of Yahweh and was so incorporated into Israel.

HISTORICAL EXPLANATIONS

How may we understand this episode? The story is legendary rather than strictly historical. We have no historical evidence to show exactly how and when Jericho fell to the Israelites, nevertheless there must be some factual kernel to the story. For, in times of prosperity, Jericho with its high defensive walls, would have been a formidable obstacle to a nomadic people (as Israel had been since its escape from Egypt) coming in from the desert. But the latest archaeological surveys discount the earlier theory (held since Garstang's excavation in 1929) that the massive walls, cracked and burned, were those of Joshua's time. Current opinion is that the city was then (circa 1250-1200 BC) sparsely populated and with insignificant defenses. What is undeniable is that Jericho, lying as it does at the edge of the great Rift Valley which stretches all the way from the Jordan, through Galilee and the Dead Sea down into the Red Sea, was always subject to earthquakes. The above factors may account for the Israelites' easy victory. Nevertheless, however it occurred, Jericho's subjugation to the invaders was of enormous significance to them. It represented the first major incursion into the Promised Land and occupation of it. It was therefore to be celebrated as an Act of God in fulfillment of His promise. It was understandable that later story-tellers, and religious historians, would want to "play it up" and present it as a major epic, in which Yahweh shows himself triumphant (as He had already done in Egypt) and in which Joshua leads Israel with the same courage and conviction as had Moses. They did so by depicting Jericho's conquest as achieved by means of a major religious ritual, a solemn procession of priests bearing the Ark, preceded and succeeded by trumpeters and warriors, repeated seven times and on seven days. They were wanting to say: "It was the power of Yahweh that caused the walls to collapse." Were the natural cause to have been a sudden earthquake, the Hebrews would not have necessarily mentioned it, since they were not much interested in secondary causes; but only in the primary cause, which, for them, was an Act of God. We may note in passing that the occurrence on the seventh day, consequent on the blowing of trumpets and the shout of the warriors, appears to have caused the writers no sabbatarian scruples. Possibly the laws of Holy War took precedence over the laws of the Sabbath.

SOME CONCLUSIONS

It will be appreciated from the above factors that this legendary account was shaped far more by theological beliefs than by any strictly historical evidence. The basic fact cannot be denied, that the Israelites occupied Canaan in a piecemeal fashion from the 13th century BC onwards. But the manner in which the story has been shaped was according to the theology of the Deuteronomistic and Priestly editors. It is therefore a theological account rather than a historical one, its purpose to implant in its hearers and readers a strong faith in God as the One who led them into this land and who still requires the Israelites of each succeeding generation to absolute faithfulness to the Torah. In view of this, all the books succeeding Joshua until 2 Kings have been rightly dubbed "the Deuteronomistic History of Israel." Inherent to them all is the message: "You occupied this land by the Grace and Power of God. He has given you the Torah as the blueprint for how you are to live in it. If you fall into idolatry and paganism, then you will forfeit your right to the land." The painful irony was that by the time of the Deuteronomists, the northern Kingdom of Israel had already been destroyed and its tribes dispersed; and by that of the Priestly writers, a yet worse fate had befallen Judah. Jerusalem had been razed to the ground, the Temple lay in ruins, its leaders had been carried into exile in Babylon and the last of the Davidic kings had died there. It appeared that the story of Israel had "hit the buffers." But, thanks to the victory of King Cyrus of the Persians in 536 BC, and his permission to the Jewish remnant to return to their land, a minor resurrection (as it was seen in the prophecy of Ezekiel, chapter 37) took place. It was probably in exile that the leading priests and prophets put in train the process by which the traditions of the past were collected and revised so as to produce first the Torah or Law of Moses and later a collection of the speeches of the prophets. All was stamped with the trenchant message: "Obey the Lord and you live; disobey Him and you die."

A CHRISTIAN UNDERSTANDING

How are we to understand the story within the overall framework of Israel's, and later, of the Church's faith? Does the behavior of the Israelites, slaughtering men, women and children wholesale, as well as helpless animals, justify such behavior for all time? Of course, other examples can readily be found. Throughout much of the Old Testament, that was the case since it was supposedly sanctioned by God. Do we find within the Old Testament any scruples of conscience about this bloody behavior? Laws for the conduct of Holy War[46] are set out in Deuteronomy 20. These represent some humanitarian consideration for Israelites caught up in the levy, permitting certain categories of them to withdraw from the battlefield; but none whatsoever for the perceived enemy. When besieging an enemy city at some distance from Israelite territory, terms of peace were to be offered its people; if accepted, then the population

---

[46] "The idea of Holy War was universal in the ancient Near East, where kings typically believed they were mandated by their gods to undertake campaigns of conquest … When armies went to war, it was a war of the god against the god(s) of the enemy." In Barton and Muddiman, *The Oxford Bible Commentary*, Oxford University Press, London 2001.

was to be taken into slavery. If it did not, then it was to be subdued, its males slain, its women and children taken into servitude, its animals taken as plunder. But as for the populations in the immediate front of Israel's advance, namely the Canaanites and their many neighbors, "you must not let anything that breathes remain alive" (Deuteronomy 20.16). The reason given is lest, in remaining alive, they contaminate Israel with their idolatry. That was the justification for their wholesale slaughter.

However draconian these regulations were, the anonymous author assumed them to have been observed to the letter. In some cases they were adhered to, as at Jericho and at Ai; but in others evidently not so. We have to bear in mind the considerable gap between the actual events of the 13th century and their recording centuries later at a time of Jewish obsession with the notion of racial purity. The rules of the Holy War represent part of this obsession. To some extent, they represent "what ought to have happened" according to the racial and religious ideology of the Deuteronomists. Whilst the "official line" of the books of Joshua and Judges is one of a sanitized Canaan wholly subdued, its pagan peoples annihilated, even within their pages that was far from being always the case.

It becomes clear that the Israelites, once settled in Canaan, adopting an agricultural life hitherto foreign to them, intermingled with the local indigenous population. The violent episodes depicted in Joshua concern only a small section of the country, that of the immediate area between Jericho and the Shephelah,[47] plus a struggle around Megiddo in Galilee. When, at the end of the book, we read the story of Joshua's renewal of the covenant at Shechem (Joshua 24), no account has been given as to how they came to occupy that area. It is notable how all versions of the Ten Commandments take cognizance of "the foreigner within your gates" (e.g. Exodus 20.10). When David captured the Jebusite city, Jerusalem, and adopted it as his capital, there is no mention of any slaughter of its population (in spite of the fact that the Jebusites are one of those marked down for such annihilation according to Deuteronomy 20.16). Indeed, the Zadok whom he appointed High Priest, was most likely the existing priest of the Canaanite sanctuary. The King's bodyguards were Kerethites and Pelethites, mercenary soldiers, the latter probably of Philistine origins, with a further 600 Gittites, i.e. men of Gath, the Philistine city from which Goliath came. David himself secured the succession of his dynasty by means of his adulterous relationship with Bathsheba, wife of his Hittite officer, Uriah, who gave birth to Solomon. It is likely that she too was a Hittite. The racial purity of the Jews was a fiction!

---

[47] Shephelah: the hill country sloping from the Judean peaks down towards the sea coast.

THE MORALITY OF HOLY WAR

How may we judge the morality of the laws of Holy War as practiced at Jericho and Ai? For Christians, there can be only one criterion of judgment, that is, in the example and teaching of Jesus. The evidence displays some slight ambivalence. On the one hand, in the Sermon on the Mount, he advocates a wholly pacifistic position. His followers are to love their enemies and pray for those who persecute them (Matthew 5.44). "Those who take up the sword will perish by the sword" (Matthew 26.52), he said in Gethsemane. He didn't yield an inch to the fanaticism of the Zealots who advocated waging a campaign of terror against the Roman occupiers. And yet, in the Temple episode, he used some force against the traders (but this was overturning tables, not people); and, according to the evidence of Luke 22.38, permitted the disciples to keep possession of two swords, one of which was evidently wielded against those come to arrest Jesus in Gethsemane. But we cannot imagine Jesus as condoning for one minute the wholesale slaughter of opponents. What appears to have been acceptable under the Old Covenant became wholly unacceptable under the New. In consequence, the Christians of the first two centuries AD refused military service in the Roman Army.

A fundamentalist is, by his own premises, bound to approve of Joshua's conduct since, according to the text, it was God who commanded it. But we would have to ask whether this was not the mistaken apprehension of the peoples of those times (unhappily of some peoples of our own time?). If God is fully revealed to us in the man Jesus Christ, and God is the same yesterday, today and for ever, then we cannot admit the old dispensationalist notion that God's expressed will has differed according to the period in question. Since Jesus taught that we should love our enemies and pray for those who persecute us (Matthew 5.44); that God causes the sun to shine and the rain to fall on good and bad alike, and taught that those who take the sword die by the sword, it is impossible to see how any form of violent warfare could be justified in his name. For Christians, dedicated to the way of their crucified Lord, there is no way in which wholesale slaughter and ethnic cleansing as practiced by the Jewish invaders of Canaan can be justified. Unhappily, their practice has been so used as a pretext by many invaders, confessedly Christian, of the territories of so-called uncivilized peoples. The treatment of American Indians, Australian aborigines, of the Bushmen of South Africa, and numerous others, remains for ever a stain on the Christian conscience. We have to conclude that the notion that God sanctioned the killing of innocents has to have been wholly mistaken.

This obliges us to ask the yet more difficult question, how does God speak to people? Did He or did He not sanction the slaughter of entire populations? There have been a number of notorious criminals who have attempted to justify their murderous deeds by declaring that God commanded them to commit their crimes: the "Yorkshire Ripper" to murder prostitutes, a young Australian to set fire to the al-Aksa Mosque in Jerusalem. Or there have been Heads of State, from Pol Pot to Idi Amin, from General Pinochet to Slobodan Milosevic, who waged murderous attacks on their enemies, using both murder and rape as political weapons. If we would have no hesitation in denouncing what went on in Bosnia or Rwanda in the name of ethnic cleansing as war crimes, don't we have equally to deplore what went on in biblical times (even though supposedly sanctioned by God)?

CHAPTER 14:
BIBLICAL INTERPRETATION (II)

Case Two: Jesus on marriage and divorce

In this second case, we will follow the main outlines of the method suggested in
the previous chapter, but without making them quite so explicit. In this case,
the historical questions are far less complicated. But, in this case, consideration
of the impact of startling modern discoveries in the fields of biology, genetics,
etc on the whole role of women in society, fields of knowledge wholly unknown
in biblical times, raises huge questions of interpretation. Here the point made
on page 178 of the previous chapter concerning the impact of modern
knowledge will loom much larger.

There is only one occasion reported in the gospels (by Matthew and Mark only)
in which Jesus made any utterance on the subject of marriage and divorce and
that was in answer to a question put to him by some Pharisees. It is ironic to
think that had such a question not been posed, then we would have had no idea
whatever of Jesus' attitude towards either marriage or divorce. It is only our
assumption that he was not either married or had ever been married. Not
surprisingly, the issues involved became of great importance in the early
Church, as is obvious within the letters of Paul.

THE QUESTION PUT TO JESUS

The question was put to Jesus: "Is it lawful for a man to divorce his wife?"
(Mark 10.1). It was possibly put to him out of curiosity, to test his loyalty to the
Torah, or, more likely, to seek his response to a matter of current controversy.
The contemporary "schools" of the rabbis Hillel and Shammai were in dispute
as to the offences which permitted a man to divorce his wife in compliance with
Mosaic teaching. Hillel's teaching permitted it for any cause whatever and the
case sometimes quoted cited the burning of his food; whereas Shammai's
position was more rigorist – a man could divorce his wife for one cause only,
that of sexual infidelity. In both cases, we need to note the common
assumption: in Jewish society only a man could divorce his wife. She had no
means of divorcing him.

Only Matthew and Mark report this interchange between Jesus and the
Pharisees; and we can only speculate as to why Luke made no use of the
material. Was he ignorant of it, or disapproving? And yet in chapter 16.17-18,
he does include a "hard-line" saying on the matter, but with no context
whatsoever given – unless as being illustrative of the eternal validity of the

Torah (as reinterpreted by Jesus?): "But it is easier for heaven and earth to pass away, than for one stroke of a letter in the law to be dropped. Anyone who divorces his wife and marries another commits adultery, and whoever marries a woman divorced from her husband commits adultery."

THE DEUTERONOMIC TEACHING

Both accounts refer to the Mosaic teaching on the subject. This is sparse indeed, to be found only in Deuteronomy 24.1-4: "Suppose a man enters into marriage with a woman, but she does not please him because he finds something objectionable about her, and so he writes her a certificate of divorce, puts it in her hand, and sends her out of his house; she then leaves his house and goes off to become another man's wife. Then suppose the second man dislikes her, writes her a bill of divorce, puts it in her hand, and sends her out of his house (or the second man who married her dies); her first husband, who sent her away, is not permitted to take her again to be his wife after she has been defiled; for that would be abhorrent to the Lord, and you shall not bring guilt on the land that the Lord your God is giving you as a possession."

This Deuteronomic teaching is probably of late origin, for there is no mention of such provision in the undoubtedly earlier versions of the Torah (except that, within the Ten Commandments, there is an outright prohibition of adultery). Deuteronomy simply presents the case of what had become customary (as if there had been no previous Mosaic teaching on the matter); i.e. that a man had the right, if he found anything displeasing in his wife, to write her a certificate of divorce which evidently gave her the right to marry another man. We can presume that the granting of such a certificate would have involved some legal procedure, probably one involving the local elders and both of the families concerned. In Ruth 4.1-12 there is an example of such a gathering at the city gate, involving matters of marriage and property. The only legislative decision given in Deuteronomy 24 is that a divorced woman, having re-married, could not be taken back in marriage by her first husband. This legislation was therefore of very limited application and hardly merits the later assumption that Moses permitted divorce. In spite of the apparent leniency of this right to divorce, it would appear that divorce was not commonplace in Jewish society, for the very good reason that a man divorcing his wife had to pay back all the dowry payment to her family.

A GOSPEL COMPARISON

So we turn to an examination of the gospel accounts of this episode, beginning with a comparative study of Matthew and Mark's versions of it. The Synoptic comparison is set out for you overleaf. We will assume the priority of Mark's account. Not only is there a considerable amount of verbal identity between them (considering only Matthew 19.3-9, since the material in verses 10-12 is

MARRIAGE AND DIVORCE:
A SYNOPTIC COMPARISON

Matthew 19:3 - 9	Mark 10:2 - 12
3. **Some Pharisees came** *to him, and to test him they asked,* `*Is it lawful for a man to divorce his wife* for any cause?' *4: He answered,* `Have you not read that the one who made them at *the beginning "made them male and female",* *5: and said,* **"For this reason a man shall leave his father and mother and be joined to his wife, and the two shall become one flesh"? 6: So they are no longer two, but one flesh. Therefore what God has joined together, let no one separate.'** *7: They said to him,* `Why then **did Moses command** *us to give a* **certificate of dismissal and to divorce her?'** *8: He* **said to them,** `It was **because** *you were so hard-hearted that Moses allowed you to divorce your wives, but at the beginning it was not so.* *9: And I say to you,* **whoever divorces his wife,** *except for unchastity,* **and marries another commits adultery.'** *[10: His disciples said to him,* `If such is the case of a man with his wife, it is better not to marry.' 11: But he said to them, `Not everyone can accept this teaching, but only those to whom it is given. 12: For there are eunuchs who have been so from birth, and there are eunuchs who have been made eunuchs by others, and there are eunuchs who have made themselves eunuchs for the sake of the kingdom of heaven. Let anyone accept this who can.']*	*2.* **Some Pharisees came, and to test** *him they asked,* `*Is it lawful for a man to divorce his wife?'* *3: He answered them,* `What **did Moses command** *you?' 4: They said,* `Moses *allowed a man to write* **a certificate of dismissal and to divorce her.'** *5: But Jesus* **said to them,** **Because** *of your hardness of heart he wrote this commandment for you. 6: But from* **the beginning** *of creation,* "God **made them male and female."** *7:* **"For this** *reason a man shall leave his father and mother and be joined to his wife,* **8:and the two shall become one flesh."** *So they are no longer two, but one flesh. 9: Therefore what God has joined together, let no one separate.'* *10: Then in the house the disciples asked him again about this matter. 11: He said to them,* `**Whoever divorces his wife and marries another commits adultery** *against her; 12: and if she divorces her husband and marries another, she commits adultery.'* **Cf. Luke 17-18:** *17: But it is easier for heaven and earth to pass away, than for one stroke of a letter in the law to be dropped. 18:* `Anyone **who divorces his wife and marries another commits adultery,** *and whoever marries a woman divorced from her husband commits adultery.*

unique to this gospel), but also chapter 19 signals the commencement of a considerable section in which Matthew follows the Marcan order of events closely.

THE MARCAN ACCOUNT

Let us examine the Marcan account (10.1-12). Some Pharisees come to Jesus with their question: "Is it lawful for a man to divorce his wife?" Mark assumes that their motivation was to tempt him, presumably as to his conformity with a provision of the Mosaic Torah. There were other such occasions of testing by Pharisees: see Mark 8.11; 12.15. Or, it might have been out of curiosity as to what position he would take with regard to the debate between Hillel and Shammai (this is more obvious in the Matthean version). As is typical in Mark, Jesus counters their question with his own counter-question to them: "What did Moses command you?" (He assumes Mosaic authorship and the binding nature of the Torah). They reply quoting the relevant stipulation of Deuteronomy 24: Moses allowed a man to divorce his wife by means of writing her a certificate to that effect. Jesus subverts the force of their reply by remarking on the "hardness of heart" for which reason alone Moses had made this concession and by appealing to God's intention in creation. In the beginning, God had created the human species, i.e. as male and female (interestingly he is appealing to the later creation account (that of Genesis 1.1-2.4a) which implies the absolute equality of the sexes rather than to the early folk-tale version in Genesis 2 (which asserts the precedence of Adam over Eve) as the ground of marriage, by which means man and woman are joined in one-ness of flesh. Possibly inherent is also the idea contained in the early Greek myth, that in marriage, the original unity of male-female had been restored. Therefore, what God had joined together should not be separated. This appears to constitute an absolute prohibition of divorce (which in effect cancels out the Mosaic provision).

It is likely that verses 10-12 comprise a later addition, originally separate from the above episode, since Mark's mention of the disciples asking Jesus about this matter "in the house" is a typical Marcan device to introduce later Church attempts to come to terms with elements of Jesus' teaching about which there was ambiguity. See my discussion of a parallel example, that of Mark 4.10-14 on page 218. What Jesus teaches (according to this interpretation) in verses 11-12 is stark: remarriage after divorce constitutes adultery. But what is quite revolutionary in Mark's account is that he assumes the equality of the sexes. Comparing with the parallels in Matthew and Luke, Mark alone declares that a husband divorcing his wife and marrying another, commits adultery *against her*, his former wife. There had never been any such notion previously within Judaism. For the Jews regarded adultery always as an infringement of a husband's prerogative. Then in verse 12, Mark envisages a wife divorcing her husband – again for which there was no precedent in Jewish law. It may be that

Mark is reflecting Roman law at this point, such as it was known and practiced in the Church community for whom he was writing.

THE MATTHEAN ACCOUNT

Matthew's account remains considerably more tied within the parameters of Jewish practice. To the question put by Pharisees to Jesus concerning the lawfulness of a man's right to divorce his wife, Matthew adds "for any reason" (Matthew 19.3). This assumes the permissibility of divorce, probing rather the causes that render it permissible. It also presupposes the near-contemporary dispute between the rabbis Hillel and Shammai. The question seeks to know with whom Jesus sides. At this point, Matthew transposes the usage made of the two biblical quotations. Mark had begun with Deuteronomy 24; but Matthew has Jesus responding first with the Genesis account of creation. He appeals to God's intention "at the beginning." In marriage, the one-ness of male and female is restored as the two "become one flesh." In verse four we may note Matthew's typically Jewish circumlocution "he who made them" in avoidance of uttering the divine name. Then his interlocutors ask, "Why then did Moses command us to give a certificate of dismissal?" (Matthew 19.7). Jesus replies that it was "because you were so hard-hearted that Moses allowed you to divorce your wives, but from the beginning it was not so." (8).

At this point, the Matthean account gives a twist to what had in Mark appeared to be an outright prohibition of divorce and of subsequent remarriage since such would constitute adultery. For Matthew19.9 adds "except for unchastity." This is Matthew's escape clause. It seems likely that this addition belongs to the discussion of the issue within the early Church rather than in the time of Jesus (as we suggested regarding the parallel passage in Mark). The fact that Luke 16.8 contains a parallel saying, more akin to that of Mark than of Matthew (except as regards equality) is further evidence that these verses were not an original part of the episode we have been considering. Evidently in the Matthean Church, divorce and remarriage had become permissible on the ground of the gross sexual misconduct of the wife. Matthew had not yet been converted to the principle of sexual equality!

IS JESUS' TEACHING APPLICABLE TODAY?

There are major issues involved here for contemporary debate amongst Christians. The Roman Catholic Church still regards divorce as prohibited in practice for Christians (although recognizing annulment of marriage in certain circumstances); and re-marriage after divorce as absolutely prohibited. So strict is its interpretation that those Catholics who have remarried after divorce are held to be in such a state of sin as to be forbidden the reception of communion. Needless to say, this draconian ruling causes enormous pain to many people already hurt by the breakdown of a marriage into which they had entered in all good faith and appears far removed from Jesus' attitude to the sinful and heart-broken. [48] Until recently, the Church of England took much the same view, but has since permitted its clergy much greater freedom in assessing the pastoral needs of divorced people. We should surely ask of every Church authority that lays down the strictest rules, because these are prescribed by the Word of God, to examine their consciences whether their rulings do not come within the category of those denunciations that Jesus leveled at the Pharisees, as reported in Matthew 23.3-4 &13: "The scribes and the Pharisees sit on Moses' seat; They tie up heavy burdens hard to bear, and lay them on the shoulders of others; but they themselves are unwilling to lift a finger to move them ... woe to you, scribes and Pharisees, hypocrites! For you lock people out of the kingdom of heaven. For you do not go in yourselves, and when others are going in, you stop them."

QUESTIONS FOR DISCUSSION
There are two major considerations that may point the way towards a more Christlike solution.

1. Firstly, Jesus appealed to what was "in the beginning." God's intention was for the indissoluble union of man and woman. But appeal to what was *"in the beginning"* is an appeal to the paradisal state of Adam and Eve, i.e. to a world as yet without sin (as the Genesis mythology puts it. In a paradisal state, marriage would presumably be equally paradisal because wholly innocent and sinless. But Jesus next reference to the Mosaic Torah's permission to divorce and re-marriage as a concession to "your hardness of heart" indicates that he fully recognized that such a paradisal condition no longer existed. Humans lived now in a society dominated by "hardness of heart." In practical terms, his reference probably had to do with women's status in Jewish society. The assumption was that a woman was always under the guardianship of a man; as a child under that of her father; as a married woman under that of her husband. Jesus' accusation of hardness of heart was probably directed against those men, who, having divorced their wives, had cast them loose into a society in which they could hardly survive (unless they were able to return to the parental home). Without male protection a woman was vulnerable to the most serious abuse.

2. A second consideration concerns the intention of Jesus' words: "What God has joined together, let no man put asunder." It appears to rule out any

---

[48] This matter is not merely theoretical. Every Free Church minister is approached by many of those for whom, within their own churches, remarriage after divorce is utterly forbidden. In my own experience, I have frequently heard from them many a case of the "irretrievable breakdown of a marriage," of the innocence (in so far as this can be assessed) of the one seeking re-marriage; and, believing the gospel (which promises forgiveness and new life) to outweigh by far the considerations of Canon Law.

possibility of divorce and remarriage amongst Christians. The saying may best be taken to mean: "Let no third party deliberately step into this relationship to destroy it." But how in fact do we know that any particular marriage constitutes what God has joined? Does one seriously consider a "one-night stand" which results in a pregnancy and a socially enforced marriage (more common in the past than today) as something "which God has joined?" Surely not! Is it religiously or morally responsible to insist that a marriage entered into in all good faith, in which one or both partners honestly attempts to live by their marriage vows, but in which one or the other is constantly betrayed by their partner; or from which all mutual love and considerateness has died, should be obliged to maintain the marital status "till death us do part?" The notion is surely monstrous. Since Jesus, by his own manifesto in the synagogue at Nazareth, declared it his aim to "to bring good news to the poor … to proclaim release to the captives and … to let the oppressed go free, to proclaim the year of the Lord's favor" (Luke 4.18-19) may we not conclude that to lock women and men into a binding relationship that has become hateful and deeply injurious to them has to be against God's purpose? The well-known parody of Jesus' saying is surely apt: "Thou shalt not officiously bind together that which God has obviously separated."

3. A general consideration involves the interpretation of much of Jesus' ethical teaching. It becomes acute in the interpretation of the Sermon on the Mount. So much of it appears utopian, inspirational but impractical. How can Jesus'disciples achieve perfection (Matthew 5.48)? Love their enemies (5.43)? Always "turn the other cheek?" Were these intended as *practical measures* that sinful humans could practice? Or were they what has been called an *interim ethic* (not for all time, but a heroic style of living for that brief period of time between Jesus' lifetime and the incoming Kingdom of God?) Or was it an *eschatological ethic* intended as descriptive of how it would be within the Kingdom of God, when God's will would be done as it is in heaven? Yet, surely in the Kingdom there would not be any coercive force demanding that you carry the soldier's pack a mile or indeed anyone likely to hit you on the cheek! The same considerations surely apply in the passage under examination. In a perfect world, within the Kingdom, we might expect marriages to be idyllic and voluntarily indissoluble. But Christians live in a most imperfect world; in which many relationships are entered into irresponsibly, in which there is as much "hardness of heart" as there ever was, and in which women especially are subject to terrible abuse both within and without the married state.

JESUS, LAWYER OR LIBERATOR?
A final consideration is this: was Jesus primarily a law-maker or a liberator from man-made laws? We cannot ignore the fact that there are many "hard sayings" attributed to Jesus. But to suppose, in the greater bulk of his teaching that he is

legislating is seriously to misunderstand and indeed to distort his message. We should weigh these against the over-all impression given within the gospels, that he brought good news, especially to all those outcast, discriminated against, those weary and heavy-laden by the harshness of life. His good news offers forgiveness and new life. It surely cannot be God's will to bind people for the entire duration of life into utterly loveless marriages. Here we are deliberately pitting the general tenor of Jesus' practice over against what appears to be the literal sense of what he said on this particular matter.

May we conclude that, ideally, marriage is for the duration of life. But because of "hardness of heart," there has to be some provision for divorce and for remarriage.

BEYOND THE GOSPELS: PAUL IN CORINTH

Issues concerning sexual relationships, marriage and divorce, continued to occupy much attention in the early Church. Paul deals with them extensively in his first Letter to the Corinthians. Corinth was a city notorious for its sexual license, with the Temple of Aphrodite prominent. The Greeks had invented a verb, to "corinthianise" meaning, to fornicate! It is understandable against such a background, that some male Christian converts had asked the apostle whether it were not advisable for men "not to touch a woman" (7.1). This is clearly a euphemism for "to have sex with." Although himself celibate (or so we assume, there is simply no evidence), Paul was sufficiently aware of the sex drive as to concede that it were better for most men and women to be married and to channel their sexual needs within that relationship.

1 CORINTHIANS CHAPTER 7

Paul's general stance in this chapter is that the celibate life is preferable for those Christians able to maintain it, but for those unable to control their sexual impulses, it were then better to marry so that the sexual needs be channeled within marriage. But on separation and divorce, he is quite specific: "To the married I give this command – not I but the Lord – that the wife should not separate from her husband; (but if she does separate, let her remain unmarried or else be reconciled to her husband), and that the husband should not divorce his wife" (1 Corinthians 7.10-11). Paul rarely if ever quotes sayings of Jesus (recall that the gospels were not yet written in Paul's day), but he evidently knows of something akin to what we have been examining in Mark 10. This was clearly a major issue in a city such as Corinth in all those cases in which only one of a couple, whether husband or wife, had become a Christian convert; for practices assumed normal in pagan society would have been illegitimate for Christians. For instance, all or most meat came from animals sacrificed in the Temple in honor of pagan gods before being sold in the market (an issue raised in 1 Corinthians 8). There would have been inevitable tensions within such a marriage. Paul advises Christian partners in a marriage not to divorce their pagan spouses; but recognizes that the case may be different when it is the pagan partner who instigates the separation (verses 12-16). In this latter case, the Christian is not bound (15); but it is unclear whether this implies that the Christian may then remarry. In verse 39 he makes clear that a Christian couple are bound together for the duration of the spouse's life; after his or her death, one is free to remarry.

Paul's whole attitude to these questions is dominated by two particular considerations: One, that Christians were living in a very limited time span, i.e. that between Jesus' resurrection and his coming again (preceded by a time of unparalleled disaster). He supposes the latter to be imminent. This factor is evident in verses 26 & 29: "I think that, in view of the *impending crisis*, it is well for you to remain as you are. Are you bound to a wife? Do not seek to be free. Are you free from a wife? Do not seek a wife … I mean, brothers and sisters, *the appointed time has grown short*; from now on, let even those who have wives be as though they had none, and those who mourn as though they were not mourning, and those who rejoice as though they were not rejoicing, and those who buy as though they had no possessions, and those who deal with the world as though they had no dealings with it. For the present form of this world is passing away." (1 Corinthians 7.27-31). Clearly Paul was mistaken as to the imminence of this expectation. Even so, this does not wholly disqualify his teaching at this point; since a certain unworldliness (in the sense of shunning the merely trivial and tawdry) will always characterize Christian behavior.

The second consideration is less time-dominated. It is the assumption that the unmarried and celibate will be wholly devoted to God's service, whilst the married will inevitably be divided in their attention between their partner and the service of God (verses 32-35). Such a consideration is supportive of those who accept a vocation to celibacy. But Paul's thinking here is surely naïve. We could propose the alternative, i.e. that those happily married may be thereby more released from personal anxieties and are therefore the more released to serve God. We may grant that there are situations into which a celibate priest may enter more easily than a married person with children to care for, but there are others where the married minister has a clear advantage. In practice, the married are not obviously more vulnerable to anxiety than are the single.

And we may believe Paul to have been unduly negative in his thinking about marriage. He, or more likely a close disciple, was more positive in the Letter to the Ephesians (see Ephesians 5. 21-33), although still insisting on the subjection of wife to husband. Whilst he advised his Corinthian converts to marry, it was as a necessary concession to the power of the sex drive and the weakness of the flesh. This led to the strange description of the purpose of marriage in the 1662

Prayer Book as "a remedy against sin and to avoid fornication; that such persons as have not the gift of continency might marry …" Modern forms of the Marriage Service commend marriage much more positively as enabling companionship and mutual support, and, within it, sex as not only the means of procreation but also as a pleasurable means of mutual enrichment. It would be a dreadful thing if it were assumed that Paul had spoken the last word on the subject of Christian marriage. It is rather one of the matters on which he remained a man of his own time, of his upbringing and personality, including we may suspect a number of prejudices. We do not have to accept his teaching as either infallible, unquestionable or for ever binding.

MARRIAGE AND DIVORCE IN TODAY'S WORLD

Are there any factors about human relationships so wholly different in today's world as to render questionable the moral stances of the ancient world? Are there Christian grounds for questioning what Jesus or the apostle Paul taught? In Jesus' case, the very paucity of the evidence should cause us to pause. Can we really base a whole philosophy of the male-female relationship on the single episode during which his opinion was sought? We cannot assume that the gospel writers infallibly reported what Jesus had said. For even Matthew and Mark disagree on the very question whether there were any permissible grounds for divorce, Matthew inserting the clause "except for unchastity." It looks as if, in the Matthean Church, divorce for that reason had been made permissible.

THE IMMINENCE OF THE KINGDOM

And were there factors at work which materially affected Jesus' attitude, such as the imminence of the coming Kingdom, and with it, the Jewish expectation that what had been in the beginning would be restored at the end? We have evidence in 1 Corinthians 7 that these factors strongly influenced Paul's thinking. Perhaps they were equally pertinent for Jesus. In which case, both may have been proposing an interim ethic, i.e. one which in effect advised converts: "Whether married or unmarried, remain as you are, faithful in your relationships, for the Kingdom is about to come in which all will be transformed." Most Christians believe that in some sense the Kingdom came in the Life, Death and Resurrection of Christ, and in the outpouring of His Spirit, such that we are called to live as citizens of the Kingdom, practicing fidelity in our relationships; but we have to acknowledge that we live also in a world that is manifestly sinful, unjust and painful for very many. Very many marriages do irretrievably break down, and because of "hardness of heart," divorces inevitably occur. To forbid them, forcing couples to remain for the duration of their lives in loveless marriages, would be displaying a greater "hardness of heart" than to permit divorce (and freely to give those affected the Church's blessing and full pastoral support).

THE ALTERED STATUS OF WOMEN

The entire situation of women has irrevocably altered, at least in the Western world, from how it was even a hundred years ago. Then it was still the case that a woman, however intelligent, educated, and gifted, could hardly survive unless dependent on the support of a man. But gradually, throughout the 19th century, women's rights came to be recognized, after a long, painful and sometimes bitter struggle. Gradually, women won the right to own property (the denial of it had meant total financial dependency), to work for a living, the right to initiate divorce proceedings, to receive a university education (even though they were for long refused Oxbridge degrees), and, eventually, in 1918, universal suffrage.

SCIENTIFIC ADVANCES IN BIOLOGY

This went alongside rapidly developing advances in scientific knowledge. In 1827 Karl Ernst von Baer identified the ovum, prior to which it had been presupposed that women played no major role in the genesis of their offspring. The womb was regarded as a seed-bed into which new life was implanted by the male (whose sperm supposedly contained all that was required for conception). Once the role of the ovaries was understood, and more recently of our genes, it has come to be understood that male and female are equally contributors of a half of the 46 chromosomes from which every cell of a baby develops. Here the sheer force of knowledge, based on irrefutable scientific evidence, must empower us to reject all prejudices based on ignorance. Women and men are equal in value, not only in the sight of God but also in their biological contribution to their offspring.

THE HUMAN TEMPLATE

Further scientific knowledge has demonstrated that female anatomy is the basic template for all humans. Every embryo is female in the earliest stages of development until such time as the coming into play of the Y chromosome produces the male characteristics in those who will be born male. Contrary to Eve being created out of Adam's ribs according to the Genesis 2 creation myth, the biological fact is rather the opposite, that man is created from woman. At last the scientific foundation had been established for full equality of status between the sexes. There is no biological basis for discrimination (whilst society rightly has to take into account the length of time a mother is occupied with pregnancy and the nursing of a new-born child). This recognition is in no way contrary to the finest of biblical insights. We could say that it has taken humanity a long time to catch up with God's having created "humankind (Hebrew Adam) male and female" (Genesis 1.26); and with Paul's deepest insight that "in Christ there is neither male nor female" (Galatians 3.28).

THE IMPACT OF CONTRACEPTION

Alongside with this has come the liberation of women made possible by the availability of safe, cheap and reliable contraception. The modern woman is at last able to control her own fertility, thus saving her from the drudgery of near continuous pregnancy. Queen Victoria was not untypical of Victorian mothers, in undergoing serial pregnancies, with nine surviving children born between 1840 and 1857. (Poor Queen Anne[49] bore 17 children, only one of whom survived childhood). Although firmly believing that marriage and childbearing were the woman's chief vocation, there were times when Victoria chafed under the drudgery of it.[50] The wholesale rejection of artificial means of contraceptive methods by the Roman Catholic Church is a tragic and blind refusal to recognize how women's lives have been liberated by its availability (whilst fully acknowledging that it can be selfishly and sinfully used). It has enabled women to advance into almost every field of human endeavor and to compete on equal terms with men (except in certain ever-shrinking pockets of male chauvinism, such as parts of the Church).

THE POTENTIAL OF MODERN MARRIAGE: FOR BETTER OR FOR WORSE?

These factors are bound to have major effects on the institution of marriage. Marriage has to be a wholly reciprocal relationship with mutually agreed sharing of roles and chores. It isn't surprising that many men find this threatening to their traditional dominance; that an alarming amount of violence occurs within marriages; and that a third or more of marriages in the UK end in divorce. But is this any worse than the pain endured in loveless marriages when divorce was not available? For some, life-long marriage meant life-long imprisonment. Historically this was not so for men. They could always seek a mistress or a prostitute. In Victorian times, there were reckoned to be 60,000 prostitutes on the streets of London, many of them hardly out of childhood.

THE CHRISTIAN IDEAL

For Christians, marriage as a life-long partnership has to remain the ideal and every effort has to be made to live up to it. Equally, children should be brought up within households in which both a mother and father are wholly involved. But genuine reciprocity is hard to achieve. There are more areas of tension, particularly conflicts of interest, which may develop into quarrels that may slide

---

[49] Queen Anne (1665-1714), wife of Prince George of Denmark. Only one child, William, survived infancy, but he died aged 12.
[50] See S Schama: *A History of Britain*, volume III, p 197. "Serial pregnancies had taken their toll of her dewy-eyed romance with which Victoria had begun her marriage," p197. The entire chapter 4, "Wives, Daughters, Widows" is a masterly summary of the gradual emancipation of women during her reign.

towards separation and divorce than was the case when the wife was subject in all things to her husband. This is surely the "hardness of heart" for which Jesus declared Moses to have permitted divorce. At the same time, real reciprocity within a caring, loving relationship, is surely infinitely more rewarding than when the relationship was one of dominance-subservience. Christians live in the tension between the ideal and the reality. But they may do so with the encouragement that flows from the selfless example of Jesus and from Paul's eulogy on the nature of love to be found in 1 Corinthians 13: "Love is patient; love is kind; love is not envious or boastful or arrogant or rude. It does not insist on its own way; it is not irritable or resentful; it does not rejoice in wrongdoing, but rejoices in the truth. It bears all things, believes all things, hopes all things, endures all things. Love never ends."

FOUR GOLDEN STEPS IN INTERPRETATION

1. The Interpreter's first duty is to determine a) what the Author intended to convey in each word, phrase, sentence or complete book that he had written; and b) what this would have meant to those for whom it was written.

2. A second task is to discover how a) and b) above were understood by later generations, by those who transmitted them orally, recorded them in writing, edited and finally redacted the book in the format that received canonical status (in which it appears in our Bibles).

3. A third task is to ascertain how the book, in its parts and as a whole, was understood, interpreted or misinterpreted throughout all the centuries of the Church's history and what lessons may be learned from that.

4. And finally, we may ask what the writing may mean for us today? How does God speak to the reader(s) through it?

COMMENTS:

Everybody who reads the Bible with serious intent is an interpreter of it, whether as a Christian wanting to read it devotionally; as a translator intending to produce a new translation; as a scholar about to write a commentary on it; or as a Minister about to prepare the Sunday Sermon.

The steps suggested above are a counsel of perfection.

❖ The devout Christian will probably not be aware of steps 1 – 3, and will likely read with the intention of going directly to Step 4. But as soon as she opens the Bible, she will in point of fact be benefiting from centuries of scholarly research into Steps 1 and 2 and of which the translation she is reading is the outcome. Further, if she uses Daily Bible Reading Notes, they will likely give some attention to Steps 1 & 2, may comment on Step 3, and suggest possible answers to the questions posed at Step 4. She will above all seek to hear what the Lord is saying to her.

❖ The Preacher preparing his/her Sermon will probably go through the first 3 Steps, but s/he will have more tools to hand, such as a Concordance, Bible Dictionary and Commentaries should s/he need to delve more deeply into the issues posed by Steps 1 – 3. Much of this will be an almost unconscious process, if Biblical study and Theological reflection have become an inbuilt habit-of-mind; nevertheless there always crop up issues that require that bit more research. It is all too tempting to leap straight from the text to Step 4, since what is more important than that the congregation hear God's message for the day? But if Steps 1-3 are neglected, the congregation may hear from the preacher's lips Eisegesis rather than Exegesis, i.e. the preacher's thoughts being read into the Bible rather than what truly emerges out of the Bible. [These key words derive from a Greek verb, 'exegeisthai', meaning "to guide or lead" in or out! What's in charge? What the Bible truly conveys or the Preacher's bright ideas?

❖ For study at the greatest depth, Steps 1 & 2 are of course the field of the Textual Critic, the Literary analyst, and the Biblical historian; with many ancillary helps such those of archaeological research, comparative linguistics, comparative studies in sociology, religion and history, all yielding evidence to take into account. As for Step 3, the Church Historian comes into play; for at different times the Bible has been understood in quite different ways. Of especial importance for us today are the changes brought about by the successive movements of the Renaissance, the Reformation and the Enlightenment, which brought about a revolution in the way we see the world around us; a challenge to institutions founded on Custom and Tradition alone; the freedom to investigate what had previously been considered "out of bounds" out which was born modern Science, modern History, and in Religion, a wholly new way of understanding the Bible.

❖ At the 4th Step, the Theologian enters the scene. Christian Theology seeks to make sense of all the data supplied by the human experience of God to which the Bible and Christian History bear witness; by elucidating what may seem fragmentary in Bible and History, by taking account of the philosophers' contributions, and by seeking to make of it a coherent system of beliefs and practice that we call Christianity.

CHAPTER 15:
MANY GENRES, MANY MEANINGS

Many people, reading the Bible for the first time, want to know: Is it true? And yet a moment's reflection reveals that the question itself is naïve, for the novel that we took out from the public library wasn't intended to be factually true. We know immediately that it is fiction. It is otherwise with the dictionary or encyclopedia that we consult. We would expect its information to be accurate. An intelligent reading of the Bible demands that we have some idea of the many varieties of literature to be found within it. What are the genres to be found in the Bible and what kind of truth does each convey?

We also assume vital differences between fact and fiction. In reality, they are not so easy to distinguish. Many a fictional work is so realistic as to be very close to the factual. The best kind of historical fiction may include episodes of historical fact, deep insights into human psychology and behavior, and descriptions so realistic as to carry the readers back into the ambience of a situation of long ago. For example, the novels by Sebastian Faulks in *Birdsong* and Pat Barker in her *Regeneration* trilogy carry their readers into the horrors of the First World War with an extraordinary realism. Fiction can convey a kind of truth. Other types of literature are neither fact not fiction. How should we classify the Psalms, or Proverbs, or the Laws of Moses?

The identification of genre is an essential key to understanding the Bible. We readily perceive the difference between prose and poetry,[51] sensing immediately that poetry is likely to convey emotion and feeling rather than the kind of matter-of-factness that we expect to find in prose. If we read Tennyson's Charge of the Light Brigade with its "onward and onward rode the six hundred" and "guns to the right of them, guns to the left," we are fully aware that this is no factual description such as might have been written by a journalist or a military historian on the spot. Awareness of the genre, i.e. in this case of epic poetry, directs us to interpret it for what it is.

Having been written over a period of some two thousand years, and by scores of authors, mostly anonymous, the Bible is a library, containing within it almost every genre of literature that one might find in the local public library. Each

---

[51] You might be as surprised as was Mr Jourdain, a character in Moliere's *Le Bourgeois Gentilhomme,* when he learned that he had "been speaking prose for forty years without knowing it." ODQ, p 478, no 16.

genre carries within it its own "rules of interpretation." What we loosely call history may include many different genres, such as contemporary reporting, chronicle, retrospective surveys, legend and myth.

1. Myth

Myth was a particularly important category of literature in the ancient world, as it still is amongst pre-literate peoples. The word itself stems from the Greek "muthos," which was the spoken part, the story-line, of the drama being enacted in Temple or theatre. It concerned the world of the gods and their relationships with human beings. It tends therefore to depict pre-historical times, i.e. in which there was not as yet any historical reporting. Not surprisingly, there is myth within the Bible, especially in the first eleven chapters of Genesis. It is particularly apparent in the stories concerning Adam and Eve in the Garden of Eden, the Flood, and the tower of Babel. But it crops up also at various places in the Old Testament: for example in the references to Leviathan in Job 3.8 and 41.8, Psalms 74.14 & 104.26; and in Isaiah 27.1. These refer to the creation story of the Babylonians, in which the world was fashioned out of the body of a great sea-monster, Leviathan, slain in battle by the god Marduk. There are possible allusions to this account in the creation story of Genesis 1.

Let us take one example, that of Adam and Eve in the Garden, Genesis 3.1-7: "1: Now the serpent was more crafty than any other wild animal that the Lord God had made. He said to the woman, Did God say, You shall not eat from any tree in the garden? 2: The woman said to the serpent, We may eat of the fruit of the trees in the garden; 3: but God said, You shall not eat of the fruit of the tree that is in the middle of the garden, nor shall you touch it, or you shall die. 4: But the serpent said to the woman, You will not die; 5: for God knows that when you eat of it your eyes will be opened, and you will be like God, knowing good and evil. 6: So when the woman saw that the tree was good for food, and that it was a delight to the eyes, and that the tree was to be desired to make one wise, she took of its fruit and ate; and she also gave some to her husband, who was with her, and he ate. 7: Then the eyes of both were opened, and they knew that they were naked; and they sewed fig leaves together and made loincloths for themselves."

What characterizes this story for it to be categorized as myth? Firstly, we have to do with a mythical man and woman. Their names, Adam and Eve are not proper names, but indicate "mankind" in general, both male and female, ("earth-creature" would be the best translation, since Adam was made from the "adamah," earth. Genesis 2.7). Eve means "life" or "life-giving." But note that throughout these stories, they are simply referred to as "the man," "the woman."

The Garden of Eden is equally mythical (Gen.2.15). It cannot be pinpointed on any map. Some archaeologists have sought to identify it with what is called "The Land of Dilmun" in the Epic of Gilgamesh and to locate this as being on the island of Bahrain. Whilst it contains trees that bear every kind of fruit to eat, it also includes mythical trees, of which one is called "The Tree of the Knowledge of Good and Evil," another "The Tree of Life" (unless these are variant names for the same magical tree). To eat of the first is to attain a knowledge equal to God's knowledge; to eat of the second is to become immortal as God is.

There is a serpent in the Garden which speaks, holding conversation with the woman and enticing her to eat of the forbidden fruit. In the ancient world, the snake was widely supposed to be immortal, due probably to the mistaken belief that by shedding its skin, it never aged and was widely worshiped as a divine being.

This story is in its origins considerably older that the version of it appearing in the Bible. A Babylonian cylinder seal,[52] from the third millennium BC, depicts a man or woman sitting in front of a tree around which a serpent is coiled, and beyond which is a god also seated, perhaps in judgment of what is occurring. There is a parallel to this scene in the world's earliest novel, the Epic of Gilgamesh. Its hero Gilgamesh's quest is to secure immortality over against death and destruction. This is to be attained by possession of a magical plant (akin to the tree of life), which Gilgamesh discovers, only to have the prize snatched from him by a serpent.

Clearly the Bible story is a version of a narrative common to all the peoples of the ancient Middle East. Why was it remembered and recorded by the Jews? They were neither isolated nor insulated from the cultures around them, so this and other mythological stories would have been well-known to them. Such myths attempted to answer questions about the origins of the world, of human beings, of life and suffering and death. Possessing little or no scientific knowledge nor tools of historical research, early peoples invented stories (supposedly revealed to them by gods or ancestors), which became deeply embedded in their cultures. Such myths were enacted in poetry, song and dance in religious rituals.

But, we should note this, the Jews (from Moses time onwards) submitted all such stories to the over-riding themes of their new-found faith. Whereas their pagan neighbors celebrated a chaos of many gods and goddesses, frequently in conflict, for the Jews there was but One God. Whereas the gods acted out of sheer caprice, the Lord God acts out of moral judgment both in punishment

---

[52] A cylinder seal comprised a round article of wood or metal, in which a pictogram particular to its owner was engraved. This was rolled onto a clay tablet, whilst still wet and thus served as a kind of signature.

and in redemption. To a considerable degree, the Bible writers demythologized the pagan myths.

How then do we interpret the myths of the Bible? If we ask, "Are they true?" the answer on a factual level would have to be "No." But in mythology, the truth question is not appropriate. The vital question is as to what the myth is intending to convey. Although a "made-up" story, myths convey the deepest beliefs and intuitions of those who guard and propound them. That is the case whether we are thinking of the biblical myths or those of Australian Aborigines or of North American Indians. Nor should we suppose that modern people have no time for and no need of myths. The most popular of many recent films have been highly mythological in content, from the *Star Wars* series through *Harry Potter* to *The Lord of the Rings*. All concern what is perhaps the most fundamental of all myths, the conflict between good and evil.

So to what human ills is the myth of the Garden of Eden attempting to supply some kind of answers? May we suggest these: why are human beings, made in the image of God, placed within a paradisal garden, nevertheless subject to unremitting toil, women to men, and all to death?

2. Legend

Legend is also common to all cultures. It has this in common with myth that it is in essence a made-up story; but has this difference in that it concerns a real person or historical event. Legend invariably grows around any person of fame and fortune. In some cases, it is hard to distinguish between myth and legend: for example, in which category should we place the stories of King Arthur and the Round Table? We may suspect that most of them are mythical for there is no hard evidence that Arthur ever lived. But with King Alfred and the Burnt Cakes, we do know that he was the first great Anglo-Saxon monarch. So the episode of the burnt cakes is doubtless legend. The word "legend" derives from a Latin word meaning "to be read;" but the concept goes back far before the era of written books. Its origin was doubtless in the story-telling of pre-literate times, when around the camp-fire, the story-teller would recount tales of famous heroes of the past such as warriors, kings or saints and the tales would doubtless grow in the telling. There are plenty of legends to be found in the Bible. Take the stories of Samson and his exploits (to be found in Judges, chapters 13-16). In no way could we read them as factually well-documented episodes of historical fact. They originate from the days of constant skirmishing on the ill-defined frontiers between Israelites and Philistines (i.e. in about the 11th century BC). There probably was such a person as Samson, who won renown by his heroic (and barbaric) deeds; but the legends are probably more fictional than factual.

Other examples concern the prophets Elijah and Elisha (in 1 Kings 17-2 Kings 13). These were undoubtedly great prophets, the champions of Yahweh, who pitted themselves against a number of paganizing kings. They were heroic, since their activities endangered their lives. There is doubtless a great deal of real historical occurrence in, for instance, Elijah's confrontation with King Ahab concerning his outrageous seizure of Naboth's vineyard (1 Kings 21) or in the dramatic encounter with 450 prophets of Baal on the height of Mt Carmel (1Kings 18). But in this latter episode, we can hardly fail to remark on the highly dramatic recounting of the story, characteristic more of the narrator's literary skill than of sober historic fact (about which we can know very little). There is enough historicity in these episodes to be sure that Elijah fought fiercely for the religion of Yahweh as against pagan gods and that he stood for social justice against a tyrannical king, but we can hardly know where fiction takes over from fact.

There are other stories in this cycle which are yet more obviously legendary, especially those told about Elisha. For examples see those in 2 Kings 2.19-25: the first (19-22) recounts how the prophet cleansed the city's water supply by the insertion of salt into the spring; the second (23-25) tells how some small boys who jeered at the prophet were mauled by two she-bears. Others are to be found at 2 Kings 4.38-41 and 42-44; in the latter, we may detect a forerunner of the story of the Feeding of the Five Thousand in the gospels. We may wonder how far stories in the gospel may have been influenced by such episodes recounted in the Old Testament. Another, in 2 Kings 6.1-7, telling how Elisha made an iron axe-head float to the surface of the Jordan, strains the bounds of credibility. In episodes such as these, the question of the miraculous is raised about which readers will have widely differing views. Some will argue that God can do anything through the hands of His servants; others question whether a God who has laid down the basic laws of the universe (discovered through science) would so lightly break them. Whatever view we take, it has to be recognized that these stories were passed on by word of mouth, possibly for centuries, before they were written down. It is sensible therefore to take account of the arts of the story-teller in embellishing the story in the direction of the spectacularly supernatural. Against that tendency, we should weigh the importance of Jesus' decision, recounted in the story of his temptations in the wilderness, to renounce the use of magical powers.

3. History

A) THE ORAL TRADITION OF ISRAEL'S PRE-HISTORY

A great deal of the Bible, the Old Testament especially, constitutes, in a very generalized sense, history. It recounts the story of the Jewish people, from the time of their founding Father, Abraham, in the early second millennium BC, until their subjection under the Greeks, in the late fourth century BC. The story is continued for a further two centuries in the books of the Apocrypha. But we have to take cognizance of the fact that for many centuries the descendants of Abraham were illiterate; therefore the story of their ancestors could only be passed on orally. Written records were hardly possible before Israel had become a settled people in the land of Canaan in the late 11th century at the earliest, more likely not until the 10th century. King David was the first monarch to establish a government, in Jerusalem, with an official designated as secretary of State (2 Samuel 8.16), who was still in office under Solomon (1 Kings 4.3). He was probably the official recorder of events at court. It may well be that it was from this time that were kept "annals of the kings of Israel," and "annals of the Kings of Judah," to which there are frequent references from 1 Kings 14.19 onwards.

There were also other compilations mentioned but no longer extant, such as "the book of the Wars of Yahweh" (Numbers 21.14-18). The references indicate that these comprised chiefly poetic utterances: e.g. "Therefore it is said in the Book of the Wars of the Lord ... from there they continued to Beer; that is the well of which the Lord said to Moses, 'Gather the people together, and I will give them water.' Then Israel sang this song: 'Spring up, O well! – Sing to it!' 18: the well that the leaders sank, that the nobles of the people dug, with the scepter, with the staff.'" The precise location of a well was of life-saving importance to a nomadic people.

Another book, "the book of Jashar," is mentioned in both Joshua 10.13 and in 2 Samuel 1.18. In the former, we have this reference to the seemingly miraculous halting of the Sun: "And the sun stood still, and the moon stopped, until the nation took vengeance on their enemies. Is this not written in the Book of Jashar? The sun stopped in mid-heaven, and did not hurry to set for about a whole day." But does not its poetic origin indicate that we have here a clear example of poetic license? We might compare it with Cornelius Ryan's account of D-Day, which he entitled "The Longest Day." The other reference in 2 Samuel 1:18-19 is again poetic: "He (i.e. David) ordered that The Song of the Bow be taught to the people of Judah; it is written in the Book of Jashar. He said: 'Your glory, O Israel, lies slain upon your high places! How the mighty have fallen!'" There follows the lamentation over the deaths of Saul and Jonathan.

B) THE POETIC TRADITION

These references strongly suggest that the earliest history was remembered in the form of epic poetry (as has been the case in most cultures, e.g. those of early Greece in the works of Homer (the Iliad and the Odyssey), c. 9th century BC; of the Anglo-Saxons in Beowulf (c. AD 1000); and of France in the Chanson de Roland (c. AD 1100). There is an excellent example of this in Judges 4 and 5. In chapter four we have a rather dry prose account of the conflict between the Israelites, under the leadership of the prophetess Deborah and her right-hand man, Barak, and the Canaanite King Jabin of Hazor, whose army was commanded by the renowned general Sisera. With his army of 900 chariots, Sisera threatened to crush the Israelite army, consisting of the men of just two tribes, those of Naphtali and Zebulon. But the Israelites put them to rout on Mt Tabor. Only Sisera escaped, but, seeking shelter in the tent of a woman named Jael, he came to a grisly end. The whole of this account reveals the hand of the Deuteronomistic editors, who fit all the stories of the Judges into their tight theological framework. A phrase such as "the Israelites again did what was wrong in the eyes of the Lord and he sold them into the power of Jabin" (4.1) immediately reveals their hand.

Chapter five is presented, by these same editors, as "A Song of Victory" rendered by Deborah and Barak. In the terms of epic poetry, this account sparkles with vivid imagery: of Yahweh marching from the south, causing the mountains to quake and the heavens to pour down rain, picturing how commercial activity had ground to a halt because of oppression, of the people (or is it the Lord?) rousing Deborah and Barak to take action against their oppressors, of the Israelite clansmen rallying to the muster (but with harsh words for the tribes that didn't respond to the call: Reuben, Gilead, Dan and Asher are all bitterly reproached). When it comes to the battle, it appears that, valiant as the tribesmen of Zebulon and Naphtali were, it was Yahweh's intervention by means of torrential rainfall that won the day. "The stars fought from heaven, from their courses they fought against Sisera. The torrent Kishon swept them away, the onrushing torrent, the torrent Kishon. March on, my soul, with might!"(Judges 5.20-21). A community called Meroz is then harshly criticized for not assisting "the Lord and his fighting men;" by contrast, Jael, the wife of Heber, is praised to the skies. By cunning and pretence of hospitality she lured Sisera to his death. In a most ironic postscript, the poet imagines Sisera's mother and her ladies explaining their hero's prolonged absence by the surmise that he is gathering loot on the battlefield. The poem ends with this flourish: "So perish all your enemies, O Lord! But may your friends be like the sun as it rises in its might."

For much of Old Testament history, whilst there is no direct corroboration from other historical sources, what the Bible recounts nevertheless fits the picture. For example, there is no evidence outside of the Bible for the existence of any biblical characters from Abraham to Moses. Whilst it is impossible to date or locate the patriarchs with any certainty, yet what is recounted of them in Genesis is not discordant with what is otherwise known about the Middle East during the first half of the second millennium BC. Migrations of people around the fertile crescent and in Canaan, living on the edge of established cities, getting into disputes, establishing treaties, buying land, going down to Egypt in time of famine, all are known and recorded. Joseph's rise to prominence in Egyptian government is most explicable if the dynasty then in power was that of the Hyksos, themselves a Semitic people (i.e. related to the Hebrew), who had invaded Egypt circa.1720; just as the subsequent enslavement of his descendants was a likely consequence of their expulsion by the Egyptians in the next century.

Independent corroboration becomes considerably easier once Israel had become an established player in Middle Eastern politics, from circa the eighth century onwards; since the rulers of Assyria, Babylonia, and later Persians, Greeks and Romans were keen to boast of their victories in massive inscriptions or in written records. The first ever mention, outside of the Bible, of the name Israel as a people settled in southern Canaan comes from an inscription by the Pharaoh Merneptah in circa 1220 BC. He boasts of having laid waste to their settlements.

C) HISTORICAL REPORTING
Is there any strictly historical reporting within the Bible? We come to something very much like it from the 10th century onwards. Read the second Book of Samuel and it is easy to imagine that we are reading the account of an eye-witness situated within the household of King David (especially in chapters 9-20). "The author seems to be writing from direct personal knowledge" so we read in the RSV's introduction to 2 Samuel. Then we come to episodes which are not only described in the most vivid terms, but for which there is also corroboration from other sources. In 2 Kings 18 we read the extraordinarily vivid account of the siege of Jerusalem by the Assyrian army under the Emperor Sennacherib, when Hezekiah was king. We read of what would have been the plight of the besieged, who would be forced to "eat their own dung and drink their own urine" (18.27) had it been prolonged; and of the Jewish officials pleading with the Assyrian negotiators to speak not in Hebrew but in Aramaic (18.26) so that the people manning the walls should not be paralyzed with fear at their words. In this case, we have Sennacherib's own account of the episode, inscribed on what is called the Taylor Prism, in the British Museum:

> "But as for Hezekiah, the Jew, who did not bow in submission to my yoke, forty-six of his strong walled towns and innumerable smaller villages in their neighborhood I besieged and conquered by stamping down earth-ramps and then by bringing up battering rams, by the assault of foot-soldiers, by breaches, tunneling and sapper operations. I made to come out from them 200,150 people, young and old, male and female, innumerable horses, mules, donkeys, camels, large and small cattle, and counted them as the spoils of war. He himself I shut up like a caged bird within Jerusalem, his royal city. I put watch-posts strictly round it and turned back to his disaster any who went out of its city gate. His towns which I had I cut off from his land, giving them to Mitinti, king of Ashdod, Padi, king of Ekron, and Sillibel, king of

Gaza, and so reduced his land. More-over, I fixed upon him an increase in the amount to be given as katre-presents for my lordship, in addition to the former tribute, to be given annually.

"As for Hezekiah, the awful splendor of my Lordship overwhelmed him, and the irregular and regular troops which he had brought in to strengthen Jerusalem, his royal city, and had obtained for his protection, together with 30 talents of gold, 300 talents of silver, precious stones, antimony, large blocks of red stone, ivory (inlaid) couches, ivory arm-chairs, elephant hide, elephant tusks, ebony-wood, box-wood, all kinds of valuable treasures, as well as his daughters, concubines, male and female musicians he sent me later to Nineveh, my lordly city. He sent a personal messenger to deliver the tribute and make a slavish obeisance."[53]

The biblical account tells us that the Assyrian Emperor had first laid siege to Lachish, a Jewish city some 25 miles from Jerusalem, to which King Hezekiah sent envoys to parley with the Emperor. The massive engraved depiction of the Assyrians' attack on Lachish can be seen in the British Museum. We see on it the various types of military hardware mentioned in the Taylor Prism and the terrible fate of prisoners; also King Hezekiah kneeling in abject obeisance before the Emperor. We are dealing here with the real stuff of history; although in the case both of the Jewish and the Assyrian accounts, we have to take account of the "spin" applied by the propaganda machines of both nations.

And what was the outcome of the siege? The fact is that Jerusalem was saved, when the Assyrian army was forced to withdraw, for what reason we cannot be sure. The biblical account tells us that King Hezekiah turned to God in fervent prayer, that the prophet Isaiah declared to him that it was the Lord's intention to save the city, in consequence of which disaster befell the Assyrians. 2 Kings 19.35-36 puts it like this: "That very night the angel of the Lord set out and struck down one hundred and eighty-five thousand in the camp of the Assyrians; when morning dawned, they were all dead bodies. Then King Sennacherib of Assyria left, went home, and lived at Nineveh." The most likely cause of such a disaster has to be disease (always the worst scourge of armies in the field) which the Jews would have attributed to God's intervention. This may find further explanation in a remark of the Greek historian Herodotus to the effect that, during the night, rodents nibbled through the soldiers bow strings. Does this possibly suggest that it was the plague bacillus carried by rats that destroyed them? But the biblical writers were not interested in secondary causes such as plague, only in first causes, i.e. the action of God.

---

[53] Taylor Prism (British Museum No 91032), p 67, in *Documents from Old Testament Times*, ed D. W Thomas, Harper Torchbooks, Harper and Row, New York.

Clearly the biblical narratives are conveying real history; but their accounts of the conflict with Sennacherib don't answer all the historical questions; and to some extent obscure what occurred. There is some discussion as to whether Sennacherib launched one or two campaigns into Palestine; if the latter then the author of 2 Kings has telescoped them into one. Nor does he mention the accusation of the Assyrians that Hezekiah had made a foolish alliance with the Egyptian Pharoah to oppose the Assyrians; that in consequence, it was on the borders of Egypt that disaster struck them (not outside the walls of Jerusalem, as we might suppose from 2 King19.35). Nor would we guess from verses 36-37 that Sennacherib was murdered by his sons 20 years later, i.e. in 681 BC! The Bible's is a very selective narration of these events.

D) HISTORY AS MORAL AND RELIGIOUS EXAMPLE

It has to be constantly remembered that every scrap of historical information that we read in the Old Testament has been selected and processed by those who edited and published the books of the Law and the Prophets. We can detect the hands of both Deuteronomists and Priests. They provide the framework within which the episodes are recounted and make the theological judgments that guide the readers' understanding. For this reason, all the books from Joshua to 2 Kings are rightly dubbed "The Deuteronomistic History," for they reflect the theological and moral viewpoint of the Deuteronomists, those anonymous reformers who judged all the leaders of Israel and Judah according to their fidelity or infidelity to the Laws of Moses and the strictures of the prophets, i.e. this is history completely subordinate to the religious interests of Israel. We could say that there is no history which isn't propagandist. Israel's story was of no interest to them as mere historical record, but only as it demonstrated the activity of God. It was of interest in so far as it demonstrated some point of moral or theological lesson.[54] To some extent the New Testament is similar. The gospels and the Acts recount a story that contains a certain core of historical fact, such as that a man called Jesus lived, preached and taught about the coming Kingdom of God, gathered disciples and was executed by crucifixion: that much can be reasonably established. But there is neither any strictly biographical or merely historical interest in the telling of the story. It was told in order to convince potential readers that, in these occurrences, God had

---

[54] That this is still the predominant outlook within Judaism is confirmed by this excerpt from Alan Untermann's *Jews: Their Religious Beliefs and Practices*: "Although the theological interpretation of history and historical events is characteristic of major sections of the Hebrew Bible, neither biblical religion nor rabbinic Judaism was interested in history as it is understood in the modern world. In line with biblical paradigms Judaism was not interested in purveying objective historical data. The value of history was its religious and ethical content, and little attempt was made to distinguish fact and interpretation. The past was continually being re-interpreted by Jewish theologians to throw light on the religious ideas of the present, and rabbinic exegesis saw the heroes of biblical religion as paragons of rabbinic religious piety." Routledge & Kegan Paul, Boston, London and Henley, 1981.

decisively acted on the human scene. Thus whilst Luke could declare his intention that his gospel should enable a certain Theophilus to "know the truth concerning the things about which you have been instructed …" (Luke 1.4); he would surely have agreed wholly with the author of John's Gospel that "these things are written that you may believe …" The gospels are evangelistic tracts. They are written to convince and convert the reader.

4. Genealogies

Genealogical lists comprise a sizeable part of the Bible. But what is a turn-off for us was of great importance to the Jewish people, for such lists determined whether a man was truly a descendent of Levi and therefore qualified to be a priest (see 1 Chronicles 5.1). Equally, the genealogies represented one's stake in the apportionment of the Promised Land. Such lists were jealously guarded by the priests.

5. Historical Fiction

At first sight, the book of Ruth wouldn't suggest itself to be a fictional tale. For it fits quite snugly into its position in our Bibles between the book of Judges before it and the first Book of Samuel after it. But the clue that it doesn't really belong there is to be shown by its position within the Jewish Bible. There it doesn't form part of the Former Prophets (as the historical books are called), but of the Khetuvim, the Writings, the third section of the Tanach; and these are all late scrolls. Ruth must have been written many centuries after the events described within it, which belong to time of the Judges. The second major clue as to the nature of this book is found in its concluding verses, containing a genealogy of the descendants of Perez (son of Judah and Tamar, see Genesis 38.29) leading us to Boaz and Ruth, which culminates in the birth of David. Why should the book's anonymous author write such a charming pastoral tale? Its conclusion, the revelation that David was grandson to a Moabitess who had adopted the religion of Israel, is the key. David was held to be the greatest of all the Kings of Israel and Judah. In what situation in Judah should the reminder that he was the descendent of a foreigner (and ancient foe of Israel) have been a potent and relevant factor? One situation fits like a glove. When, after the return from exile, the tight-knit community living in and around Jerusalem in a ghetto-like situation, fearful of its aggressive neighbors, became xenophobic to the point of expelling the many foreign wives of its citizens. Read the account of this terrible act of ethnic cleansing in the book of Ezra 9 and 10.

Although this deed is presented as one to which the entire community gave its assent, there must have been at least one dissenting voice, i.e. the author of the book of Ruth. How could the People of God, themselves of mixed racial origins, behave in so racist a fashion? We cannot hide from the fact that such argument, such division of both belief and practice, is inherent within the Bible. Throughout much of the Bible we find the tension, deeply embedded, between the exclusivism which supposes that salvation is only for the Jews and the inclusivism that understands God's Love to be for all human-kind. Ezra belongs to the first position; the author of Ruth to the second. If the book of Ruth is fictional, it is fiction with a moral and religious purpose.

It is likely that the Book of Jonah is of similar origins and intention. Nor should we forget that there is fiction with a purpose in the New Testament, notably, in the Parables (about which see further). We understand these to be made-up stories. Most of them are so true-to-life as possibly to have been based on true events. It cannot have been uncommon for a merchant to be mugged and left for dead on the road between Jerusalem and Jericho. Whether factual or fictitious hardly matters since Jesus told them so as to convey his teaching about the Kingdom of God. Parables are stories with a purpose.

6. Legal Material

It is clear that a great deal of the Old Testament consists of legal material, for which cause the Torah (the first five books) is usually translated as The Law, or the Laws of Moses. The consideration of these laws (variously described as commandments, statutes, instructions, precepts, etc) should never be separated from their function within the covenant relationship God had established with Israel at Sinai. They are the expression of God's purpose, that having adopted Israel as the People whom He has saved and to whom He offers protection, they in response should honor Him and obey his commandments. Therefore these include legal regulations covering everything to do with Temple worship (which are unlikely to have been recorded till after the Temple had been built under King Solomon, i.e. centuries after Moses' time), and those regarding the ethical behavior of his people and their usage of the land. Since we neither offer animal sacrifices nor live off the land, much of this material is of little obvious relevance for Christians today. Of much greater relevance are the principles behind much of this legal material, both concerning the nature of God's provision and of our human relationships; always remembering that whenever we have to make hard choices, the example and teaching of Jesus has to be the chief criterion of what is right or wrong in any given situation. But a chapter such as Leviticus 19 comes very close to the spirit of Jesus. It is from verse 18 that his quotation of "Thou shalt love the Lord thy God ..." as the first of all the commandments was immediately followed by "... and thy neighbor as thyself" as the second.

Scholarship on the laws of the Torah has distinguished between two types of material to be found there. The first is called "Apodictic" law, from a Greek word meaning "clearly established," "beyond dispute," i.e. that is law of the "Thou shalt ..." and more frequently "Thou shalt not ..." variety. This is the type of law most characteristic of the Jewish religion, for these are requirements of God. They are found most obviously in the Ten Commandments, but are also scattered around the rest of the Torah. For other examples, see Exodus chapters 22 and 23. The other type is "Casuistic" law, i.e. laws made case by case, as and when occasions demanded. Not only does this make up the majority of the legal rulings contained in the Torah, but is also of a type common throughout much of the Middle East. Many of the laws given in what is called the Book of the Covenant (Exodus 21-23) are similar to those in the Babylonian Code of Hammurabi, who was King of Babylon in 1792-1750 BC. They begin typically with "If a man does so-and-so..." or "When such and such arises, then ..." you should do this, that or the other. It is evident that such rulings, mostly governing the agricultural way of life of the Hebrews after their settlement in Canaan, could not have been made by Moses centuries beforehand, but represent an accumulation of legal precedents made as and when required.

7. Poetry

We have already alluded to the earliest historical remembrance being conveyed in poetic form and cited Judges 5 as an excellent example. But even when the Israelites became a sedentary and civilized (which means no more than city-dwelling) people, much of their utterance was still delivered in poetic form. This was particularly the case with the oracles of the prophets. From early days, there was the phenomenon that when God spoke to his inspired servants, it was in the form of poetic oracles. The poetic format, with its frequent alliterative quality, was a particularly awesome, attention-catching and memorable means of conveying the message. There are parallels to this in pre-Islamic Arabia, in which the spirit-inspired man covered his head with his cloak and uttered his message in rhythmical poetry. Of this, Mohammed was the master, such that the recitation of the Koran is said to have an almost hypnotic effect on its listeners. This was held to be the mark of inspiration. The case must have been similar with the Hebrew prophets. This was obscured in almost all English translations till modern times; only in the latter do we have their oracles printed as the poems that they are.

The chief characteristic of Hebrew poetry is what is called **parallelism**: a particular thought is expressed in a usually brief, terse phrase, which is then reinforced in one or more parallel phrases with the same or closely similar idea, of identical grammatical structure but in slightly varied wording. This hammers home the idea in most memorable fashion; and is to be found especially in the prophets and in the Psalms. Some examples are:

The Lord is my light and salvation: whom shall I fear?
The Lord is the stronghold of my life: of whom shall I be afraid?

Psalms 27.1-2

Come now, let us reason together, says the Lord:
Though your sins are like scarlet, they shall be white as snow;
Though they are red like crimson, they shall become like wool.

Isaiah 2.18

How lonely sits the city that once was full of people!
How like a widow she has become, she that was great among the nations!
She that was a princess among the provinces has become a vassal.

Lamentations 1.1

Nor should we forget that such a way of speaking came naturally to Jesus and is one reason why his teaching was so memorable:
Ask, and it will be given to you; search, and you will find;
knock, and the door will be opened for you.
For everyone who asks receives, and everyone who searches finds,
and for everyone who knocks, the door will be opened.

Matthew 7.7-8

Poetry was also a most fitting vehicle for worship and as such was the format of the Psalms, which constituted the hymn book used in Temple worship. These could convey in a powerfully emotive manner both the praises of God and the emotional outpouring of the worshipers, whether expressing pain, sorrow, anger and anguish, or thankful remembrance and joyful outbursts of praise. It could also be used to convey the deepest emotions connected with human suffering. Thus the book of Job, begins and ends with a prose setting and conclusion to the matter unfolded in the sufferings of Job, but the detailed philosophical argument is carried forward in the poetic form. By contrast, the Song of Solomon was in origin an outpouring of passionate erotic love, which may well have originated in the courtly circles of King Solomon. It would seem doubtful to have found its way into scripture, had it not been early (at least in the Christian Church) understood as an allegory concerning the mutual love of God and the human soul. But it is a reminder that Hebrew religion had no hang-ups about the goodness of sexual love (as sadly was to disfigure much later Christian thinking – under the pernicious influence of gnosticism). These four examples remind us that the Hebrew soul didn't express itself in coldly analytical thought but rather in passionate outpouring and in highly pictorial imagery.

For which reason, its message should never been understood in a wholly literalistic manner. Only by entering into the emotions, reliving the experience, sharing both in the hope and in the despair, can we hope to interpret rightly the message being delivered.

8. Mashal

A) ALLEGORY

Mashal covers a wide variety of literary forms that we might translate variously as allegory, parable, or riddle. In biblical times, the wise man employed many such forms of speech. It used to be supposed that the Jews never went in for allegory. In allegory, one or more characters in the story represents one of the participants in whatever the situation is under consideration; it is told in order to illuminate its hearers as to the reality of the situation. There is an excellent example in Judges 9.7-15. It tells of the situation in which the Israelites, sore pressed by their enemies, had asked Gideon (who also bore the pagan name Jerubaal) to assume the Kingship over them, which he refuses (Judges 8.22-23). The same Gideon had 70 sons by a number of wives and one bastard son called Abimelech (which means, "My Father is king"). After much conspiracy, this man engineered the death of all his brothers but one, in order to rule over Israel unopposed. But the escapee, Jotham, ascended Mount Gerizim above Shechem, and from its summit, addressed the people of Shechem with an allegory. It concerns the trees of the wood desiring to appoint one of their number to rule over them. In turn they approach the olive tree, the fig tree and the vine, asking each in turn to become king of the forest; but each declines, preferring to produce their respective nutritious fruits. So they approach the wild thorn, offering him the kingship. His response is that, from him, fire will burst out that will devour the tallest trees. Jotham then addresses the people of Shechem directly: have they treated Gideon's memory and his children justly? He warned them of what the consequences of Abimelech's rule would be. Had Jotham's listeners got the point? Certainly not immediately. In time the consequences for them were grizzly. Taking shelter in their watch-tower, the citizens were burned to death by a fire set alight by Abimelech's men. Shortly afterwards, Abimelech was trying to deal with the inhabitants of Thebez, also enclosed in their tower, in the same way, when a woman hurled down a millstone which cracked his skull. For the shame of being killed by a woman, his bodyguard finished him off.

B) PARABLE

An excellent example of a parable occurs in the Old Testament, at 2 Samuel 12.1-9. It was told by the prophet Nathan to King David, at a time when the King appeared utterly remorseless over his adulterous union with Bathsheba and the consequent engineering of her husband's murder so as to cover up his evil deed. Nathan was prompted by God to tell the king this story: "There were two men in a certain city, one rich and the other poor. The rich man had very many flocks and herds; but the poor man had nothing but one little ewe lamb, which he had bought. He brought it up, and it grew up with him and with his children; it used to eat of his meager fare, and drink from his cup, and lie in his bosom, and it was like a daughter to him. Now there came a traveler to the rich man, and he was loath to take one of his own flock or herd to prepare for the wayfarer who had come to him, but he took the poor man's lamb, and prepared that for the guest who had come to him." Such was the parable, a cleverly devised verbal trap into which David fell headlong. His anger aroused, David replied to Nathan: "As the Lord lives, the man who has done this deserves to die; he shall restore the lamb fourfold, because he did this thing, and because he had no pity." Still unwitting that he had condemned himself, the prophet pounced: "*You are the man!* Thus says the Lord, the God of Israel: I anointed you king over Israel, …I gave you your master's house, and your master's wives into your bosom, and gave you the house of Israel and of Judah; and if that had been too little, I would have added as much more. Why have you despised the word of the Lord, to do what is evil in his sight? You have struck down Uriah the Hittite with the sword, and have taken his wife to be your wife, and have killed him with the sword of the Ammonites". Only then did David become conscious of the evil he had committed and turn to God in repentance.

This example demonstrates that a parable was no entertaining story for the children. It was a story designed to provoke its listeners to a consideration of their conduct. It demanded a response. It challenged a person to decision. This needs to be borne in mind in the case of Jesus' parables. Look out for what clues there may be as to the situation in which the story was being told; to whom it was addressed; and what was the response? If in David's case it led to repentance; in others it led rather to fierce anger. For a New Testament example of a parable that provoked an extremely hostile reaction, see Mark 12.1-12, the parable of the vineyard. How did this parable expose the evil intentions of some of those listening to it? (See Mark12.12).

C) PARABLE AND ALLEGORY

There are doubtfully any true allegories in the New Testament, but there was a tendency for the gospel-writers to treat some of the parables of Jesus as if they were allegories. A true parable conveyed one main point, which is usually clear in its very last words (just like the "punch-line" of a joke). A parable like that of the Sower (Mark 4.3-9 & //s), originally bore the message: "Although much of the good seed, scattered liberally over all types of soil, failed to germinate or to come to fruition, in spite of such loss, there was nevertheless an excellent harvest from the seed that fell on good soil." A first century audience gathered around Jesus would have understood perfectly the point he was making. Peasant farmers that they mostly were, whose practice was first to sow and then to plough, would have understood perfectly well that however much seed was lost, you would still normally get some harvest (except, of course, in exceptional times of drought). Its extension of meaning within the Church would have been clear. Jesus proclaimed the good Word of God; some of it produced little or no response, but other produced "a harvest of souls" as people responded to it joyfully. All that would have been recounted, discussed and debated, in the Aramaic language, without any danger of misinterpretation.

But the gospels weren't written till 30, 40, perhaps 50 years later, and then in the Greek language and heard by people unfamiliar with the farming practices of Palestine. It seems likely that the very notion of parable was not well understood in the Graeco-Roman world. This becomes evident in Mark's Gospel. It is likely that Mark 4.10–20 is not original, deriving not from Jesus but from the early Church. Verses 10-12 show the Church grappling with the question: "If Jesus was the Messiah, who brought God's rich word to the Jewish people, why was it that so many either failed to hear it or rejected it?" For elucidation, they turned to the prophet Isaiah's words about "listening but understanding nothing." And he said, "Go and say to this people: 'Keep listening, but do not comprehend; keep looking, but do not understand.' Make the mind of this people dull, and stop their ears, and shut their eyes, so that they may not look with their eyes, and listen with their ears, and comprehend with their minds, and turn and be healed." (Isaiah 6.9-10) The passage is part of the story of Isaiah's call to be a prophet, following his dramatic vision of the Lord's glory in the Temple (Isaiah 6). Both concerning the prophet and Jesus' preaching of the gospel, it would seem strange to propose that God deliberately hardened hearts and closed ears so that the listeners should neither understand nor come to salvation. But the Hebraic way of understanding would have supposed that God foresees all that will come to pass; and that so foreseeing, he would have foretold its occurrence.

In the Greek-speaking world, the Church understood the parable as an allegory, as we see demonstrated in Mark's Gospel, for, from verses 13-20 (cf Matthew 13.10-23 & Luke 8.9-15) we have a full blown interpretation of the parable. Each item here represents an element in the story. The Seed is the Word (i.e. the gospel message), made most explicit in Luke's version (see Luke 8.11). The different qualities of soil represent the varying spiritual capacities of Jesus' hearers to comprehend and respond appropriately to the message. The factors that make for unbelief are personalized – in Matthew as "the evil one," by Mark as "Satan," by Luke as "the Devil" who snatches away the good seed. What we have in each of the Synoptics is how the original parable was understood as an allegory in three different Christian communities some five to six decades after Jesus' lifetime, i.e. we are overhearing examples of early Christian preaching.

D) RIDDLES

These are more characteristic of the Old than the New Testament. The best examples occur in the book of Judges, concerning Samson, the Hebrew strongman. In the days of strong antipathy between Hebrews and Philistines, Samson evidently lived in the border between the two ethnicities. So began a fierce competition, not only involving deeds of physical prowess but also in verbal cunning. Propagandist ploys preceded military conflict. On one occasion, Samson was courting a Philistine woman. A feast was proposed. The episode continues (Judges14.10-12): "Samson said to them, 'Let me now put a riddle to you. If you can explain it to me within the seven days of the feast, and find it out, then I will give you thirty linen garments and thirty festal garments. But if you cannot explain it to me, then you shall give me thirty linen garments and thirty festal garments.' So they said to him, 'Ask your riddle; let us hear it.' He said to them, 'Out of the eater came something to eat. Out of the strong came something sweet.' But for three days they could not explain the riddle."

The Philistines put pressure on Samson's wife to wheedle the answer out of him; which she succeeded in doing. On the appointed day, the townsmen confronted Samson and astonished him by explaining the riddle thus: "What is sweeter than honey? What is stronger than a lion?" And he said to them, "If you had not plowed with my heifer, you would not have found out my riddle." Samson was so enraged at the betrayal of his secret, that he went down to Ashkelon, slaughtered 30 of its men and handed over the festal garments to those who had correctly solved the riddle. Such stories bear no moral or religious message, but originate in a wholly amoral folk-tale tradition.

Some of Jesus' sayings are riddle-like. For examples, see the sayings in Mark 2.18-22 about the inappropriateness of fasting at a wedding feast, about patching old clothes with new cloth, or putting new wine into old wineskins. How do you suppose those listening would have understood these riddles? And how appropriate were they to the critical comments of the Pharisees?

9. Proverbs

These were also a popular medium of conveying traditional wisdom, so much so that they are to be found in a book of that name, as well as others such as the book of Ecclesiastes. The inclusion of this book in the canon is surprising, since it conveys a world-weary cynicism about life, characterized by the expression that "there's nothing new under the sun." The last verses of the scroll are thought to be an editorial postscript, which includes this downbeat advice for would-be authors: "Of making many books there is no end, and much study is aweariness of the flesh."(12.12). Hopefully this will not have deterred you, the reader, from persisting to this point any more than it has me, the author.

Some concluding thoughts

Every conceivable type of literature is to be found within the library which is the Bible. Each type poses its own problems, demands its own rules of interpretation, conveys its own kind of truthfulness. What is most characteristic of the Hebrew language, therefore of biblical thought, is its multiplicity of figurative, pictorial, and metaphorical ways of expression. This should constantly remind us that to think of everything within it too literalistically is most likely to misinterpret it. On the other hand, the backbone to the entire biblical story, is a series of historical events whose essential veracity is vital to both the Jewish and Christian faiths.

CHAPTER 16:
A CRITIQUE OF
FUNDAMENTALISM

Origins of fundamentalism

The term "fundamentalism" stems from the early years of the 20th century. A group of American evangelical Christians, alarmed at what they saw to be the baleful effects of a liberal, modernist theology, issued a rallying cry to Christians to return to the fundamentals of the faith. They published a series of booklets setting out what they perceived to be "the fundamentals" These were declared to be:

❖ The inspiration and authority of scripture
❖ The deity, virgin birth, supernatural miracles, atoning death, physical resurrection, and personal return of Jesus Christ
❖ The reality of sin, salvation by faith through spiritual regeneration, the power of prayer and the duty of evangelism[55]

We might consider how far these items provide an adequate summary of Christian belief. Not that we should assume these items are supposed to embrace the whole of evangelical belief. They were more probably those items of belief which they felt to be most distinctive of evangelicalism and most at risk from liberalism. Nevertheless, is it not alarming that they say not a word about the Love of God or about Jesus' manifest concern for the marginalized members of society? Do they not reduce Christian faith to a set of dogmatic statements (some of dubious validity) rather than as having to do with a living relationship with God, empowered by the Spirit? These are matters which I will pursue later in my theological critique. Modern critics of fundamentalism argue that it is essentially a modern heresy; being a product of the positivistic temper of mind that stems from the Enlightenment. People of biblical and pre-

---

[55] Another statement of these beliefs was issued at a gathering of the General Assembly of the Northern Presbyterian Church in 1910, these five items being declared to be "the fundamentals of faith and of evangelical Christianity." I have highlighted the words or concepts that go beyond the statement given above.

They were:
the inspiration and *infallibility* of Scripture
the deity of Christ
His virgin birth and miracles
His *penal* death for our sins
His physical resurrection and personal return

Enlightenment times knew very well that literature could bear many strands of meaning, such as the mythical and legendary, metaphorical and parabolic as well as the factual and historical. So that the literalist interpretation of scripture typical of fundamentalism is an aberration. Packer[56] rejects this criticism, maintaining that "conservative evangelicalism" (a designation which he prefers to fundamentalism because of the latter's derogatory overtones) is the historic Christian position, going back to Christ and the apostles.

On what grounds do fundamentalists believe the Bible to be an infallible[57] book?

1. Within the New Testament, the passage most often cited in justification of the evangelical doctrine is found at 2 Timothy 3.15-16, in which Paul writes to Timothy, saying "… from a child thou hast known the holy scriptures, which are able to make thee wise unto salvation through faith which is in Christ Jesus. All scripture is given by inspiration of God, and is profitable for doctrine, for reproof, for correction, for instruction in righteousness: that the man of God may be perfect, throughly furnished unto all good works."(KJV). Verse 16 provides the chief ground for the doctrine of scriptural inspiration. Nevertheless these verses do not justify the weight of doctrine placed on them. The translation itself is uncertain. Behind the word "inspiration" is the Greek word "theopneustos," literally "God-breathed." Since the Greek language has no verb "to be," it has to be decided whether 'theopneustos' serves as an adjective or a verb. If it were the former, then the translation should read: "Every God-breathed scripture is profitable for doctrine …" etc. In this case, the question as to which writings are "God-breathed" is an open question. If the latter it should read: "Every scripture is God breathed (i.e. inspired)…, etc." By scripture here is undoubtedly meant the books of the Old Testament, for as yet anything recognizable as the New Testament did not exist. The Christian writings that did already exist, e.g. Paul's letters and one or more gospels were only gradually recognized as "God-inspired" over a period of several decades.

We may compare two modern translations. That of the NRSV goes for the first, traditional option: "All scripture is inspired by God and is useful for teaching, for reproof, for correction," etc. A footnote gives the alternative translation: "Every scripture inspired by God is also …" The REB takes the second option: "All inspired scripture has its use for teaching the truth and refuting error …" etc. But neither of these translations justifies the fundamentalist position. Whilst 2 Timothy 3.15-16 asserts inspiration it makes no claim whatsoever as to infallibility. We do not have to believe in the verbal infallibility of the Bible to

---

[56] J I Packer: *Fundamentalism and the Word of God*, Inter-Varsity Fellowship, 1958.
[57] Another adjective frequently used is "inerrant," ie incapable of being wrong.

agree readily that the scriptures "have power to make us wise and lead us to salvation through faith in Christ Jesus." That they are "useful for teaching the truth and refuting error, for reformation of manners and discipline in right living, so that the man of God may be capable and equipped for good work of every kind" (REB translation) is hardly in dispute. What these verses claim falls far short of asserting that the scriptures are infallible and verbally inerrant.

2. More weighty is the evidence adduced from the passages which attribute scriptural verses to the agency of the Holy Spirit. A number of New Testament quotations from the Psalms especially are introduced by the expression: "as the Holy Spirit said …", e.g. in Acts 1:16 Simon Peter addresses these words to those assembled in Jerusalem: "Friends, the scripture had to be fulfilled, which *the Holy Spirit through David* foretold concerning Judas, who became a guide for those who arrested Jesus." These words refer forward to verse 20, in which Psalm 69.25 is quoted, implying Peter's assumption that the Psalms were composed by King David under the Holy Spirit's inspiration. Whilst such an assumption was then perfectly intelligible, it is no longer. Few modern exegetes would suppose either that all the Psalms were written by David or that this one was directly prophetic of Judas' defection and terrible fate. We can appreciate that the New Testament writers, just like those who inscribed the Dead Sea Scrolls, supposed that all the scriptures referred directly to the events of their own times.

3. The weightiest argument is that Jesus himself, Paul and the authors of the gospels all believed (so we may induce) in the inspiration and authority of the Old Testament scriptures. They appeal to those scriptures as evidence for the divine prediction of what was to be fulfilled in and by Jesus. To which, conservative Christians will add that this was the universal assumption of all Christian theologians throughout the early Church and down the centuries to the Reformation. Therefore, for liberals to approach the scriptures on any other assumption is to part company with the apostolic tradition. This may appear a water-tight case, but it is deceptively so.

Rebuttal of the fundamentalist position

We will contend that it was no more possible for pre-modern Christians to question the assumption of the divine authorship of scripture than it was for them to believe in a spherical Earth or in the centrality of the sun within our solar system. Prior to the European Enlightenment, nobody (with the exception of some of the pre-Christian Greek philosophers) could view the world from a scientific viewpoint. There was never any discussion amongst the Jews as to the authenticity of the scrolls that made up the Old Testament; their inspiration, authorship and authority were simply taken for granted. Neither Jesus nor any of the New Testament writers would have had any grounds for questioning such assumptions. They would have been imbibed with their mother's milk. For Jesus to cite a quotation from Genesis or Exodus as "Moses said ..." was simply to employ the current way of referral. It is unlikely that he gave the matter of their authorship any thought whatever. We cannot expect people of the first century to have asked either 17th or 21st century questions. But it is clear that he claimed to possess an authority higher than that of Moses, an authority derived directly from God. This gave Him authority both to approve and to call into question what Moses had written (according to those assumptions). It was not until the Enlightenment[58] (from the 17th century onwards) that the ascription of Mosaic authorship could be questioned. Only then could serious biblical criticism get under way, eventually obliging a completely new understanding of biblical authorship.

If therefore, we today have to part company with the apostolic tradition, with the assumptions of the medieval Church and of the Protestant Reformers, (or in my case, with my grandparents) in how they understood the scriptures, it is no more remarkable than that as modern people we long since had to part company with Galen on matters of medicine, with Aristotle on matters of philosophy, and with Ptolemy on those of astronomy. But, we may claim that by so doing, we have been able to rid ourselves of mountains of theological "junk" and actually to recover the essentials of the Christian faith. Looking at the Bible with the new eyes of modern research (into which we may believe that the Holy Spirit has led us), we are able to draw closer to the heart of Christian faith than was ever possible within the blinkered assumptions of fundamentalism.

QUESTIONS WE HAVE TO POSE TO FUNDAMENTALISTS
(In this section we will address issues that concern what used to be called Lower Criticism).

• •

Lower Criticism concerns the scholarly work that has to take place before we can begin to interpret the books of the Bible. It concerns the establishment of an accurate text by textual criticism, the scientific study of languages, etc. **Higher Criticism** concerns the interpretation of the text once established, asking such questions as, who wrote it, when, where, for what purpose, etc, and then how it may be understood.

• •

---

[58] "For Luther as for Bacon or Descartes, the way to truth lay in the application of human reason. Received authority, whether of Ptolemy in the sciences or of the church in matters of the spirit, was to be subject to the probings of unfettered minds." Extract from *Encyclopedia Britannica* 2002, article on the Enlightenment.

1. We should have to ask fundamentalists which version of the Bible it is that is infallible? It cannot be any particular English translation in spite of the attempt by many to exalt the KJV to the status of "the inspired text," such an evaluation depending on the supposed (but wholly erroneous) perfection of the so-called Textus Receptus on which it was based. There are undoubtedly some translations better than others, but of none could we say, "This is the inerrant Bible." In practice, fundamentalists generally concur that the inerrant text is that originally written.

2. But what was the text originally written? It cannot be any particular manuscript of the Old or New Testaments extant today, since no two manuscripts are identical. The Church adopted the Jewish canon of Old Testament scripture and the text standardized by the Masoretes (in the early centuries AD). We know from the Dead Sea Scrolls that, even in Jesus' day, the texts were not yet standardized. To give but one example, there are amongst the scrolls three manuscripts of the book of Jeremiah, yet one of these is a third shorter than the other two. Which of these is the authentic manuscript? We cannot say. The case is yet more confusing as regards the New Testament. None of the original orthographs exist. All modern Greek texts of the New Testament are the result of patient sifting and evaluation by textual critics, but we cannot say of any one that it is, without doubt the original, infallible text. If such did exist, we probably wouldn't recognize it. This makes a nonsense of the Universities and Colleges Christian Fellowship's adherence to "the divine inspiration and infallibility of Holy Scripture, as originally given."[59] F F Bruce, having quoted this statement explains that "The phrase "as originally given" does not imply that the qualities of inspiration and infallibility belong to some lost and irrecoverable stage of the biblical text." I do not see what else they can mean.

3. How can we treat as infallible a text which is in places obscure? The internal evidence of the Bible does not support the notion of an inerrant text. At various points within the Old Testament in any reliable modern translation, we come across the translator's notes such as these: "Hebrew unintelligible" (e.g. at 2 Samuel 7.23); or, "Hebrew word of uncertain meaning" (e.g. 2 Samuel 17.20); "probable reading" (2 Samuel 17.28); "Hebrew obscure" (2 Samuel 22.44) or, that the Hebrew lacks a word which has been conjecturally supplied by the translator, usually from a Greek or Syriac translation, e.g. 2 Samuel 23.18, where the Hebrew gives the number "three" but the Syriac gives "30" which makes better sense within the context.[60] Let us take an example from the New

---

[59] In F F Bruce, *The Canon of Scripture*, Chapter House, 1988, p 287.
[60] All these examples are from the Revised English Bible.

Testament: how does Mark's Gospel end? Almost all scholars accept that whatever is printed in our Bibles beyond chapter 16.8 was not written by Mark. Are the shorter or the longer endings, both supplied by another hand, to be considered as truly scriptural? From such examples it becomes clear that the text is plainly not infallible. That being the case, it would be illogical to ascribe infallibility to the whole Bible.

4. Is it surely demeaning to God to ascribe to him the errors, contradictions, repetitions, and apparently approved immoral behavior that are undoubtedly present in the biblical text once we open our eyes to notice them? I will justify this statement with some examples.

a. Errors? Mark 2.23-28 reports the episode in which, one Sabbath day, Jesus' disciples plucked and ate ears of corn whilst walking through the field. When the Pharisees accused them of Sabbath-breaking, Jesus defended them by referring to an episode in the Old Testament when David's men entered the Temple at Shiloh, and, in their hunger, ate the shewbread that was reserved for priests only. Jesus is reported to have described the event as taking place "when Abiathar was high priest." But if we look at this episode in 1 Samuel 21.1-6 we will see that the high priest at this time was Ahimelech (Abiathar's father). This is clearly an error; but whose error? That of Jesus, of the oral tradition, or of Mark?

b. Contradictions? (1) The last chapter of 1 Samuel tells the story of King Saul's death on the battlefield. Rather than being captured and killed by the Philistines, Saul directs his own armour-bearer to kill him. The man refuses to do so, whereupon Saul falls on his own sword (1 Samuel 21.19). This is crystal clear. But in the first chapter of 2 Samuel, a wholly different account is given of the King's death. He urges an Amalekite (apparently on the battlefield by chance) to kill him, which he does. This is what the Amalekite tells David when he questions him. Of course, it could be that the Amalekite was lying in order to curry David's favor. But David takes him at his word and has the Amalekite killed on the spot. These are two inconsistent accounts.

(2) There are similar discrepancies concerning the manner of Judas' death. In Matthew 27.5, Judas hanged himself, having repented of his act of betrayal and thrown down the 30 pieces of silver in the Temple; subsequently the priests bought a field with this money. But according to Acts 1.15-19, Judas himself purchased the field, in which he then fell, his stomach burst open and he died.

(3) We might imagine that there could be no possible doubt as to who killed the giant Goliath of Gath. Who has not heard of young David's exploit recounted in 1 Sam. 17? And yet 2 Sam.21.19 ascribes it to an Israelite called Elhanan. "Then there was another battle with the Philistines at Gob; and Elhanan son of Jaare-

oregim, the Bethlehemite, killed Goliath the Gittite, the shaft of whose spear was like a weaver's beam." A possible explanation may come from the Anglo-Saxons. Their warriors used to ascribe all victories and spoils of battle to their chieftain. Might this explain how the conquest of Goliath came to be attributed to David?

c. Repetitions? These are considerable. The books of Chronicles repeat most of the content of the books of Kings, but with a different slant (they represent the priestly viewpoint as opposed to that of the Deuteronomists). This is no different from how, in English history, Whigs differed from Tories, or in the USA, Republicans from Democrats, in their accounts of historical episodes. This is a reminder that there is no uniform viewpoint in the history of Israel or that of the early Christian Church, but several, sometimes representing conflicting interests.

Such repetition is also to be found within single narratives. For example, the content of Genesis 6.5-8 is repeated in verses 11-13 (but note "God" in the latter, "the Lord" in the former section).

d. Immoral behavior? Lot was Abraham's nephew, who had parted company with his uncle and had settled himself and his family in Sodom. Because of the extreme wickedness of its population, God decided to destroy Sodom and its neighboring city of Gomorrah. He sent messengers (human or angelic?) to warn both Abraham and Lot of the cities' impending doom. When the messengers arrived in Sodom and took shelter in Lot's house, they were besieged by the men of the city, intent on sexually assaulting Lot's male guests. Lot refused to permit this, but, in order to assuage the men's lust, offered to hand over his virgin daughters to them! It was always a sacred duty to shelter and defend one's guests, but how could a father offer to subject his daughters to gang-rape? Yet this father was supposedly a righteous man, worthy to be rescued from the doom about to befall the city. The way the story is told implies that the story-teller counted women as being of little value and therefore disposable. This is further exemplified in Lot's wife being turned to stone; and further on, in the incestuous relations of Lot's daughters with their father. This is employed so as to demonstrate why the Moabites and the Ammonites (originating in incest) were a thoroughly bad lot, always enemies of Israel.
I have not been gratuitously looking "to pick holes" in the biblical narrative. But such errors and inconsistencies are present and we have to be able to account for them. The fundamentalist position rigorously maintained would have to lay all these faults at God's door. Better to accept that God alone is infallible, and that all errors and confusion are to be laid at the door of his human servants, in which respect we recognize that the Bible writers were little different from ourselves. If we recognize the Bible as the human book that it is, then the errors

pose little problem. In our daily newspapers, there will be conflicting accounts of what happened yesterday, yet alone 50 years ago. To err is human. But human testimony to what God has done can still carry conviction even though there may not be any unanimity in the telling of the tale. The reader of the Bible is not unlike the juryman or woman in the law court. His and her task is to sift through the conflicting evidence and to come to a conclusion. The author's conviction is that despite all human faults and failings, the Bible nevertheless testifies to the Acts of God within human history and within individual lives.

5. Ascribing authorship to God necessarily obscures the personal, sometimes idiosyncratic characteristics of its human authors? The notion of "accommodation," by which it is proposed that God's inspiration accommodates itself to the personality of each human writer, is most unconvincing. It is yet more unconvincing to suppose that inspiration could possibly imply a complete take-over of an author's brain-cells, reducing a human being to a mere cipher! That is not how God relates to human beings, nor is it the impression given by any of the biblical authors.

6. Detailed study of the Bible reveals that its anonymous authors did not themselves treat the Scriptural text as if it were infallible. The fundamentalist assumption as to the manner of divine inspiration is not apparent within the processes by which the books of the Bible were actually written, once these are examined with the tools of modern scholarship. Study any section of the Torah in detail. The Ten Commandments as presented in Exodus 20 and Deureronomy 6 provide a good starting point. Whatever part Moses played in their promulgation, close examination makes it clear that we have here two highly edited versions of them. The mention of slaves being present within Israel, and to "the aliens within your gates" indicate that they cannot have been composed in the wilderness of Sinai, but centuries later when the Israelites had settled in Canaan. The evidence for this has been explained more fully in Chapter 6. Whatever Moses originally formulated, every generation of priests, prophets and law-givers felt it their responsibility to revise, up-date and reformulate what had been passed down to them. It wasn't until the fifth century or later that the priests and scribes gathered around Ezra, having by then lost all historical understanding as to how the Torah had been put together, ascribed it all to Moses and declared it be untouchable because the holy Word of God. It was only at that stage that the notion became enshrined in Jewish religion such that the written pages took on a hallowed glow and were declared to be infallible. Fundamentalism only arose in retrospect.

7. The same is the case with the New Testament. Examine the ways in which Matthew and Luke made use of the manuscript of Mark's Gospel that lay before them and you will observe the liberty with which they went about their task.

Mark's was not yet so sacred a text that it couldn't be altered which I have demonstrated in Chapter 10. Nor is there any hint whatsoever that Paul understood his letters to be in any way on a par with scripture. He believed that he was commissioned by God to be an apostle and was therefore authorized to address his congregations with authority. Nevertheless, he differentiated between what the Lord had said from his own opinion (although even on that he claimed "to have the mind of Christ").

8. Already in the second century AD, some within the Christian community were making comparisons and noting the differences between the gospels. Some even objected to John's Gospel on the ground of its incompatibility with the Synoptic accounts. So it is not true to assert that gospel criticism only began in the 17th century. There was considerable discussion within the early Church as to which books were acceptable within the canon of the New Testament. In the end, familiarity, antiquity and supposedly apostolic authorship decided the content of the canon. It was therefore a long process before the books of the New Testament were regarded with the same reverence as had been those of the Old Testament. In time, they too were regarded as works of divine inspiration and therefore inerrant.

9. The fact is that fundamentalism is wholly dependent on the initial premise from which we began this study, but have shown to be faulty. If the approach is that of the *Deductive Method*, and we assume, as fundamentalists do, a) that Christians need an infallible authority and b) that that authority *is* the Bible, then the actual reading of the Bible undertaken on the basis of that assumption is necessarily blinkered. The brain is remarkably adept at screening out what has been made unacceptable to us by means of teaching received in childhood or by the kind of brain-washing practiced by some of the cults. Many a cult is coercive in its catechesis of converts. Every seeming discrepancy, contradiction, plain error of fact or ambiguity is explained away (by some extraordinarily casuistic thinking). But drop the assumptions, adopt the *Inductive Method* (the method of all scientific research), study the text as far as possible without prior assumptions, take seriously the discrepancies, the contradictions, the repetitions, etc, and seek for the most likely explanations of them, and the major results of modern scholarly work on the Bible can be arrived at for oneself.

Theological critique of fundamentalism (Addressing what used to be called the Higher Criticism)

I have already voiced some generalized criticism of the original statement of the "fundamentals" as an arbitrarily selected and inadequate account of Christian belief. I will make these further specific points:

❖ The fundamentals turn out to be a quite arbitrary selection of Christian beliefs. They are not based on any serious consideration of the historical roots of Christian faith. Treating the Bible as if a compendium of infallible statements (without regard to context and background), they thus misrepresent the Bible that is supposedly their authority. They ignore the fact that the Bible essentially tells a story, of God's interaction firstly with the people of Israel and then with those who followed Jesus. The story itself invites a response of faith and obedience. It doesn't itself propose specific items that those who hear the story are then obliged to believe on pain of excommunication if they don't. The entirety of the Old Testament never proposes any credal statements other than those that re-enact the Exodus from Egypt, for Old Testament religion was concerned with practice rather than with belief. It demanded always a practical response. If Micah raises the question: "What does the Lord require of you?" the Lord's response is not, "You must believe this, that and the other …", a notion wholly foreign to biblical religion, but rather: "He has told you, O mortal, what is good; and what does the Lord require of you but to do justice, and to love kindness, and to walk humbly with your God?" (Micah 6.8). But we note that justice, kindness and walking humbly with God don't figure amongst the fundamentals.

❖ And it is much the same with Jesus. There is not a single incident in which he quizzed anybody on what precisely he or she believed. He frequently commended faith, which he and his hearers would have presumed to indicate an absolute trust in the faithfulness of God. In the case of the Roman centurion whose servant (or son) Jesus healed, he spoke approvingly of his faith (evidenced by the fact that he had only to believe Jesus' words to know that his son was healed) as being greater than any he had met with amongst the people of Israel. Clearly faith here implied belief in Jesus as the one to whom God had entrusted the authority to heal. After many healings he declared to the person concerned: "Your faith has healed you." Jesus appears not to have been interested in doctrinal statements. The only creed he commended was that of the two greatest commandments: that we should love God and our neighbor as ourselves (Mark 12.30-31). Loving or trustful deeds impressed him more than words. He asked for nothing more than a non-defined faith. In the Old Testament and the gospels, faith always means "an active trust in God" – never any system of doctrinal beliefs that we could summaries as "the Faith."

❖ Let us mention, for closer examination, just one of these fundamentals, that headed as *The Virgin Birth*. The term is itself a misnomer. For what is in question is the manner of Jesus' conception, not of his birth (although the Catholic and Orthodox Churches did go on to declare that even his birth was without parturition, i.e. it involved none of the physical processes of labor). But to exalt his virgin birth to a major object of belief is to do what the earliest Christian proclamation never did,[61] for it formed no part of the kerygma[62] of the early Church (being unknown to Mark as to Paul and to John), which centered wholly on the salvific nature of his death and resurrection.

❖ It is also to misinterpret the intention of Matthew and Luke's birth narratives. Neither of them, in their respective gospels, propose for us any doctrine of Virgin Birth. Each is writing a largely legendary[63] account of Jesus' birth to express their belief in the uniqueness of Jesus as the Son of God, presenting it as yet more wondrous than all the stories of miraculous births recounted in the Old Testament. They are not recounting biology (the biological data which explains how conception occurs were not known until the early 19th century); but as the creative artists that they were, they were rehearsing the wonderful acts of God in such a way as to bring their readers and hearers to "wonder, love and praise." To create of this a dogma – which the authors of the Apostles' and the Nicene Creeds had done by the fourth and fifth centuries – is largely to misrepresent the gospel stories. It would be akin to taking a Rembrandt painting, say, of the Holy Family, and reducing its value to that of the chemical components of the paints he used. The New Testament never proposes that every Christian had to believe in the Virgin Birth (the notion is foreign to it). Sadly, the Church of those centuries was fast losing sight of its Jewish roots and becoming pre-occupied with its attempt to analyze the faith in the terms of Greek philosophy. This was the stage at which the language of adoration was turned into the language of dogma, and Christian behavior became more a matter of what you believed (deteriorating to the point where you could be burned for heresy if you didn't) than of the Christ-like way you lived.

❖ Belief in the inspiration of the scriptures doesn't need to assert inerrancy. Do we not, in Christian worship at its best, experience moments of inspiration when it is as if God is speaking to us through the mouth of his human servant? Just as we also recognize occasions of inspiration in a piece of prose or poetry, in a piece of music or a great painting; yet we wouldn't dream of ascribing infallibility to any of them. If that is how God's Spirit operates within the Christian community today, it is surely not unreasonable to suppose that in biblical times He operated in a very similar manner.

---

[61] Of course, the Church did eventually; for the Virgin Birth is declared in both the Apostles' and the Nicene Creeds; but since the Apostles' Creed did not see the light of day until the fourth century, it dubiously represents the faith of the apostles.

[62] Kerygma, a Greek word meaning "a public proclamation." In Biblical study, kerygma stands for the message preached by the early Christians – its content can be most clearly discerned in the speeches attributed to Peter in the Acts of the Apostles and in the letters of Paul.

[63] We have to describe it as legendary (if not mythical) since the accounts of Jesus' ministry in all four gospels display no knowledge of Jesus' birth. The few references to his mother Mary give no indication whatsoever of there having been anything unusual about his birth.

❖ To expect infallibility in anything human, whether in people or in institutions (even supposedly holy ones) is to expect more than we have any right to expect. If Paul could write in his great passage on the nature of love (1 Corinthians 13): "For now we see through a glass, darkly; but then face to face: now I know in part; but then shall I know even as also I am known." (1 Corinthians 13.12 KJV). Or, as it is put in the REB: "At present we see only puzzling reflections in a mirror, but one day we shall see face to face. My knowledge now is partial; then it will be whole, like God's knowledge of me." Paul's statement demolishes any notion that we need absolute knowledge or infallible authority. He declares the limitations of our earthbound knowledge yet looks forward to the perfection of vision that will be granted us in the hereafter, when we shall know God as fully as He knows us. On earth "we walk by faith and not by sight" (2 Corinthians 5.7). Fundamentalism assumes that we have a right to total vision and certainty of faith. The biblical witness offers us no such thing.

❖ It should be asked whether the craving after infallibility, after an absolute assurance of faith, does not constitute a form of idolatry? The craving whether for infallible book or infallible church is a seeking after sight rather than faith; in effect a rejection of the sufficiency of faith.
Such craving is to behave as the Israelites did in the wilderness, who, wearying of Moses' absence up the mountain, rebelled against the God who was invisible to human eyes and preferred to construct their own god, a golden calf. For many, the infallible Bible is such a golden calf.

The essence of idolatry is that it refuses trust in God alone and fabricates its own god, which being a human artefact, is itself manipulable The idol, whether of metal or mental construction, is something we control, to which we give orders, which exists to serve our will. It is a puppet at the service of our egotism.

What are the consequences of fundamentalism?

1. Fundamentalism trivializes the concept of inspiration. The Bible is like a landscape of huge variety, with high mountains and deep valleys, flat plains and mighty river courses; which fundamentalism reduces to one level. It trivializes the concept by reducing to one level all the multi-faceted literature found in scripture. Whilst all Christians would surely recognize the extraordinary levels of inspiration in 1 Corinthians 13's eulogy of love, in Jesus' teaching at the Last Supper table or in the Johannine depiction of Christ as the true Vine; what inspiration did the apostle Paul require when he wrote: "When you come, bring the cloak that I left with Carpus at Troas, also the books, and above all the parchments"? This gives an intriguing insight into the daily life of Paul. Is it possible to deny that there are in the Bible many pages of wholly commonplace

information, instruction or regulation which neither required inspiration nor can be of any relevance whatsoever today?

2. Fundamentalism encourages the irresponsible quotation of single verses of scripture without regard for the context in which they are set. This could hardly have been done before the mid-16th century, for it was only then that editions of the Bible were printed with verse divisions, with each verse commencing on a new line. For its proper interpretation, a verse has to be understood within its context.

3. Fundamentalism fails to perceive the many voices which are to be heard in the pages of scripture. To cite but one example: the story of Jesus' Temptations in the wilderness can be read in both Matthew and Luke's Gospels, in chapter four of each. Within the narrative we clearly discern three voices: there is the voice of the narrator relating the story; secondly that of Satan (who, be it noted, is adept at quoting scripture to his advantage); in third place, we hear Jesus' response. He also quotes scripture in repudiation of the satanic suggestions. To propose that God is merely playing the ventriloquist, that each voice is in fact God's voice, makes a nonsense of the reality of Jesus' experience. Throughout the scriptures of the Old and New Testaments, a multitude of voices are heard, amongst them that of God (through his human intermediaries). That can only be discerned if we learn to distinguish it from the clamor of human voices, some truly representing God, some misrepresenting Him.

4. A more serious charge to be laid against fundamentalism is that it confuses the relationship between Old and New Testaments. If all is inspired, then what is written in the Old Testament should be considered quite as authoritative for Christians as what is in the New Testament. This wholly fails to recognize what was innovative in the teaching of Jesus or why any new covenant was necessary. The early Church had speedily to resolve the question whether the Mosaic Torah was binding on Gentile converts to the faith; it concluded that it was not. We too have to recognize that much of the Old Testament has authority only for Jews. But even as a Jew, Jesus paid scant regard to a number of its prescriptions. I will say more about this in Chapter 19.

5. Fundamentalists are frequently people of an authoritarian state of mind, who, out of personal insecurity, need a dogmatic framework of belief. We have only to think of certain tele-evangelists in the USA or politicians in Ulster as examples of those who manipulate their spurious authority either for personal gain or for political power in situations of insecurity. They prey upon the ignorant, the gullible and the vulnerable, offering them a bogus sense of security. Sadly, many such people look for an institution that can direct their lives in every respect. To them, an infallible book or infallible church is attractive, for by obeying its precepts, they give up on personal responsibility

and having to take their own decisions. For this reason the fundamentalist sect, with its infallible leadership wielding its infallible book will always be attractive to insecure persons, but this is also potentially extremely damaging. Instead of being set free, they adopt the path of servitude to a bogus ideology.

A Shameful History

It has to be noted that many of the most shameful attitudes and deeds performed by Christians down the centuries have frequently occurred and been justified by fundamentalist readings of scripture.

1. HOLY WAR

Christians have gone to war and committed the most heinous atrocities, justifying their actions by the example of episodes from the Old Testament, as if these were exemplary for Christians. The prime example is from the Crusades. The Crusaders supposed themselves to be in the tradition of the Holy War. Some of them were responsible for pogroms of Jewish communities in central Europe; the wholesale slaughter of Jews and Muslims, men, women and children, when at last they captured Jerusalem on July 15, 1099; and the sacking, looting and massacre of Orthodox Christians in Constantinople (the peoples to whose rescue they had supposedly gone) under the Fourth Crusade in 1204. They supposed that they were doing no more than had been commended in the books of Joshua and Deuteronomy. The repercussions of such violence are readily embodied in Middle Eastern politics to this day, wholly souring relations between Muslims and Christians.

2. TERRITORIAL CONQUEST AND GENOCIDE

Many migrant communities, Christian in name, encountering aboriginal peoples during the colonization of supposedly virgin territories, have regarded themselves as the new Israelites, invited by God to take possession of these lands and have not hesitated to slaughter indigenous peoples who have appeared to them as barbarous (because alien) and pagan. So North American Indians, Bushmen and Bantus in Southern Africa, Aboriginals in Australia have been slaughtered, their lands seized, their survivors enslaved, in the name of the God who commanded the Israelites to slaughter the Canaanites. In such situations, it has been to the Old Testament rather than to the New that fundamentalist Christians have looked.

3. SLAVERY

The infamy of slavery was long justified because it was supposedly scriptural. It was Christian slave traders from Europe who traded guns and rum for slaves throughout West Africa, transporting them by the millions to the Caribbean and North America, justifying their actions on the ground of the Bible's apparent toleration of slavery. We should not forget that much of the United Kingdom's prosperity, which financed the Industrial Revolution and so made Britain the most powerful nation in the world, was achieved on the economic basis of the huge profits made both from the slave-trade and from the plantations worked by slaves. Genesis 9.25 was frequently quoted, a passage which depicts God as cursing Canaan, the son of Ham, to perpetual servitude for the sin of having looked on his father's nakedness whilst the latter was drunk! It is difficult to see why this was supposed so heinous a deed to have suffered so dire a punishment! Originally the episode was used in order to justify the subjection of the Canaanites (i.e. those who had not been slaughtered) to perpetual slavery. Recall how the Gibeonites, because of their deception, were rendered "hewers of wood and drawers of water" (Joshua 9.21-27). There was no justification whatever for the later assumption that Ham was the father of the black races! This was a Christian fiction, cynically invented to justify the enslavement of all the black races.

It was to the credit of evangelical Christians around William Wilberforce that they campaigned and succeeded in abolishing, first the trade, and later the institution of slavery in territories under the British dominion, in the 19th century. But Christians had tolerated it and profited by it for centuries. Many of their opponents (equally Christian) pointed out how it was commonplace for the patriarchs to keep slaves and that the institution of slavery had persisted for centuries in Israel. They would have added that Jesus was not known to have said anything about it and that Paul apparently tolerated it. But more attention should have been paid to the apostle's letter to Philemon, in which he commends this well-to-do Christian to receive back Onesimus, his run-away slave. He demands that he be received as a "brother in Christ." And he declares in Galatians 3.27-28: "As many of you as were baptized into Christ have clothed yourselves with Christ. There is no longer Jew or Greek, there *is no longer slave or free*, there is no longer male and female; for all of you are one in Christ Jesus." It is shameful that it took 18 centuries for Christians to put into practice what Paul had demonstrated in principle.

4. APARTHEID

The practice of apartheid in South Africa arose from the same roots as those which justified slavery for so long. The Dutch Reformed Church (predominant in South Africa) had always been an extremely conservative body and was politically hand-in-glove with the Nationalist Party which swept to electoral victory in 1948. It was the heir to the old Boer traditions that saw the entry of their forbears into South Africa as being akin to that of the Israelites into the Promised Land. Being wholly ignorant of the culture of the Bushmen and Hottentots, and later of the more sophisticated Zulu and other Bantu peoples, it assumed them to be both pagan and inferior but also highly desirable as forced labor. They found their attitudes powerfully reinforced by their reading of the Old Testament. The Bantu and others were fit only to be "hewers of wood and drawers of water;" and when such a stereotype was challenged by the fact of the rising expectations of the African populations and proven capability of many, conveniently invented the doctrine of apartheid (meaning "separateness") so as to subject them to a position of permanent inferiority in South African society. A group of 150 mostly younger theologians broke ranks with their seniors, declaring (in the Kairos document of 1985) "why the Church should stand against the civil authorities on the side of the oppressed against the apartheid regime," and was one of the factors that led to the overthrow of the system and the election of Nelson Mandela's African National Congress.

5. ANTI-SEMITISM

There was nothing anti-Semitic in the teaching and behavior of Jesus. How could there have been, since he was himself a Jew and understood his mission to be to "the lost sheep of the house of Israel" (Matthew 10.6)? He felt free to criticize sternly the leadership of his people as "false shepherds" of the sheep. But undoubtedly, anti-Semitism had crept into Christian attitudes and even into the pages of the New Testament within 50 or so years of his lifetime. How else to account for the playing up of the Jewish role in his crucifixion and the attendant whitewashing of Roman responsibility for it, apparent especially in the gospels of Matthew and of John. In the latter, his opponents are regularly starkly termed "the Jews" (as if he were not one) and these as being hateful to God. It is highly probable that all such passages stem from the mid-80s to 90s AD when Jewish Christians had been excommunicated from the synagogues and attitudes between Jew and Christian had deteriorated from tolerance to suspicion and hatred. It was easy too, ever since the Roman sacking of the Temple in AD 70 to interpret this as God's final judgment on the Jewish people. So a text such as that of Matthew 27.24-25, telling how Pilate, at the conclusion of Jesus' trial before him, publicly washed his hands, declaring himself to be innocent of Jesus' blood, upon which "the people as a whole" answered: "His blood be on us and on our children," was taken to be vindication of the notion that whatever ills befell the Jewish race were the nemesis brought upon themselves. How chilling that throughout Christian history until quite recent times, some Christians have supposed it their right to kill Jews without compunction. And almost as chilling that it was not until 1965 that the Roman Catholic Church officially lifted its interdiction on the Jewish people, declaring them to be not collectively guilty of the death of Jesus.[64] Anti-Semitism has been a very dark stain on Christian history.

6. ANTIFEMINISM

The Christian Church has been deplorably marked by anti-feminism through the ages and in some quarters still is to this day. This was the result of the marked patriarchalism of the Old Testament; to the fact that Jesus chose only males to be apostles (thought by some to be an insuperable objection to the ordination of women) and more specifically to the negative thinking of Paul in some of his letters. Women should not be permitted to speak in Church, which effectively debarred them from ministry (1 Corinthians 14.34-36). He taught a wholly submissive status for women in respect of their husbands; "just as Christ is the head of the man, so the husband is the head of his wife." Further on we read that the woman is the reflection of the man and was created for the sake of man (1 Corinthians 11.3-16), the whole based on a literalist understanding of the second creation story in Genesis 2. Had he heeded the equality of male and female declared in Genesis 1, he could not have uttered such an absurdity. Add to this the Manichean attitudes towards everything bodily that invaded the Catholic Church from the fourth century onwards; hence the elevation of celibacy (eventually its enforcement on all who would be priests) and its all too frequently misogynist attitude towards women. Women were seen as Eve-like temptresses, to be permanently subjugated to inferior status, because so dangerous. Statements by medieval theologians are almost incredible: "Woman is an occasional and incomplete being, a misbegotten male. It is unchangeable that woman is destined to live under man's influence and has no authority from her Lord." Thus wrote Thomas Aquinas,[65] the greatest Catholic theologian of the Middle Ages.

Although the matter of women's ordination isn't necessarily a matter of feminism or anti-feminism, in practice it has been much affected by it. Although the Church of England passed measures to ordain women as priests in 1992, many of their women priests still suffer discrimination. In the Roman Catholic Church, Pope John Paul II has ruled out of order even any discussion within church circles as to the possibility of ordaining women. As for Jesus having chosen only men to be apostles, has it not occurred that he also chose none but Jews? Some of the Free Churches ordained women almost a hundred years ago and in principle seek to assure an absolute equality of opportunity for men and women in ministry.

7. HOMOPHOBIA

This remains a matter of extreme sensitivity causing much pain. Issues concerning the possibility of permitting same-sex marriages or ordaining as clergy men and women known to be homosexual threaten to split churches. On

---

[64] In its Declaration on the relationship of the Church to Non-Christian religions (2nd Vatican Council, 1965): "Even though the Jewish authorities and those who followed their lead pressed for the death of Christ (see John 16.6), neither all Jews indiscriminately at that time, nor Jews today, can be charged with crimes committed during his passion." Vatican Council II, Constitutions, Decrees, Declarations p 573. General Editor: Austin Flannery, OP.
[65] In Lavinia Byrne, *Women before God*, p 6, SPCK, London 1988.

the one side are attitudes wholly condemnatory, chiefly based on biblical passages from the Book of Leviticus and from the teaching of Paul. To biblical conservatives, no sexual practice other than that of male and female within marriage is permissible. On the other side, there are those who argue for a more permissive (and they would argue, more Christian) attitude on a number of grounds: *One*, that there is no record of what Jesus thought or said on the matter. Whereas there is considerable evidence that he befriended those who in his own day were considered outcast, being called "the friend of tax-collectors and sinners." *Two*, that to be of homosexual orientation is not in itself sinful, but is a matter of genetic inheritance (for which a person can hardly be blamed) rather than a perverse inclination. *Three*, now that homosexual practice between consenting adults is no longer a criminal offence, note has to be taken of the not inconsiderable proportion of males and females who are of homosexual orientation, amongst them many who make a considerable contribution to society, especially in the fields of art, music and literature. Amongst them are many who believe in and practice Christian faith. Are these to be permanently discriminated against? Four, the fact is that there are many Christian clergy, and probably always have been, who are both "gay" and highly regarded as caring pastors (many of them ordained before any questions were asked about one's private life). Whilst it is understandable that Christians differ sharply on what is permissible to homosexuals, homophobia can never be justified.

8: THE STATE OF ISRAEL

This last example is given in illustration of the fact that fundamentalism can still be a major contributor to hot political issues. With the historical background of widespread anti-Semitism amongst Christians, it would seem surprising to find large numbers of American fundamentalists giving ardent support to successive Israeli Prime Ministers in their repressive measures against the Palestinians. But such is the case. Fundamentalist Christians have always been strongly drawn to the apocalyptic passages in the Bible. The expectation of the imminent return of Jesus in clouds of glory, with true believers being lifted up in the rapture, has been much heightened by current events in the Middle East. A wholly unhistorical and uncritical reading of Old Testament prophecies has lead to the belief that what is happening in Israel are "signs of the end." The consequence is that we see fundamentalist Christians joining forces with ultra Orthodox Jews, openly supporting the mass influx of Jews into the Promised land, no matter what dispossession, oppression, and brutal mistreatment is inflicted on the indigenous Palestinian population, amongst them the tiny remaining community of Arab Christians. A television documentary in 2002 reported that when President Bush was demanding that Israel withdraw its forces from the West Bank, a phone-call from Gerry Falwell, claiming to have 70 million evangelical Christians behind him, urged him to lay off. Mr Sharon should be given total freedom to deal with the Palestinians as he wished. It has been said that Orthodox Jews discover to their surprise that "their safety belt is the USA's Bible belt."

In 1999 I heard Dr Edward Shehardeh, Medical Director of BASRA (the Bethlehem Arab Society's Hospital for Rehabilitation) express the sentiment that "God had forgotten his Palestinian Christians" and urged our pilgrim group not to do so. Evidently 70 million Christians have done so, a wicked betrayal of their brothers and sisters in Christ.

In all or most of the above attitudes and activities of Christians through the centuries there have doubtless been very many different causes, but in every one of them a fundamentalist reading of scripture has been powerfully argued in justification of them, thus adding to the sum total of prejudice, violence and evil in the world.

The following article, posted on the Internet, was printed in the monthly newsletter of Oxted United Reformed Church in the United Kingdom.

This tongue-in-cheek, hilarious, but also deeply serious, contribution, points up the hypocrisy of picking out just one extract from a book of the Bible, whilst wholly ignoring other stipulations in the same book. If we were to follow rigorously every injunction within the Old Testament, we would be not only executing homosexuals, but stoning adulterers and Sabbath-breakers, burning witches, even executing disobedient children! Does any Christian seriously suppose that we should be doing all that ?

LEVITICUS AND ALL THAT!

Laura Schlessinger is a US radio personality. Recently, she said that as an observant orthodox Jew, she believed homosexuality to be an abomination according to Leviticus 18:22 and therefore could not be condoned under any circumstances.

The following is an open letter to Dr Laura penned by a US resident* ...

Dear Dr Laura,

Thank you for doing so much to educate people regarding God's Law. I have learned a great deal from your show, and I try to share that knowledge with as many people as I can. When someone tries to defend the homosexual lifestyle, for example, I simply remind them that Leviticus 18:22 clearly states it to be an abomination. End of debate. I do need some advice from you, however, regarding some other specific laws and how to follow them.

1. When I burn a bull on the altar as a sacrifice, I know it creates a pleasing odour for the Lord (Lev.1:9). The problem is my neighbours. They claim the odour is not pleasing to them. Should I smite them?

2. I would like to sell my daughter into slavery, as sanctioned in Exodus 21:7. In this day and age, what do you think would be a fair price for her?

3. Lev 25:44 states that I may indeed possess slaves, both male and female, provided they are purchased from neighbouring nations. A friend of mine claims that this applies to Mexicans, but not Canadians. Can you clarify? Why can't I own Canadians?

4. I have a neighbour who insists on working on the Sabbath. Exodus 35.2 clearly states that he should be put to death. Am I morally obliged to kill him myself?

5. A friend of mine feels that even if eating shellfish is an abomination (Lev. 11.10), it is a lesser abomination than homosexuality. I don't agree. Can you settle this?

6. My uncle has a farm. He violates Lev 19:19 by planting two different crops in the same field, as does his wife by wearing garments made of two different kinds of thread (cotton/polyester blend). He also tends to curse and blaspheme a lot. Is it really necessary that we go to all the trouble of getting the whole town together to stone them? (Lev 24: 10-16) Couldn't we just burn them to death at a private family affair like we do with people who sleep with their in-laws? (Lev 20:14)

I know you have studied these things extensively, so I am confident you can help. Thank you again for reminding us that God's word is eternal and unchanging.

Your devoted disciple and adoring fan, ...

---

* Of course we would gladly attribute this piece to its author if we only knew it.

CHAPTER 17:
BIBLICAL CRITICISM – ATTACK
AND DEFENSE

The counter attack

When Alan Richardson wrote his classic *Christian Apologetics* some 55 years ago, he could assume that against all other methods of interpreting the Bible, that of literary-cum-historical criticism had "won the field". He would surely have been both surprised and disturbed to know that some 30 years later, its very foundations would come under severe attack. To readers in touch with the world of biblical criticism over these last years, the very content of this book may seem like "old hat." Of course, in this book I have been able to outline only the main lines of the critical approach, without mentioning the many caveats and criticisms made of it.

The main attack has been along these lines:

1. That biblical criticism originated in the mind-set of those who launched the Enlightenment in the 18th century, accepting its values, mostly hostile to revealed religion, too readily.

2. That biblical criticism has encouraged an all too rationalistic, skeptical and negative attitude, virtually tearing any traditional understanding of the Bible. to shreds.

3. That biblical criticism had the effect of destroying any proper understanding of the Bible as the authoritative scripture of the Christian Church. So we have heard the cry: Let's get back to scripture! This has been reinforced by a theological movement that promotes what it calls "Canonical Criticism." How valid are these criticisms?

1. The Enlightenment

The Enlightenment marked a huge intellectual leap forward, whereby the more educated and thoughtful people in most countries of Western Europe and North America rejected the stranglehold that authoritarianism in church and state had long exercised over men's and women's minds. This freed them to investigate life and nature for themselves. Consider what had happened to

Galileo Galilei. He had built up a formidable body of evidence to support Copernicus' hypothesis that the sun and not planet Earth was central to the solar system. Because the Roman Church assumed the right to control men's thoughts, especially when it came to their publication, it hounded and harassed poor Galileo into recantation of what he knew to be true. Enlightenment man refused to accept such gagging. The consequence was an outburst of free-thinking. In America, this inspired the principles of American democracy; as James Barr writes[66] : "… the greatest single social document of the Enlightenment … is without doubt the Constitution of the United States." But, not surprisingly, it also produced many attacks on Christianity. It led on the continent to Atheism and in England to Deism (i.e. to belief in a Deity who had created the universe, on mechanical principles, then left it to its own devices). It created the illusion that Humankind was perfectible (inventing the idea of "the noble savage") and that ignorance and superstition could be dispersed by the free exercise of human reasoning. Humanity didn't need any special revelation of God – it could work out everything necessary for itself. (The writings of Charles Darwin and of Sigmund Freud in the 19th and early 20th centuries were to demolish these illusions). But without that liberation of the spirit, the development of modern science would have been impossible as well as any rational understanding of the Bible. As long as the tradition of "Holy Bible," off-limits to rational criticism was maintained, there could have been no understanding of the Bible intelligible to modern people. The Bible itself would have remained a promoter of ignorance and intolerance.

But it was not only the Enlightenment that had launched biblical criticism. Its roots go back to the earlier Renaissance, dating from circa 16th century in Italy, when the scholarly cry was "Ad fontes," "Back to the Sources," i.e. of European culture. The movement was considerably accelerated by the re-discovery of the writings of the Greek dramatists and philosophers and hence of the Greek language. The writings included manuscripts of the Greek New Testament. Their study convinced scholars such as Desiderius Erasmus (1469-1536) that the official Bible of the Catholic Church, the Vulgate, was seriously flawed as a translation with the consequence that many abuses within the Church were traceable to ignorance of what the New Testament really said. This was a major cause of the Reformation, for Martin Luther's eyes were opened by his study of the Psalms in Hebrew and of Paul's Letter to the Romans in Greek. Even a century and half before that, the Wycliffite Bible (see further at page 259) in the late 14th century had encouraged priests and lay folk to read the Bible for

---

[66] In J Barr, *Holy Scripture: Canon, Authority, Criticism*, OUP, p 124. Barr further commented that "The Enlightenment … is a deeply essential part of our heritage. The world of critical theology, in which free biblical research is an essential part and historical criticism a small but highly symptomatic element, is as much part of our tradition as is the thought of Calvin or the world of the Fathers."p125.

themselves (at huge personal risk) and so to compare its teaching with that of the Church.

Of course, the values of the Enlightenment are not to be swallowed without discrimination. On the whole, I regard the Enlightenment as, in the language of *1066 and All That*, a Good Thing! It liberated the human spirit from fear and superstition, opening eyes to the wonders of God's universe, including to the possibility of a fresh understanding of the Bible and consequently of a Christian faith in harmony with (rather than opposition to) the scientific revolution in human knowledge.

2. Criticism, negative or positive?

A charge frequently made is that biblical criticism is excessively negative. That it deliberately engenders a spirit of skepticism. Perhaps we need to remind ourselves that the word "criticism" is not innately negative, but implies discernment both positive and negative. However, there is as Ecclesiastes puts it, "a time to break down, and a time to build up" (Ecclesiastes 3.3). Sometimes, old attitudes and old suppositions have to be dismantled before there can be any breakthrough to new ones. It cannot be denied that there always have been and are scholars whose temperament is to be skeptical and whose intention is to be destructive of Christian faith. The fact is that, faced with a large assemblage of data, the conclusions any particular scholar arrives at often depend more on his or her philosophical presuppositions than on the data before him. That is of course as true of committed Christians as of those who are atheists, agnostics or of another religious faith. All scholars should be honest as to what their presuppositions are.

Certainly the critical climate has changed. Fifty years ago, the presupposition in most gospel criticism was that you could assume the reported words of Jesus to be accurate unless there were strong reasons to think otherwise. For example, few scholars supposed that Matthew 28.19, with its reference to "baptizing in the name of Father, Son and Holy Spirit" could have been spoken by Jesus, because its Trinitarian phraseology was nowhere else apparent in the gospels and was probably an editorial insertion made at a time when the doctrine of the Trinity was developing. But for the past 20 or so years, the criterion of authenticity (as all such discussion is termed) is rather: "Accept nothing as authentically words of Jesus unless there are very strong reasons to believe them to be such."[67] When a further measure of judgment was to accept nothing as authentic if it could be paralleled in contemporary Jewish writing, we had reached a "reductio ad absurdum" – for what could be expected from a first century Jew whom the "common people heard …gladly" (Mark 12.37 KJV) than that he should have spoken in their everyday language. Every word of the Lord's Prayer may be paralleled in sayings of the Rabbis, but the prayer remains unique in the particular linking together of the petitions that we find in Matthew 6.9-13 and Luke 11.2-04. I adhere to the older view, i.e. to the bias that assumes gospel wording to be accurately reported, unless we have Synoptic evidence that the wording has been altered or good reason to suppose that the text represents the thinking of the early Church of decades later than Jesus' time. Even then, if we suspect that a saying is more likely that of the Jerusalem Church of the 40s or of the community that lies behind John's Gospel in the 90s, it is still evidence of how the early Church regarded Jesus. That is as much constitutive of the early faith of Christians as are precise words of Jesus himself.

3. Rebuttal

As to the charge that biblical criticism had effectively destroyed the possibility of regarding the Bible as the chief source of authority, I will seek to deal with that criticism in my chapters 19 to 21. The fact is that, long before the emergence of a modern critical approach, the Bible's authority was already ambiguous. For, within the thought-world of literalism, by what criteria did churchmen decide as between Old and New Testaments when, on a number of issues, they clearly clashed? The greatest fruit of the critical method is to have revealed the gospel at the heart of the Bible more clearly than had been possible before.

New approaches

Over the past 30 or so years, there have emerged many radically new approaches that have typically begun with sharp criticism of just the type of biblical criticism that I have been commending. Fashions come and go in theological study as in most other walks of life. It is understandable that the "young Turks" in university circles challenge the "old codgers." How else may young and ambitious academics justify their existence? In this section, I am indebted to the contributors to *The Cambridge Companion to Biblical Interpretation*,[68] published in 1998, for their judicious review of the more recent developments.

The Bible as Literature

Some of the new approaches have originated in secular quarters (some but not all hostile to religious belief and practice). From about the mid-70s, there was

---

[67] This attitude is epitomized especially in the Jesus Seminar in the USA. In its meetings, after prolonged discussion, a vote is taken of all the scholars present as to whether a particular saying of Jesus is to be regarded as certainly authentic, possibly authentic, more likely inauthentic, or certainly inauthentic. In a book published in 1993, this resulted in the following scores given for Mark's Gospel: 1, 18, 66, 92. How skeptical can you get! This and other approaches are well summarized in Mark Powell's book, *The Jesus Debate*, a Lion Book, 1998.

[68] *The Cambridge Companion to Biblical Interpretation*, ed John Barton, CUP 1998.

evidence of considerable interest in the Bible as literature regardless of its theological and religious significance. The most obvious fruit of this was the publication in 1987 of *The Literary Guide to the Bible*,[69] edited by Robert Alter and Frank Kermode, two of the leading lights in this movement. Its justification was that the Bible is a repository of magnificent literature, which deserves to be appreciated (regardless of religious belief) together with other great literature. (To be ignorant of the Bible is to be ignorant! To give but one example; who, ignorant of the Bible, could understand and chuckle at many of P G Wodehouse's brilliant one-liners? He knew the Bible as well as he knew the mind of the admirable Jeeves!) This had an almost immediate effect on biblical criticism. Whereas the greater part of scholarly interest had been in the origins, source and development of each book of the Bible, now the demand was to accept the text as the finished product that it is, allowing its literary quality to speak to the reader directly for itself. The implication was that much biblical criticism had been so preoccupied with the trees as to miss the wood! We then heard of "reader-response". It was telling us that the reader's immediate reaction to the text was just as important as the author's intention in writing it. And attention to the reader him/herself was of importance. With what presuppositions, prejudices, and expectations did s/he approach the text? Here the insights of psychology and sociology shed invaluable light.

To cite my own practice, I always set my students the task of reading through Mark's Gospel at one sitting. The discussion that then ensued was always illuminating. Nor did those who heard Alec McCowen's recitations of a complete gospel quickly forget the impact the full-bodied narrative made on them. We may reflect on how much Church congregations miss when they hear no more than tiny "snippets" in the Bible lections. There should perhaps be more experimentation in reading, say, the whole of second Isaiah (chapters 40-55) or the entire Sermon on the Mount or a complete gospel. But then much attention would have to be given to the presentation and to the quality of reading.

Reader-response is important, but, it has to be said that for Christians, the reader's response cannot be the sole or the chief criterion of what the text means. Carried to an extreme, reader-response is a typical post-modern delusion, that the only Truth is whatever is true for me. Therefore there are as many truths, or meanings, as there are people reading. This is the hermeneutic of Humpty Dumpty: "When I use a word," Humpty Dumpty said, in a rather scornful tone, "it means just what I chose it to mean – neither more nor less." "The question is," said Alice, "whether you can make words mean so many different things." "The question is," said Humpty Dumpty, "which is to be

---

[69] Published by Fontana, an imprint of Harper Collins, 1987.

master – that's all." Exactly! In reading the Bible, the truth the Christian believer seeks is God's truth.

Another catch-word with its origins in literary criticism is for "synchronic" (as opposed to "diachronic") reading of texts. The key here is "chronic" deriving from the Greek "chronos," meaning "time," the time we read off the clock. A diachronic reading is one that seeks to discern the different layers of text, from the inception of the writing, perhaps in very remote times, through all the stages of re-writing, adding or deleting, until the book reaches its final stage, that of publication. As you will have noted, my approach, typical of most biblical scholarship over the past 200 years, has been for diachronic reading. The proponents of synchronic reading say in effect: "Forget all that, read the text as it is, in its wholeness, as a finished product." Of course, that is how our forbears read the Bible. It is beneficial to allow the scriptures to speak to us and for us to listen intently to what "word from the Lord" may be heard in them. But, the fact is that once we begin to delve more deeply into them, literary questions inevitably rise up demanding answers which inevitably lead us into literary criticism; and with them, historical questions as to how and why and when this scripture was written. Any serious study of the Bible cries out for a diachronic approach.

The greatest theological consequence of this approach was in the emergence of what was called "Canonical Criticism" (on which, see further on p250-253).

Ancillary disciplines

It was not surprising that scholars, coming to biblical study from other academic disciplines, should bring their professional expertise, whether in anthropology, sociology, psychology, psychoanalysis, linguistics or literary criticism, to their understanding of the Bible. Those with archaeological and sociological expertise have come to question many of the assumptions of an older scholarship, especially as to the early history of Israel. Fifty or so years ago, there was an evident hunger amongst Christians for confirmation that the biblical record was historically reliable. A book such as Werner Keller's *The Bible as History* [70] fed this desire. I have already cited the example of Garstang's excavation at Jericho in the 1920s appearing to have uncovered the very walls that had collapsed at the sound of Joshua's trumpets! And so apparently to vindicate the account of the event given in Joshua chapter six. More recent research has shown those conclusions to be largely mistaken. Yet more recent research in Palestine reveals no obviously significant dislocation as between the Canaanite settlements supposedly replaced by those of the invading Hebrews,

---

[70] W Keller: *The Bible as History*, Hodder and Stoughton, London, 1956.

putting a question-mark over the historical veracity of the accounts of Joshua and Judges. Moreover the paucity of significant remains of Israelite civilization dating from the early years of the Monarchy, i.e. of the period of David and Solomon, raises the question whether the books of Samuel and of Kings exaggerate the greatness and magnificence of these Kings. This has led some scholars to doubt whether those biblical books were written as early as had been supposed, with the consequent supposition that the historical books were more likely written in the Persian period (sixth century BC) or later, presenting a retrospective and idealistic view of the early monarchy. It is suggested that these books represent the vested interests of the priestly aristocracy in Jerusalem. Needless to say, later rather than earlier dating of Old Testament writings makes very little if any difference to Christian faith. The precise accuracy of the historical detail of Israel's history is of little importance for those who seek the Word of God in Torah and Prophets.

Alternative perspectives

Others have brought not so much another discipline as another perspective from which to approach the Bible. A fresh perspective from that of traditional standpoints may reveal facets of the biblical story previously unnoticed. The one that most catches the eye is that of "feminist criticism." Not surprisingly, many women have regarded the Bible as irremediably patriarchal and "macho" in its subjugation of women to perpetually subservient status. And that such an attitude was carried forward into the New Testament, being further promulgated by Paul; which explains how and why much of Church history has been marred by misogyny, chauvinism and violence against women. Some feminist critics have examined those Bible passages in which women have a minor role, suggesting that their real importance had been suppressed by the biblical writers. Feminists (who of course are not necessarily women) bring out aspects that most male commentators had totally missed. It seems likely that such new ways of thinking contributed to opening the way for women to be ordained to the priesthood in the Church of England (some Free Churches such as the Congregational had ordained women since 1917). Clearly their insights are of considerable value for those Churches seeking to further eradicate sexual discrimination.

Other perspectives are those under the banners of "Liberation Theology" or "Black Theology." Both originate in the observation that most biblical study and theological research in the past has been carried out by WASPS (white, Anglo-Saxon Protestants) to which we would have to add usually "male, comfortable, and middle-class." The full force of this struck me in Klaus Klostermaier's brilliant book *Hindu and Christian in Vrindaban*.[71] In his chapter entitled "Theology at 120°" he contrasts the typical European academic working in the comfort of his air-conditioned study with his colleague toiling amidst the heat, dust, and squalor of Vrindaban just before the breaking of the monsoon. Herewith a taste of it:

> "A short, uncomplicated article on the Christian idea of God had to be done for a Hindu magazine. The subject had been discussed in all the theological textbooks, of course. All that need be done is to argue a few single points a little. However, what was written there and what one had studied with adequate zeal only a few years ago now seemed so inadequate, so irrelevant, so untrue. Theology at 120° F in the shade seems, after all, different from theology at 70° F. Theology accompanied by tough chapatis and smoky tea seems different from theology with roast chicken and a glass of good wine. Now, who is really different, theos or the theologian? The theologian at 70° F in a good position presumes God to be happy and contented, well-fed and rested, without needs of any kind. The theologian at 120° F tries to imagine a God who is hungry and thirsty, who suffers and is sad, who sheds perspiration and knows despair. But all this is already too hinduistic. The theologian at 70° F and with a well-ordered life sees the whole world as a beautiful harmony with a grand purpose, the church as God's kingdom on earth and himself as promoter of the real culture of humanity. The theologian at 120° F sees the cracks in the soil and the world as a desert; he considers whether it wouldn't be wiser to keep the last jug of water till the evening ..."

It is hardly surprising that those living in the heat and squalor of Vrindaban, or in the shanty towns of Sao Paulo, Nairobi or Calcutta, in wholly unjust societies, in which the only livelihood to be made is by scavenging through the rubbish dumps, will read the Bible (if literate!) with quite different perceptions from those of us who have hardly experienced a day's discomfort in our lives. And that they find in the Bible a message of liberation, of ancient wrongs needing to be put right and that such readings may well have revolutionary consequences.

Hermeneutics

Hermeneutics is currently the big word in everything to do with literary criticism. It stands for "The Theory and Art of Interpretation," coming from the Greek verb, "hermaneuo," I interpret. It has been mainly the concern of the philosophers, but has undoubtedly impinged on biblical study. Since the whole enterprise of biblical study involves the interpretation of ancient documents, it has to be aware of the issues involved. As the content of this chapter has

---

[71] Klostermaier: *Hindu and Christian in Vrindaban*, SCM Press, 1969, p 40.

demonstrated, the presuppositions that any scholar brings to his or her researches inevitably affects the evaluation of evidence and the conclusions reached. Lest the reader should suppose that such matters are of concern only to academics, a little reflection shows that that is far from being the case. Every time you chat with a neighbor or exchange letters with a friend, there is the possibility that something you have spoken or written may have been misunderstood. Did you employ a word that might have been understood quite differently by neighbor or friend? Were you describing an experience that your interlocutors had never experienced? In either case, there is a problem of hermeneutics. The preacher faces these problems every time s/he declaims from the pulpit. You will doubtless have heard the story of the two neighbors fiercely arguing over the garden fence, to whom an innocent observer remarked: "The trouble with you two is that you're arguing from different premises!" In many a theological argument, sometimes leading to disastrous breakdown of relationships and schism between churches, the different premises from which discussion has taken place have made for unbridgeable misunderstanding. That was always the case as between the Western and the Eastern Churches, between Catholicism and Protestantism, between "conservative evangelicals" and "liberal modernists." Joint study of hermeneutics might enable some bridges of understanding to be built.

Canonical criticism

Closely related to the movement which urges primary attention to the text as it is (rather than into the search for historical origins, sources, and development) has been Canonical Criticism. The term is associated particularly with the name of B.S. Childs, Emeritus Professor at Yale University. His approach declares that the scholar's duty is to interpret a book, say that of Genesis, as the finished product that it is in our Bibles; for it was that finished product that was received by Judaism and by the Christian Church into its canon (i.e. the official listing of books deemed authoritative). And thereby to regard all matters of origin, of literary sources, and stages of development as of lesser importance. It is an attempt to break the dominance of literary-cum-historical criticism and to re-establish the authority of the Bible as scripture. I cannot but suspect that, having thrown Biblicism out of the front door, canonical criticism is a means of sneaking it in again through the back door.

In Chapter 19, I will express strong reservations about selecting the recording of biblical material in written form as the moment "par excellence" of inspiration. I have similar objection to shifting the key moment to a book's "canonization" (meaning by whatever process it was accorded authority status). As James Barr demonstrates,[72] regarding the Old Testament, there is no evidence of any such formal process ever taking place in Judaism. The Torah of Moses was always accorded the highest status of authority, certainly from the time of Ezra, yet there is no report of any debate on the matter nor on the gradual addition to it of the Prophets and the Writings. Nor did the Rabbis at Jamnia make any pronouncement on the matter (as we used to suppose). It would appear rather that canonization was a concept foreign to Judaism, so it was rather the Christian Church that accorded the Hebrew scriptures canonical status as its Old Testament.

To exalt the moment of canonization to that of highest authority is to commit a number of errors:

1. It is to ignore the fact that there was never total agreement as to the content of the canon. There were varying versions of it. The Hebrew canon (if such existed) was confined to the 22 scrolls. The Qumran community included all of these (except for Esther) and many more. It is likely that its members regarded their own writings, such as the Community Document, as also being inspired writings. Greek-speaking Jews recognized far more books than that. The Septuagint translation included those books printed in our Apocrypha in addition to the Hebrew books. The Roman Catholic and Orthodox Churches accepted this longer list. But Martin Luther, by contrast, adhered to the Hebrew Bible in his Old Testament, to be followed by all the Protestant Churches. It is surely a weakness for any doctrine of Authority based on the canon if the very content of that canon is uncertain.

2. It is to create an artificial and quite arbitrary division between books that were included in the Canon and those that were not. And to assume in consequence that books in the Canon were wholly inspired, and those outside, wholly uninspired. This suggests without warrant that at some point after Pentecost, God suddenly withdrew the Holy Spirit from his People. This is unacceptable. As a matter of common observation, there are books within the Canon that strike many readers as singularly uninspired, whilst there are numerous classics of Christian testimony down the ages widely regarded as inspirational. We might cite Augustine's *Confessions, The Revelations of Divine Love* of Mother Julian, John Bunyan's *Pilgrims Progress* and Bonhoeffer's *Letters and Papers from Prison* as examples from across the span of Christian history; or from the musicians, the works of J S Bach and the hymns of Isaac Watts or Charles Wesley, of Pratt Green or John Bell.

3. The drawing up of the Christian canon has little to do with inspiration. Canonization was always a practical, but not a theological, necessity. Its finalization at the Council of Carthage in AD 387 was useful in drawing a line

---

[72] James Barr, in *Holy Scripture: Canon, Authority, Criticism*, Clarendon Press, Oxford, 1983.

under the writings held to be constitutive of the origins of the Christian faith. The 27 books listed became scriptural largely because their authors happened to be the people "in the right place at the right time." Not eye-witnesses themselves (as has been demonstrated), but close enough to those who had been, their writings give us a kind of "ground plan" of the shape of the newly emerging faith. For that reason, they are unique, irreplaceable and invaluable. Whilst some of their writings read as exceptionally "inspirational" – from the New Testament we might pick out the birth narratives, the Sermon on the Mount, the parables, the story of the crucifixion, the impassioned letters of Paul, the profound meditations of John – they are on the whole neither more nor less inspirational than the work of dozens of other inspired authors through the ages. From that perspective, their canonization was artificial. The Holy Spirit had not ceased to speak because of the closing of the canon!

4. The canonical approach obscures the fact of the diversity of writings that constitute the Bible.[73] We have to hold in balance both its unity and its diversity. There is a unity, in that all the books of the Old Testament relate to the covenant mediated by God through Moses to the people Israel; and those of the New Testament to the new relationship offered by God through Jesus. Provided we never lose sight of the unifying thread of the Bible Story, we need equally to grasp that the Bible embraces a many-faceted spectrum of genres of literature, of voices expressing their faith and yearnings, their joy and their grief, and as many viewpoints as there are voices heard. To propose that only the final stage of the process that produced the books of the Bible is worthy of our full attention is, reverting to our metaphor of the New Testament as an archaeological "dig" (which could have been equally used of the Old Testament), to say that we should scrabble about on the top of the "tell" but are forbidden to dig inside so as to uncover its secrets. It is to reduce what was three-dimensional (and thus vibrant with life and energy) to a flat two-dimensional image. This is to drain the life and vitality out of the biblical story, for it is biblical criticism, detecting the relics of oral tradition, revealing the different literary layers, each representing a different theological understanding, that makes the Bible story come truly alive.

5. The Canonical Approach shunts the Bible off into a siding marked "Holy," "Special," "Different" (recall our discussion on p8-10). It ghettoizes Christian faith as if it has little to do with the real world of human "blood, sweat and

---

[73] However, Raymond Brown, in his "Introduction to the New Testament" makes an opposite observation on this point, ie that enclosing 27 books of such diversity within the Canon yields the positive value that their very diversity is thereby sanctioned. We have to recognize that the Gospels differ from each other, that Paul and James differ sharply on the matter of justification by faith or by works, etc. There has never been a time when all Christians were wholly at one in what they believed and how they behaved. And yet all is canonical.

tears." One could make a similar observation about the style of biblical theology that used to address what it called "Salvation history," as if biblical history was somehow unrelated to ordinary history. It would be nonsensical to write as if all that occurred to Israel was somehow unrelated to the empires that surrounded it, Egypt, Babylonia, Assyria, Greece and Rome – whereas the very opposite was the case. There could not have been any salvation for Israel that didn't entail salvation from slavery in Egypt as the foundational story of the Exodus recounts. Nor could Jesus' gospel be meaningful to the people of Galilee unless it had addressed (however obliquely) the heavy burden of Roman occupation. That he should have died by Roman execution only underlines the point.

Christians should affirm that the Bible belongs to the real world. It is a part of all the mess and mayhem that is human history. The Church doesn't comprise a ghetto except in so far as a fundamentalist theology creates one. The "saved" can huddle in their mental ghetto, largely ignoring the world, looking forward to the rapture, when the Lord, at His coming, will snatch them out of this wicked world doomed to destruction. An incarnational Christianity (one which sees "the Word made flesh" (John 1.14) as central to Christian believing and living) accepts that we are called to be the "hands and feet" of Christ in mission and service, inspired by his Spirit, in the real world. Not by escapism from it. Christians should be found where the action is: demanding justice, seeking peace and striving for the integrity of creation. Our theology should determine how we behave as responsible stewards of God's creation.

A major principle of this study is that the Bible plus Christian history constitutes one continuous span of the story of faith, beginning with Abraham, continuing through Old and New Testament times, through the centuries of Christian history down to our own time. To repeat the metaphor I used earlier on, we live by the side of an immense river, which has flowed now for more than three thousand years, with many tributaries contributing to its life and bifurcations tending to disperse its flow. The tradition of faith is the thread of continuity, linking us to our spiritual forbears. We read the Bible for no antiquarian reason, nor with any scientific disinterest, but with rather the passionate desire to learn from our forbears in the faith. Against the charge of negativism, as if our whole concern were to discern and analyze the events of the remote past, we should affirm to the contrary, that we only analyze the struggles, the defeats and the triumphs of our forbears so as better to understand the situation in which we try to live the life of faith for today.

Conclusions

In this chapter, I have given a brief review of some of the many new methods of approach to the study of the Bible. Whatever the insights uncovered by these new methods of enquiry, there can be no abandonment of a truly scientific approach to the Bible, that is, of literary-historical enquiry. There has to be Literary Criticism, because, whatever else it may be, the Bible is literature. There has to be Historical Criticism because, at its core, there is the story of a particular people, Israel and of a particular man, Jesus of Nazareth. These were embedded in the history of the Middle East in the two millennia BC, just as the Church has been a visible institution within history, down to our present time. Neither Judaism nor Christianity are the products of fiction, neither fairy-tales nor fantasies, neither philosophies (whose truth or falsehood is not related to the circumstances in which they were founded) nor merely theories. They were born and developed within historical, therefore social, economic, political and other circumstances. Therefore the Bible cannot be understood without paying considerable attention to the histories involved. It is the case that, in many instances, we cannot be certain of the history behind the stories; especially when the biblical account is not matched by any corroborative evidence from extra-biblical sources. However, we can still enquire as to whether the biblical story is compatible with what is known of the conditions prevailing at or around about the period concerned.

To cite an example, but one of crucial importance. How can we know for sure that a man called Jesus of Nazareth ever lived? We have no corroborative evidence for the existence of Jesus from outside of the New Testament until early in the second century. But when the Jewish document "bSanh 43a"[74] from the Tannaitic[75] period pinpoints the reasons for the "hanging" of the Nazarene; and the writing of the Roman historian Tacitus[76], circa AD 110, mentions the execution of Jesus under the procuratorship of Pontius Pilate – neither Jew nor Roman thinks of denying that such a man existed. On another front, there is nothing in the gospels that conflicts with, say, the known history of the Roman occupation in Palestine. All the gospels report that the Roman procurator who condemned Jesus to death was Pontius Pilate. The name of Pilate is well-attested in Roman records, as being procurator from AD 26-36, just the right period; and his character as one little concerned with justice is attested by the Jewish philosopher Philo. When a major world religion, Christianity, which certainly did not exist before the first century AD, points back in near unanimous testimony in the New Testament and in Christian history, to Jesus as its source and inspiration, it would be folly to deny his existence. It would be like accepting the Complete Works of Shakespeare, whilst denying that Shakespeare wrote it. If not Shakespeare, then who else?[78] If not Jesus, then who else? When we see a road bridge carrying heavy traffic over a wide river, we are

---

[74] In *The Historical Jesus*, G Theissen & A Merz, SCM Press, London, 1998, p75.
[75] Tannaitic: ie from the first two centuries AD, the sayings of Jewish doctors of the Law whose opinions were recorded in the Mishnah or other writings.
[76] *The Historical Jesus*, G Theissen & A Merz, SCM Press, London, 1998, p82.

obliged to assume that it must have been built on solid foundations. Christianity is wholly inexplicable without Jesus being that "foundation stone" as it is put in 1 Corinthians 3.11: "For no one can lay any foundation other than the one that has been laid; that foundation is Jesus Christ."

Trustworthy scholarship

Some of the new approaches have been advanced by scholars in principle hostile to Christian faith. A strong impression from reading *The Cambridge Companion to Biblical Interpretation* is as to how few of the exponents of new methods (with the honorable but possibly misguided exception of the canonical critics) appear to have any interest in the religious message of the Bible. Some of the reviewers of their methods themselves express misgivings about the motivation of their research. Whilst Christians should always be ready to recognize truth no matter from what quarter it comes, such methods cannot ultimately be of much interest to those who read the Bible seeking to discern in it "the Word of the Lord." It is not as if the old established and well-tried methods have failed. In most university departments of theology or of biblical studies, there are still many scholars admirable both in their scholarship as in their Christian discipleship.

To cite a number of examples of recent biblical scholarship, which employ the old tools of literary and historical criticism, yet with many strikingly new insights from newer disciplines: **Raymond Brown's**[78] *Birth of the Messiah, Death of the Messiah* and two-volume commentary on John's Gospel will remain classics for years, heading the huge contribution of Roman Catholic scholars since restrictions were removed from their activities. His Introduction to the New Testament won immediate acclaim. **Walter Brueggemann**, Professor Emeritus of Old Testament at Columbia Theological Seminary, is a Christian scholar held in huge respect on both sides of the Atlantic. He is a deep theologian, relating his researches to the needs of pastors and preachers working in the cold climate of post-modernism. His latest publication, An *Introduction to the Old Testament*[79] (subtitled *Canon and Christian Imagination*), gives a brilliant running commentary through the Old Testament, sparkling with fresh insights. The work of Anglican scholars, **James Barr** and **John Barton**, both of Oxford University, has been outstanding, precisely in so many of the issues I

---

[77] Of course, there are those who believe that somebody other than Shakespeare wrote the plays that bear his name. A good friend of mine, David Caruth, cites Edward de Vere, the 17th Earl of Oxford (1550-1604), as his preferred candidate. If that were the case, we should still want to assert that the author of the Works of Shakespeare was a genius. In Jesus' case, there is no other candidate in sight.

[78] Raymond E Brown, SS (a member of the Order of St Sulpice), died in 1998, a huge loss to biblical scholarship.

[79] W Brueggmann, Introduction to the Old Testament, Westminster John Knox, ©2003.

have been outlining in this book. Barr's *Holy Scripture: Canon, Authority, Criticism; Old and New in Interpretation; The Bible in the Modern World*, and *Fundamentalism* are all illuminating. John Barton wrote, together with Robert Morgan, *Biblical Interpretation* in the Oxford Bible Series, and edited both the *Cambridge Companion to Biblical Interpretation*, and more recently, with John Muddiman, the *Oxford Bible Commentary*. **Tom Wright**, recently installed Anglican Bishop of Durham, severely critical of aspects of Enlightenment thinking, of conservative "bent" of mind and yet of scholarship of huge erudition, has produced a trilogy of considerable importance: *The New Testament and the People of God; Jesus and the Victory of God*; and recently, *The Resurrection*; as well as many smaller books addressed to the thinking public, including the first volumes of a series of popular Bible commentaries intended to cover the entire New Testament. **James Dunn** is a Methodist scholar: after several influential books, such as *Unity and Diversity in the New Testament; The Makings of Christology*, and commentaries on Romans, Galatians and the Acts of the Apostles, his *Theology of Paul the Apostle* is the finest exposition of Paul's thinking for 50 years and more. **Graham Stanton**, Lady Margaret's Professor of Divinity at Cambridge University, is also an Elder of the United Reformed Church. He has written a number of scholarly but accessible books such as *The Gospels and Jesus; Gospel Truth? Today's Quest for Jesus of Nazareth* and an erudite study of Matthew's Gospel, *A Gospel for a New People* setting it within its context in the church and world of the first century.

Beside these major works of scholarship, within the noble tradition of biblical criticism allied to Christian faith and personal commitment, some of the recent approaches are illuminating but others appear distinctly trivial.

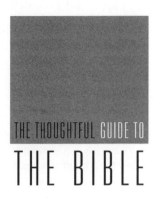

THE THOUGHTFUL GUIDE TO
THE BIBLE

THE ENGLISH BIBLE

CHAPTER 18:
THE STORY OF THE
ENGLISH BIBLE

The Bible of our ancestors

Our theme is the English Bible. I sometimes like to imagine the experience of my ancestors over all the past centuries. My immediate forbears, the generations of my parents, grandparents and their parents were staunch nonconformists (going back how many generations I do not know); but at some time in the past, whatever their private beliefs, they must have worshiped in their local Parish Church (because the law required them to do so). Even when they were permitted to build and use their own Chapels, they still had to pay their Church tithes and could only get married in the Church. Then think back to the time before the English Reformation, when all those parish churches were in communion with the Bishop of Rome. Then, my ancestors (who would have numbered more than a million people in the early 16th century) and yours in all probability, were technically Roman Catholics. They would have been so ever since the coming of Christianity to Britain from the end of the sixth century AD onwards.

The Latin Vulgate & Anglo-Saxon

All through those centuries that we call the Dark Ages that became the Middle Ages, the only version of the Bible that our ancestors could have known was the Latin Vulgate. This Latin translation, the work of Jerome, completed in AD 405, was the Bible of Christendom for well-nigh a thousand years. "Vulgate" means "common" or "popular." It may have been that for the Romans, but it certainly wasn't for the Britons and Anglo-Saxons. The Latin Bible would have been intelligible only to the tiny elite of educated people in the land. The common folk would have been familiar with its teaching only through what the parish priest chose to tell them, from the performances of wandering actors in the Mystery Plays, from story-tellers and from what was depicted in the wall paintings and statuary in their churches. There had been some translation into the Anglo-Saxon tongue. King Alfred did so with the Ten Commandments as a preface to his law-code, whilst the Venerable Bede supposedly translated John's Gospel shortly before his death. Nevertheless, the vast majority of our forbears were illiterate. To them the rhyming couplets of the Northumbrian shepherd Caedmon, sung to the harp, would have been more popular.

Not all remembrance of the Vulgate Bible has been erased from our minds, even in post-Reformation England (especially not for those familiar with Anglican Psalmody). You may surprise yourself by your knowledge of Latin if you will jot down the answers to these questions (in Latin please!). The answers are to be found at the end of this chapter:

1. In the Christmas story, what did the shepherds hear angels singing?
2. What did Mary sing (when she was visiting Elizabeth)?
3. What did the aged Simeon pray in the Temple?
4. What is the Latin for *"Come"*?
5. What is the Latin for *"Rejoice"*?

The Wycliffite Bible

The first complete English Bible is associated with the figure of John Wycliffe (1330-1384). By the 14th century a major crisis had developed in the Roman Church. Because of upheavals in Italy, the Popes, largely controlled by the French monarchy, fled to Avignon in the south of France. For a lengthy period there were two Popes in rivalry; for a short time, even three. All over Christendom, voices cried out for reform. Foremost among them were John Hus in Bohemia and John Wycliffe in England.

Wycliffe was an Oxford Professor, the most learned man of his day and an outspoken critic of the Church. He denounced its malpractices fiercely, so much so that he was eventually denounced as a heretic, deposed from office and posthumously condemned, his mortal remains burned.

Wycliffe believed that the only sure way to reform a corrupt Church was for the English people to be able to read the Bible in their own tongue. He therefore instigated its translation. It seems the work was carried out by his close associates Nicholas of Hereford and John Purvey. They used the Vulgate as their text since Greek manuscripts would not have been available to them. In any case knowledge of the Greek language had been largely lost in Western Europe). The first translation was strictly word for word because Wycliffe regarded the Bible largely as a legal code, hence there was necessity for a word for word concurrence with the Latin text. A second version, for which Purvey was responsible, rendered a much more intelligible English. In spite of the fierce hostility of the Church, backed by legal force, hundreds of hand-written copies were made and passed round in secret, thus beginning to influence people towards an eventual reformation. Wycliffe has been rightly called "The Morning Star of the Reformation."

During his lifetime, Wycliffe trained and sent out hundreds of so-called Poor Preachers. They were nicknamed "Lollards" (the word being derived from the Dutch for "babblers") by their detractors. They preached from village to village, encouraging the literate to read the Bible to their illiterate neighbors and kinsfolk. So small groups of dissidents (the prototypes of nonconformity) were formed and were especially active in the south-east of England, including East Anglia. They suffered much persecution. The Oxford Constitutions of 1408 "forbade anyone to translate, or even to read, a vernacular version of the Bible in whole or in part without the approval of his diocesan bishop ..." These were designed to stamp out Lollardy, which they did by enforcing the provisions of "De Heretico Comburendum" (1401), which prescribed the burning of heretics. In those days, even to possess a Bible was presumptive of heresy. I recall my horror as a teenager at seeing the monument in Brentwood, Essex, to a 14-year-old boy, who had been burned to death; his crime, daring to read the English Bible! Lollardy was certainly established in the Waveney Valley (on the Norfolk-Suffolk border in the UK near to where I am writing) where three people suffered the extreme sanction. It is probable that the "Seven Sacrament" fonts to be found particularly in East Anglian churches, for example, at St Peter's, Brooke (my village in Norfolk), were intended as a rebuttal of Lollardy. Whereas the Lollards taught, on the basis of scripture, that the Lord instituted only two sacraments, those of Baptism and the Lord's Supper, the Church depicted the seven sacraments as defined by the Catholic Church for all the illiterate to see.

The extreme reaction taken by Church and State against Lollardy is explicable on the grounds of the expected consequences of their beliefs. Pope Gregory XI's condemnation of Wycliffe was because he deemed his views to be subversive of all authority. That the Peasants' Revolt broke out within Wycliffe's lifetime, in 1381, would have underscored this allegation, for radical religion and radical politics have always gone hand in hand, as was to be illustrated yet more vividly during the English Civil War of the 17th century.

For the information of readers in East Anglia (UK), there is a copy of the Wycliffe Bible in the Norfolk Heritage Centre, part of the Forum in the heart of Norwich.

Printing and the revival of Greek studies

In the 16th century some major developments had taken place that were to revolutionize the dissemination of the Bible and to prepare the ground for the Protestant Reformation. The first was the invention of printing. It is difficult for us even to imagine what it had been like, until that invention, to be dependent on the hand-copying of every book and document. It made books both rare and expensive. But in 1450 Johannes Gutenberg set up his printing press in Mainz and thus opened the floodgates for the wider dissemination of knowledge. The very first publication was that of the Latin Vulgate. Not so long afterwards, William Caxton was setting up his press in London. His early publications were overwhelmingly those in high demand in Catholic England. There was nothing inherently Protestant in the technology of printing! But it made available a tool for the diffuse broadcasting of any new and revolutionary ideas and thus served the message of Protestantism admirably.

The second factor is not at all so obvious. In 1453, the Ottoman Turks captured Constantinople, the great capital of Byzantine Christianity for more than a thousand years. To Greek Christians, this event was as calamitous as had been the sacking of Rome by the Vandals in AD 410. The West was largely indifferent to its fate (except in so far as it aroused a new fear of Islam). But the fall of Byzantium produced some most beneficial effects in the West. Numbers of Greek scholars fled to the West, bringing their manuscripts with them, also, of course, their Greek language and culture. This cultural influx stimulated the revival of learning throughout the West, sparking the so-called Renaissance (the New Birth). It involved a return to the sources of western culture, as the writings of the Greek philosophers and playwrights became available; but more importantly for our purposes, a renewed interest in the Greek origins of the New Testament. It did not escape notice that the all so-familiar Vulgate Bible sometimes diverged considerably from the underlying meaning of texts in Greek.

Desiderius Erasmus

Desiderius Erasmus, the greatest humanist[80] scholar of his age and renowned throughout Europe, took an immediate interest in the Greek text of the New Testament, publishing and printing it in several editions during the years 1516-1535. He was aware of critical problems, but hadn't the resources to resolve them. He therefore published editions that were in time to become the basis of the Textus Receptus. In Britain, the Universities appointed lecturers in the Greek language for the first time; thus, at Cambridge, the lecturer, Richard Croke, had amongst his students a brilliant young man called William Tyndale. In London, the gifted Dean of Westminster, John Colet, began lecturing directly from the Greek text of Paul's Letter to the Romans. Much the same was happening in Germany. When his Augustinian superior, Staupitz, instructed Martin Luther to give University lectures, it was to the Hebrew of the Old Testament and to the Greek of the New that he turned. In both he discovered rich resources for a fresh understanding of Christian faith that had long been obscured by the Roman Church's dependence on the Latin Vulgate.

---

[80] Humanism was a noted feature of the Renaissance. It involved turning away from the medieval obsession with the supernatural, with the dogmas and practices of the Catholic Church, to a more human-oriented program. This was considerably boosted by the rediscovery of the writings of the Greek philosophers and playwrights.

William Tyndale, father of the English Bible

The Reformation, anticipated by both Hus and Wycliffe and boosted by a long-felt desire throughout Christendom for reform, broke out with full force in Germany. Martin Luther, for whom the study of the Bible in its original languages had opened his eyes to the full import of the gospel, first came into conflict with the Catholic Church over the matter of indulgences. The Church, intent on rebuilding St Peter's Basilica in Rome, was not too bothered as to how it raised the large sums of money required. It authorized the sale of indulgences[81] and Friar Tetzel was authorized to do so in the region of Wittenberg. Incidentally, both Gutenberg and Caxton found the printing of indulgence forms a most profitable business! Luther saw this practice as constituting a denial of the gospel truth that men and women are saved by the Grace of God alone, implying as it did, that they can pay their way out of Purgatory. He nailed his famous 95 theses on the Church door of Wittenberg, the customary way of challenging his opponents to debate. This act sparked off a controversy that rocked the Medieval Church to its foundations. And when Luther's life was obviously in danger, his friends spirited him away to a castle called the Wartburg and it was from this hide-out that he set to the translation of the Bible into German. He also poured out tracts which, thanks to printing, found their way around Europe.

In England, there were groups of students (amongst them Tyndale) and the rising class of merchants who eagerly studied Luther's writings and embraced the cause of reformation. Tyndale had already proved himself an able translator with his version of Erasmus's "Enchiridion" ("The Christian Soldier's Armoury" was its English title), in which Erasmus had pleaded that every Christian should be encouraged to read the Bible in his own language. Tyndale took this plea to heart. It was reinforced by the sort of obfuscation he met with from die-hard traditionalists. The story is told that a so called "learned man" said to him: "It were better to know the Pope's laws than the laws of God," to which Tyndale riposted: "If God spares my life, before many years I will cause the boy who drives the plow to know more of the Scripture than you do." He approached Bishop Tunstall of London, requesting permission (as the Oxford Constitutions required) to translate the Bible into English. It was refused; in consequence, he took the decision to cross the Channel to Germany where the Reformation was gaining faster ground and where, so he thought, his work could proceed without hindrance. After some time in Wittenburg and Hamburg, he completed

---

[81] Indulgences were certificates, authorized by the Pope, which stated that for whatever sum of money had been donated, the donor would receive so many years of remission from the pains of purgatory either for himself or for deceased relatives. The sellers of indulgences played on people's fear of purgatory so as to extract considerable sums of money which went towards the rebuilding of St Peter's Basilica in Rome.

his translation in Cologne, using Erasmus' Greek text, with the Vulgate and Luther's translation to hand for reference. The printer Peter Quentel had set up the first 10 sheets of typescript when Tyndale was warned that the city authorities intended to seize it. He just had time to make his get-away with the precious scripts. However, copies of the Cologne printing which comprised the Gospel of Matthew as far as chapter 22 (some evidence suggests the whole of it) and the entirety of Mark's Gospel, were soon reaching England. The translation was prefaced by a prologue entitled "A Pathway into the Scripture," for Tyndale realized that his readers would need some guidance in understanding. This edition also included marginal notes, mostly of simple explanation, but some of highly polemical content, reflecting a decidedly Lutheran interpretation of the New Testament. He didn't hesitate to identify the Pope with the Antichrist! It was therefore in Worms that, in February 1526, the first complete printed English New Testament was produced. The British Library printed a facsimile copy of it in the year 2000. Its editor declares that, in his opinion, this was "arguably the most important single event in the history of the English Reformation" (p ix). I applaud this as a counter to the notion that the English Reformation was of wholly political origin, in Henry VIII's determination to divorce his wife. But the Worms edition had abandoned both the prologue and the annotations.

The authorities of church and state reacted with extreme hostility. Tyndale's translation was immediately denounced as Lutheran and therefore heretical. Bishop Tunstall adopted the policy of buying up as many of these New Testaments as he could in order to have them burned in public. Ironically, the policy suited Tyndale well, for it provided him with a steady cash-flow wherewith to continue printing yet more of them on the continent. Foremost in criticism was Sir Thomas More. In a pamphlet he referred to "the pestilent sect of Luther and Tyndale" as the work of Antichrist. The substance of his critique was that Tyndale had abandoned age-old Church tradition in translating the Greek "ecclesia" as "congregation," not "church"; Greek "presbuteros" as "elder" rather than as "priest"; the Greek "metanoia" as "repentance" and not "do penance." Modern translators would wholly back Tyndale's judgment as against that of More.

Tyndale then turned his attention to the Old Testament, completing the five books of Moses and Jonah. There were some notable felicities such as this: "The Lord was with Joseph and he was a lucky fellow." Meanwhile, in England, the tide was turning towards the Reformation. With the fall of Thomas More on account of his refusal to support Henry VIII's divorce and consequent proclamation of himself as Supreme Governor of the Church of England, and the rise of Thomas Cromwell, the English vernacular Bible was more highly favored. But Tyndale was not to benefit personally from this. In 1535 he was kidnapped in Antwerp and handed over to the authorities in Brussels, an area directly under the jurisdiction of Emperor Charles V. The following year, he was condemned as a heretic, strangled and burned at the stake on October 6. His last prayer was said to be: "Lord, open the eyes of the King of England". It would appear that his prayer was speedily answered.

Myles Coverdale

One of Tyndale's associates, Myles Coverdale, took up his work in the more favorable conditions now pertaining in England. He revised Tyndale's translation and himself completed that of the Old Testament in 1535 (although he was not competent in Hebrew). His translation was said to be from the "douche," which meant in those days what we would call German, with some side reference to the Vulgate. His was the first complete English Bible to be published. Its preface began with a flattering obeisance to the King. This was doubtless the price he had to pay for publication under "the King's most gracious license." How ironical that a translation, basically that of the "heretic" Tyndale, completed by Coverdale, should receive the royal approval (thus overturning at one blow the provisions of the Oxford Constitutions). So felicitous was Coverdale's translation of the Psalms that it was his version which was used in the English Book of Common Prayer and is therefore still sung in cathedral and parish choirs to this day.

The Great Bible

1537 saw further fulfillment of Tyndale's prayer. Another of his associates, John Rogers, working under the pseudonym of Matthew, revised the Tyndale-Coverdale translations to produce the Matthew Bible. This met with such approval that only some further slight revision of it was published in 1538 as the "Great Bible," with explicit instruction that it was to be of sufficient size to be clearly visible on Church lecterns and that a copy of it was to be displayed in every Parish Church in the land. The second edition of it in 1540 contained the line: "appointed to be read in churches," which implied both royal and ecclesiastical approval. This was not to last for long. The accessibility of the Great Bible caused a sensation, as crowds swarmed around the lecterns to hear it being read aloud to them. This happened even during the daily services, so a further decree forbade its public reading while services were on. Indeed, King Henry took fright. If Tom, Dick and Harry could so openly read the scriptures for themselves, they might well get big ideas into their heads and form their own opinions. Trying in vain to push the genie back into the bottle, he issued a decree that forbade the reading of scripture either in public or in private by "women ... artificers, prentices, journeymen, serving men of the degrees of yeoman or under, husbandmen or laborers," though noble and gentlewomen might read the Bible in private! The legislation, masterminded by Bishop

Gardiner, was entitled "For the Advancement of True Religion." And, as a throwback to the past, the Act provided that persistent clerical offenders could be burned at the stake and lay people suffer seizure of goods and perpetual imprisonment.

King Henry's death put an end to this oppression. With the young Edward VII on the throne, and reformers prominent in his government, the green light was on for further progress. Cranmer was able to push through reforms, most notably with his introduction of the first English Service Book, the Book of Common Prayer (1547), to replace the old Catholic liturgies. It was the English Bible that was to be read alongside the English prayer book.

Mary and the Catholic reaction

With Edward's premature death in 1553, Mary Tudor, a devout Catholic, came to the throne and immediately instituted a reaction. Zealous reforming bishops were replaced by Catholics. Some of the former, as well as many priests and layfolk, were accused of heresy and accordingly more than three hundred were burned at the stake. But, Mary never rescinded the order that an English Bible stand on the lectern of every parish church. The effect of this reaction was that large numbers of Protestants, especially amongst the aristocracy and the clergy, fled the country, as earlier, Roman Catholics had been forced to do. Most of these took refuge in those continental cities in which the Reformation was most securely established, such as Geneva, Basel and Strasbourg. Here they came under the direct influence of the great Reformers, such as Calvin and his successor, Theodore Beza. It was in Geneva that William Whittingham set about producing a fresh translation. He was able to employ manuscripts more accurate than those previously known and to consult with many reputed scholars. The result was the publication in 1560 of the Geneva Bible.

The Geneva Bible

The Geneva Bible was of significance for a number of reasons. Although referring to the earlier English versions, it was more innovative than any of the other translations since Tyndale's. It was the first printed Bible to include the verse divisions devised by Stephanus and with each verse commencing a new line (useful for cross referencing but a retrograde step in that it suggested each verse had a meaning regardless of its own regardless of context). In the wide margins, it inserted both explanatory notes and extensive theological commentary, strongly representing the theology of the Reformation. It was this that made it so controversial in England. Since Geneva was a republic, these notes were frequently condemnatory of wicked kings and attacked the practices of Catholicism. It became popularly known as "the Breeches Bible," from its translation of Genesis 3, reporting that Adam and Eve "sewed themselves fig leaves and made themselves breeches." There is a Breeches Bible on display in Holy Trinity Church, Loddon, in Norfolk.

The Bishops' Bible

In the meantime, Elizabeth I had come to the throne and the exiled Protestants were able to come home, bringing the Geneva Bible with them. It became the most widely read version in England and was to be the Bible used and quoted by John Bunyan and William Shakespeare. But Queen Elizabeth's religious policy was to steer a middle way, keeping both Roman Catholicism, and the extremer forms of Protestantism, at bay. Many of her bishops regarded the Geneva Bible with aversion and in consequence promoted a revision of the Great Bible as the only one to be authorized for reading in church services. This was known as the Bishops' Bible. Many in England heard the Bishops' Bible in Church, but read the Geneva Bible in the privacy of their homes. It was the latter that promoted a Protestant understanding of the faith.

The King James Bible

We might have supposed that Christians couldn't go on forever producing new versions of the Bible. And yet they did, chiefly because no translation was ever perfect and the nature of the English language was changing rapidly throughout these years. In 1603 James the VI of Scotland had become James I of England. With the recent death of Queen Elizabeth, English people were fearful of what the religious policy of the new king might be. He was after all the son of Mary Queen of Scots, a deposed and executed Catholic Queen. But James was content to accept the "Elizabethan Settlement" and, like Elizabeth, to steer a middle way. This was to annoy the Puritan faction in the Church, a considerable group which wished the Church to be more distinctively Protestant in its belief and practice. It was supposedly to determine what reforms were necessary in the Church that James I called together an assembly of Church leaders at Hampton Court in 1604. It was a Puritan leader, Dr Reynolds, who proposed that the King should authorize a new translation of the Bible, the which he was eager to do. For he detested the Geneva Bible, not because of its translation, but because of the avowedly anti-monarchical views that appeared in so many of the marginal commentary. Recalling his mother's fate, he did not appreciate the sort of comment concerning the terrible death of Queen Jezebel, that read "thus God deals with tyrants." James was a firm believer in the Divine Right of Kings, i.e. that he was King by God's anointing and was not answerable to human laws. We should recall that that belief was totally rejected some 40 years later by those who tried, condemned and executed his son, Charles I. We may guess that the regicides would have been readers of the Geneva Bible.

MAIN VERSIONS OF THE ENGLISH BIBLE

c. 1380:   John Wycliffe, 1st Ed. (poss.Nicholas of Hereford)
c. 1385:   John Wycliffe, 2nd Ed., John Purvey.

The Tyndale/KJV Tradition HENRY VIII (1509 to 1547)

1525 :   Martin Luther, German Bible
1526 :   William Tyndale, NT 1st Ed.
                 OT (Gen - Chron)
1534 :   William Tyndale, NT 2nd Ed.
1535 :   Myles Coverdale, 1st Ed. (first complete printed Eng. Bible)
1537 :   Matthew's Bible (=John Rogers)
          Coverdale, 2nd Ed. (rec'd King's licence)
1538 :   The Great Bible, - set up in every Parish Church
1540 :   The Great Bible, 2nd Ed. "*appointed to be read in all the churches*".

EDWARD VII (1547 to 1553)

1547:   Book of Common Prayer, 1st Ed.

MARY 1 (1553 - 1558)

ELIZABETH I (1558 - 1603)

1560 :   The Geneva Bible - first with verse divisions
1568 :   The Bishops' Bible (revision of Great Bible)

JAMES I (1603 - 1625)

1611 :   King James' (or Authorized) Version

The Independent Tradition

1768 :   John Wesley's NT (rev. of KJV)

The American Tradition

1881 :   Revised Version (rev. of KJV)
1901 :   American Standard Version
1913 :   James Moffatt NT
1924 :   James Moffatt   OT
1947 :   JB Phillips "*Letters to Young Churches*"
1952 :   Revised Standard Version
1961 :   New English Bible
1962 :   The Living Bible
1966 :   Jerusalem Bible (RC)
1966 :   Today's English Version
1976 :   Good News Bible
1979 :   NIV   New International Version
1982 :   Revised King James' (Authorized) Version
1989 :   Revised English Bible (rev. of NEB)
1989 :   New Revised Standard Version

I have listed the English monarchs whose political power was crucial for the work of Bible translators and for publication of the Bible.

As to who should carry out this new translation, James out-maneuvered the Puritans. He himself chose the scholars who should execute the translation, confiding the management of it to Richard Bancroft, Bishop of London. Since neither king nor parliament could finance the operation, the scholars were given to understand that their reward would be that of preferment to vacant bishoprics. Bancroft himself became the next Archbishop of Canterbury. This factor goes some way to explain the extraordinarily sycophantic language of the translators in their dedicatory epistle to the King. King and bishops laid down from the outset that their version was not to contain any marginal notes, except those explanatory of some obscure words.

It is a pity that the longer preface is rarely printed nowadays, for it set out clearly what the translators were attempting, not to produce a wholly new translation, but rather to revise and improve on the previous translations of the English Bible. They declared themselves to be standing "on the shoulders of giants." It is the case therefore that much of the work of Tyndale, Coverdale and others reappeared in new guise. The appraisal of one scholar is that 60% of its wording derives from previous translators (including some 18% from Tyndale and 19% from the Geneva Bible). It is a surprise to discover that all biblical quotations in this preface are straight from the Geneva Bible.

Why this translation ever became known as the Authorized Version is a mystery. Apart from the King's initial authorization of the project, it was never authorized by any act of parliament which under the Elizabethan Settlement would have been necessary. The preferred designation nowadays is to refer to it as the King James Version.

The new translation was published in 1611. It did not meet with immediate popular acclaim – far from it. It was badly printed and expensive, whereas much better and cheaper copies of the Geneva Bible were still easily imported. Readers complained of the many misprints. Some of these achieved notoriety. An edition of 1630 earned the sobriquet of "The Wicked Bible" for the printer had missed out "not" in the seventh Commandment and had to pay a fine of £300 for his error. Holy Trinity Church in Blythburgh, Suffolk used to display[82] a so-called Judas Bible. In the 23rd chapter of Matthew's Gospel, the printer had inadvertently printed the name of Judas rather than that of Jesus!

How and why did the KJV triumph? It did, but not until some 50 or 60 years after publication. During that period, the Geneva Bible remained the popular version. The reason for the eventual triumph of the KJV has to do with the

---

[82] I write used to, because in circa 2000, some miscreant broke into the showcase and vandalized this unique Bible.

aftermath of the English Civil War. The failure of the Commonwealth established by Oliver Cromwell, which, having executed Charles I, had abolished both monarchy and episcopacy, and gone to such excesses as the abolition of Christmas, led to an eventual backlash. The Geneva Bible must have been associated in the popular mind with such excesses. In 1660, James II was restored to the throne to huge popular acclaim. The restored episcopate and landed gentry returned to power with a vengeance (of which the imprisonment of John Bunyan is evidence). The Puritan faction was defeated, and with it, we may suppose, the popularity of the Geneva Bible. But the fact that the KJV was without marginal notes of an inflammatory nature must have commended itself to a majority of Christians. Thus by the end of the century it had become *the* English Bible and remained so for the best part of three centuries. The fact was that the translators had done an excellent (though not faultless) job. Many literary critics would say that in its pages the English language had reached its epitome; that in the Bible and the works of William Shakespeare it had reached its finest heights of expression.

Quite how and why it was exalted into almost idolatrous status in some Christian circles (as it still is today) is difficult to tell. Recently I was looking for the KJV Bible on the Internet, and I came across it on one web page, with the subheading: "This is the true Word of God." In some conservative American churches, any attempt to revise it (as in the Revised King James' Version) has been met with vitriolic opposition. It is well to remember how an Irish Archbishop in the late 19th century once held up a Bible in an assembly of his clergy and declared, "This is not the Bible" (which was met with shocked expressions) and went on: "It is a translation of the Bible." Quite so. No translation is perfect. I am happy to believe in the inspiration of many a translation, but in the infallibility of none.

The necessity of continuing revision

Why cannot we remain forever content with the KJV? It will remain for ever a literary treasure, for its translators had a great felicity in choosing phraseology that reads pleasantly to ear and eye. But even here, there are obscurities that require revision if it is to be understood. Much of its language was bordering on the archaic even in 1611. The "thees" and "thous" written into the text were fast disappearing from spoken English even as it was being translated. Much of its language can hardly be understood by today's readers (unless trained in the language of bygone years). Few today would understand that "prevent" meant "go before" in the speech of the early 17th century.

But the main criticism of the KJV has to be regarding the inaccuracy of its textual basis, for which its translators bear no blame. No translation can be better than the text on which it is based. They could employ only what manuscripts were then available; and those were days before the art of serious textual criticism had begun. They were able to use only those manuscripts that had been available to Erasmus (which he recognized to be defective) and to the Parisian printer Stephanus. They had collated a number of manuscripts which had been printed in various editions in the 16th century and whose 1633[83] edition was advertised as the "Received Text" (known generally as the Textus Receptus), which misled some to suppose it to be in some way officially authorized. These manuscripts were mostly of the Byzantine (or Koine) family of texts, which subsequent research has demonstrated to be amongst the least trustworthy.

Within two decades of the KJV's appearance, scholars had access to a manuscript which gave, at many points, readings differing from those of the Textus Receptus. In 1628 Patriarch Lucar of Constantinople had sent to King Charles I a manuscript subsequently known as Codex Alexandrinus. It was of the Alexandrian "family," up till then hardly known in the West. This was of course two centuries before Tischendorf's discovery of Codex Sinaiticus and before the Vatican revealed its possession of Codex Vaticanus; both manuscripts of the fourth century in excellent condition and which have enabled the establishment of a much more reliable textual basis for modern translations.

Why so many modern translations?

My own recollection is that, until about 1950 or thereabouts, the only version widely used by individuals and by churches, was the KJV. There were some others available, like the Revised Version of 1881 (useful as a study Bible, because it adhered closely to the underlying Hebrew and Greek text; but for the same reason, didn't read well in public); or the Moffat Bible, the work of a Scottish scholar, James Moffat, a brilliantly idiosyncratic work, which had been published before the war. It had the distinction of using variable type-face to indicate the different sources within the text of the Pentateuch.

From 1950 onwards, there came a seeming explosion of new English translations. A S Duthie, in a book published in 1985, lists 17 translations of the whole Bible and 15 of the New Testament since 1945, and we may wonder how many have there been since then.

---

[83] Metzger, *Text of the NT*, p 106: the 1633 edition had printed quite misleadingly: "the reader has the text which is now received by all, in which we give nothing changed or corrupted." As an advertising gimmick, this wording was intelligible, but as a factual statement, quite false.

Why the multiplication of new translations?

We can adduce several reasons:

1. The 1939-1945 war had impeded scholarly progress, with shortages of manpower and paper. With the war ended, there came about the feeling of entering a new age, in which a new society had to be built on solid foundations. A sign of this was the Butler Education Act of 1947, ensuring that Religious Knowledge, wholly Christian and Bible-based, would have its place in the British school curriculum. For this brave new (but dangerous) world, the Bible message should be presented anew.

2. There had been significant discoveries of Hebrew and Greek manuscripts, yielding yet more resources to the textual critics. In foremost place was the discovery of the Dead Sea Scrolls in 1947 but of course it was to be decades before their secrets would be fully disclosed to the scholarly world. More important initially were the Egyptian papyrus discoveries from early in the century. The excavation of ancient rubbish heaps turned up amazing treasures; of thousands of fragments of papyrus (which could only have survived in so dry a climate) covering almost every aspect of the daily life of two thousand years ago. The Greek used in these fragments was very similar to that to be found in the New Testament; proving that both were written in what was known as "koine" or common Greek, not that of the high-flown poets and philosophers but of the common people.

3. Our knowledge of the ancient languages and of the environment of the Middle East is constantly increasing. If the meaning of a Hebrew word is uncertain, its equivalent in another Semitic language, whether Syriac, Coptic or Babylonian, is often revealing. Finds amongst the papyri were revealing. In the Lord's Prayer, there occurs a word "epiousios," of uncertain meaning, but usually translated "daily" (hence, "Give us our daily bread"). The word occurs in the fragments as clearly indicating the soldier's "daily ration," immediately illuminating our Lord's meaning (that is, of course, on the assumption that it accurately translated what Jesus had said in Aramaic).

4. Add to that the fact that our own language is also constantly changing. Imagine all the words commonplace in our language today which would have been unintelligible to our grandparents, words like "email," "megabytes," "euros," "x-ray" etc. If the biblical message is to be heard by today's people, it has to be expressed in today's language.

5. The translator's work is never finished, for no translation can be perfect. A Latin tag has it that "traductore est traditore," to translate is to betray. We may feel irritation that no sooner have we become used to the New English Bible

than it is superseded by the Revised English Bible. Similarly with the Revised Standard Version; within years of its publication, it has been replaced by the New Revised Standard Version. There's nothing new about this. No sooner had William Tyndale published his English New Testament than he began on the revision that would replace it. This was the case with the King James Version. Within its year of publication, there were three editions printed, each making minor amendments.

Two Main Approaches: I the Tyndale Lineage

Amongst all the modern translations, there are two main lines of approach taken. Some attempt no more than to revise a previous translation; others set out to translate "de novo," as if on a clean slate. In the first category, we can trace a clear "genealogy" stemming from the original work of Tyndale. A whole succession of 16th-century translations fall into this category; beginning with Tyndale, we continue with Coverdale, the Matthew Bible, the Great Bible, the Bishop's Bible and the King James Version. It has been calculated that even the KJV uses 18% of Tyndale's words and yet more of his sentence constructions[84]. And this continues into modern times. The Revised Version of 1881 didn't set out to be anything other than a revision of the KJV. The principle was: "Don't alter anything that is perfectly clear unless new textual or philological evidence demands it." The famed American versions followed much the same principle: thus the American Standard Bible (ASB) led to the Revised Standard Version (RSV) and more recently to the New Revised Standard Bible (NRSV). This explains why so many of us brought up on the KJV usually feel more comfortable with the translations coming out of this inheritance. Within them we can still discern the echo of Tyndale and the KJV and yet in translations that disclose the best of modern scholarship.

II : Fresh Translations (without regard to previous ones)

❖ J B PHILIPS

There ever remains the danger of familiarity breeding not contempt but somnolence. Jesus' teaching of parables had the effect of jerking people's attention (perhaps getting "under their skin"), so as to hear "the word of the Lord" in a new way. Don't we need translations that do just this? Four post-war attempts to do that deserve our close attention. J B Philips was an Anglican vicar with a brilliant flair with words. Throughout the war years he was working

---

[84] In a recent major study, "*The Bible in English*, Yale UP 2003. Professor D. Daniell argues that the proportion is far higher. He cites a computerized study as demonstrating that, in the KJV, 83% of the NT; and 76% of the OT is dependent on Tyndale." See p. 448.

on a translation that would really convey the message of Paul's epistles in modern idiom. His chief principle was that the translator's task was to perceive Paul's meaning and then to convey it in whatever idiom would be most easily understood by today's readers (even though that meant departing far from biblical language). It is therefore paraphrase rather than strict translation. *When Letters to Young Churches*, his translation of the epistles, was published in 1947, it caused quite a sensation. I advise you to read its preface (its paperback version is easily found in most second-hand bookshops) as well as the translation. It throws almost contemporary light on Paul's genius. His book *Ring of Truth*, also makes for exciting reading as he shares his reflections on translating the New Testament. Both are classics.

❖ THE NEW ENGLISH BIBLE

At much the same time, the British Council of Churches believed that it was the appropriate time to launch a wholly new English translation on an ecumenical basis. It drew together the best scholars from all the churches, under the chairmanship of Dr C. H. Dodd, a Congregationalist scholar. The Roman Catholics eventually joined the team, first as observers, later as full members; a significant fact as the first time Protestants and Catholics had worked together on a biblical translation. The result was the New English Bible (1970). Again, nothing stands still. It was no sooner finished than the work of revision began, resulting in the publication of the Revised English Bible in 1989. This is an excellent translation for giving fresh insights that you might have missed within the Tyndale – KJV lineage; but it has never wholly caught on within the public worship of the Church. Many people in pews miss the cadence of the Tyndale lineage, for example, in the REB's translation of the opening words of John's Gospel: "In the beginning the Word already was. The Word was in God's presence, and what God was, the Word was." Brilliant translation, but does it sound right? But does sounding right matter?

❖ THE JERUSALEM BIBLE

This was the first major post-war translation to emerge from within the Roman Catholic Church and it signifies a modern development of huge ecumenical significance. It marked the eruption of the finest Catholic scholarship into the full light of day, unfettered by the hitherto heavy hand of the Vatican. In the early years of the 20th century, a number of fine biblical scholars had been harshly repressed within the blanket condemnation of Modernism. Now, in the post-war years, Catholic scholars were permitted to engage in the international and ecumenical world of biblical scholarship, with the most fruitful results. The Jerusalem Bible largely stemmed from the work of the Ecole Biblique in Jerusalem; whose scholars were heavily engaged in the study of the Dead Sea Scrolls as well as in biblical research. Like the New English Bible, this too set out to translate directly from the Hebrew and Greek text, without reference to earlier translations. It therefore read as a wholly fresh product. One controversial decision was to translate the Hebrew "tetragrammaton," the sacred letters of the name of God, as it was believed to have been pronounced, i.e. as Yahweh. One has to wonder whether this was not offensive to Jews, amongst whom the name of God should never be spoken aloud in public. It is too sacred. In its place they always substituted "Adonai," in English, the Lord.

❖ THE GOOD NEWS BIBLE

At the forefront of all Bible translation are the United Bible Societies, the descendents of what began life as the British and Foreign Bible Society. With their strong motivation to provide Bibles both intelligible and affordable to people all round the world, they took account of the fact that many millions spoke hundreds of different languages yet understood and spoke English as their second language. They set out to produce an English version which would be easily understood by such people, i.e. with a fairly basic English vocabulary. The result was "Today's English Version" which in time became the Good News Bible (GNB). This has been phenomenally successful and was adopted by many churches as their pew Bible. It succeeds admirably in rendering lucid what in previous translations had been opaque. It is easily understood. At times, its translation is clumsy. For example, in the gospels, it regularly translates what used to be rendered as "leper" as "a man with a skin disease," technically correct since the biblical references do not equate with what modern medical practice would term leprosy, but nevertheless clumsy.

❖ THE NEW INTERNATIONAL VERSION

There are many modern versions of which I have made no mention at all. An extremely popular version is the New International Version (NIV). I cannot comment on what I have not seriously read, but the fact that all the translators had to subscribe to a narrow doctrine of verbal inspiration renders me suspicious of it. Integrity demands that the scholar translate on the basis of the textual evidence alone and not according to any preset dogma. In other words, this version is the outcome of the "Holy Bible" assumption that I have criticized in the opening chapter of this book.

Without a doubt, yet many more new translations have appeared since I wrote the paragraph above. Each one has to be assessed on its own merits.

Appendix: the remnants of the Vulgate Bible.
1. What did the shepherds hear angels singing? *Gloria in excelsis Deo.*
2. What did Mary sing? *The Magnificat.*
3. What did the aged Simeon pray in the Temple? *Nunc dimittis.*
4. What is the Latin for "Come"? *Venite.*
5. What is the Latin for "Rejoice"? *Jubilate.*

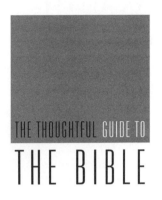

THE THOUGHTFUL GUIDE TO
THE BIBLE

THE AUTHORITY
OF THE BIBLE

CHAPTER 19:
THE BIBLE AS AUTHORITY:
is it the Word of God?

What is authority and where is it to be found?

1. GOD, THE SOURCE OF ALL AUTHORITY

The word authority derives from the idea of authorship. In the theology of creation, God is thought of as the creator/author of all that exists. He is thereby the ultimate and only supreme authority. On the human level, and by analogy, we recognize the inventor of, say, a new type of motor engine, a creative artist, or the author of a novel, as being authorities over the product of their creation.

On an occasion of crucial importance, Jesus appealed to the direct authority of God (rather than to any human institution) in justification of his actions. The episode is recorded in Mark 12.27-33. Jesus was questioned by the Temple guardians as to his authority for acting there as he did – this presumably refers to his demonstration against the Temple traders and money-changers as well as to his teaching the crowds as if he were a licensed teacher. He responded, as he did frequently, by putting a counter question to them: "By what authority did John baptize repentant sinners in the Jordan?" The case of John was clearly not dissimilar from that of Jesus. This silenced his critics. Had they said, "It was clearly from God," he could have demanded to know why they didn't believe his message. If they had replied, "He did it on his own authority," they feared the crowd for John was esteemed as a great prophet of God. They replied: "We do not know," to which response Jesus refused to disclose by what authority he acted as he did. Was he not in essence declaring that his authority was like that of John's, an authority conferred directly by God (and therefore in the prophetic tradition) and not dependent on any status of family, of training or ordination conferred by the chief priest? His authority, derived from God, was self-authenticating as all true authority is.

2. AUTHORITY UNDER GOD

From the biblical perspective, all human authority, whether that of persons, of human institutions such as nation-states or churches, is by delegation from God. Paul makes the clearest statement about this in Romans 13.1 where he wrote: "Let every person be subject to the governing authorities; for there is no authority except from God, and those authorities that exist have been instituted by God."[85] Authority and power go hand in hand. Whoever has authority has power to put it into effect.

Under the heading of delegated authority, we may cite that of reigning monarchs, in the modern world mostly replaced by parliamentary democracies. In the United Kingdom, the Queen is the nominal authority in that no legislation is valid until it has received her signature; but in practice, Parliament is sovereign. In the United States, the Constitution of 1788 is paramount, of which the Supreme Court is the guardian. Even the President, powerful as he is, can only rule according to the Constitution. Similar to this is the authority of many types of governing bodies, charged with the direction and control of an institution. We may think readily of the governing bodies of schools, of hospitals, of sports clubs, etc, and, of course, of churches. For Roman Catholics, such authority is vested in the Office of the Pope; for churches of the Reformation in democratic assemblies such as General Assemblies. Whoever has "the final say," or takes the executive decisions, is the controlling authority for that institution.

3. AUTHORITY BY COMMISSIONING

Another kind of authority is a diluted form of the above. A ruling body may delegate some part of its own authority to a subordinate. An Army officer receives the President's or the Queen's commission. As such s/he represents all that his presidential or her royal office entails. His orders to the soldiers under his command have to be obeyed because his authority is delegated from the sovereign. The Roman centurion in Capernaum (Matthew 8.5-10) recognized that Jesus had that sort of authority, deriving as it did from God and that it was superior even to his own delegated to him from the emperor.

In most churches, it is this type of authority which is conferred on those ordained as ministers. In all churches, the candidating procedures attempt to discern a candidate's vocation to ministry, recognizing that a calling by God is *the* most vital factor, but it is ordination which confers the Church's (delegated) authority to preach and teach and administer the sacraments in its name.

4. THE AUTHORITY OF SPECIAL INSIGHT AND KNOWLEDGE

A different kind of authority, moral rather than legal, is recognized in some

---

[85] Paul's words may well appear astonishing in view of the fact that the ruling emperor at the time he wrote his letter to the Romans (c AD 58) was Nero. But Paul was proud of his Roman citizenship. Roman officials had frequently protected him against many an angry mob; and, the first five years of Nero's rule were quite beneficent. The empire was peaceful. One wonders whether he could have written as he did after the events of 64, when Nero launched the first and fiercest persecution of Christians, had he survived it. According to Roman tradition, he did not.

people. We will hear it said that Professor So-and-So is "the authority" on, say, molecular biology; meaning that he or she knows as much as can be known within that field of science and can speak about it in such a way as to carry conviction. This kind of authority is particularly that of the great men of God in the Bible: of Abraham, Moses, David, Elijah, Isaiah, of Paul and, supremely, of Jesus. It is characteristic of them that each received a calling from God. They were His appointees and therefore spoke with His authority. In the case of Jesus, the gospels bear testimony that the common people recognized this quality in him, as is reported of the worshipers in the synagogue in Capernaum "They were astounded at his teaching, for he taught them as one having authority, and not as the scribes."(Mark 1.22). In him they recognized a true authority coming directly from God, contrasting it with that of the scribes whose authority would have depended on rabbinical training and certification. He knew God in so intimate a sense as to carry immediate conviction to his hearers that he bore God's own authority. This was made quite explicit in his claim to forgive sins and to make the lame walk (Mark 2.1-12, especially verses 9-11). The expression he used of himself, "Son of Man" designates (in the Jewish thinking of its time) the one to whom God has delegated His own authority as His agent in the coming Judgment of the world.

What came to be the common Christian conviction is summed up at the conclusion of Matthew's Gospel, when the author represents Jesus as telling his disciples: "All authority in heaven and on earth has been given to me."(Matthew 28.18) The same understanding is expressed symbolically in the story of the ascension, as in the Apostles' Creed's declaration that "he is seated at the right hand of the Father." In an Eastern court, only the heir apparent or the chief minister would sit at a monarch's right hand. For all practical purposes then, *Jesus' authority is regarded as equal to that of God the Father*. He shares in the exercise of God's authority.

5. THE EXERCISE OF AUTHORITY

Jesus enunciated a particular attitude towards the exercise of authority which is characteristic, especially by comparison with the worldly use and abuse of authority. He himself exemplified this in word and in deed. On a number of occasions, he advocated humble service rather than self-assertion. In Mark's Gospel, when James and John were arguing over precedence in the kingdom, he said: "You know that among the Gentiles those whom they recognize as their rulers lord it over them, and their great ones are tyrants over them. But it is not so among you; but whoever wishes to become great among you must be your servant, and whoever wishes to be first among you must be slave of all. For the Son of Man came not to be served but to serve, and to give his life a ransom for many." (Mark 10.42-45). In John's Gospel this was exemplified in his washing of the disciples' feet. As also in Paul's Letter to the Philippians where the apostle urged Christians to imitate the humility of Christ, who "though he was in the form of God, did not regard equality with God as something to be exploited, but emptied himself, taking the form of a slave, being born in human likeness. And being found in human form, he humbled himself and became obedient to the point of death – even death on a cross."(Philippians 2.5-8). This sets a bench-mark for all Christian exercise of authority.

How do these definitions of various levels of authority apply to the Bible?

In the above discussion, I have cited the Constitution of the USA as an example of supreme authority vested in a legal document. Magna Carta (from 1215) still lays down the basic principles of English law; as in contemporary world affairs, the United Nations' Declaration of Human Rights sets a goal for the rights that should be available to all (but which are sadly denied to many). Does the Bible constitute the Supreme Authority for the Christian Church (as the United Reformed Church's Basis of Union declares)? The Bible has been so regarded in the Churches stemming from the Reformation. We have to enquire whether this is justifiable?

God as Author of the Bible?

The traditional understanding of the Bible as supremely authoritative was on the assumption that it had been written either directly by God or by men at his dictation. It has therefore been customary to speak of God as being the Author of the Bible and still is in some circles. The Westminster Confession (1643), cornerstone of the Presbyterian brand of English nonconformity, declares in its first article: "The authority of the Holy Scripture ... dependeth not on the testimony of any man or Church; but wholly upon *God* (who is truth itself) *the author thereof.*" And quite recently, in his preface to *The Interpretation of the Bible in the Church* (published by the Pontifical Biblical Commission in 1993), Cardinal Ratzinger refers to God as "the genuine author." As did the document "Verbum Dei" emanating from the Second Vatican Council.

Whilst we may continue to believe that God is the creator of all that exists, I have already argued throughout this book that to view Him as in any realistic sense as the author of the Bible is unhelpful. Otherwise, we should have to regard Him as equally the author of the Works of Shakespeare, of the paintings of Michelangelo, or the inventor of the Concorde aeroplane, indeed of every human artifact that exists. This does not accord in any way with how the divine-human relationship actually operates. In creation, God "lets be" everything that He has made to exist, so that whilst it is dependent upon Him yet it has its own life. He does not control every article of His creation as a puppeteer controls his

279

puppets. He respects our human freedom. Even the inspiration of His Spirit does not over-ride our human personalities. It is therefore not helpful in practice to speak of God as author of the Bible. The authors of its books are independent authors, nevertheless authors in the service of God.

Is the Bible's authority dependent on the stature of its authors?

The traditional attribution of authority to the Bible was considerably based on the understanding that it had been written by great men of God, themselves authority figures. Since, according to the traditional theory, Moses penned the Pentateuch, David the Psalms and Solomon the Wisdom writings; and in the New Testament, apostles (or their associates such as Mark and Luke) wrote the gospels as did Paul all the writings appearing under his name, their authenticity (hence authority) was supposedly guaranteed. As I have demonstrated at some length, historico-literary criticism has largely demolished these attributions of authorship. Moses may well be the originator of the traditions at the root of the Pentateuch, but the final product as we have it took several centuries and was the product of scores of anonymous priests and prophets, scribes and officials. Equally, in the light of modern criticism, the gospels in their final form were not the product of either apostles or other eye-witnesses (although doubtless the testimony of such witnesses must lie in the very earliest sources at their disposal). The fact is that the early Church left little or no evidence as to how or why the gospels were written (except for that which lies embedded in the text, which is the data of greatest importance to scholars); such that the efforts of the Church in the second century to attribute their authorship to apostles were somewhat suspect attempts to give them legitimacy.

To traditionalists, such biblical criticism has destroyed the credibility of the Bible (hence their fierce hostility to it). But this was an unnecessarily extreme reaction. As Moses lies behind the Pentateuch, so the apostles stand behind the gospels. If the Pentateuch and gospels as we have them were the product of scores of hands rather than very few, why should they appear diminished? If the Spirit that was in Moses befell the 70 Elders (Numbers 11.25) so as to share in his inspiration, isn't it acceptable that the Books of Moses may have been written by many anonymous writers? If it is established (from the evidence within them) that neither Matthew nor John, apostles, wrote the gospels which bear their name, can we not accept that their anonymous authors were just as faithfully committed to proclaiming the gospel as were those apostles? The authority of what is written is not diminished if it is the case (as we believe that it is) that they were written by anonymous preachers and teachers rather than by named apostles. The message is greater than the messengers!

The Bible is a human product, a work of great inspiration, a trustworthy record of its authors encounters with the living God, which thereby conveys to us "the Word of God," but which remains nevertheless a book marked by every kind of fault and failing to which human authorship is prone.

Is the Bible the Word of God?

It has been customary, especially amongst Protestants, to designate the Bible as "The Word of God" or "The Word of the Lord." This has become habitual whenever, in the liturgy, the reader of each biblical lection concludes with "This is the Word of the Lord," to which the congregation responds "Thanks be to God." It would not be surprising that many listeners take this to imply that the Bible was written either by God or at His express command. We might call this the traditional sense in which the expression is used. An alternative and more rational understanding is that through its authors' testimony, God conveys his message without being identical with it. In writings of the early Church Fathers, the process of inspiration was described as being like the playing of a flute. It is the breath of God that produces the sound and human fingers, as moved by God, which determine the notes played. An alternative version of this metaphor would say that the biblical authors listened intently for the Word of God, and moved by the Spirit, played the music as it resounded in their hearing and by their fingering. But it was their version of the music that we hear.

• •

What is the Word of God? It is time that we examined what is meant, in the Bible itself, by the expression "Word of God." Does it ever refer without ambiguity to the scriptures? Or may it convey a more dynamic meaning, such as that the Bible conveys or contains the Word of God?

• •

Within the Bible, we find these usages of the expression "Word of God"

1. THE WORD OF GOD IS ACTIVE IN WORDS AND DEEDS

God as revealed within the biblical story is a God who communicates with his creation. In the Hebrew Bible, the main word employed is "dabar" (plural debarim), which can equally well be translated as "word," "saying" or as "thing, act or event." The second flows from the first, for the word spoken achieves the action performed. This is beautifully portrayed in Isaiah 55.10-11: "For as the rain and the snow come down from heaven, and do not return there until they have watered the earth, making it bring forth and sprout, giving seed to the sower and bread to the eater, *so shall my word be that goes out from my mouth*; it shall not return to me empty, but *it shall accomplish that which I purpose*, and succeed in the thing for which I sent it."

Above all, His Word works wonders, both in creation and in redemption. In the creation stories, God has only to speak the words, "Let there be Light" and there is Light. In redemption, He calls Abraham to be the founding Father of the Jewish race, through whom blessing is to be conveyed to all humankind. By mighty deeds, He punishes the Egyptians, liberates the Israelites from slavery, leads them across the Sea of Reeds, and gives them the Torah on Mt Sinai by which they are to live. It was in such events that the biblical authors perceived the activity of God.

We could say that God's actions speak louder than words. In general then, "the Word of God" indicates God's activity in creation and redemption. The expression is indicative of a quite advanced stage of theological thinking, when the biblical authors, fearful of taking the divine Name in vain, substituted for it a periphrasis. Thus, in place of "the heavens were made by God" we have instead "By the word of the Lord the heavens were made, and all their host by the breath of his mouth."(Psalms 36.6) The difference may appear to us over subtle, yet to the pious Jew it was deeply meaningful.

2. THE WORD, GOD'S MESSAGE, IS ALSO CONVEYED THROUGH THE LIPS OF HUMAN BEINGS

From the call of Abraham onwards, God spoke to those whom He had called and conveyed his Will to them. This becomes especially the case with the Prophets. The English word derives from Greek "prophetes," meaning "one who speaks on behalf of another," i.e. of God. Typically the prophets prefaced the messages they were given with "Thus says the Lord ..." or ended them with "This is the Word of the Lord." It was not to deliver their private opinions but a message received from God that they spoke. In chapter 7 I have discussed the means by which the prophets discerned God's message. The Word of God is then a message from God conveyed by his spokesman. Even within biblical times, the question arose as to how bystanders could know whether God had really given the message the prophet proclaimed. There was the occasion, reported in 1 Kings 22.1-40, when two self-professed prophets gave contradictory advice to a King eager to know the Lord's Will as to whether he should go into battle or not. This raises the question of false prophets (a matter with which Jeremiah had much to say). The general answer discernible within the pages of the Old Testament is that the Word of a true prophet comes to fruition; that of a false prophet does not. A deeper principle of discernment was cited by Jesus in the Sermon on the Mount: "Beware of false prophets ...you will know them by their fruits."(Matthew 7.15-16)

3. THE WORD IN SYMBOLIC ACTIONS

It was not only through spoken words that prophets conveyed the Lord's message. It was also by means of *symbolic deeds*. Jeremiah smashed an earthenware jar in the Temple (Jeremiah 19.1 & 10) so as to give visual warning of what God would do to the Temple. And it went further than outward deeds. The message was also lived out within the life and sufferings of the prophet. Hosea was commanded to take as wife a woman who was notoriously promiscuous (Hosea 1.2); thus the prophet felt within himself all the agony that God feels in His love for a faithless people. Jeremiah's sufferings anticipate those of the Servant of the Lord in Isaiah's prophecies (and thence in Jesus' agony in Gethsemane). This means of communication is not therefore significantly different from that described in the previous paragraph: both constitute the "debarim" of God, whether in words or in deeds.

4. THE WORD COMMITTED TO WRITING

In some very few cases the prophet is directly bidden to commit the message to writing, so here we have the first indication of the Word as identifiable with words written on a scroll. Such was the case with Jeremiah when refused entry to the Temple (in Jeremiah 36). He was given very specific instructions: "… this word came to Jeremiah from the Lord: Take a scroll and write on it all the words that I have spoken to you against Israel and Judah … from the day I spoke to you, from the days of Josiah until today. Then Jeremiah called Baruch son of Neriah, and Baruch wrote on a scroll at Jeremiah's dictation all the words of the Lord that he had spoken to him. And Jeremiah ordered Baruch, saying, 'I am prevented from entering the house of the Lord; so you go yourself, and on a fast day in the hearing of the people in the Lord's house you shall read the words of the Lord from the scroll that you have written at my dictation'" (Jeremiah 36.1-6). In the event, the king deliberately destroyed the scroll, casually throwing it, piece by piece, onto the fire; only for the prophet, at God's behest, to dictate a further copy of it to the faithful Baruch. But even in this very precise sequence of events, the scroll itself is never designated as "Word of God." It remains the most explicit (and rare) mention of how a piece of Old Testament scripture came to be written.

Isaiah too had been directly commanded to commit some of his prophetic message to writing. In 8.16 we read: "Bind up the testimony, seal the teaching among my disciples." The testimony which the prophet had declared to the people, which they had rejected, was to be consigned to a scroll, which would then be tied and sealed – as a permanent and tangible witness against the people. A traditionalist viewpoint would say that there had been earlier precedent, that of Moses' recording of the words of the covenant at Sinai; but we may suspect that the writing of these accounts is post-Exilic. But even in these accounts, from the books of Exodus and Deuteronomy, there is some ambiguity as to whether the Decalogue was supposedly written by God (but how?) or by Moses at God's dictation.

Apart from these two historical instances, it is remarkable that there are no other obvious attributions of divine authorship to the books of the Old Testament. The inference is that the vast corpus of Old Testament scriptures was of human authorship, to which, in time, varying degrees of divine inspiration were attributed. We cannot sensibly extend the meaning that certain writings were recorded at God's express command to the notion that the entire corpus of the Bible constitutes words written or dictated by God.

5. THE WORD OF GOD IN PERSON

The culmination of the process described above by which God conveys his message is fulfilled, from the Christian perspective, in the coming of Jesus. Jews still await the coming of the Messiah. The significance is clearly conveyed in the opening lines of the Letter to the Hebrews: "Long ago God spoke to our ancestors in many and various ways by the prophets, but in these last days he has spoken to us by a Son, whom he appointed heir of all things, through whom he also created the worlds."(Hebrews 1.1-2) Jesus comes as the climax and pinnacle of all that had come before him. God reveals himself finally in a person, Jesus Christ. John's Gospel expresses the significance of his coming. The start of the gospel directs us to consider that "in the beginning was the Word," that the Word "was with God" and "was God." So we are led to think of the Word as God's self-expression, the outgoing nature of which creates the universe as the sphere within which His purpose is to be expressed; and the climax comes in verse 14 where we are told that "the Word became flesh and dwelt among us, and we have seen his glory, the glory as of a father's only son, full of grace and truth." The culmination of God's revelation is in Jesus Christ, a man of flesh and blood. He is the Word of God in person.

The same truth is declared in a more enigmatic form in the Revelation of John. In a vision, the heavens are opened and the seer is shown "a white horse! Its rider is called Faithful and True … He is clothed in a robe dipped in blood, and his name is called The Word of God."(Revelation 19.11-13).

OTHER USAGES

In the New Testament, the "Word" has become synonymous with "the gospel," the essential Christian message (the "kerygma"[86] of the earliest Christian preaching). So, in the interpretation of the parable of the Sower, we read that

---

[86] Kerygma is the Greek for "a public proclamation," an "official announcement," deriving from the verb "kerussein," usually translated "to make an public announcement" or "to preach." In NT studies, the term is used in description of the core message of early Christian preaching. C H Dodd publicized the word in his seminal study *The Apostolic Preaching and its Developments.*

"The sower sows the word" (Mark 4.14) or "the seed is the Word of God" (Luke 8.11). The imagery is clear: just as the sower flings the seed widely so as to fall on every part of the field, so Christian preachers broadcast the gospel to all who will hear it. In Luke 1.1-4, "the servants of the word" come immediately after "the eyewitnesses" as the foremost proclaimers of the gospel whose witness Luke was finally going to record in writing. It is important to note that in all such cases, the Word is nothing static, not letters inscribed on papyrus but is always associated with verbs descriptive of action: flinging out seed, preaching the gospel, etc. Other variants are as follows: "the word of the gospel" (x 3), "the word of the kingdom"(x 6), "the word of salvation" (x 2), "the word of life"(x 8, e.g. 1 John 1.1), "the word of truth;" in every case the expression clearly means "the word about, or which conveys, the gospel, the message of salvation, the truth," etc. In no case did it ever, at this stage, indicate words written in a book.

What conclusions can we draw?

From our study of the Bible's own usage of the expression Word of God, it becomes clear that the concept is absolutely central to the message of the Bible, but that **there is little or no justification for making the simple identification that the Bible is the Word of God, or, that for us today, the Word of God is the Bible**. Indeed to make that identification would be dangerous, for it encourages an idolatrous usage of the Bible.

The derivative nature of the Bible

It follows that the Word of God written in a book is a secondary (if not tertiary) stage by which God communicates with us. When the Word, that was initially an event embodied in a person who spoke inspired words, became a written record of that experience and of those words, it takes on an inevitably derivative form. To some extent what was originally a living experience becomes a fossilized form of it. We could imagine a great spiritual revolution as being like a spectacular volcanic eruption. The initial explosion throws red-hot material into the air; the lava begins to flow down the mountain-side, channeling out pathways before it. Gradually the molten rock cools and solidifies where it lies. Are not many spiritual revivals similar? The day of Pentecost witnessed a great outpouring of spiritual energy and power which brought the Christian community to birth, from which the gospel radiated outwards from Jerusalem. But can we doubt that when Luke wrote his account of those events in his Acts of the Apostles, that in itself marked a slowing down and cooling off of the initial ardor. The written account of the event inevitably conveys only a pale reflection of what it must have been like to have been personally present at the time. However inspired the writing, it can hardly match the inspiration of the lived experience.

It is for this reason, that whilst the words of scripture undoubtedly can and do inspire men and women to faith, they mostly do so in the context of Christian preaching and teaching, in which the action of the Holy Spirit brings to life the words which would otherwise have remained lifeless on the page.

A SIGNPOST TOWARDS THE TRUTH

We should never forget the provenance of the written words, as once living words. To fail to do so, by over-exalting the written record, is to confuse the signpost with the destination to which it points. It is to confuse our reading of the tourist's guide to Venice with the experience of actually being there, walking the piazzas or worshiping in St Mark's. This is where a mere Biblicism becomes a snare and a delusion, leading us into the cul-de-sac in which those Jews chided by Jesus in John 5.39 had been led.

And yet we need the signposts as we need the guide book. We, within the Church, are like people living in an impressive mansion, slowly built up over many centuries, who need, from time to time, to carry out repairs and alterations. But woe betide us if we don't continually consult the original ground-plans, particularly of the foundations on which the entire structure stands and the title deeds by which we have the right to occupy the building. Whatever its imperfections, the Bible constitutes such title deeds and ground-plans – without which we could easily go astray. They are the unique record of the history and foundational events of Christian faith, the tradition within which we stand.

We may then conclude that **the Bible conveys the Word of God**, as it also contains the Word of God, meaning that throughout its broad sweep from Genesis to Revelation, we can discern in its pages a gradual unfolding of the way in which God has addressed himself, firstly to the Jews, ultimately to all humankind, setting out His way of salvation. We have no difficulty in agreeing with the sentiment expressed by Paul (or one of his disciples) in reminding Timothy that "the sacred writings … are able to instruct you … for salvation through faith in Christ Jesus." (2 Timothy 3.15). We don't have to be fundamentalists to believe that the Bible conveys a clear message for humankind, to Jews as the Torah, to Christians as the gospel.

How does the Bible convey authority?

We may consider this under four headings:
1. What in the Bible is not authoritative?
2. What in it was once authoritative but is so no longer?
3. What in it is ambiguously authoritative?
4. What in the Bible is authoritative to the highest degree?

We will begin from the negative and move towards the positive.

1. What is *not* authoritative in the Bible?

Until some one or two centuries ago, Christians generally assumed the Bible to be completely authoritative in the entire field of human knowledge. It gave, so they supposed, an accurate account of the creation of the world; of the function of sun, moon and stars in the firmament; of the origin of every species of animal as of humankind; of the origins of the major ethnic divisions and the many languages; of the earliest history of humanity; of the earliest practices of agriculture and of city dwelling; of all the attendant arts and crafts practiced within them. Our forebears of not so many generations ago turned to the Bible much as we today would turn to the *Encyclopedia Britannica*, expecting to find truthful answers for practically every question we might put to it. That notion had to be abandoned long ago.

The Fallacy of Creationism: Most Christians today, at least in Western Europe, realize that such assumptions are quite mistaken. An exception perhaps is that of those who call themselves *Creationists*. These still read the first chapter of Genesis as a literally factual account of how God created the world; and for that reason reject all the accumulation of evidence as to the origins, nature and evolution of the universe culled by the scientific enterprise of the past three centuries. I don't know which is more misguided, their science or their religion. Their science would assume that the cosmological knowledge of the Babylonians of three millennia ago (which is the cosmology underlying Genesis chapter one) is superior to that garnered thanks to the Hubble Space telescope and the Joddrel Bank Observatory and all the observations that have led to the theories of the Big Bang origin of the universe, of Einstein's Relativity and of Particle Physics, etc. Their religion assumes that Genesis 1 was intended to be a factual scientific account; and that, accepting that as God's Word, every other explanation has to be rejected out of hand. This is a level of literalism that is crass in its absurdity. The Hebrews had no access whatever to any scientific information; for this reason, they borrowed that of the Babylonians. But they believed, as we may believe, that behind the mystery of the universe, lay the creative power of God. Theirs was a statement of faith, which is neither provable nor unprovable. We don't have to pitch it against whatever is the current scientific hypothesis, which sets out to explain *How* the universe in which we live came to be, but which is not able to give any explanation as to *Why* anything came to be. Their declaration of faith was expressed in the form of a poem in seven strophes (which is what Genesis 1 is) the whole leading up to the celebration of God's creativity on the Sabbath day. It's highly likely that the poem was composed for a great annual festival in the Temple, in which both creation and Sabbath were joyfully celebrated. Genesis 1 is pure religion; it has nothing to say about science. It is perfectly feasible for a Christian to accept the Big Bang theory on the evidence of science; and adhere to the belief that behind it all lay the creativity of God on the basis of the quite different kind of evidence that Christian faith proposes.

The fact is that humankind has made a huge leap forward in knowledge in almost every sphere of human life. I doubt very much whether the most ardent evangelical/fundamentalist, discovering that he has a nasty skin rash would seek out a priest to heal it; or, visiting a department store, would reject a particular shirt because it is made of mixed fabrics; or, attending a restaurant, would scan the menu to make sure he ate only the flesh of an animal that had divided hoofs, cloven feet and which chewed the cud. The Bible contains a load of rules and regulations that covered every aspect of the everyday life of Jewish people in the first millennium BC which the great majority of Christians long since gave up observing. It is inconsistent, to say the least, to defend with "might and main" a literalist view of creation, whilst having long since abandoned every other position in the line. Most Christians regard those parts of the Bible as no longer authoritative. And they have the authority of Jesus for taking this attitude. Christians are, after all, people of the New Covenant and not of the Old.

2. What in the Bible *was* authoritative but is so no longer?

The Mosaic Torah contains a great deal of precise information as to how the Temple was to be built, about the furnishings it was to contain, about the different kinds of sacrifice that were to be offered on its altars, and about the priests, their qualifications, their vestments, and the duties they were to perform. All of these regulations were obviously of huge importance for so long as the Temple stood in Jerusalem. They were the authority for all that took place there. But once the Roman army had stormed and destroyed the temple in AD 70, all of that sacrificial system collapsed and was never revived.

But Christians had no reason to have any interest in the rebuilding of the Temple (still a desired goal of many Orthodox Jews) and in the restoration of the sacrificial system. For them, Christ's death on the cross, regarded as the supreme sacrifice on behalf of humankind, had rendered all such animal sacrifices null and void. Hence the emphasis, in all of the gospels but made most explicit in that of John, in connection with the accusation laid against Jesus that he had intended to destroy the Temple, that God's dwelling place on earth was no longer situated in the Temple but in the body of Christ. See John 2.21's rather mysterious "He was speaking about the Temple of his body." The Letter to the Hebrews develops the theme. Christ's sacrifice has put an end to the validity of all other sacrifices. The point is clear: this entire section of the

Torah, once hugely authoritative, is so no longer. Some Christians may still use aspects of this in their preaching and teaching, in a typological sense, i.e. that they see in some aspects of the sacrificial system truths or values that help to explicate the meaning of Christ's death.

3. What in the Bible is ambiguously authoritative?

We cannot evade the fact that for various reasons some parts of the Bible, considered as a source of authority, are ambiguous. I will outline some of these reasons quite briefly:

1. The writing of the Bible was completed almost 1,900 years ago. Whilst we may assert that God has not changed (our perceptions of Him may have done so), nor has human nature, the fact remains that much of the Bible is addressing people whose ways of living and thinking were vastly different from ours. The Bible is an ancient book. It does not directly address many of the great issues facing humanity today.

2. There is the lengthy span of time, covering almost 2,000 years of history which the biblical narratives record, stretching from the call of Abraham in the early to mid second millennium BC until the post-apostolic age at the end of the first century AD. This is a time-span as long as that separating us from the days when the Romans occupied Britain. We have to ask how a record covering such a lengthy time-span can be universally authoritative; when, within that period, there have occurred huge changes, political, social, economic, cultural, and religious? We wouldn't expect many laws propounded by the Romans to be still legally valid today. In like manner, we could hardly apply any or many of the Jewish laws circumscribing the practice of agriculture in Canaan (such as are given in Exodus and Leviticus) to the modern farming industry.

3. In chapter 15, I reviewed the many different genres of literature which are found within the books of the Bible. We saw that each genre conveys its own kind of meaning. It would be foolish to confuse a parable with a historical record or the differences between prose and poetry. Each genre carries its own kind of authority and has to be evaluated appropriately. You might look back at the many genres outlined in that chapter and ask, "In which of these is the Word of God most clearly conveyed?" It is surely conveyed most clearly in direct teaching mediated by Moses, by the prophets or by Jesus, less obviously so in historical chronicles, in genealogies or in worship songs (however inspiring these may be).

4. The juxtaposition of Old and New Testaments in the Christian Bible seriously highlights the ambiguity of their relationship. From a Jewish perspective, the Christians highjacked their Bible and proceeded to interpret it

in ways quite foreign to their own way of understanding it. From a Christian perspective, God had opened their eyes to see the meaning of the Torah clearly whilst the minds of Jewish readers remained veiled (this is Paul's argument in 2 Corinthians 3.12-18). Sadly, this was a condition of stalemate as regards any common understanding of the scriptures.

❖ Clearly this is a major issue in the pages of the New Testament. In Matthew 5.17, following immediately after the opening themes of the Sermon on the Mount, Jesus is reported as declaring: "Do not think that I have come to abolish the law or the prophets; I have come not to abolish but to fulfill. For truly I tell you, until heaven and earth pass away, not one letter, not one stroke of a letter, will pass from the law until all is accomplished." (Matthew 5.17-18). The Torah stands secure – until all is accomplished. And yet the gospels indicate that now is the time – "the Kingdom of heaven is upon you" (Matthew 4.17) – that Jesus is now fulfilling the promises of God. In the very next paragraph of the Sermon, Jesus contrasts what "our forefathers were told" (By whom and where? By Moses in the Torah) with what he now declares. No wonder that opponents heard that as the abolition of the law! Jesus' disciples saw it as fulfillment of the law!

❖ There was high tension in the early Church and the above passage surely reflects that tension. Some have seen the next verse, about "whoever breaks one of the least of these commandments, and teaches others to do the same, will be called least in the kingdom of heaven …" as taking a side-swipe at Paul. That goes beyond the evidence, but the early Church in Jerusalem was divided between the "Hebrews" who kept rigidly to the Torah and the "Hellenizers" (Greek speakers) who took a more liberal line. At the ensuing council of Jerusalem, the Hellenizers lead by Paul won the debate that Gentile converts to the faith should not have to submit to the rite of circumcision nor be subject to the entirety of the Torah.

❖ The fact is that Jesus himself chose to ignore, reinterpret or actually to flout some of the legal requirements of the Old Testament. Whilst he observed the Sabbath day, he challenged the Pharisaic rulings as to what was permissible to do on it. He ignored the kosher regulations, by consorting with people who were technically unclean by reason of their occupation, immorality or illness. He declared all foods to be clean (unless this is Mark's editorial comment, Mark 7.19) thus breaking the strict regulations of Leviticus. There is no indication that he ever attended any of the daily sacrificial rituals in the Temple (an argument from silence, yet whatever the significance of his cleansing of the Temple, his attack on the buyers and sellers of animals could not have been seen in any other light than as an attack on the Temple sacrifices).

❖ The early Church largely followed Jesus down this path. How soon we cannot tell, but quite early the Sabbath was abandoned as an obligatory holy day, the first day of the week being observed instead as the day of the Lord's resurrection. And the Church took a momentous decision, as early as circa AD 50 when it decided that Gentile converts to the faith should not have to submit to the rite of circumcision. This was the most decisive factor that led to an eventual and inevitable schism of the Church from Judaism.

❖ This decision largely decided how the relation between Old and New Testaments would be understood within the Christian Church. The Old Testament had reported what was the Word of God to Israel over many centuries. Through the mouths of the prophets, God had prepared a people for the coming of His Son. What came next was radically new. The disciples saw Jesus as the fulfillment of all God's promises, who had inaugurated a New Covenant with them and with all who would come to follow him. The Old Testament was authoritative but only in so far as it was read in the light of His coming and the Spirit's illumination.

4. What in the Bible *is* truly authoritative?

Bearing in mind the reservations that have been expressed, it remains the case that the Bible is the major source of authority for Christians. It is so for reasons such as these:

1. The Bible is the unique record of the foundational events in the life of Israel, of Jesus and the early Christian Church. This constitutes what we may consider the blueprint of two great world religions, Judaism and Christianity.

2. The Bible tells a compelling *story* of "the Acts of God" on the human stage and of that inspired succession of men and women[87] of God who interpreted them over a thousand years and more, whose witness, at first passed on by word of mouth, was recorded within its pages.

3. The Bible holds up *a mirror to all humanity*. There is virtually no facet of human behavior, no kind of wickedness, no aspect of goodness that is not recorded somewhere within its pages. The Bible is wholly realistic about the human condition. It depicts humans as creatures made "in the image of God," all too prone to temptation and deeds of wickedness, and yet, by the grace of God, redeemable.

4. The Bible comprises a collection of writings which convey to us a true *Revelation of God*. This is what we would call "special revelation," i.e.

---

[87] It is the case that in the recording of Israel's history and of the early Church by men, the women mentioned are all too few, but we may still recognize the important roles of Deborah and Huldah in the OT, of Mary the mother of Jesus, Mary Magdalene, and of women prominent in the Church in Rome, such as Prisca, Junia, Julia and another Mary, and of Lydia in Phillipi, within the NT.

conveying a knowledge of God which, apart from God's initiative and the Holy Spirit's influence, could not have been discovered by the ordinary use of our human faculties. This is the key reason for biblical authority – its pages reveal to us in a unique fashion the nature and purposes of God.

5. The Bible depicts a gradual dawning of a *monotheistic concept of God*, of an understanding of His attributes and of His purposes for mankind which was translated, on the human side, into ways of worship, in recognition of His moral demands expressed in Torah, and of His loving purpose for the salvation of all people expressed in the gospel ...

6. The Bible discloses *God's initiative* in inviting people into a close relationship with Him. This was expressed in the covenants He offered to all humanity through Noah, to the Jewish people through Abraham and Moses; and in the new covenant through Jesus' life, death and resurrection for all who come to believe in him. In that relationship, Jesus' followers are empowered to know God intimately as "Abba, Father." This is experienced as sheer grace on God's part, inviting faith on ours.

7. The Bible recounts the unique story of the *life, words and works of Jesus*, in the gospels. Related in four different accounts, with varying emphases and occasional differences, they nevertheless convey a compelling account of one who was the friend of sinners, healer of the afflicted, teacher of wisdom, bearer of "the sins of the world," savior from sin and death, Lord of all who love him, even God incarnate on earth.

8. In the Bible, we find ourselves personally challenged – through Christ's call to discipleship, in his challenge to our pride and prejudice to give ourselves to the service of the poor and needy and to the search for justice in the world.

It is a fact of compelling witness that huge numbers of people have come to a lively faith in God and have been called to follow in the way of Christ, through the reading of these scriptures. They may still speak directly to hearts and minds today.

The sole criterion: Jesus Christ

In spite of the reservations expressed in the previous pages, we should not ignore the enormous continuing value of the Old Testament. Jesus consistently quoted from it, especially from the books of Deuteronomy and the Psalms. It will for ever remain a source of inspiration, of examples both heroic and dastardly, of a gradual unfolding of the purposes of God within a nation's life. Within it God's Word is still heard. And yet it remains pre-Christian. There would have been no necessity for a new covenant if the old had fulfilled all that

God purposed. Its people remain our spiritual ancestors, whom we rightly honor and from whom we have much to learn; nevertheless, Jesus instituted a new covenant and it is this that is the foundation of Christian faith. It follows that the Old Testament must always be subordinate to the New. And the most important factor of all is this: *the sole criterion of judgment on every matter concerning Christian faith and life, belief and behavior, is Jesus Christ*. His teaching and example are the touchstones whereby we judge what is truly Christian. Whatever is incompatible with that, whether in the Old Testament or any other source, is to be rejected as sub-Christian. He is the supreme authority. He is the Word made flesh, the Word of God in person.

Nobody has expressed this more clearly than Hans Kung. Having discussed and rejected the claims of either Bible or Church to infallibility, he wrote this:

"What do we really believe in? What is the real basis of Christian faith? Is it the Church or the Bible? It is neither, for that is a false alternative. The ground of faith is God himself in Jesus Christ; it is thus Jesus Christ himself who is attested in the Bible and is constantly proclaimed anew by the Church. The Christian does not believe in the Church, or in the Bible; he believes in God, in Jesus Christ. He believes, not in the Gospels, but in the gospel and in him who speaks through it. Thus Jesus Christ remains the Lord also of scripture; as the source and yardstick of its authority, he is the ultimate authority in matters of faith and theology. It is he who is the spiritual power of scripture, with the result that the latter, notwithstanding all biblical criticism, as the history of exegesis shows, constantly asserts and gains recognition of its truth anew. Thus I do not, for instance, first believe in scripture or in the inspiration of the book, and then in the truth of the gospel, in Jesus Christ. I believe in the Jesus Christ who was originally attested in scripture and, by thus experiencing Scripture as gospel in faith, I see how filled and permeated with the Spirit Scripture is. My faith in Jesus Christ originates in Scripture, because Scripture testifies to Jesus, but it is not based on Scripture; Jesus Christ, not an inspired book, is the ground of faith."[88]

Further Considerations: that need to be taken in to account when evaluating the Bible as Word of God.

---

[88] In H Kung: *Infallible?*, Collins Fount Paperback, 1971, p 179. This was the book that got Hans Kung, Swiss Roman Catholic priest and theologian, into "hot water" with the Vatican and led to the withdrawal of his license to teach as a Catholic theologian. Fortunately, the Ecumenical Faculty at Tubingen gave him a ready platform to continue to propagate his thinking to an international audience. Re-printed by permission of HarperCollins Publishers Ltd. © Hans Kung 1971

A) IS CHRISTIANITY NECESSARILY A BIBLE-BASED RELIGION?

Our reforming forebears assumed that the Christian religion was, from its origins, a Scriptural religion, i.e. a religion which looked to certain written scriptures as their authority. Some of these assumptions have to be questioned in view of new understandings gained through biblical criticism.

1. The Faith of Israel

The point is powerfully argued by James Barr that the majority of people, Jews or Christians, living within biblical times, were not themselves "scriptural" peoples. They didn't look to any written scriptures for what they believed and how they served God. No written records served as their source of authority. For the simple reason that, during their life-time, no official scripture as yet existed. This is particularly the case with regard to the Old Testament, with the tendency of recent study to push the actual writing of the oral traditions to an ever later period, i.e. to suppose that little if any of the OT was written before the Persian (from the late sixth century) or even the Greek periods (from the late fourth century) of their occupation of Palestine. It is a remarkable fact that throughout the historical books of the Old Testament (especially from 1 Samuel through to 2 Kings), and throughout the books of the Prophets, you will find no quotations whatsoever from the books of the Mosaic Torah (which, according to the Tradition, had been written by Moses centuries before the events lying behind these historical and prophetic books). You may recall (from Chapter 6) the conclusion drawn by Wellhausen, that the Torah (in its completed form) did not as yet exist. A prophet like Hosea appeals to the foundational events of Israel's story, to the exodus from Egypt and the wilderness years, about which he knew presumably through the oral tradition of them. In chapter 4.2 he condemns sins named in the Ten Commandments, i.e. those of "swearing, lying, killing, stealing, adultery and murder" and yet his order is not that of the Commandments, suggesting that the prophet didn't know them in that form. The point is made, that most of the people within scripture didn't have any scripture. Their authority was that of a strong oral tradition, of which particular people such as priests and prophets and story-tellers at the local Temple, were the guardians.

The Jews didn't become a scriptural people until the discovery of "the book of the law" in the Jerusalem Temple during the reign of King Josiah in circa 621 BC (i.e. quite late in their history). This initiated what we might call a Scriptural revolution which culminated in Ezra's promulgation of the completed Torah some century and a half later. Only at that stage may we think of the Jews as having become the People of a Book. The point is clear: it was possible for a people to be faithful (more or less) to God over many centuries without having recourse to an authoritative book.

2. The Faith of Christians

The case is not so different as regards the New Testament. We used to suppose that for Jesus and his disciples, as for the early Christians, their authority was the Old Testament scriptures. But, as James Barr again makes clear,[89] the early Christians did not regard or employ the scriptures as their ultimate authority. They searched its pages and quoted from them frequently in support of their new-found faith in God's revelation to them in the life, death and resurrection of Jesus. This was their ultimate authority: everything that Jesus had come to mean to them. What he had done and said was held in their memories before being written down in the gospels and only gradually did these come to be regarded as scriptural, on a par with the scrolls of the Old Testament.

For at least a century and a half (till the time of Irenaeus, Bishop of Lyons, in circa AD 180) their authority resided largely in the oral traditions of the Church, Papias being witness to the fact that even well into the second century these were still more highly regarded than the written form of them. We cannot speak of an authoritative New Testament until the end of the second century at the earliest. Even then, the chief authority referred to was not the scriptures but what was called the *Rule of Faith*. This was a summary of the chief beliefs of Christians, encapsulated in the baptismal creeds taught converts and recited by them at their baptism. It was these confessions of faith that developed eventually into the Creeds, such as the Apostles' and later the Niceno-Constantinopolitan (usually referred to as the Nicene) Creed. If challenged as to the validity of such beliefs, they would have quoted the scriptures in support of them. But to give the scriptures prime place would be to have put the cart before the horse!

As with the Old Testament, so also with the New. It was possible for Christianity to be a dynamic, growing faith, ever-expanding into the Graeco-Roman world, over a hundred years and more without written scriptures playing any dominant role. Their authority was Jesus himself, what they had experienced in him and through the outpouring of the Holy Spirit on them. And this continued for the best part of two centuries.

3. Canonization as indicating a loss of faith and vision

I have already suggested that, in the case of the Torah, its written format and its promulgation by Ezra coincided to some extent with a failure of nerve and of faith. It coincided with the ghettoization of the Jewish people within Jerusalem

---

[89] In "Holy Scripture: Canon, Authority, Criticism", Oxford University Press, 1983.

and its immediate surrounds, hemmed in by enemies, and with the supposition that God had withdrawn his Spirit from them – that the voice of prophecy had ceased. This marked a low point in Israel's story. We cannot be so sure in the case of the New Testament how and why the 27 books came gradually to be recognized and canonized. But it is noticeable that the later books written, such as Jude and 2 Peter, the Johannine letters and Revelation, no longer bear witness to the kind of freshness of faith, the confidence and vibrancy of the earlier New Testament writings. The dynamic of the Spirit doesn't come over with such sparkle as it had previously. As I have asserted before, to some extent, canonization is the point at which the once living, dynamic faith became fossilized. It can be brought to life again only by the mediation of the Holy Spirit (see p.308)

4. The usefulness of authorized scripture

But, the scriptures were written and in time became authoritative statements of the faith. In their favor, we may cite several factors. Once the scriptures were in written form, they could be disseminated into places into which as yet no Christian missionary had penetrated. After the death of the apostles, as of the entire first generation of Christians, they did encapsulate the witness of those first Christians. Whilst the faith was spread chiefly by word of mouth, and into places ever more distant both in time and in place, there was a danger that the message might have been diluted, or re-fashioned, or wholly misrepresented. There is evidence both within and without the New Testament of sectarian groups, variously named as Judaizers or Gnostics, who infiltrated the Church and tried to subvert its message. A considerable reason for canonization (and hence authorization) of the New Testament scriptures was so that they could provide a bench-mark, against which heretical teachings could be evaluated and repulsed.

And it is the case that the Christian Church has always been in danger of succumbing to the temptation of abandoning its gospel in favor of accommodation to other competing ideologies. Such a danger point was when, after centuries of persecution of Christians, the Roman Empire adopted the tactic of "If you can't beat 'em, then join'em". The Church supposedly evangelized the empire, but the empire struck back. When the Roman imperial machine took over the Church, it imported values wholly at variance with those of the gospel. The clergy were duly "Romanized," priests began wearing what we call the "dog-collar," part of the uniform of the Roman civil service; bishops, the purple vestment, which signified the exercise of imperial power. Did the Church convert the empire, or the empire convert the Church? The scriptures always stood as a witness to the Word of God and to the gospel, calling the Church to repentance and renewal of faith and commitment to Christ.

5. The source of Christian renewal

As such, the scriptural witness has been at the origins of every significant movement of Christian renewal throughout history. It was after pondering the story of the rich young ruler that Anthony abandoned his life of luxury, went out into the Egyptian desert and so founded the monastic movement. It was the chance reading of one of Paul's letters in a Milanese garden that brought Augustine to conversion. Spurred by the same passage that had touched Anthony, Francis abandoned his father's home and dazzling prospects, adopted the simple brown habit and called the Church to repentance. Similarly, Peter Waldo and John Wycliffe and John Hus, started reforming movements, wishing to reform a corrupt Church that had wandered far from the gospel. It was the study of the scriptures, in Hebrew and Greek, which opened Luther's eyes to the essential message of the gospel, which had been obscured within the Roman Church and so to press for reform and so to spark off the Protestant Reformation. In this way we could continue into modern times. There has been no significant movement of Christian renewal that has not been initiated by a rediscovery of the Word of God in scripture; and which has not itself reawakened the Church to its scriptural foundations.

6. Treasure in earthen vessels

To have examined reasons why the Bible cannot carry quite the authority that it did to our forebears is not to trash the Bible – but rather to conclude that, in spite of all the signs of human fallibility within it, it still carries within it a clear message from God and about God. It is, as St Paul wrote of his ministry amongst the people of Corinth, that "We have this treasure in earthen vessels"(2 Corinthians 4.7: literally "clay jars," as NRSV translates). Of what treasure was he speaking? This is clear from the previous verses: it concerns "the light of the gospel of the glory of Christ" (verse four); it proclaims "Jesus Christ as Lord" (verse five); it speaks of "the God who said, 'Let light shine out of darkness,' who has shone in our hearts to give the light of the knowledge of the glory of God in the face of Jesus Christ." (verse six). All of these expressions summarize what most Christians would recognize as the gospel that is the treasure of which he writes. But what is the clay jar? In the context, this indicates Paul's own human weakness. He was evidently under attack from some of his own converts. In self-defense against their accusations, he claims to "have renounced the shameful things," "we refuse to practice cunning or to falsify God's word;" "we commend ourselves to the conscience of everyone in the sight of God." Then following the verse under discussion, he reverts to his own sufferings in the service of the gospel: "We are afflicted ... but not crushed; perplexed, but not driven to despair; persecuted, but not forsaken; struck down, but not destroyed; always carrying in the body the death of Jesus, so that the life of Jesus may also be made visible in our bodies." (2 Corinthians 4.8-10).

It is surely not perverse to apply these words to the Bible. Is it not also like a clay jar, of human construction, fallible and fragile (being reminded of those clay jars in which the Dead Sea Scrolls had been secreted) and yet containing priceless treasure, the glorious gospel of Jesus Christ?

THE WORD OF GOD DIAGRAM

In the diagram opposite, I have tried to encapsulate the above discussion in visual form. In it, we have three columns of text. The central column tells the story of how God's communication of His Word relates to the various stages of God's revelation of himself, beginning with the Patriarchs and Moses, through Jesus and the apostles, to the writing of the Bible, through the story of the Church down to the present day and age. Hopefully within this sequence, the reader may sense that the biblical period is not somehow separate from the rest of historical time, but that we, Christians of the 21st century, stand within that continuous tradition.

The two outer columns enable us to see how that communication can be perceived as one continuous process (rather than as separated stages), on the one hand as a matter of divine initiative, through the Holy Spirit, and on the other as a human response to that initiative, within the traditions of Israel and the Church. These two are simply the reverse sides of one and the same coin, i.e. that God communicates with humanity in many ways to which humans respond in equally varied ways.

THE WORD OF GOD AND THE BIBLE

The Divine Initiative

↓

The Continuing Activity of the Holy Spirit

↓

The Spirit is the invisible presence at every stage of the process

↓

Calvin : It is "the inner testimony of the Holy Spirit" which conveys to the believer what was first uttered by priest or prophet, recorded in Scripture and preached in the Church.

↓

1. God communicates in Deeds:
a. at Creation:"God said. Let there be Light...(Gen. 1. 3)" "In the beginning was the Word..."John 1. 1)
b. in Redemptive Acts, as in Liberation of Israelites from Egypt; in Life, Death and Resurrection of Jesus. His actions speak louder than words.
c. in symbolic acts of prophets.

2. The Word of God as inspired utterances conveying his message: through Patriarchs, Prophets, in the teaching of Jesus (Heb.1. 1-2) and his apostles. Prophets ('those who speak on behalf of God') declared: "Thus saith the Lord..."

3. The Word of God became personal in experiences of prophets, e.g. Hosea's marriage, Jeremiah's suffering; esp. in Person of Jesus Christ (the Word made flesh, Jn.1.14) - also Mark 1.22, John 5. 39 & Rev. 19.13.

4. The living Word was passed on by Oral Tradition over centuries or decades.

5. The Word of God as written record (i.e. the BIBLE) of the above events penned by inspired but fallible witnesses
a. In Hebrew and Greek language
b. In MSS that no longer exist but which had been faithfully copied by hand till printing.
c. As recognised by Church consensus and decision over many centuries. Ch. Councils decided the Canon (official list of MSS received as scripture)
d. In translations of best available "text" - always imperfect, always requiring revision and new translation.

6. The Word of God as preached and taught within the Church - not judged by private interpretation (2 Peter 1.20-21) but by the "magisterium" (whether of Pope or Bishops or believers who seek "the mind of Christ" & commended to the individual conscience of believers).

5. The Word recreates the living experience of God as it was at stages 2 & 3 above. The Word is thus the dynamic "presence" in the Church.

The Human Response

↓

All is conveyed within the Tradition, at first, of Israel, and later, of the Christian Church

↓

The Tradition continues within the Life of the Church Today

↓

The Book that changes lives

1. THE STORY OF TOKICHI ISHII

Tokichi Ishii was a Japanese convicted murderer on death row. Two Canadian missionaries visited him. They were not allowed into his cell because he was so violent. He would not talk to them despite several visits. Conversation being impossible, they pushed a copy of a gospel through his cell bars and left.

There can be no more boring place than prison. With no other books to read, Tokichi began to read the gospel. Having begun he could not stop and eventually came to the story of the crucifixion and the words: "Father, forgive them. They do not know what they are doing. He said: I was stabbed to the heart as if pierced by a six inch nail. Shall I call it the love of Christ. Shall I call it the birth of compassion in me? I don't know what to call it. I only know my heart and life were changed."

He was duly hanged. But it was a different man who died than the man first put into prison; a man who saw life differently, faced death differently.

2. THE LEARNED PROFESSOR

A professor of languages was asked to help translate the New Testament into Mongolian. He agreed, was paid for the job which he undertook purely as an academic exercise. Missionaries who worked with him thought him a hard, unyielding man, doing a job for the job's sake, unwilling to talk about the meaning of the words he was translating. It was the same words, words of forgiveness from the cross that broke him down or perhaps made him up and turned an academic task into a journey of discovery and Christian conversion.

3. SIGNOR ANTONIO

From Brazil comes the story of Signor Antonio. A friend gave him a Bible to read. He hadn't the slightest desire to read such superstitious nonsense (as he called it). Reaching home, he threw the book onto the fire. It wasn't easy to burn; a closed book is a very solid object. So he opened the pages that they might more easily catch fire. They opened at Matthew 5, the Sermon on the Mount. He noticed the words: "Blessed are the pure in heart, Blessed are the peace-makers." He took the charred book from the fire to see why they were all so blessed. He sat for two hours reading it and later could say: "Now I understand, now I believe."

Donald Hilton

The stories supplied by the Rev D H Hilton, have been gathered over a period of many years from a variety of now unidentifiable publications. If any of them are copyright, we apologise. If further information is provided, appropriate acknowledgement will be made in any future editions of this book.

CHAPTER 20:
PROTESTANTISM: BIBLE, TRADITION AND THE SPIRIT

There is no doubt that the Protestant Reformers employed the expression "Word of God," indicating thereby the entirety of the Bible as their chief source of authority. Although their usage of the Bible was what we today would call fundamentalist, since they regarded everything within it as directly inspired by God, they did not use it uncritically.

A canon within the canon

Whilst Luther accepted the canon[90] of the Hebrew scriptures, he firmly set aside the apocryphal books as of lesser inspiration and as the source of some erroneous Catholic teachings. Nor did he accept all the New Testament writings as being of equal value. In effect he operated with a canon within the canon. The criterion by which he judged the value of every book was as to whether he found in it a clear presentation of the doctrine of justification by faith.

This was for him no merely theoretical matter. It was by the dawning of the truth, as he prepared his lectures on the Psalms and on Paul's Letter to the Romans, that we are saved by the sheer grace of God to which we respond with faith – over against the erroneous emphasis in medieval Catholicism on human "works" such as pilgrimages and penance and the purchase of indulgences, that he had come to an evangelical conversion. It was the truth of Justification that led him to his full-scale revolt against the Church. By this criterion, he adjudged the letter of James with its emphasis on "works" to be "an epistle of straw." By the same criterion, he would have lessened the authority of Hebrews and Jude and the Book of Revelation. This was clearly demonstrated by the fact that, in his German translation, he assigned these four books to the end of the New Testament (Jude and Revelation were already there) which ordering was followed by Tyndale in his English translation.

The other great Reformers, Calvin and Zwingli, were less critical, accepted the canon without demur, and gladly exalted the Bible as Word of God over against

---

[90] Canon: a Greek word that indicated a length of papyrus that could be used as a measuring stick. It went on to describe what had been measured. It came into Christian usage as the term for the collection of books that were deemed "scriptural," hence authoritative in the Church, ie the 27 books of the New Testament. Each of these can be said to be "canonical."

the authority of the Roman Church. This was entirely comprehensible. In rejecting the awesome authority of the Roman Catholic Church, backed up as it was by the military power of the Holy Roman Empire, the reformers were forced to seek a counter-balancing source of authority, which they did in a literalist reading of the Bible.

The Word of God versus the traditions of men

The Reformers belief in the authority of the Bible was expressed in their slogan:. "Sola Scriptura" (by scripture alone) which became their watchword. The authority of scripture as the Word of God set down in ink was at the epicenter of their revolution against the Roman Church which had dominated Western Christianity for a thousand years. Whilst the medieval Church theoretically owned the scriptures to be the source of its authority, in practice it had considerably obscured its centrality. It had promoted the Vulgate translation as its only official text, with its faulty textual basis and frequently erroneous translations. In the Vulgate (the Latin Bible), the Greek "metanoia" was rendered "do penance." Thus "metanoia" as "conversion of heart and mind," a complete turning to God, had been misrepresented as doing so many "Hail Marys" and paying so many Peter's pence.

Furthermore, the Roman Church had in practice exalted what it called "Tradition" to have in effect greater authority than the Bible. Tradition implied that the Church had access to other written sources, which could supplement wherever the Bible's teaching was unclear. To give one example, there is little doubt that the apocryphal "Protevangelium of James," which purports to recount the full story of Mary's origins and her "immaculate conception,"[91] had enormous influence in both promoting Mary to virtual semi-divine status in her role as "Mother of God" and to the exaggerated glorification of virginity and hence of clerical celibacy. And since the Church alone, in the person of the Pope, could rightly interpret both scripture and Tradition, the authority of the Church was thereby limitless. To the Reformers, the Church had thus usurped the true source of authority, replacing it with "the traditions of men."

Commandments of God and traditions of men

What this contrast implied is most clearly illustrated in two episodes reported in Mark 7.1-13. In the first the Pharisees noticed that Jesus' disciples had not performed the ritual washing of hands (the latter explained by the narrator as

---

[91] The Roman Catholic belief that Mary's own conception had been miraculously without any transmission to her of her parents' sinful nature. She was thus enabled to give birth to a sinless child, Jesus.

one of "the traditions of the elders") before partaking of food, and criticized them for it. Jesus riposted by accusing them in the words of Isaiah as hypocrites who honored God with their lips whilst their hearts were far from Him. He concluded thus: "In vain do they worship me, teaching human precepts as doctrines. You abandon the commandment of God and hold to human tradition." (Mark 7. 7-8).

The second instance occurs immediately after. In this Jesus took the initiative: "Then he said to them, 'You have a fine way of rejecting the commandment of God in order to keep your tradition! For Moses said, "Honor your father and your mother;" and, "Whoever speaks evil of father or mother must surely die." But you say that if anyone tells father or mother, "Whatever support you might have had from me is Corban" (that is, an offering to God) – then you no longer permit doing anything for a father or mother, thus making void the word of God through your tradition that you have handed on. And you do many things like this.'" (Mark 7.9-13). The practice of Corban was one in which a Jew took an oath to give a specified sum of money to the Temple treasury (like a deed of covenant). The circumstance envisaged here is one in which the donor could no longer afford both to pay his Temple gift and to support his aging parents. Apparently a Pharisaic dictum ruled that his prime duty was to fulfill his Corban oath. Jesus took the opposite view. The fifth commandment to "honor father and mother" should take precedence over Corban. This was an example of how "they made void the word of God by adhering to what was only a human tradition."

The point is clear, but it covers only a rather specific notion of tradition, i.e. the attempt by the Pharisees to define various practical measures by which a commandment could be observed. Its intention was not to make void the Word of God, but rather to offer practical guidance as to how it could be better observed. The clearest example is that of the fourth Commandment: how should one observe the Sabbath Day? The commandment forbade any work being done on that day. But what constituted work? The elders devised a list of 37 actions that were not to be performed on that day: they included such items as cooking, carrying any weight, reaping corn, and walking more than a very short distance (the so-called Sabbath-Day's journey). It was on the basis of these traditions that the Pharisees charged Jesus with "sabbath-breaking" when he healed the sick on the Sabbath day. Clearly to him, the restoration of a person's life and health which led to the joyful praise of God was an entirely proper use of the Sabbath.

"The traditions of the elders" were then not evil in intention. But these instances stand as a permanent caution to us, lest our best intended interpretations of the Bible might actually subvert the original meaning of God's Word.

Sola scriptura?

But the great Reformers were not wholly opposed to the influence of Tradition. For they still interpreted the Bible through the selective lenses of the early Church Fathers. They fully accepted and themselves taught the great dogmas of the fourth – sixth centuries, i.e. those which propounded the doctrines of God as Holy Trinity, in which Father, Son and Holy Spirit are each truly God, and of the two natures of Jesus Christ, as fully divine and fully human. Whilst it may be claimed that the primary data for such dogmas are present within the pages of the New Testament, they are not certainly promulgated within it. Where, according to Matthew 28.19, we have Jesus commanding his disciples to "Go therefore and make disciples of all nations, baptizing them in the name of the Father and of the Son and of the Holy Spirit" there are few scholars who don't regard this as an editorial gloss on what Jesus' instructions may have been. This is developed Christian theology read back into Jesus' lifetime. Neither of these dogmas could have been set forth, as they are, in the terminology of Greek philosophy before the fourth century at the earliest – which is why they appear so alien to both biblical and modern ways of thinking and speaking. A "paradigm shift"[92] had occurred as between the interpretation of the Bible rooted in the Hebrew and Aramaic tongues and its intellectualization within the world of Graeco-Roman culture.

Whereas the great "magisterial"[93] Reformers, as Luther, Calvin and Zwingli are called, were happy to continue interpreting the doctrines of the faith through the teaching of the great Church Fathers (such as Basil, the two Gregorys and Augustine[94]) and so didn't in practice wholly adhere to the principle of "sola scriptura," the so-called Radical Reformers, like Thomas Muntzer and the Anabaptists refused to accept any doctrine not wholly legitimized within their reading of the Bible. The practical consequence of this was that most of them went way "off-stream" and ended up as heretical, anarchical and dubiously Christian sects. Most of the modern sects, such as Jehovah's Witnesses, Christian Science, Seventh Day Adventists and others proclaim the authority of the Bible,

---

[92] The concept of paradigm shift is much used by philosophers of science. It stands for a radical revision of all previous thinking once new evidence convinces the scientific community that the traditional theories are wrong. The most obvious example is that of Copernicus' realization that the sun is at the center of our solar system and not, as had been previously assumed, the Earth. That obliged a huge paradigm shift. We could describe the Reformation as marking such a paradigm shift, at least for Protestants.

[93] The term "magisterial" properly applies to those Reformers who believed the city magistrates to be the local authorities of God's appointment and therefore the right bodies to put into effect their instructions for the reformation of the Church. This sets them over against the more radical reformers who refused any co-operation with such local authorities.

[94] The "Fathers:" Basil of Cappadocia, 329-379; Gregory of Nyssa, 335-394, Gregory of Nazianzus, c 330-389 and Augustine, Bishop of Hippo, 354-430 were the most important theologically.

but assume that they can leap backwards in time to the first century AD and thereby recreate the conditions of the apostolic Church – as if the intervening centuries did not exist, as if the entirety of Christian history had achieved nothing, learned nothing, and was valueless except as a horrible warning of where the Church had gone wrong. Thus history and tradition were abolished. From a mainstream perspective, all such sects can be dubiously considered to be Christian.

Finally, in thus exalting the Bible over against the Roman Catholic Church, the Reformers could hardly do other than interpret it in a literalistic manner. It is unreasonable for us to suppose they could have been other than men of their own time, living before the Renaissance and Enlightenment forged the tools of a properly literary and historical criticism. They were after all still medieval theologians. For all that, Luther's critical stance suggests that he for one would not have opposed a critical approach to the Bible.

Re-evaluation of Tradition

It used to be assumed that the great difference between Roman Catholic and Protestant understandings of authority was over the place of Tradition in the Church. It used to be said naively that "Protestants believe the Bible;" "Catholics believe the Church" (or Tradition). Neither statement is even remotely true, as we realize now. The Roman Catholic Church has rediscovered the Bible (if it had ever lost it), whilst Protestant scholarship has come to acknowledge the huge role played by Tradition. I have already discussed (in chapter nine) the considerable importance of Tradition for the apostle Paul. He was determined to pass on the essentials of the gospel that he had received from the Church leaders in Jerusalem to his converts in Corinth. This was Tradition in action. Tradition stands for the entire process by which Jews and Christians, beginning from the time of Abraham, have passed on the stories of their faith to succeeding generations. For centuries, this was largely an oral process whereby parents to their children, story-tellers around the camp fire or at the city gate, priests in their sanctuary, prophets to their followers, Christian apostles to their converts, handed on the essentials of the faith. A major consensus within biblical studies is that the periods of oral tradition, regarding both Old and New Testaments, were vital to the shaping of the material that would, eventually, be written down. When it was written down in the scrolls of papyrus and parchment that would eventually be the books of our Bible, this was the Tradition taking different form – we could call it positively the crystallization of the Tradition, or, more negatively, the fossilization of the Tradition.

One of the methods of study that I discussed with regard to both Old and New Testaments was that of "the history of traditions," which I find the most fruitful of all. In it, we seek to trace the development of a biblical theme from its origins (where that is discernible) through its various phases until it reaches its apogee (or perhaps disappears from view).

TRADITION AS CONTENT

The word Tradition is also used in another sense – as the content of what was passed on. Of course, what is passed on has to have content. In the two cases cited from Paul, the first, in 1 Corinthians 11, concerned what occurred at the Last Supper with the institution of the eucharist; the second, in the same letter chapter 15, concerned the core beliefs of the early Church, i.e. "that Christ died for our sins ... that he was buried, that he was raised on the third day..." etc. (1 Corinthians 15.3-8). This earliest of all Creeds, going back to the Jerusalem Church within less than 20 years since Jesus' death and resurrection, was the Tradition that Paul handed on to his Corinthian converts. In this sense then, Tradition is synonymous with the earliest definitions of the faith.

Tradition lives on

The recording of the Tradition in the books of the Bible didn't put a stop to its ongoing continuance. The Spirit didn't cease to speak through the mouths of apostles, evangelists and preachers simply because the ink had dried on the parchments. I have already criticized the notion that canonization denoted a point of terminus to the Christian mission – far from it. Papias wasn't the only Christian, who, in the second century, still preferred to hear the gospel from the mouths of living witnesses rather than from the inscribed pages of a book. Christian teaching and preaching and neighbor-to-neighbor evangelism continued – as it does to this day. It is important therefore to realize that we, the Christians of the 21st century, are still part of the living Tradition of the Christian faith. Week by week, Christian parents, ministers, Bible class leaders and Sunday school teachers are continually involved in the passing on of the Tradition.

We should also recognize the particular role of biblical scholars and theologians, for the various disciplines of studying and commenting on the Word of God in scripture is in itself a continuance of the Tradition. So the Church Fathers, in particular Augustine of Hippo, through to Thomas Aquinas, Martin Luther and John Calvin, down to Karl Barth and Dietrich Bonhoeffer, seeking to interpret the Bible so as to be meaningful in every century, have magnificently continued and enriched the Tradition. So as Christians seeking guidance and enlightenment, we don't simply turn to the pages of the Bible and leap straight from them into our present world. We have also to listen intently to the voices of Christian witness all through the ages for the illumination they shed on the biblical text. This may be beyond the capacity of most Christians, but this is where we wisely listen to the voices of our present-day biblical scholars and theologians. Some, such as William Barclay[95] and, today, Tom Wright, have exceptional gifts for sharing their scholarship with people without much learning or theological training.

Where Protestants will differ from Roman Catholics is in restricting what is acceptable as Tradition to that which is biblically well-founded and in conformity with the gospel of Christ. Protestants regard with suspicion a great deal of popular and devotional Catholicism, especially that regarding its dogmas about the Virgin Mary, the infallibility of Papal encyclicals, the enforcement of celibacy on its priests, and its procedures for making saints as unfounded, untrue to the biblical witness and therefore unacceptable.

Tradition with a small "t"

We have to recognize that many Christian beliefs, customs and practices are also described as being "traditions" which may be confused with Tradition as described above. We should consider these traditions as being characteristic marks of our diversity of beliefs and practices which do not affect the essentials of Christian believing and practicing. I will illustrate this with how two churches, the Church of England (hereafter C of E) and the United Reformed Church (hereafter URC) speak and act with regard to the Holy Communion.

The C of E celebrates the *Eucharist* (its preferred term. It also speaks of Holy Communion) with the worshipers *walking* forward, *each* to receive the *wafer* and *chalice* from the hands of the *priest* or a *server*. In the URC observance of "the *Lord's Supper*" or "*Holy Communion*" (both terms are used) the worshipers remain *seated*, are served with the *bread* and *wine* (in a minuscule cup) by an *elder*, then eat and drink *together* at the invitation of the minister. Each of the emphasized words indicates a "tradition" distinctive of these two churches. In the latter, even the wine is probably unfermented, due to a strong tradition of teetotalism in nonconformist churches. Such traditions carry their own history. Until the late Victorian period, nonconformist churches regularly used the common cup, the *chalice*; that is, until teetotalism became almost an article of belief – this in protestation against the evil effects of drunkenness in British society. Adopting only non-fermented wines, the chalice was then no longer acceptable for reasons of hygiene – hence the adoption of the tiny cup. Few people in our churches are aware of this history.

It will appear at first that there are no major conflicts or matters of principle in these respectively different ways of serving the Communion meal. But there

---

[95] William Barclay's NT commentaries were rightly famous, as, I guess, will be those of Tom Wright with titles such as *Mark for Today*.

may be some matters of principle lurking beneath the surface; for instance that the URC's practice of receiving seated and eating and drinking together is more reminiscent of how Jesus' disciples were ranged around the table at the Last Supper. At another level, some Anglicans will more readily believe in some kind of "transubstantiation" taking place at the consecration of the bread and wine, whereas most URC members will more likely take a "memorialist" view of what is occurring.

"Traditions" (small "t") are those minor but not insignificant practices which distinguish one church from another. And they certainly do. Most experienced observers could enter almost any nonconformist chapel, and, without having seen the notice board, sense immediately whether this building was originally Methodist (of Wesleyan or Primitive flavor), or URC (of Congregational or Presbyterian origins) or Baptist. The differing traditions bear their own unmistakable marks.

Calvin on the Holy Spirit and Scripture

We do not have to look far to perceive situations in which, to this day, the scriptures can be used in a largely negative sense, as means of browbeating the faithful and exercising social control over them. The scriptures can be beneficial, healing and helpful only in so far as they are illuminated by the Spirit so as to convey life rather than death.

It was to the credit of John Calvin to stress the role of the Holy Spirit in his famous epigram "testimonium sancti Spiritui" (the testimony of the Holy Spirit). In chapter seven of his *Institutes of the Christian Religion*, Calvin wrote: "… the Scriptures are the only records in which God has been pleased to consign his truth to perpetual remembrance, the full authority which they ought to possess with the faithful is not recognized, unless they are believed to have come from heaven, as directly as if God had been heard giving utterance to them." (Vol I, p 68). And how are they so to be believed? Arguing against the thesis that the Bible owed its authority to the Church (and was accordingly subordinate to it); or to the conscience that might or might not recognize it, Calvin contended that "…God alone can properly bear witness to his own words, so *these words will not obtain full credit in the hearts of men, until they are sealed by the inward testimony of the Spirit! The same Spirit*, therefore, who spoke by the mouth of the prophets, *must penetrate our hearts in order to convince us* that they faithfully delivered the message with which they were divinely intrusted." (p72).

Here Calvin established a most important principle: that, if evangelicalism has always cited the act of writing as the supreme moment of inspiration (a view which I have criticized), it was equally required that the Spirit be present at the moment of reading the scripture if we are to hear within it the Word of God. Only the Spirit can make "the dead letter" become "the living word."

Continuing in the same vein, Calvin wrote: "Let it therefore be held as fixed, that those who are inwardly taught by the Holy Spirit acquiesce implicitly in Scripture; that Scripture, carrying its own evidence along with it, deigns not to submit to proofs and arguments, but owes the full conviction with which we ought to receive it to the testimony of the Spirit! Enlightened by him, we no longer believe, either on our own judgment or that of others, that the Scriptures are from God; but, in a way superior to human judgment, feel perfectly assured as much so as if we beheld the divine image visibly impressed on it that it came to us, by the instrumentality of men, from the very mouth of God." (p72).

In Calvin's thinking then the inner testimony of the Spirit convinces the Bible's reader that it was a book of wholly divine origin. I can no longer accept his fundamentalist presuppositions, but will readily endorse his thinking as to how the Spirit enlightens the mind, not in proof of dogma, but rather in making the biblical witness come alive for its readers in the here and now. This is not to deny that anybody may find in the Bible matters of interest, but beyond that, the Christian who turns to it seeking in its pages encouragement or guidance, will be the more ready to receive the Spirit's help. In Christian worship, the attempt is deliberately made to create such conditions of reverence and expectation by which God's Word may be the more readily heard and understood. The reading and preaching of the Bible message can only come alive as and when the Spirit makes the words live, bringing them home to the heart and mind of those who read or hear them. Every preacher will know of occasions when he or she may have been wholly unaware of how the sermon with which one had struggled in the preparation may have spoken to the exact needs of somebody in the congregation. After all the background reading, the study that goes into the making of one's sermon, its effectiveness does not lie in its eloquence, the cogency of its argument, its humor or lack of it, but on the Spirit's enlivening of what is heard by the listener.

Inspiration of the few or the many?

We surely need a wider understanding of the Spirit's operation than Calvin envisaged. Just as I have argued for a more diffuse picture of biblical authorship, i.e. by the many rather than the few, so we might recognize the Spirit's presence in far wider circles than just that of the authors. And accept that the Spirit's influence does not completely override our human capacity for confusion or error. Indeed, the ancient notion of the biblical writers operating as virtual puppets on a string, manipulated by the Holy Spirit, is to make a mockery of the entire process. One thing has been made abundantly clear by modern biblical criticism and that is the human dimension of scripture. King David and the apostle Paul were mightily used by God, not because of but rather in spite of their humanly flawed personalities.

In an address delivered in Dublin Cathedral in 1977, Hans Kung declared his preference for the word "indestructibility" rather than "infallibility" (when speaking of either Bible or Church), explaining, "This means that, in virtue of the promise, the Church is maintained in the truth of the gospel and never definitively falls away – not because we would not make any mistakes, but despite our mistakes. The basic infallibility of the Church consists, then, in the persistence of the Church in the truth of Jesus Christ, despite all errors of individuals ... even the Pope."[96] Although addressing primarily the Roman Catholic claim to papal infallibility, his remarks are equally fitting to those who assume the Bible to be inerrant. The Bible becomes God's Word for us, not because it is faultless, but because despite all faults, it clearly conveys to us the way by which we are offered salvation.

The diversity of spiritual gifts

Once we perceive this, and desist from attributing overpowering inspiration to the biblical writers (other than that made available to all who seek to serve God), then we may understand that the inspiration of the Spirit may be recognized in every stage of the process by which we receive the Word of God through the Bible:

❖ in the original occasions on which prophets discerned messages from God and proclaimed them in public.
❖ in the minds of those who heard them, treasured and memorized them.
❖ in those who eventually wrote them down on papyrus or parchment.
❖ in those who recognized them as inspired writings and so collected them together.
❖ in those who read them aloud in synagogue and church.
❖ in those who faithfully copied them by hand through many centuries.
❖ in those who set up the type-face so as to reproduce them in printed Bibles.
❖ in those who translated them from Hebrew and Greek into English and a thousand other languages.
❖ in the work of the textual critics who, by meticulous study of manuscripts, seek to restore a text as close to the original as possible.
❖ in the historians and archaeologists who uncover the historical and cultural background of these writings and the theologians who interpret their meaning for today.

---

[96] On the back cover of H Kung, *Infallible?* Op cit.

❖ in those who publish the Bible in its many modern versions.

❖ in those who, in the privacy of their home, seek to find in its words what God would say to them today; as in the work of preachers and teachers who strive to do the same for Christian congregations.

❖ in those who, encouraged and challenged by the Word of God, live out a positively Christian life-style in their daily living.

Hans Kung has made the same point in other wording: "... so is it wrong in the case of Scripture to restrict the working of the Spirit of God to any particular statement by an apostle or biblical author. The truth is rather that the whole process, the origin, collection and transmission of the word, the acceptance in faith and further proclamation of the message, is under the guidance and control of the Spirit. In this sense not only the history of the writing of the Scriptures, but the whole of their prehistory and subsequent history is inspired by the Spirit; not dictated by it, but soaked and filled with it."[97]

How are we then, in practice, to study this ancient book in such a way that we may receive in it a Word from God for today?

Does it apply today?

How can we apply the Word given long ago to that which needs to be heard today? The attempts nowadays by a large number of conservative evangelical believers to ransack the pages of the prophets for prediction of what is occurring in the world today, and more, to predict the immediate future is largely misguided. This turns the Bible into something magical, a sort of *Old Moore's Almanac*, as if within it is a coded message in which the entire future of the world is set out. It is a quite different matter to investigate the historical circumstances in which any particular prophecy was given, to attempt to perceive what was meant as uttered by the prophet and as heard by the people, and finally what echo of that "Word of God" may still be heard. We may then seek to apply it to our own times by asking what similarities there are between the situation in which that Word was given and that in which we live; and to apply to it the expression of Prof Leonard Hodgson: "If God so spoke to those people long ago, what would He say to us today?"[98] There may be no relevance to our times at all. But, since God is "the same yesterday, today and for ever," and human behavior has changed little since biblical times, there will likely be many situations in which God's message via the prophet will apply with equal force to our situation.

---

[97] H Kung, *Infallible?* p 177.
[98] L Hodgson: *For Faith and Freedom*, Pt III, pp 15-16, SCM Press Ltd, 1968.

The Particularity of the Word

We have to note another factor of great importance. Almost all the prophecies issued as "the Word of the Lord" were quite specific to a particular time and situation. To take but one famous example: the prophet Isaiah's message to King Ahaz that "a young woman will conceive and bear a child and you will call his name Immanuel" (Isiah 7.14). What situation gave rise to this prophecy and what were the consequences of it? The occasion was quite specific. Judah was in peril, threatened by her two more powerful neighbors. The King, in some state of panic, went to seek Isaiah's advice. Not content with the prophet's words of consolation, the Lord (via the prophet's mediation) told the King to demand a sign, which he refused. In response, the prophet declared that God would give him a sign. The sign given consisted of those words, "The young woman will conceive ..." etc. It went on to predict that before the child to be born would have been weaned, at the age of two or thereabouts, these invading powers would have retreated in disarray. The King cannot have been in any doubt as to the meaning of this prophecy. The young woman in question was undoubtedly his wife; the child born was probably Hezekiah who was to succeed Ahaz on the throne. His birth-name "Immanuel" (God is with us) signified the promised blessing of God in saving the nation from its enemies. That this same prophecy was employed centuries later to apply to the birth of Jesus need not detain us here: we are making the point that its origin was quite specific to a particular historical situation.

The Letter that kills, the Spirit that makes alive

Paul was the author of these familiar words. He was contrasting the new covenant, with its law inscribed on human hearts and minds by the Spirit of God with the old covenant whose commandments had been engraved on tablets of stone. Behind them lay the whole of Paul's admittedly ambiguous, sometimes tortuous, attitude to the role of the Torah in God's plan of salvation. Although he describes the law as "holy and just and good," he sees it nevertheless as an instrument through which mankind was condemned to spiritual death. In verse seven he refers to "the ministry of death, chiseled in letters on stone tablets." Just prior to that expression he used the words "the letter kills, but the Spirit gives life." (2 Corinthians 3.6). Since no man, by his own efforts, could obey every letter of the Torah's prescriptions (all 613 of them!), the effect of such effort was condemnation – in effect the words of Torah killed! In contrast, whenever people turned to God in faith, relying not on themselves but on the grace of Jesus Christ, there was the gift of life freely given. This was brought about by the action of the Holy Spirit. The Spirit gives life.

My concluding thought is this: God's Word for today is not to be sought for exclusively in the pages of the Book, although it is within it that we should commence our search. For faithfulness, in the myriad new situations facing Christians today, does not so much require discovering the appropriate quotation of a verse found in scripture but rather what God would say to us today. We cannot pretend that scripture, even those parts of it termed "prophetic," foresees everything that could or would happen in today's world. That is one of the greatest fantasies pursued by many fundamentalists. It represents a failure of faith to suppose that God has said the last word on every possible matter 2,000 years ago and has since maintained a stony silence (we may be tempted sometimes to suppose that He has). We have rather to seek for whatever the Spirit may be saying to the churches in our day, as was the message communicated to the churches of Asia Minor towards the end of the first century: "Let anyone who has an ear, listen to what the Spirit is saying to the churches."(Revelation 2.7).

CHAPTER 21:
AUTHORITY IN PRACTICE – A
CASE STUDY OF TWO CHURCHES

Having considered some of the issues involved in taking the Bible as our chief source of authority as to what Christians should believe and how they should behave, I propose examining how this works out in practice. We will look at churches at almost opposite ends of a spectrum of mainstream Christianity: on the one hand, the Roman Catholic Church and on the other, the United Reformed Church. On the first, I write critically as an outsider; towards the second, I write as an insider, but hopefully with my critical faculties equally alert. I cannot pretend to be wholly objective towards either. I would hope that readers belonging to churches at other points on the spectrum might compare how they recognize and exercise authority within their communities.

Authority in the Roman Catholic Church

I will illustrate this from one of the major documents emanating from the Second Vatican Council (1962-65) called by Pope John XXIII in 1958. "Good" Pope John initiated this ecumenical[99] council against the advice of many of his senior cardinals, wishing to commence what he termed a process of "aggiornamiento" which he explained as "throwing the windows open" to the world. Thus began a momentous process of reform within the Catholic Church, received amongst the faithful with both excitement and alarm.

One or two sources of Revelation?

In its document on revelation entitled "Verbum Dei," the Word of God, the Council reworked and reworded what had been the assumption since the First Vatican Council (1869-1870), i.e. that the Church recognized two sources of revelation (and hence of authority), being the holy scriptures and the Tradition. The Bible was received as Tradition written under the inspiration of the Holy Spirit. By Tradition was meant a separate stream of teaching handed down in the Church but remaining unwritten. This was disingenuous, since many of

---

[99] It was termed an ecumenical council because the worldwide Catholic community was represented by their cardinals and bishops. It was not ecumenical in the sense of calling together representatives of all the mainstream churches within Christendom; although it had invited other Christians to be present as observers. Their presence did represent a new spirit of openness.

these traditions had been written down, especially by the early Church Fathers,[100] in the decisions of ecumenical councils, especially those that defined the nature of God as Holy Trinity and the person of Jesus as both human and divine; and in the consequent ecumenical Creeds. But when, in 1870 the Church defined the dogma (i.e. a teaching from which no dissent is permissible on pain of excommunication) of Papal Infallibility; and, prior to that, in 1854 that of the Immaculate Conception of the Virgin Mary; and later, in 1950, that of her Bodily Assumption, Protestants could justifiably protest that by Tradition the Roman Catholic Church could fabricate whatever it wanted regardless of any evidence to be gleaned from the Bible.

But Vatican II, strongly influenced by the open-minded spirit of the new pope and by the background influence of a number of outstanding young theologians present there as "periti" (experts) such as Hans Kung and Karl Rahner, declared that there is but one source of revelation, namely, the Word of God. This flows, like a bifurcating stream, in scripture and in Tradition, coming from one source and flowing towards one goal.

Herewith some of the most important statements published under the title of Verbum Dei, the Word of God:

Regarding the Bible

In chapter three on "Sacred Scripture: its divine inspiration and its Interpretation," these statements are made: "Those things revealed by God which are contained and presented in the text of sacred scripture have been written under the inspiration of the holy Spirit. For holy mother church, relying on the faith of the apostolic age, accepts as sacred and canonical the books of the Old and the New Testaments, whole and entire, with all their parts, on the grounds that, written under the inspiration of the holy Spirit (see John 20:31; 2 Timothy 3:16; 2 Peter 1:19-21; 3:15-16), they have God as their author, and have been handed on as such to the church itself. To compose the sacred books, God chose certain men who, all the while he employed them in this task, made full use of their powers and faculties so that, though he acted in them, it was as true authors that they consigned to writing whatever he wanted written, and no more.

"Since, therefore, all that the inspired authors, or sacred writers, affirm should be regarded as affirmed by the holy Spirit, we must acknowledge that the books

---

[100] These were the great theologians of the early centuries, from Origen in the third century to John of Damascus in the seventh. Their importance is that it was their thinking that defined the chief doctrines of the Christian Faith.

of scripture, firmly, faithfully and without error[101], teach that truth which God, for the sake of our salvation, wished to see confided to the sacred scriptures." (p104-5, no 11).

And from chapter six on "Sacred Scripture in the Life of the Church:"
"It (i.e. the Church) has always regarded and continues to regard the scriptures, taken together with sacred tradition, as the supreme rule of its faith. For, since they are inspired by God and committed to writing once and for all time, they present God's own word in an unalterable form ... It follows that all the preaching of the church, as indeed the entire Christian religion, should be nourished and ruled by sacred scripture ..."

"Access to sacred scripture ought to be widely available to the Christian faithful. ... since the word of God must be readily available at all times, the church, ...sees to it that suitable and correct translations are made ... from the original texts of the sacred books. If, when the opportunity presents itself and the authorities of the church agree, these translations are made jointly with churches separated from us, they can then be used by all Christians."

"Sacred theology relies on the written word of God, taken together with sacred tradition, as its permanent foundation ... The sacred scriptures contain the word of God, and, because they are inspired, they truly are the word of God; therefore, the study of the sacred page should be the very soul of sacred theology."

Here we will recognize the most powerful statements concerning the status of the Bible which may well surprise many Protestants. There could hardly be a more totally "evangelical," even fundamentalistic account of the divine origins of the Bible. The scriptures are "the very Word of God," "the supreme rule of faith" and "the soul of sacred theology." There are unresolved ambiguities, such as the statement made that they (the Old and New Testaments) have "God as their author" and then in the next clause, that "to compose the sacred books, God chose certain men who ... made use of their powers and faculties so that ... it was as true authors that they consigned to writing whatever he wanted written and no more." That reads to me as a contradiction; and in view of the main argument of this book, not one that can be resolved.

Although some concessions are made to the insights of modern biblical criticism (such as that we have to take account of the different genres of literature), the document is not untypical of many encyclicals and documents

---

[101] The attempt of some led by Cardinal König of Vienna to remove or amend the words 'without error' was defeated. All too few at Vatican II were trained in Biblical Criticism.

emanating from the Vatican which yield evidence that they have been written by dogmatic theologians and canon lawyers rather than by biblical scholars. Hence the quaintly sounding expressions of pre-critical attitudes towards the Bible. This is hardly surprising since it was only in 1943 (in the encyclical Divino Afflante Spiritu) that the Vatican belatedly set its biblical scholars free from the shackles in which they had been tied down for the previous century and so enabled them to employ the tools of modern criticism. In my view the fruits of biblical scholarship have not yet seriously affected the mind-set of the curial officials in charge of the Vatican.

ON SCRIPTURE AND TRADITION

"Sacred tradition and sacred scripture, then, are bound closely together, and communicate one with the other. Flowing from the same divine well-spring, both of them merge, in a sense, and move towards the same goal ... Thus it is that the church does not draw its certainty about all revealed truths from the holy scriptures alone. Hence, both scripture and tradition must be accepted and honored with equal devotion and reverence. Tradition and scripture make up a single sacred deposit of the Word of God, which is entrusted to the Church ...".

So we learn that scripture and Tradition have co-equal status; together they form a single sacred deposit of the Word of God.

ON THE TEACHING OFFICE (THE MAGISTERIUM)

"... the task of giving an authentic interpretation of the word of God, whether in its written form or in the form of tradition, has been entrusted to the living teaching office of the church alone. Its authority in this matter is exercised in the name of Jesus Christ. This magisterium is not superior to the word of God, but is rather its servant. It teaches only what has been handed on to it ... All that it proposes for belief as being divinely revealed it draws from this sole deposit of faith. It is clear, therefore, that, in the supremely wise arrangement of God, sacred tradition, sacred scripture, and the magisterium of the church are so connected and associated that one of them cannot stand without the others."

We see here that every statement concerning the scriptures is immediately balanced by others giving equal status to the Tradition and is further conditioned by the Teaching Office as having the sole right of interpretation. In all, there appear to be three sources of authority: Bible, Tradition and Magisterium, but in Vatican-speak, these coinhere. They speak with one voice.

In response to these declarations, Protestants are likely to feel both pleasure and some suspicion. We have to take more seriously than in the past the undoubted role of Tradition of which the Bible is a part, also that of the Teaching Office of the Church. For there has to be some agreement as to who may interpret the scriptures and how this should be done. If the three, Bible, Tradition and Teaching Office are truly to speak with one voice, there would have to be some clear delineation between them. Protestants would insist that the biblical witness must form the foundation on which Tradition and Teaching Office have to build. The suspicion is, particularly with the three dogmas already mentioned in mind, that on occasions the Roman Church has proclaimed dogmas which have little compelling biblical foundation at all. To cite another example, the Pope beatifies and canonizes saints (presumably because that has been the Roman tradition for many centuries), a process that runs counter to the entire tenor of New Testament teaching on sanctity. In it, the saints are all those called by God to be His own, not the exceptionally heroic. The Roman practice runs counter to what is scriptural. We cannot therefore take entirely seriously the statement that the Magisterium teaches nothing but what has been divinely revealed. Our perception is that frequently Tradition (often in the guise of popular devotion) speaks louder than the biblical witness would justify.

Some consequences of Vatican II

The Second Vatican Council took many decisions with immense consequences in the life of the Church. Just to mention those of greatest interest to Protestants: for the first time, it authorized saying the mass in the vernacular, with the priest facing the congregation (rather than, as previously, with his back to it), with the laity taking an active but subsidiary role in the liturgy. It encouraged that the Bible be made easily accessible to the laity and that they should be encouraged to read it. (This was in complete contrast to what I had heard from a young Belgian Colonial official in the Congo who told me that, when he was a boy, it was considered a sin to read the Bible). Protestants will surely applaud that permission was given for Catholic scholars to co-operate fully with Protestants in the task of biblical translation. Fully ecumenical versions are a huge fillip to ecumenical dialog; as is the fact that biblical scholarship has long since transcended the old sectarian boundaries. In its teaching on the Church, it emphasized the Church as the people of God, as being made up of all its members, all of whom have a role to play in the liturgy; and the Church as being fully present in the local as in the universal sphere. Furthermore, Pope John referred to Christians outside of the Roman communion as "our separated bothers and sisters."

The reader will realize that in such measures, the Church had conceded to several of the major demands of the Protestant Reformation. So it wasn't only Catholics longing for reform who welcomed such changes with open arms, but Protestants committed to the goal of reuniting the divided Body of Christ, who hoped that John's "aggiornamento" might herald a new day in ecumenical relations. I had evidence of this in the remoteness of the Congolese jungle before I was even aware of the Vatican Council's existence. As both foreign and Protestant, we British missionaries had been regarded with suspicion and generally cold-shouldered. Overnight, this changed. We were embraced by our local Catholic missionaries and treated as brothers and sisters.

Many years later it was still possible to meet with huge enthusiasm amongst Catholics for the positive advances made at Vatican II. In Oxted, Surrey, the Council of Churches decided to prepare jointly for the impending first-ever visit of a Pope on British soil in 1981. Canon Denis Corbishley chaired an open meeting for a discussion as to how our different churches regarded the varied forms of ministry, including that of the Papacy. When a number of Anglican vicars and Catholic priests had had their say, I rose to speak with some trepidation as the only nonconformist in the meeting, thinking of myself as being a Daniel in the lions' den. In so far as I can recall, I said: "I am the sole representative here of Protestantism of the Reformed tradition. In our tradition, we approach the matter of Church and Ministry bottom-up rather than top-down. We see the Church not as an hierarchy composed primarily of shepherds looking around to find some sheep for them to lead and feed; but rather as the Body of Christ, of which the laity is the foundational component, the sheep of Christ's flock, from amongst whom God selects and calls some to be shepherds of the flock." What happened next astonished me. A sizeable group of members of the local Roman Catholic parish rose to their feet and said unanimously, "That's what we believe" and proceeded to give me a standing ovation! Such an occasion prior to the Second Vatican Council would have been unthinkable. It has to be a matter of huge regret, felt equally amongst many Protestants as amongst Catholics, that much of the considerable impetus given by that Council towards reform was slowly and deliberately stifled by high officials in the Vatican, from the time of Paul VI onwards, who took fright when they saw their own power and authority slipping from their fingers.

The Bible in the Church

The Church still proclaims its commitment to the principles of the Second Vatican Council and many of its fruits remain visible and welcome. This has been the case in the field of biblical scholarship; in which over time, Catholic scholars have learned to employ all the methods of literary and historical criticism, including many of those described in Chapter 17, first pioneered by Protestant scholars. One visible fruit of this is the excellent one-volume *New Jerome Biblical Commentary*.[102] These methods were officially approved in a publication of considerable importance issued by the Pontifical Biblical Commission in 1993, entitled *The Interpretation of the Bible in the Church*. It

---

[102] *New Jerome Biblical Commentary*, ed Raymond E Brown, Joseph A. Fitsmayer, & Roland E Murphy, published by Geoffrey Chapman, London, 1989.

embraced all these methods, of course with the proviso that they were employed in the service of the Church and under the direction of its Teaching Office. No Catholic biblical scholar or theologian can work without knowledge that the Vatican is watching over his shoulder, and many are those who have been carpeted by the Congregation for the Doctrine of the Faith (which still operates with all the arcane secretiveness of its medieval predecessor, the Inquisition).

In his edited version of this publication, the Anglican scholar, Leslie Houlden[103] asks this vital question: "... there is an area of difficulty about which ... the document is inclined to be bland and even, unusually, to resort to pious platitude... It is a difficulty that none of the great churches has yet summoned the energy to tackle much. And here, for all its diplomatic language, much of the document could prove to be a time-bomb. The difficulty goes like this. If you go in for a historical approach to scripture as a necessary dimension of modern interpretation, you soon discover that many traditional formulations of doctrine, and sometimes doctrines themselves, were grounded on what must now seem erroneous interpretations of scripture. This faces you with a dilemma. You can either adopt a strong view of Providence in the church, producing truths even by what now appear wrong thought-processes; or you can be relaxed about the doctrine in the light of your new understanding of its pedigree. The existence of this nettle is never quite acknowledged in the Vatican document, and it is certainly not grasped; but many readers will see it lurking in the undergrowth."

I have already cited some of the dogmatic definitions the scriptural justification for which most Protestants find flimsy or non-existent. They would see such dogmas as proof that in the Roman Church, Tradition is more important than biblical evidence and that, ultimately, it is the Magisterium which is the supreme authority. For this reason, Hans Kung was entirely justified, in his publication Infallible? in focusing on this single issue. He argued that if the Pope is really infallible in his "ex cathedra"[104] pronouncements, then the Church could never admit to error in its past dogmatic pronouncements and thereby precluded itself from ever putting them right. This is the sharp point of Dr Houlden's question.

The assent of the faithful

Roman Catholic dogma requires the unreserved assent of all the faithful. The Church excommunicates those who refuse such assent (as happened with the

---

[103] In *The Interpretation of the Bible in the Church*, ed J L Houlden, SCM Press Ltd, London, 1995, p 110.
[104] It is important for Protestant readers to understand that, in Catholic teaching, the Pope's pronouncements are only infallible when declared "ex cathedra", ie from the papal throne, meaning, when he is speaking officially on behalf of the Church on matters concerning faith and morals. It is not as if his private opinions are supposed to be infallible.

Old Catholics when they refused to accept the decree on papal infallibility). But this requires that there is proper consultation with the Catholic faithful before dogmas are proclaimed. In the notorious case of the Papal decree called "Humanae Vitae," banning Catholics from the use of artificial means of contraception, Pope Paul VI chose to ignore the majority recommendation of the commission of experts (including lay and married men but no women!) he had appointed to examine the issue. Within more recent times, John Paul II has ruled out even the permissibility of discussing issues of obligatory clerical celibacy, of the acceptance of married priests and of the ordination of women to the priesthood; issues about which opinion polls demonstrate that a majority of Catholics, even in traditionally Catholic countries such as Italy and Spain, are quite open-minded. I would not be so foolish as to expect the Church suddenly to become democratic (democracy was one of the errors condemned by Pope Pius IX (Pio Nono) in his infamous Syllabus of 1864. The same Pope had declared that "error has no rights"). But what can "assent" or "consent" mean if the views of the laity are ignored? Even those lay people called to Rome for consultations find themselves more "talked at" rather than "listened to" (as recent letters to the *Tablet* (i.e. in August 2003) demonstrate. The Church as "the People of God" remains a fine-sounding slogan from Vatican II. It has not yet been securely established at ground level, so much so that considerable numbers of lay Catholics in Austria and Southern Germany have organized themselves under the banner "We are the Church". They are officially ignored.

The status of the pope

Roman Catholic teaching on authority is clear. All authority continues to lie with the Pope as the successor of Peter and thereby the Vicar of Christ on earth. Its reality lies quite as much with the arch-conservative bureaucracy of the Vatican. The much discussed principle of collegiality, whereby the pope operates in concert with the whole College of Bishops, and they with him, is not much practiced. Behind it all is an ill-founded notion of the origins of the papacy.

In the Roman Catholic view, Simon Peter was instituted by the Lord as the first pope. That is how the account of Matthew 16.13-19 is understood, especially verse 18 in which Jesus said to him: "And I tell you, you are Peter, and on this rock I will build my church, and the gates of Hades will not prevail against it. I will give you the keys of the kingdom of heaven..." There has been endless debate as to the precise meaning of this event. It is undeniably the fact that Peter enjoyed a certain primacy amongst the apostles. He is always the first named in every listing of the apostles. In other passages too he is given some kind of special role to be fulfilled after the Lord's death and resurrection: notably in Luke 22.31-32 spoken at the Last Supper table; and at John 21.15-19, when Jesus commissions Peter "to feed my sheep." But, whilst in Matthew 16.19

Peter alone is given some authority of "binding" and "loosing" (i.e. exercising disciplinary powers), in John 20.22-23 the same power is delegated to all of the apostles present. This latter is the root of the concept of "collegiality." However, there is nothing in the rest of the New Testament to give any impression of Peter as exercising any kind of dominant leadership role. In the first part of Acts, he is shown as an active missionary, recognized at the Council of Jerusalem as being supremely the apostle to the Jews. But he does not preside over that Council. He is later described by Paul somewhat disdainfully, as "one of the pillars of the Church" together with James and John (in Galatians 21.18-2.10). Paul also describes a blazing row that he had with Cephas (as Peter is called in this section) in which he accuses him of treachery in refusing to sit at table with gentile Christians.[105] There is nothing Pope-like in the entire presentation of Simon Peter in the New Testament. It cannot be passed over, in a Church enforcing celibacy on its priests that, in his travels, Peter continued to be accompanied by his wife (1 Corinthians 9.5).

The papacy in contemporary debate

The Roman Church next assumes that Peter handed on his supreme role to a successor such that every Pope is thereafter in a direct apostolic succession. This claim is made without a scrap of evidence to support it. In a remarkable lecture[106] delivered at the *Tablet's* Open Day in 1998, Eamon Duffy, the foremost Catholic historian in Britain, challenged his Church to face up to the implications of applying the tools of historical and textual criticism to the origins of the Papacy. Over two centuries these had been applied to the Bible, with a resultant total re-evaluation of the role of figures such as Moses, David, and even Jesus (such as I have been describing in this book). The early origins of Catholicism should be approached in the same way. Addressing what he calls "the foundation myth of the papacy," he outlines what is a historically verifiable account of its beginnings: "The Church established itself in Rome some time in the AD 40s: we now know that for the best part of the century that followed, there was nothing and nobody in Rome who could recognizably be called a pope. Christianity in Rome evolved out of the Roman synagogues, and to begin with it was not so much a single Church as a constellation of independent churches,[107] meeting in the houses of wealthy converts or in hired halls and public baths, without any

---

[105] It is strange in a Church supposedly founded jointly by the apostles Peter and Paul that in practice all power has been confided in Peter whilst Paul is largely "bound and gagged" – one wonders whether Peter is taking revenge on Paul's outspoken attack in Antioch!
[106] Abridged version published in the *Tablet*, July 4, 1998. Eamon Duffy is the Professor in Church History at Cambridge University. His thesis can be read more fully in his book, *Saints and sinners: A History of the Popes*, Yale University Press, 1997.
[107] So perhaps we who were Congregationalists (before entering the United Reformed Church) were the true heirs of the early Church in Rome!

central ruler or bishop." "… in the first century, episcopacy emerged as the dominant form of church order … but Rome…was very slow to adopt this system." Further on he writes: "… the recognition of the bishops of Rome was the result … of a long and uncertain evolutionary process …" This "surely rules out any absolutist understanding of the nature of papal authority." As an example of such absolutism, Duffy cites the saying of Boniface VIII (1294-1303) to the effect that it was "altogether necessary to salvation for every human creature to be subject to the Roman pontiff." "The modern papacy … is … the result of a historical catastrophe, the French revolution. The revolution swept away the Catholic kings who had appointed bishops and ruled Churches." That duty fell perforce to the pope. "This means by which the Pope controls the entire Church from Rome dates only from the Canon Law of 1917."

But Professor Duffy is a Roman Catholic historian. It is most important therefore to hear him state: "It is not my argument that the papacy is built on false claims and ought to be dismantled: the papacy is a fact … one of the concrete forms in which order, unity and fidelity to the truth have been preserved within the Church: … the papacy is the way things have worked out." My choice of quotations has had necessarily to be selective. His lecture deserves to be read in full. I pick out one further quotation: "Getting the story right can … illuminate for us the character of the institution which has resulted from the historical process."

Look forward in hopefulness

This lecture appears to me as a remarkable response to Dr Houlden's challenge (p.320 above). In his encyclical "UT UNUM SINT," "That they may be One," Pope John Paul II recognized that to many Christians, the papacy as an institution is a stumbling block on the road to Christian unity and invited theologians of other churches to comment. One wonders how far Professor Duffy's thesis is understood and accepted within the Roman Church. If it were, it would provide a firm foundation for ecumenical discussion on the possible place of the papacy within a reunited Church. A further contribution of huge significance had already been made by Hans Kung towards the close of his book, *Infallible?* It would be a shame if Catholics were so deterred by the negative (as traditionalist Catholics probably saw it) core of this book's argument as to have missed the positive conclusion to it, i.e. in his chapter headed "Look forward in hopefulness," he described what a truly reformed papacy and Church that lived by the gospel would be like. His final chapter, "Portrait of a Possible Pope" set out on the basis of some proposals put forward by Cardinal Suenens in 1969, included this: "The Pope that we have in mind would take a genuinely evangelical and not a juridical-formal and static-bureaucratic view of the Church. In the light of the gospel, he would see where the secret of the Church lies; he would see it, not as a centralized administrative unit in which the bishops are merely the Pope's delegates and executive agents, but as a Church whose authentic life is in the local churches (of parishes, towns, dioceses, countries) that everywhere combine to form the community of the one Church of God and, are thus linked with the Church of Rome as the center of their unity."

This would be highly promising if it were not for the fact that Kung, whom many consider the finest apologete for the Christian Faith in the Western world during the past 50 years, is still banned from speaking as a Catholic theologian. There is little reason to suppose that the Vatican is as yet ready to pay heed either to the voice of its own prophets or to the historical research of Professor Duffy. Until it does so there can be no very meaningful ecumenical conversation.

The United Reformed Church

Origins: The United Reformed Church (hereafter the URC) was formed by the coming together, in 1972, of the former Congregational Church in England and Wales and the Presbyterian Church of England. It was later joined by the Churches of Christ in 1982 and the Scottish Congregational Church in 2001. The former two churches traced their origins from the later years of the 16th century, as parts of the turbulent English Reformation. The Congregationalists were amongst the more radical Reformers, rejecting not only the Papacy, but also the right of monarchy or parliament to govern men's souls. They formed "gathered communities" of Christian believers, elected their own pastors, and sought direction for their godly living in the pages of the Bible. The Presbyterians desired to establish a National Church, but one without pope or bishops; the Church to be led by elders both lay and ordained. Both groups led an uneasy existence vis-à-vis the Church of England, some remaining officially within its orbit; others setting up entirely independent Christian communities. Some of their ministers remained clerics of the Established Church until their ejection as a consequence of the Act of Uniformity in 1662. Almost 3,000 clerics, lecturers and schoolmasters refused to conform and either left or were expelled from the Church of England. Hence they were termed "nonconformists," although for long the term "dissenting independents" was more generally used of them. The Churches of Christ were a quite small localized denomination in the UK, of more recent origin, practicing "Believers' Baptism" and stressing lay ministry.

The basis of union

As part of the Act of Union (which had to receive parliamentary approval), the two bodies devised what was termed *The Basis of Union*. I am using this example since it is likely to have been the only mainstream Church in Britain required to define its concept of authority in comparatively recent times. Within its statement concerning the nature, faith and order of the United Reformed Church, the third clause declares: "The United Reformed Church acknowledges the Word of God in the Old and New Testaments, discerned under the guidance of the Holy Spirit, as the supreme authority for the faith and conduct of all God's people." Note that the reference is to the Word of God, not directly to the Bible, although the latter is immediately identified by reference to the Old and New Testaments. We will seek to elucidate what this may mean, especially as to how such authority is to be discerned.

It was understandable that the Act of Union of, initially two nonconformist churches originating in the Protestant Reformation, should look back to the Bible as their chief source of authority as a unifying factor. But it immediately poses a problem (that to this day has not been resolved) that the biblical revolution that has been the subject of this book has intervened between us and the 16th-century Reformers such as Luther, Calvin and Zwingli. They could not have been anything other than literalist in their thinking about the Bible – whereas we have the tools forged in the transition from Renaissance through Enlightenment into the modern world by which we may approach the Bible quite differently. My suspicion is that the URC accepted a dogmatic definition of authority, of which Calvin would have approved, but based on a literalist understanding of the Bible at a time when in practice a majority of our ministers and members cannot so regard it in view of the biblical scholarship of the past three centuries. We can no longer think as Calvin or Zwingly thought. Of course, the declaration of the faith, order and nature of the URC could not be other than succinct and thereby lays itself open to misinterpretation. On occasions therefore it probably needs to be "fleshed" out. But let us note what it does not say before we consider what it does.

❖ *It acknowledges the Word of God in the Old and New Testaments.* It does not equate the Word of God directly with the Bible, but discerns it within the Bible. It defines the Bible as Old and New Testaments, by which we can assume that it takes Luther's line in subordinating the Apocrypha to a less than scriptural position.

❖ It qualifies the above by a principle of interpretation: as "discerned under the guidance of the Holy Spirit." This we might consider as a useful "escape clause" from the clutches of fundamentalism. If the statement "in the Old and New Testaments" suggests an ambivalence as to their respective authority, "discerned under the guidance of the Holy Spirit" may offer illumination as to how to resolve those ambiguities.

I propose now to examine the URC's statement by comparison and contrast with the Roman Catholic positions outlined in "Verbum Dei."

A STATEMENT CONCERNING THE NATURE, FAITH AND ORDER OF THE UNITED REFORMED CHURCH

1) The United Reformed Church confesses the faith of the Church Catholic in one God, Father, Son and Holy Spirit.

2) The United Reformed Church acknowledges that the life of faith to which it is called is a gift of the Holy Spirit continually received in Word and Sacrament and in the common life of God's people.

3) The United Reformed Church acknowledges the Word of God in the Old and New Testaments, discerned under the guidance of the Holy Spirit, as the supreme authority for the faith and conduct of all God's people.

4) The United Reformed Church accepts with thanksgiving the witness borne to the Catholic faith by the Apostles' and Nicene Creeds, and recognises as its own particular heritage the formulations and declarations of faith which have been prepared from time to time by Congregationalists and Presbyterians in which they have stated the gospel and sought to make its implications clear.

5) The United Reformed Church testifies to its faith and orders its life, according to the Basis of Union, believing it to embody the essential notes of the Church Catholic and Reformed. The United Reformed Church nevertheless reserves its right and declares its readiness at any time to alter, add to, modify or supersede this Basis so that its life may accord more nearly with the mind of Christ.

6) The United Reformed Church under the authority of Holy Scripture and in corporate responsibility to Jesus Christ its everliving head, acknowledges its duty to be open at all times to the leading of the Holy Spirit and therefore affirms its right to make such new declarations of its faith and for such purposes as may from time to time be required in obedience to the same Spirit.

7) The United Reformed Church, believing that it is through the freedom of the Spirit that Jesus Christ -holds his people in the fellowship of the One Body, upholds the rights of personal conviction. It shall be for the Church, in safeguarding the substance of the faith and maintaining the unity of the fellowship, to determine when these rights are asserted to the injury of its unity and peace.

8) The United Reformed Church declares that the Lord -Jesus Christ, the only king and head of the Churc-h has herein appointed a government distinct from civil government and in things spiritual not subordinate thereto, and that civil authorities, being always subject to the rule of God, ought to respect the rights of conscience and of religious belief and to serve God's will of justice and peace for all men.

9) The United Reformed Church declares its intention, in fellowship with all the Churches, to pray and work for such visible unity of the whole Church as Christ wills and in the way he wills, in order that men and nations may be led more and more to glorify the Father in heaven.

The Bible in the URC

We have seen that the URC accepts "the Word of God, in the Old and New Testaments, as the supreme authority for the faith and conduct of all God's people." I question the appropriateness of employing the epithet "supreme" in this context, on the ground that the only Supreme Authority is that of God alone. We might allow its appropriateness when applied strictly to the expression "The Word of God" (understood in terms of the discussion of its meaning in Chapter 19), i.e. whenever it indicates every means by which God communicates with us. But not so if applied directly to the Bible per se. For even "the Word of God" is known to us only by the human reporting of it. The distinction may be over-subtle, but we walk here along a precipitous ridge. It is well to avoid any hint of bibliolatry.

The Guidance of the Spirit

But how is the Word of God discerned and by whom? My view is that this could have been made clearer in the URC's Basis of Union. For the URC to declare its supreme authority to reside in "the Word of God in the Old and New Testaments, discerned under the guidance of the Holy Spirit ..." leaves it open to the charge of Biblicism. Recent debate over the highly emotive matter of the ordination of people of homosexual orientation and practice, with much over-dependence on the quotation of highly selective texts, illustrates how uncreative and unfruitful such debate can become. Crucial in this statement is the reference to the guidance of the Holy Spirit. This has been the universal belief of the Church and was particularly stressed by John Calvin. In his teaching, it is "the inner witness of the Holy Spirit" that brings conviction to the hearts and minds of believers. The Word of God in scripture may be little more than a dead letter, unless and until the Spirit causes it to be heard again as a living Word.

How we are to discern the witness of the Spirit?

It should be acceptable in denominations whose contribution to biblical scholarship has been considerable and which have always valued a scholarly ministry, that they should regard the entire modern enterprise of biblical scholarship as a massive effort in such discernment, an enterprise in which its own scholars (such as T W Manson, Charles Dodd, George Caird, John Marsh in New Testament studies; Wheeler Robinson, Harold Rowley and others in Old Testament studies) have played, as others still do, a considerable role. Rather than regarding the Enlightenment as a retrograde step into rationalism and skepticism, I believe that we should regard it as a liberationist movement of the Spirit in no area more so than in the study of the Bible. The greatest fruit of such study has enabled us to discern far more clearly what is the essence of the gospel over against beliefs and practices which were merely customary and traditional within the worlds of Israel and the early Church. One obvious example is that of the overwhelmingly patriarchal assumptions of both. One has to ask how far Paul's ethical teaching was more influenced by these than by the radical newness of Jesus' gospel. I include amongst the chief fruits of such liberation a more just and egalitarian appreciation of the role of women and men in the Church.

Of course, the Word of God may also be discerned wherever Christians seriously and humbly seek the mind of Christ. The authenticity of such discernment will largely be known by the fruits that it bears. Wherever, in study and meditation, in prayer and preaching, the Word comes alive, is heard as if freshly minted, is completely in accord with the practice and precept of Jesus and is for edification of the whole Christian body, then it is surely the work of the Spirit. To which I have to add an important rider: that what is of the Spirit is always subject to the judgment of the Church. Whilst individuals may have a startling revelation of God's Word for them, this has always to be subject to the enquiry and consensus of the Christian community.

The URC values Tradition

With the wholly new appreciation of Tradition as outlined in the previous chapter, as both prior to scripture and operative after scripture, it follows that we are not so far removed from the Catholic notion as we used to suppose that we were. We give "pride of place" to the Word of God found principally but not solely within the pages of the Bible. But we also value Tradition. This is made evident in the first clause of the Statement when it declares its adherence to "the faith of the Church Catholic in one God ..." The word "Catholic" here means "universal" rather than having to do specifically with the Roman Catholic Church. The URC regards itself as, by the Grace of God, a part of the historic Christian Tradition traceable through two thousand years of history. And in the fourth clause: "The United Reformed Church accepts with thanksgiving the witness borne to the Catholic faith by the Apostles' and Nicene Creeds, and recognizes as its own particular heritage the formulations and declarations of faith which have been prepared from time to time by Congregationalists and Presbyterians in which they have stated the gospel and sought to make its implications clear." The URC claims to be within the Tradition which produced the great ecumenical creeds of the early Church; and, more recently, that of our dissenting forbears who penned the Westminster and other confessions of faith. But whilst we acknowledge them, we are not bound by them. We accept them as honest but time-bound and time-conditioned attempts to define the essence of Christian faith in the language and ideology of their own day and age. Our task in the 21st century is to delineate the essentials of the faith for our own time.

However, Christians of our tradition would not give equal status to scripture and Tradition. Whilst valuing the latter, we would always regard the former as having primacy. This is for the reason that the Word of God discerned within the Old and New Testaments sets out the foundational documents of the Christian faith. They constitute the blueprint, the ground plans of the building on which later generations of believers have built. The faithfulness of our building is in its conformity with the ground plans. We would generally consider any traditions incompatible with the plain witness of the scriptures to be illegitimate; unless there are very strong reasons for believing that new situations demand new responses which were simply not within the sight of biblical authors. This is a major caveat, since humankind today faces challenges and dangers in the spheres particularly of scientific research and its consequences which could not possibly have been foreseen in biblical times.

How do we practice discernment?

Where does the URC stand in relation to what the Roman Catholic Church terms the Magisterium, the Church's Teaching Office? The very notion indicates that the interpretation of Bible and Tradition is a weighty matter such that the Christian faithful require guidance. Catholics may feel with justification that, when it is assumed that every Christian can interpret the scriptures for him or herself, then there is the recipe for confusion and sectarianism. The multiplication of "Bible-believing" sects is proof of this. Some of the early Protestants were fully aware of this. Martin Luther was alarmed at the fissiparous dangers inherent once Church authority was rejected and thundered mightily (but in vain) to prevent them. William Tyndale significantly wrote a small tract of practical guidance entitled *A Pathway into Scripture* for those about to read his "novel" *New Testament in English*.

By its Basis of Union, the URC seeks the help of the Holy Spirit in order to discern the Word of God in the Old and New Testaments. This practice of discernment is carried out within the various levels at which the Church lives. The URC, as every Church, has in practice to have some kind of Magisterium (to use the RC word) which thereby exercises authority. But this authority is advisory, exhortational rather than juridical. A situation in which every member of the Church made his or her own decisions on matters of faith and practice (other, of course, then those which are of a purely private nature) would indeed lead to anarchy. It would have been little use at the Reformation, having dethroned the Pope as supreme authority, to have instead every member arrogating to him or herself such authority. As 2 Peter 1.20-22, duly warns: "... no prophetic writing is a matter for private interpretation. It was not on any human initiative that prophecy came; rather, it was under the compulsion of the Holy Spirit that people spoke as messengers of God." Verses 21-22 rather obfuscate the plain sense of verse 20: have we not experienced those who claim the inspiration of the Spirit to promote some personal agenda? The spirits have to be tested and personal opinions to be evaluated within the body of the Church. Since Christianity is in its essence a social faith, a body with many limbs and organs, it can only operate by a high degree of consensus.

The role of church councils

In the United Reformed Church, there is a tradition of deference to the views of those trained and ordained as ministers who are thereby authorized to speak with some authority on matters of faith and doctrine. But, in the Church Meeting, which brings together all who have become members on confession of faith, all have the right to speak and to vote on any matter according to their conscience. Where there are matters beyond the competence of the local congregation, or of wider than local concern, the focus of discussion, debate and decision is in the District Meeting; at a higher level in Synod (covering a wider area akin to an Anglican diocese); at the highest level, at the General Assembly of the Church. In the URC, the faithful (i.e. the members at local level) have theoretically a full voice at every level of discussion, but this does raise serious questions as to how adequately they are represented especially at General Assembly. Appointed representatives cannot wholly represent (how could they?) every member unless there has been extensive prior consultation.

The Rights of Conscience

The rights of private conscience are written into the Basis of Union. No Christian can be coerced into the acceptance of any particular belief or practice. For this reason, most churches do not impose any rigid tests of doctrinal belief on their members (although whenever an adult joins the Church by Baptism or by Confession of Faith, s/he is expected to give assent to a simple Trinitarian formula). URC churches very rarely recite the Apostles or Nicene Creeds. In fact, it would be true to say that most nonconformist Christians are suspicious of such creeds. Faith that is in essence an act of trust cannot be adequately expressed in words (just as few married couples could easily explicate verbally their experience of love). Just as it is accepted that no form of human words can adequately express the Christian faith, so is it that no two persons' understanding of it will be identical. But if such a person's belief or behavior deviates so far from what is acceptable to the congregation, the Church (meaning the assembled members of it) has the right to withdraw such a person's membership.

---

[108] For the circumstances in which Newman made this remark, see *The Victorians*, by A N Wilson, Hutchinson, London, 2002, p 375.

We should recognize at this point that the Roman Catholic Church also teaches that no Christian can be expected to obey Church teaching against the dictate of his/her own conscience. Yet it isn't at all clear how this is compatible with a Catholic's necessary assent to a dogma which is essential to one's salvation! It is by this defense that large numbers of lay Catholics (so we may guess) in the Western world ignore the papal prohibition on the use of artificial methods of contraception and yet otherwise remain loyal adherents of their Church. There was the famous occasion when John Henry Newman, who converted to the Roman Catholic Church in 1845, declared: "I shall drink – to the Pope, if you please – still, to Conscience first, and to the Pope afterwards."[108]

The authority of one's conscience

In practical terms, it has to be said that all genuine authority has to be self-authenticating. If it does not convince a person's heart and mind, then it cannot be believed or followed. People are rightly resistant to indoctrination and will not give assent to matters with which they do not wholly and voluntarily concur. Experience teaches that faith, or any particular belief, is not arrived at by a conscious effort of the will, but rather by a dawning of the truth, as something given or revealed to one's heart and mind. It isn't so much that "I grab the truth;" but rather that "the truth grabs me." There may be some necessary groundwork, some preparatory effort required, such as conversing with a convinced believer, reading some helpful literature, perhaps spending time in prayer and meditation; these may prepare the ground by positioning myself in the place or situation in which that truth may disclose itself to me. There is then a sense in which the ultimate authority is neither Bible nor Church but one's own heart and mind, one's own powers of reason and the decision of one's own conscience. This is not a surrender to solipsism (as if what I believe or think is all that matters) since the Christian experience is that coming to faith in God, Father, Son and Holy Spirit, is to be born into the Christian community. If and when we come to faith, we realize that it is through the Christian Tradition that the faith has been conveyed to us. The most common means by which people come to faith is from their involvement within the life of the Church.

The conscience is not some innate quality, but is itself the consequence of a gradual formation of the moral side of a person's nature by upbringing, education, example, life experience and, finally, by personal conviction. A Christian's conscience will have been informed by and within the family, school and church so there will be a predisposition (or, let's admit, sometimes an aversion) to Christian belief and action. Nevertheless, there still has to be genuine personal conviction. We cannot finally separate between conscience and one's powers of reasoning. If the reason persuades, then the conscience commits the will to its pursuit.

In the light of these considerations, I hold that our dependence on written scripture may be exaggerated. The "Word of God" is more than words in a book; it is rather a living encounter with God in Christ. "For me to live is Christ …"(Philippians 1.21) as the apostle declared, or, as he reminded his friends in Colossae, "Christ in you, the hope of glory" (Colossians 1.27). The experience is what matters most, perhaps mediated through scripture, through prayer or preaching, or perhaps whilst strolling the hills with the dog or walking along the beach.

Semper Reformanda

Reformation thought adopted the slogan "Semper Reformanda," implying that Christians had constantly to be reforming their faith and practice in conformity with the Word of God. The URC takes seriously that, if it is to be faithful to God and to the tasks of the gospel, it has always to be listening to the voice of the Spirit. And always to be prepared to amend, restructure, reform, whatever is required, in order to be a more fitting instrument of the gospel. It can never sit back and think: "We reformed all that was necessary so many centuries ago." It has to heed what is God's Word for now.

It is important therefore to recognize that the Christian Tradition never dies. It is not something that occurred in the past (so that interest in it is simply antiquarian) which came to a halt so many years ago. It is rather the ever-flowing mighty river that carries us as it carried Abraham and Moses, David and Isaiah, Jesus and Paul through the biblical years, then Augustine and Francis, Wycliffe and Tyndale, Luther and Calvin through to Bunyan and Wesley, down to Pope John XXIII, Martin Luther King and Desmond Tutu in our own times. This is the movement of the Spirit which has brought us through more than three thousand five hundred years of history. If we are to be faithful witnesses to this Christian Tradition, we have to seek to express the gospel in language intelligible in this 21st century; for which reason the URC "affirms its right to make such new declarations of its faith and for such purposes as may from time to time be required in obedience to the same Spirit." (para.6).

The URC statement: is it adequate for the 21st century?

---

[109] Quoted from memory in an address delivered at the Norfolk Theological Society in 1999 or thereabouts.

We have seriously to ask whether the URC's Basis of Union, affirming the authority of the Word of God in Old and New Testaments, is adequate, if we are to face all the challenges of the new millennium. The Reformers, being men of their time, could hardly have read the scriptures in any other way than what we would term "fundamentalist." As I have argued throughout this book, we who have learned to read the Bible "with new eyes," thanks to three centuries of enlightened biblical scholarship, have to part company with them, not on the essentials of Christian belief and trust in God as Father, Son and Holy Spirit, but in their unhistorical and over-literalistic reading of it. We can't turn the clock back. There are questions facing us that simply weren't so much as conceived by them, including questions for which there is no solution whatsoever given within the pages of the Bible. I have already mentioned some of these: in the role of women in society in general and the Church in particular, in the whole area of sexual ethics, especially those to do with homosexuality, with contraception, abortion, and treatments for infertility; with the possibilities of stem cell research, genetic engineering and cloning. Nor can we afford to overlook the huge ecological questions, the excessive population growth, the dissipation of natural resources, pollution of air, earth and water, the threat of nuclear warfare and terrorism: all of which threaten humankind's very survival. To which we need to add the question of our relationships with women and men of other faiths. "There can be no world Peace without Peace between the religions" is a dictum of Hans Kung, motivating his search for a global ethic that will unite all peoples of good will. All such matters require us to be as well informed in areas of new scientific knowledge and in other faiths (about which the people of biblical times knew nothing) as we have been in biblical studies.

Can there be a Word of God heard outside scripture?

The URC statement declares "the Word of God" to be the supreme authority. Can this possibly mean something bigger and wider than "the Old and New Testaments?" If the answer is "No," then there are areas of life in which we will be left floundering in the dark. If the answer is "Yes," we will need to qualify and define what other sources of authority there might be. May I remind you from what has already been written in this study, that "the Word of God" was heard and heeded (by many) in Israel before ever a word of the Old Testament was written; and that "the Word of God" in person walked and talked in Palestine before a word of the New Testament was penned. There is precedent for acknowledging the Word of God as not confined to the pages of a book. Is there precedent for the Word of God being heard after the completion of the scriptures? Surely we can affirm that it is so heard. The words of Dr Houlden still ring in my ears: "I find it distinctly odd to suppose that God spoke the final word on every matter 2,000 years ago."[109]

The Wisdom literature

Is there any biblical basis for the recognition that God's Word may be heard beyond the confines of the book? There is a section of the Old Testament to which, in this study, I have made very little if any reference. Amongst the writings, the third and last section of the Old Testament to come to the fore, are some books assigned to the Wisdom Tradition. These include Proverbs, Ecclesiastes, Job, and other books forming part of the Apocrypha, such as the Wisdom of Solomon. At first sight, these appear as an almost alien intrusion into the biblical narrative. They make little or no reference to the great events of Israel's history and don't fit easily into the most distinctive features of Jewish faith. Some disclose a tradition of homespun, worldly wisdom; set out moral maxims employed in the education of the young; some exude a world-weary skepticism; some introduce concepts from the Greek philosophical tradition. There is just a hint that they introduce what might appear to be an almost secular attitude to life. Are they introducing "a parallel universe" to that of the Jewish religious faith which we also need to acknowledge?

An embryonic science?

I suggest that we may glimpse in this the emergence of a kind of detached scientific approach to life which may be complementary to religious faith. 1 Kings 4 summarizes the international fame achieved by King Solomon; in it we read "... that Solomon's wisdom surpassed the wisdom of all the people of the east, and all the wisdom of Egypt ...his fame spread throughout all the surrounding nations. He composed three thousand proverbs, and his songs numbered a thousand and five. He would speak of trees, from the cedar that is in the Lebanon to the hyssop that grows in the wall; he would speak of animals, and birds, and reptiles, and fish. People came from all the nations to hear the wisdom of Solomon; they came from all the kings of the earth who had heard of his wisdom. (I Kings 4.30-34).

It is perhaps far-fetched to suggest that verse 33's reference to trees and animals and birds suggests a new interest in the natural world out of which, eventually, the sciences would emerge. But there appears in the Wisdom literature an inkling of the notion that not all knowledge stems directly from the "special revelation" disclosed to Moses and the Prophets, to Jesus and the apostles. Simple observations about life and social behavior can yield a kind of complementary knowledge (which, developed, will be called "general revelation"). In the Wisdom of Solomon (7.17-22), the author extols the fruits of wisdom in a direction more suggestive of the scientific spirit: "For it is he who gave me unerring knowledge of what exists, to know the structure of the world and the activity of the elements; the beginning and end and middle of times, the alternations of the solstices and the changes of the seasons, the cycles of the year and the constellations of the stars, the natures of animals and the tempers of wild animals, the powers of spirits and the thoughts of human beings, the varieties of plants and the virtues of roots; I learned both what is secret and what is manifest, for wisdom, the fashioner of all things, taught me." This does indicate an embryonic scientific approach to life's mysteries.

In Proverbs, also traditionally attributed to Solomon, there is a remarkable passage in which Wisdom is personified as a being at God's right hand, God's assistant in the very act of creation: "The Lord created me at the beginning of his work, the first of his acts of long ago. Ages ago I was set up, at the first, before the beginning of the earth. When there were no depths I was brought forth, when there were no springs abounding with water. Before the mountains had been shaped, before the hills, I was brought forth – when he had not yet made earth and fields, or the world's first bits of soil. When he established the heavens, I was there, when he drew a circle on the face of the deep, when he made firm the skies above, when he established the fountains of the deep, when he assigned to the sea its limit, so that the waters might not transgress his command, when he marked out the foundations of the earth, then I was beside him, like a master worker; and I was daily his delight, rejoicing before him always, rejoicing in his inhabited world and delighting in the human race." (Proverbs 8.22-31)

God's book of Nature:

There is a close correlation between this concept of Wisdom active in creation and that of the Logos (Word) in John's Gospel. "Logos" emerged out of the Greek philosophers' attempts to account for the creation of a material universe by an immaterial divine Being. Wisdom-Word was at God's right hand. No Jew could have thought of Wisdom or Word as another being besides God; but he could as a personification of God's creative activity. Logos was the expression of God's mind, of God's communication with the world of His creation. It is not without significance that so many words indicative of our different intellectual disciplines are compounded with the "logos" suffix. Thus we have theology (from "logos" about "theos," God) on the one hand; and biology (logos about "bios," living things), zoology (logos about "zo-os," living creatures), cosmology (logos about the "cosmos," the universe) etc on the other. In the Middle Ages, all such intellectual disciplines would have been considered as so many pathways towards the knowledge of God. Even when the sciences were beginning to

---

[110] In *Galileo's Daughter*, by Dava Sobel, Fourth Estate, London 1999, on p 63.
[111] Above, on p. 65

establish themselves as autonomous disciplines, it was common for a genius such as Galileo to perceive them as constituting what he called *God's Book of Nature*, to be studied alongside of *God's Book of Scripture*.

The Wisdom of Galileo

In a letter written to a colleague in December 1613 Galileo probed the relationship of truth discovered in nature to revealed truth in the Bible. He wrote: "... it seems to me that it was most prudently ... established by you, that Holy Scripture cannot err and the decrees therein contained are absolutely true and inviolable. I should only have added that, though Scripture cannot err, its expounders and interpreters are liable to err in many ways ... when they would base themselves always on the literal meaning of the words ..."[110] Here Galileo, employing the currently literalist view of scripture (for there was no other), realized and expressed doubts as to the over-literalist interpretation of it.

Further on, referring to the controversy as to whether the sun had literally stood still in the sky (as per Joshua 10.12-14) he explained "that the Bible spoke to a more important purpose" (i.e. than to God's intervention in a cosmic event). "I believe that the intention of Holy Writ was to persuade men of the truths necessary for salvation ... such as neither science nor any other means could render credible, but only the voice of the Holy Spirit. But I do not think it necessary to believe that the same God who gave us our senses, our speech, our intellect, would have put aside the use of these, to teach us instead such things as with their help we could find out for ourselves, particularly in the case of these sciences of which there is not the smallest mention in the scriptures; and, above all, in astronomy, of which so little notice is taken that the names of none of the planets are mentioned. Surely if the intention of the sacred scribes had been to teach the people astronomy, they would not have passed over the subject so completely."[110]

Here was the first truly modern scientist claiming the independence of the scientific method, not in opposition to the teachings of holy scripture, but in complementing areas of human concern and interest in no way dealt with in the Bible. If Galileo could make such a claim four hundred years ago, in a time when the Bible could not have been understood in any other way than that of either a crude literalism or of the most fanciful allegorization, how much more may we, having discarded the premises of biblical fundamentalism, regard the scientific disciplines as ways to authentic knowledge, not of God but of God's creation. Within a monotheistic faith, there cannot be any truth whatsoever which is not God's truth. If it is God's truth about the way the universe is, then that too has to be authoritative.

What is truth, asked Pilate?

The concept of truth is itself ambiguous and much discussed by philosophers. Do such scientific concepts as the Big Bang Theory or that of Evolution by Natural Selection themselves constitute truth? I mention these two since they have both notoriously been battlegrounds as between the fundamentalists of both science and religion. Certainly the theories have been promoted after the most exhaustive research and accumulation of evidence over many centuries, all of which evidence is open to public investigation. All science is based on the minute examination of data and the theories are propounded to best explain the data. But they remain theories. Theories are by their nature provisional. The evidence of the researches of the past century strongly points to the essential correctness of the Big Bang Theory. But, no genuine scientist would be so bold as to deny that there might emerge data that could throw the theory into doubt. Every astronomer knows that a considerable enigma in current theory is the fact that 90% of the matter in the universe is still wholly hidden from us. This "dark matter" still requires examination and explanation. It is unlikely that this should challenge the Big Bang Theory (for which the accumulated evidence is considerable) but that there are mysteries yet to be resolved. Authentic science always holds open the possibility that fresh evidence, or the re-examination of old evidence, might yield data that would oblige corrections to current theory or even their overthrow.

This attitude, fundamental to true science, should serve as an admirable example to all who engage in Christian theology – with its dreadful history of dogmatic intolerance in the not so distant past.

The truth as final arbiter

Finally, we have to recognize that the truth (from whatever quarter it may come) is the highest authority, since all truth must be God's truth, whether it concerns Quantum Physics, the Map of the Human Genome, or God's revelation of Himself in Jesus Christ. This does not negate our understanding and use of the Bible. The Bible was recognized as the Church's main source of authority because, so Christians decided, it contains the truth about God and the truth of God. For reasons I have already discussed, today we can no longer suppose that the Bible contains the truth on every single matter – it manifestly does not. The Christian claim to its remaining value is solely on the grounds that within its witness God reveals Himself as He does not in any other sphere. This may be arguable. Some will say that God reveals him/herself in other religions; others that he may be known by direct mystical experience. I do not wish to dispute either possibility. But a specifically Christian picture of God is derived through His self-disclosure depicted in the pages of the Bible. Christians come to God through Christ. God is thus the ultimate source of all truth. But a vast range of what we might call secular knowledge is available to us not through the Bible, but through all the investigative tools and techniques devolved over the past three centuries. This too yields truth, not the truth of God directly, but the truth of God's creation. Whatever is true, from whatever source, is thereby authoritative. We cannot therefore pitch biblical knowledge over against secular knowledge. But we may gratefully accept that all knowledge is ultimately of and from God.

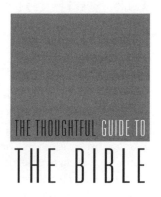

THE THOUGHTFUL GUIDE TO

THE BIBLE

POSTSCRIPT

CHAPTER 22:
THE HORIZONS OF OUR VISION

The Small World of the Bible Story

"In the beginning God created the heavens and the earth …" (Genesis 1.1) On Christmas Eve 1968, a space-capsule from the Apollo 8 Shuttle went into orbit round the moon. That evening, the American astronauts aboard, Frank Borman, Jim Lovell and Bill Anders broadcast their Christmas greetings to the world, seen or heard by millions. Each of them read selected verses from the first chapter of the book of Genesis; surely the most extraordinary reading of it ever made. In the following year, Neil Armstrong and Buzz Aldrin landed and walked on the Moon, marking "one small step for man, one giant leap for mankind." They carried out a number of scientific experiments, but they also took Holy Communion on its surface. Aldrin left the text that he had written out from Psalm 8. 3-4 underneath a rock on the moon's surface: "When I look at your heavens, the work of your fingers, the moon and the stars that you have established; what are human beings that you are mindful of them, mortals that you care for them?"

These historic events marked a quite spectacular meeting of two cultures, the ancient culture of the Bible and that of modern scientific and technological achievement. It would seem that these astronauts, evidently Christians, had no difficulty in reconciling the two cultures within their own thinking. They can hardly have believed in the cosmological suppositions of the ancient Babylonians (which could never have landed anybody on the moon) which form the background of the biblical account. They must have been fully conversant with the latest scientific account of the origins of the universe. They knew all that and yet still felt it appropriate to believe that, "in the beginning" was God.

I have already posed a number of questions, on p.81, which we have to resolve if we are to understand this biblical account of creation. We saw that Genesis 1.1–24b is one of the latest parts of the Old Testament to be written; that it was written by a priest of the Second Temple probably towards the end of the fifth century BC; and that it was designed as the script for a great annual New Year Festival which celebrated the goodness of God's creation and the joy of the Sabbath day. Our priest was a learned man, steeped in the traditions of Israel, but also in the mathematical and astronomical knowledge of the Babylonians (which he would have learned during his time in exile) and a skilled poet.

What was to be *the format* of his poem? It was simple. The Jews had adopted the seven-day week from the Babylonians; the Temple Festival lasted seven days. What could be more natural than to celebrate the creation in a poem comprising seven stanzas, one for each day of creation? So each day concludes with a variable refrain: "And there was evening and there was morning, the first day …" etc.

What was to be *the content* of the poem? It was to portray God's creation against the background of the cosmological knowledge the Jews had learned from the Babylonians. This supposed the world to be a cake-shaped plateau, built on pillars going down into the abyss, and with a dome (the firmament) overarching it. The abyss above and beneath the earth (what we call space) consisted of water from which rain fell down and springs gushed up. Above the dome were the heavens, into which God had placed the sun, moon and stars – the former two daily tracking across the sky from east to west. On the earth, God created the varying species of creatures: of fish, birds, animals, and lastly, of mankind. But all of this pre-scientific information formed only the backdrop to the drama being described; it was not itself the chief content. That was the activity of God in creation and His relationship with humankind.

Nevertheless, the people of Bible times could still stand in awe before the vastness of the night sky above them. In times before air pollution and electric lighting, they would have seen far more stars than we can with the naked eye. In God's promise to Abraham, it is remarkable that he is promised as many descendents as the stars in the heavens and that they are as numerous as the grains of sand on the seashore (Genesis 15.5, 22.17, 26.4). And a shepherd such as Amos was wholly conversant with the night sky, naming God as "he who made the Pleiades and Orion" (Amos 5.8).

What was *the theology* of the poem? This was undoubtedly the matter of greatest importance to our priest-poet. He probably knew the creation story present in our Bibles from Genesis 2.4b onwards – stemming probably from the early Yahwistic (J) tradition. He may have regarded it as naively amusing, possibly embarrassing. He had learned from many centuries of Jewish faith and experience no longer to think of God in simple anthropomorphic terms (e.g. as a man walking in the Garden of Eden); but rather as a transcendent being, the Lord of Heaven and Earth, as He had been portrayed by a great prophet such as Isaiah (see, for example, Isaiah 40.12-31). Nor could he possibly accept the absurd notions of the polytheistic peoples of surrounding nations who worshiped the idols they had manufactured and regarded the sun, moon and stars as deities. Our priest has demythologized all that. In his creation poem, God had only to speak in order to create: "God said: Let there be light and there was light." Sun, moon and stars are as much created objects as the birds and the

bees. Last of all, God created humankind, comprising male and female (no
distinction here, no subordination of one to the other). It is in their
togetherness that they reflect God's image. The climax of it all is in the
completion of God's creative work, which listeners and readers were invited to
celebrate on the Sabbath day. Life was not intended as a matter of unending toil,
but one in which, our tasks accomplished, we should take rest. All in all, Genesis
1 is a huge intellectual-cum-spiritual leap forward from Genesis 2.

How can we understand such a passage today?

Genesis 1 is not a scientific account of creation and was never intended to be.
With the huge limitations of the scientific knowledge available 2,500 years ago,
how could it have been? However grandiose its conception, the biblical world
was a small world: with God in the heavens, Earth the focus of God's sole
attention, man the pinnacle of His creation, His steward ruling over the
kingdom of the animals. Sun, moon and stars were just the fairy-lights strung
across the firmament like so many Christmas decorations. But then it was a
poem written as the text for a religious drama, a work of poetic imagination. It
was written not for factual instruction so much as material for joyful
celebration in the Temple and a quiet Sabbath's contemplation.

How can we meaningfully use it today? Our scientific knowledge is immensely
greater than could have been dreamed of in biblical times (or even one hundred
years ago). We can meaningfully use the text of Genesis 1 only in so far as we
are able to substitute for its ancient Babylonian cosmology that made available
to us through the scientific discoveries of the past century. The astronauts on
Apollo 8 must have made such a substitution in their thinking. They will have
learned to marry their scientific "know-how" with faith in God as creator of a
universe incomprehensibly huge. We can be sure that they were fully conversant
with the latest understanding of the "Big Bang" origins of the universe, of the
ever expanding cosmos, of the moon as a "reject" from planet Earth's formation
some 4.5 billion years ago; and yet they could still read it with evident emotion
and belief that, however created, God was the power behind and within it all.

The big universe of modern cosmology

We now live in a very big universe, indeed so enormous that it largely defies our
imagination, with the Hubble Space Telescope picking up light that has taken 15
billion years to reach it. The Bible should never be used as the refuge of lazy or
frightened minds, as if we could possibly go on believing in the cosmological
notions of ancient civilizations. The way in which we read and understand the
Bible has to take into account the current state of knowledge as to how the
universe came to be what it is.

The Bible's embedment in local cultures

One of the realizations resultant on the modern study of the Bible is how deeply embedded is its entire narrative within the cultural environment of the Middle East. To cite Professor Ernest Wright's quotation from W F Albright, "No longer is the situation what it was 150 years ago when 'from the chaos of prehistory the Bible projected as though it were a monstrous fossil, with no contemporary evidence to demonstrate its authenticity and its origin in a human world like ours.'"[112] The accumulated evidence since then demonstrates that "the monstrous fossil" is deeply embedded in its surroundings. We have already seen that the Jewish people were always affected by the cultures surrounding them. The Babylonians believed that their great corpus of laws, many of them remarkably similar to those of the Hebrews such as that of "an eye for an eye and a tooth for a tooth," was the gift of their god Shamash. The story of the Great Flood could never have originated in Canaan, a dry land of mostly barren hills, but was wholly understandable stemming as it did from the great flood plains of the Euphrates and Tigris rivers. It wasn't only the Hebrews who came to a monotheistic belief in God. The Egyptians had arrived at monotheism (albeit briefly) when Aten was proclaimed the sole God, Lord of heaven and earth. A section of the book of Proverbs (22.17–24.22) is remarkably similar to the 30 proverbs contained in the Egyptian "The Instruction of Amen-em-ope" and was probably borrowed from it. Since much of the biblical message is emphasizing the distinctness of God's Chosen People from the pagan peoples around them, this other evidence cannot be ignored.

The Church's embedment in culture

The Christian Church too (in its myriad varieties) has also always been embedded in the prevailing cultures of each age. It is as if Christianity cannot be taken "neat" but has to be mixed in with other cultures (with the consequent danger of being so diluted as to become indistinguishable from them). The churches set within the Greek cities of the Middle East were markedly different from those later established in the West (from which stemmed eventually the schism between Roman Catholicism and Eastern Orthodoxy). All denominations inevitably reflect something of the social, economic, political and cultural environments of their origins. This is why each denomination has its distinctive features, some of which are less the consequence of theological preferences than of those reflecting cultural differences. For example, Methodism (especially that which was originally termed "Primitive") still reflects something of the fact that Wesley's preaching was particularly successful amongst solidly working-class communities, of Durham miners, Cornish china-

---

[112] G E Wright: *Biblical Archaeology*, The Westminster Press, 1962, p 18.

clay workers and farm laborers, and with huge consequences. Since the British Labour Party emerged from within such communities, the saying that "the Labour Party owed more to Methodism than to Marxism" is wholly justified.

Such is still the case. Most churches, especially in the Western world, are strongly influenced by the prevailing cultures of the 21st century and it could not be otherwise. There are some sects, such as the Amish Mennonite communities of the USA, who try "to stop the clock" and to freeze their entire way of living to that of the period of their foundation in the 17th century. To quote the *Encyclopaedia Britannica*: "The Amish are best known for their severely plain clothing and their nonconformed way of life. The men wear broad brimmed black hats, beards – but not moustaches – and homemade plain clothes fastened with hooks and eyes instead of buttons. The women wear bonnets, long full dresses with capes over the shoulders, shawls, and black shoes and stockings. No jewelry of any kind is worn. This cultural nonconformity is thought by the Amish to be obedience to biblical strictures, but it is primarily the continuance of 17th-century European rural costume. The Amish also shun telephones and electric lights and drive horses and buggies rather than automobiles. They are generally considered excellent farmers, but they often refuse to use modern farm machinery.[113]

Their way of life will seem attractive to many, but could hardly be followed by the majority of Christians in the West. These latter fly in jet aircraft, drive smart cars, prepare their lunch in the microwave, work much of the day at a computer, watch the world news on digital television, and can, if they are so interested, see what the weather is doing on the planet Jupiter, thanks to NASA. Much of our life's energy is spent within the parameters of our modern Western technologized society. How does the Bible get a look-in within this kind of world? Not that we should forget that the majority of Christians live in dire poverty in the Third World, without any access to the technology we take for granted.

The fact is that the biblical world was confined within the very narrow parameters of the limited knowledge available two thousand years ago. Just ponder the fact that to the people of Bible times, the Earth was the only planet known to them. It was at the center of God's creation. They knew of nothing beyond it. We today live in a very different world. The culture is overwhelmingly scientific and technological (at least is so in the West) although we cannot deny the bizarre recrudescence of superstition and sheer paganism within it. The saying is true that "those who reject belief in God don't believe in nothing – they believe in anything!"

---

[113] Reprinted with permission from *Encyclopaedia Britannica*, © 2003 by Encyclopaedia Britannica, Inc.

The Horizons of our Vision

By way of contrast with the biblical world, let us reflect on the horizons of our vision. We know, chiefly from the discoveries of the past century, the following:

❖ That the universe came into being some 15 billions years ago.

❖ It began with what is metaphorically called the "Big Bang" – from which space and time were born.

❖ From the "singularity," a super-heated density of sub-atomic particles, eventually emerged the simple elements of hydrogen, helium and lithium. During a period of "inflation," dense clouds dispersed in all directions, condensing into whirling galaxies, in which stars and planets were born. In the hot interiors of such stars, the heavier elements such as carbon, phosphorous, etc (essential to the eventual emergence of life) were cooked. The explosions of super-novae scattered these elements throughout their galaxies, including, of course, ours, the Milky Way. About which Polkinghorne wrote: "Every atom of carbon in every living being was once inside a star, from whose dead ashes we have all arisen."[114]

❖ About four and a half billion years ago, our solar system was born; within it the planets, including Earth and its satellite, the moon.

❖ For millions of years, Earth was a wasteland without possibility of life because of intense volcanic activity, electrical storms and deadly radiation from the sun.

❖ Only gradually were the protective layers of the ionosphere and the biosphere (i.e. an atmosphere in which life could emerge) able to envelope the planet.

❖ Life forms, at first very primitive, began appearing about two billion years ago. The various animal orders began in the sea, eventually invading the land.

❖ Hominids, the forerunners of Homo Sapiens, emerged out of the several species of primates, some two-three million years ago.

❖ Homo Sapiens come "onto the stage" within the past 200,000 years, creatures endowed with a brain three times the size of its ancestral species.

❖ From about 10,000 years ago, human beings have learned to make sophisticated tools out of flaked stone; hence to manufacture tools for agriculture, weapons for the hunt, and to make clothes and personal adornments.

❖ From about 8,000 years ago, human beings launch what we call "civilization" i.e. living in towns that become cities, in which rapid developments take place in the crafts of building, in various arts and crafts, in language skills, in irrigation of the land, in political and military organization, and in religious beliefs and practices. A religious attitude to life (mixed in with much superstition and magic) seems to be innate amongst all evolving humans. It is one characteristic that distinguishes us

---

[114] J Polkinghorne, *Science and Christian Belief*, SPCK, London, 1994, p 72.

from all other species. From their emergence, humans practice rituals expressive of social solidarity; of a sense of communication with "spirit" forces and pay special attention to the burial of their dead. These are obvious pointers to the beginnings of religious belief.

❖ From circa 5,000 years ago, forms of writing have been invented, at first pictorial, and then in an alphabetic script, significantly, in the Middle East. This made possible the eventual recording of historical events and human communication on a scale never possible before. It is against this background that the Bible Story commences, with God's calling of Abraham fitting appropriately into the Middle Eastern scene of the early to middle second millennium BC.

This is necessarily a sketchy account of what is by its nature a hugely complex story. Much of the scientific evidence is exceedingly difficult for those of us not scientifically trained to comprehend. Nevertheless, there are many easily accessible books, such as those of Isaac Asimov, of Philip Davies, John Polkinghorne and others, which will fill out the picture. What is immediately and starkly obvious is that we, members of the Human Race, have only just turned up! It's almost as if one has sat in a theatre for a three hour performance of a drama, and the famous actor we had paid our ticket to see appears on stage just five seconds before the final curtain comes down. We might feel like demanding our money back.

But that is not how we as humans normally see things. Nor can we know how God views the scene. Certainly, in view of our last five seconds arrival, that on a planet which orbits round a quite minor star, on a spiral wing of a galaxy that is just one of billions, we have to feel humble before the facts. We appear not to be the king-pins of creation that we had supposed ourselves to be. It may be, it seems increasingly likely, that there are considerable numbers of planets similar to ours, in other solar systems, in which life-forms may have developed, many possibly far superior to ours in knowledge and achievement. We may wonder: how does God relate to them?

Nevertheless, there is much that is remarkable about our situation. Some scientists are impressed at how much of our knowledge of what occurred at the Big Bang and subsequently points towards the notion that the eventual emergence of creatures such as ourselves was "in-built" from the start. This has led some to propose what is called "the anthropic principle," Some features of the physical universe give the appearance of being so exceedingly "fine tuned" (like tuning a radio to pick up the signals) to the emergence of life as to suggest that our appearance "on the stage" was foreseen from the beginning. This was expressed by Freeman Dyson: "The more I examine the universe and the details of its architecture, the more evidence I find that the universe in some sense must have known we were coming."[115]

We are literally the first generation of human beings to have a scientific knowledge of where we come from. Every human culture, from the most primitive onwards, has had its own origin stories, expressed in story-telling, in ritual, song and dance. Ours is the first generation to possess a scientific account of it. The consequences of this fact are immense. We know now that: 1) ... the physical laws which govern the world are universal, i.e. they are the same everywhere. 2) ... Creation did not occur as a once-off event in the far distant past, but is a continuing reality. 3) ... the universe is still expanding (contrary to all previous human assumptions that it was a stationary and unchanging system). 4) Humankind is a very late-comer onto the stage.

The Universe Story

All of this comprises what we should now learn to consider the *Universe Story*[115] (the title of a book by Brian Swimme and Thomas Berry) which should be required reading for all who have any influence over human affairs, for, rather like the satellite positioning devices, it shows us where we, the human race, are at and how we got here. The book represents a remarkably integrated understanding of the human situation, in the light of what we can only call the scientific revelations of the past two hundred years. It delineates for us the horizons of our thinking. And it should not unduly disturb those of us who believe in the biblical Revelation of God. Both authors maintain that the story cannot be adequately told without taking full account of both the scientific evidence and of what they term "the mythic dimension" – for the facts themselves are awesome.

Creation in flux

Even Albert Einstein assumed the universe to be a solid, stable, unchanging entity; but he had the humility to accept (on the basis of Edward Hubble's discoveries) that it is in constant flux, that we live in an expanding universe. Creation is therefore not something that occurred once and for all "x" number of years ago: it is continuous throughout the universe. So we should not speak nowadays of the "cosmos" (as if a completed object) but rather of

---

[115] Quoted in J Polkinghorne, Science and Christian Belief, SPCK London, 1994, on p 76, the quotation coming from F J Dyson, Disturbing the Universe, Harper & Row, 1979.
[116] *The Universe Story (From the Primordial Flaring Forth to the Ecozoic Era – a Celebration of the Unfolding of the Cosmos)*, by Brian Swimme and Thomas Berry, Arkana Penguin Books, 1994. © Brian Swimme. The book is the outcome of the authors' work at the Center for the Story of the Universe at the California Institute of Integral Studies in San Francisco – to which large numbers of scientists, philosophers and others contribute. The book is not an easy read for those, like myself, without a scientific education.

"cosmogenesis," a universe which is constantly in process of becoming. Every particle within the universe is directly linked together: it is one unity, one body (to use the biblical terminology). A remarkable unity underlies all that exists, as was so eloquently stated by the authors of *Only One Earth:*[117] "Not only are all forms of energy interchangeable. In the last analysis, energy and matter are interchangeable, too. The material universe of which we ourselves, our peoples and our planets are phantasmal parts is made up of a single sweeping pulsing force of energy, existing for eons in the spinning galaxies of the firmament, for minute flashes of time in our physical bodies and questing brains – but all parts of a common throbbing impulse of unimaginable force. The scientist's vision of orderly law, the philosopher's dream of overarching unity, the sage's sense of a single cooperative order are not baseless imaginings. They are facts, not dreams."

For the religious believer, this vision of an all-embracing unity is entirely consistent with the biblical image of the universe as God's creation.

Stewards of God's Creation

Just as the authors' purpose, in both the above books, is to awaken readers to our awesome human responsibility for our planetary home, so do they echo the biblical injunction, as God charged humankind with the stewardship of God's creation: "God blessed them, and God said to them, 'Be fruitful and multiply, and fill the earth and subdue it; and have dominion over the fish of the sea and over the birds of the air and over every living thing that moves upon the earth.' God said, 'See, I have given you every plant yielding seed that is upon the face of all the earth, and every tree with seed in its fruit; you shall have them for food. And to every beast of the earth, and to every bird of the air, and to everything that creeps on the earth, everything that has the breath of life, I have given every green plant for food.' And it was so. God saw everything that he had made, and indeed, it was very good. And there was evening and there was morning, the sixth day." (Genesis1.28-31)

It was unfortunate that human beings should exploit the words "subdue" and "have dominion over" as invitations to an all-out rape and ravishment of the natural world from which we are now reaping the catastrophic consequences. If, a hundred years ago, it was possible for our forbears to suppose that the Bible could serve as handbook and guide to the entirety of human living, it is clear that it cannot do so any more. It alone teaches us the true knowledge of God.

---

[117] *Only One Earth, The Care and Maintenance of a Small Planet* by Barbara Ward and Rene Dubois, Penguin Books in association with Andre Deutsch, pp 71-2. © The Report on the Human Environment Inc.

SYNTHESIS: A CHRISTIAN UNIVERSAL VIEW

GOD

THE UNIVERSE OF GOD'S CREATION

ALL TRUTH IS GOD'S TRUTH

GENERAL REVELATION	SPECIAL REVELATION	GENERAL REVELATION
The World of Scientific Research Discovery & Technological applications	God reveals Himself through Patriarchs, Prophets and Priests	The World of Human Endeavor
Each discovery offers "knowledge of good and evil"	In Jesus & through Apostles, Preachers Teachers, conveyed in the Biblical Record	In the great World Religions and
For good or evil? Genetic Modification Cloning: for medical purposes Information-sharing via World-wide Web Space Research	Revelation is received by the	Philosophies, Cultures, Arts and Crafts, in Literature. Art and Music
Dangers: World over-population Shrinkage of resources Pollution of air, earth, water Global Warming War and Terrorism	Illumination of the Holy Spirit, by conviction of the Mind, the assent of the Conscience within the Community of God's People	? The will to forge an international community, without Racism, Sexism, Ageism 'No peace between nations without peace between the Religions'

For explanatory notes, please see Appendix 354

But as parameter for our wider secular knowledge, it has to be replaced by *The Universe Story* (not the book itself – it isn't a substitute for the Bible – but the story it contains). Within it, the Bible remains hugely important. For, however spectacular are the findings of science and the technological fruits of science (such as the computer at which I am writing), science by itself can make no theological or moral judgments. Science can neither prove nor disprove God. The fact is that every fresh scientific discovery offers once more "the knowledge of good and evil" (Genesis 2.17). It can provide us with reams of evidence, it can offer us numerous options, but, it cannot decide whether to take this pathway or that. An immediate illustration concerns the genetic modification of plants. Trial plantings are already yielding important evidence as to whether the herbicides used on GM crops damage wild life more than do those employed in conventional farming. To date, the evidence is ambiguous. When scientists try "to play God," they can make the most awful mistakes for which humanity has to pay terrible costs. Most of the moral decisions we are obliged to take depend not so much on the facts, but on our evaluation of human life and its impact on the environment. To believe that "the earth is the Lord's and the fullness thereof" (Psalms 24.1), that all life is sacred because God-given, and that we are responsible before God for the decisions we take, will in the end weigh more heavily in our judgments than the mere facts of the case.

Salvation: individual or collective?

Much of Christian thinking, especially of the more evangelical sort, during the 19th and 20th centuries, saw the Christian mission in terms of the salvation of souls. A missionary like Hudson Taylor was obsessed by the vision of Chinese men and women dying without knowledge of Christ, so much so that he spent a lifetime in China rescuing "brands from the burning." There were others who, beyond their deeply religious commitment, accepted their moral obligation to address pressing social problems, as did Wilberforce, Shaftesbury, Barnardo and William Booth. But even these would have seen themselves as seeking to change individual lives rather than trying to change society at the political and national level. That was rather the vision of the Christian socialists such as Kingsley and Maurice.

This individualistic way of thinking prevailed well into the 20th century. Christianity was largely seen, both within and without the Church, as an individual option, a harmless hobby, having little effect on how one earned one's living, voted in elections, or had any repercussions on society at large. This is one of the facets of Christianity in the Western world which most bewilders adherents of other faiths, such as the followers of Islam or Sikhism, in which religion is completely communitarian, social, definitely not a matter of private option. No wonder they perceive our society as godless, immoral and anarchic (without appreciating how far Christian faith, as leaven in the lump, still permeates many of our institutions and influences lives that are not overtly Christian).

It is clear that for the 21st century, the individualist notion of Christianity is not adequate to face the challenges of our century. It is not true to the biblical roots of our faith. It is the case that, within the world of the gospel, men and women asked the question, "What must I do to be saved?" and received the reply, "Believe in the Lord Jesus Christ." Yet such a person was immediately bound into the Christian community. The solitary Christian is unknown in the New Testament. I would not deny for one moment that we are invited to be in a personal relationship with God in Christ and that that is the surest foundation for one's life. But every Christian, being baptized into Christ, is thereby made a member of His body. The teaching of Paul in 1 Corinthians makes plain that each member of the body is both supported by the rest of the body and has within it a vital role to play.

The world today faces crises of such mega proportions that only a concerted effort which eventually involves every person on the planet can hope to address them.

Universal Salvation

As Christians, we have to alter our perspective so as to seek corporate salvation, ecological salvation, environmental salvation. This is in line with biblical thought. However naively expressed in terms of ancient mythologies, Genesis chapters 1-11 speak of the entire world as God's creation, of Adam as the prototypical father of the human species, of the whole race as involved in wickedness and therefore in need of redemption, and even after the disaster of the Flood, offers all humankind a covenant in which God binds Himself to the salvation of the whole race. Even the calling of Israel to a special relationship with God is not, ultimately, for its own aggrandizement, but so that "in you all the families of the earth will be blessed" (Genesis 12.2). The later calling of the Church is not for its own benefit but so as to be the hands and feet and lips of Christ in bringing blessing to all peoples to the ends of the earth.

There is an apt biblical image for this notion of the Christian mission. It is to be found in the narrative of Paul's shipwreck off the coast of Malta, in Acts 27. The imagery of the Church as the Ark or ship of salvation has been much used in the past. Medieval lithographs depicted smug-looking Christians, "the saved," on deck, whilst the "damned" swam desperately in the ship's wake. The image is no longer appropriate. For the situation in today's world, threatened with storms on every side, is that we all sink or swim together. What is at stake is the salvation of the human species, and with it, every other species of creature with which we share our planetary home. Martin Rees, the Astronomer Royal, has recently published a book entitled *Our Final Century: a Scientist's Warning.* Reviewing the imminent dangers from many different quarters, his assessment is that humankind has no higher than a 50% chance of surviving the next hundred years. In such a context, Paul's shipwreck is an informative depiction. With the ship in danger of breaking up on rocks, the crew on the point of abandoning ship (leaving its passengers to their fate), the Roman soldiers on the verge of putting their prisoners to the sword lest any should escape, Paul saves the situation. "When neither sun nor stars appeared for many days, and no small tempest raged, all hope of our being saved was at last abandoned. Since they had been without food for a long time, Paul then stood up among them and said, 'Men, you should have listened to me and not have set sail from Crete and thereby avoided this damage and loss. I urge you now to keep up your courage, for there will be no loss of life among you, but only of the ship. For last night there stood by me an angel of the God to whom I belong and whom I worship, and he said, "Do not be afraid, Paul; you must stand before the emperor; and indeed, God has granted safety to all those who are sailing with you." So keep up your courage, men, for I have faith in God that it will be exactly as I have been told.'"(Acts 27.20-25). After yet more hazards, the narrative concludes: "And so it was that all were brought safely to land."

Christians should abandon any narcissistic attention to their own souls, remembering Jesus' words: "For those who want to save their life will lose it, and those who lose their life for my sake, and for the sake of the gospel, will save it. (Mark 8.35) We have to accept our true mission, not to behave as a holy huddle of "the saved," but rather, to be as "leaven in the dough" and "salt in the dish" working as God's secret agents in the business of the salvation of the world and everything within it.

God so loved the world

The core belief cherished by most Christians is that "God so loved the world that he gave his only Son, so that everyone who believes in him may not perish but may have eternal life." God did not send the Son into the world to condemn the world, but in order that the world might be saved through him."(John 3.16-17). This text that we trip off our tongues so lightly may, with emphasis on the "whoever believes," suggest an individualist notion of salvation. But if we stress rather "the world" which God so loved, the whole world, and by extension the entirety of the universe and the intention "that the world might be saved," we have a vision of the universal salvation willed by God. If that is God's purpose, then we as Christians have no option other than to strive towards that goal in cooperation with all men and women of goodwill.

Appendix (referring to p.349)

Notes on Synthesis: a Christian universal view

1. There is something a little ridiculous in trying to summarize an entire philosophy in one simple diagram, but here it is. I think it important in a universe of such complexity to be able to hold one unified vision of it. The scientific realization that everything from atoms to elephants to galaxies is a unity fits in well with the Christian conviction that everything is the creation of the One God.

2. By placing 'God' within a black cloud is both in line with the Biblical view of God as mysterious, as being as much hidden as revealed, dwelling in the darkness of the 'Shekinah'[118] ; and with the Christian mystical tradition of the "The Cloud of Unknowing", the work of an anonymous English mystic of the 14th Century. God "may be well be loved, but not thought".[119]

3. Within this tradition we only know God because He has chosen to reveal himself to us. Christian theology has traditionally distinguished between **general** and **special revelation**. By the former is meant that we can know something of God through all that He has created. The apostle Paul stated this clearly in Rom.1.19-20: "*For what can be known about God is plain to them, because God has shown it to them. Ever since the creation of the world his eternal power and divine nature, invisible though they are, have been understood and seen through the things he has made.*" This carries the corollary that all Truth is God's Truth, as much in scientific research as in theological study. There is nothing in the Universe that can be alien to God.

4. But the Judeo-Christian tradition has always held that God chose to reveal himself to a particular people in a particular situation, namely to Abraham and his descendents, the Jewish people; and, in a fresh development, in Jesus of Nazareth and the embryonic Christian community that gathered around him. This is **special revelation.** Its intention was never exclusivist. God's choosing of Abraham was with the intention that, through him, all the peoples of the earth should be blessed (Gen.12. 3). Nor was Jesus' message and mission exclusively to the Jewish people. His Gospel was to be proclaimed to the ends of the earth.

---

[118] This Hebrew word stood for the notion that God's holiness was so radiant as to be unbearable to human eyes; therefore God in His mercy appeared to the Israelites as a dark cloud, such as hung above Mt. Sinai (Ex. 19.9, 18, 21) or in the Tabernacle in the desert.
[119] The Cloud of Unknowing: ed. Clifton Walters, Penguin Classics, London, 1961.

5. But 'general' and 'special' are not mutually antagonistic.[120] Secular truth and religious truth are not mutually exclusive. Many scientists have felt that the moment of discovery came as 'a flash of recognition', i.e. as the revelation of some aspect of reality. And it is the case that much theological study has to use the same inductive tools as do the sciences, i.e. by the accumulation and evaluation of data, the testing of them against other data, then the drawing of conclusions. Of course, religious experience is not so easily evaluated, except that the newer tools of psychology and sociology are rightly applied to religious phenomena as to any other. But there are areas of religious experience which are not accessible to scientific investigation. God is not discernible through telescope or microscope. Stephen Jay Gould has argued powerfully that Science and Religion should respect each other's rightful autonomy.[121]

6. Therefore I would like there to be 'fuzzy edges' both to the concepts of general and special revelation, as also to the three columns beneath them. I have placed centrally a Christian view of God's revelation, from God's initiative in sending his messengers to Israel as recorded in the Old Testament; and in the coming of Jesus and the founding of the Christian Church in the New. In the second box, I summarize how revelation is received: by the Spirit's help, bringing conviction to the mind, assent to the conscience, within the shared community of the Church. But I cannot deny that adherents of other religions would regard themselves as being equally the recipients of special revelation. The matter of the relationship between the different world faiths is far beyond the scope of this book.[122]

7. My left-hand column takes for granted the precarious situation that our entire Planet now faces, with many dangers threatening to overwhelm all living species (including ours) unless drastic action is taken by all of humankind together. And it takes for granted that every scientific breakthrough offers humanity further knowledge of 'good' and 'evil'. It behooves those of us who believe both that *"the earth is the Lord's and the fullness thereof"* to accept that human beings have a major responsibility as stewards of it. We need vigilance to ensure that the new technologies are used for the environmental good; and not misused for selfish vested interests.

---

[120] Colin Gunton deals lucidly with all the issues in his "A Brief Theology of Revelation", T & T. Clark, Edinburgh, 1995.

[121] S.J. Gould, Rocks of Ages: Science and Religion in the Fullness of Life, Jonathan Cape, London, 1999.

[122] But an excellent starting point for investigation and discussion is to be found in "The Faith of Other Men" by Wilfred Cantwell Smith, a Mentor Book, The New American Library, New York, 1962. He takes a simple notion of faith as 'trustfulness in Life' to be fundamental to most or all religions.

8. The right hand column exemplifies the rich diversity of human skills and cultures. In the situation mentioned above, Christians need to be wholly ecumenical in outlook, spurning all narrow sectarianism and therefore allying ourselves with all organizations that promote the welfare not only of the human species but of every species with whom we share this planet. It is to the huge credit of Hans Kung to have established his Institute for a Global Ethic[123]; one of the few theologians to be promoting a truly global approach to the world's problems, knowing full well that mankind does not lack the knowledge and the skills to tackle world problems, but only the Will. As President Kennedy reportedly said: "To feed myself is a material matter; to feed the world is a spiritual matter".

---

[123] Hans Kung, Global Responsibility: in Search of a New World Ethic, SCM Press, London, 1990.

Acknowledgements

I gladly acknowledge the help and advice of many friends and colleagues, in particular the Revds. Donald Hilton, Bruce Waldron and fellow Church members Sheila Inwards, Jethro Free and Ken Jones, who have read my script in draft, corrected mistakes and offered many wise comments and suggestions; and to all who have sat through my lectures at the Oxted Christian Centre and at Emmanuel Church, Bungay, whose questions and comments have stimulated my thinking. Of course, I alone am responsible for the views expressed.

1. I am grateful to those Publishing houses which have permitted the quotation of Bible passages from various versions of the Bible as follows:
a. Scripture quotations are from the *New Revised Standard Version of the Bible* (except where indicated otherwise), copyright © 1989 by the Division of Christian Education of the National Council of the Churches of Christ in the USA. Used by permission. All rights reserved.
b. Scriptures and additional materials quoted are from the *Good News Bible* © 1994 published by the Bible Societies/HarperCollins Publishers Ltd.,UK. *Good News Bible* © American Bible Society 1966, 1971, 1976, 1992. Used with permission. Quotation from the Good News Bible, 2nd Edition. The maps included at pages 61, 63, 115 & 136 are by kind permission of the Bible Society.
c. *Revised English Bible* © Oxford University Press and Cambridge University Press 1989.
d. *Biblia Hebraica*, edited by Rudolf Kittel, 3rd Edition, © 1937 by Wurttembergische Bibelanstalt Stuttgart.
e. *Synopsis Quattuor Evangeliorum*, edited by Kurt Aland, 1st Edition, © 1963 by Deutsche Bibelgesellschaft Stuttgart.

2. I acknowledge and thank those Churches and Publishing Houses which have given me permission to quote from their publications: especially to the United Reformed Church in Great Britain for "The Statement concerning the Nature, Faith and Order of the United Reformed Church".
Mr. Terence Copley for permission to use three cartoons from *The Bible: the story of the book*, Bible Society 1990, © Terence Copley; and the Revd.E.W.L. Davies, for his personal permission to use his cartoons under the name of "Taffy Davies".

I am obliged to the following Publishers for the permission to quote from the following sources:
a. The Oxford University Press for permission to use extracts from T*he Text of the New Testament* by Metzger,B.M.© 1964; *Holy Scripture: Canon, Authority, Criticism* by Barr, J. © 1983, (UK Rights); *The Oxford Dictionary of Quotations*

for one quote from Moliere; and *The Oxford Bible Commentary* edited by Barton, J. & Muddiman, J. © (2001).

b. The SCM-Canterbury Press (17/12/03) for quotations from *Hindu and Christian in Vrindaban,* by Klaus Klostermayer, © 1969; *The Historical Jesus,* G.Theissen & A. Merz, © 1998; *For Faith and Freedom,* L. Hodgson, © 1968; *Christian Apologetics,* A. Richardson, © 1955; and *The Interpretation of the Bible in the Church,* edited by L. Houlden, © 1995

c. The Westminster John Knox Press; for quotations from *Holy Scripture: Canon, Authority, Criticism.* ©1983 James Barr. Used with permission from Westminster John Knox Press. (US Rights) Also for *New Testament Apocrypha,* North American English language rights only.

d. HarperCollins Publishers for extracts from *Infallible?,* by Hans Kung, reprinted by permission of HarperCollins Publishers Ltd. © 1971 William Collins Sons & Co Ltd. London

e. The Lutterworth Press: *New Testament Apocrypha,* Vol.1, E. Hennecke, © 1959 J.C.B. Mohr (Paul Siebeck) Tubingen, English Translation © 1963 Lutterworth Press (UK Rights).

f. Wm. B. Eerdmans Publishing Company for quotation from *Fundamentalism and the Word of God* by J.I. Packer, © The Inter-Varsity Fellowship, 1958

g. Mr. Alan Untermann for one quotation from *The Jews: their religious beliefs and practices,* published by Routledge & Kegan Paul, Boston, London and Henley 1981.

h. *The Tablet,* the international Catholic Weekly, for permission to quote from Eamon Duffy's Open Day lecture published in *The Tablet* on 4th July 1998. For queries, please contact http://www.thetablet.co.uk

i. Chapter House Limited, for a quotation from *The Canon of Scripture,* by F.F. Bruce, © 1988 F.F. Bruce.

j. The SPCK for brief quotations from *Women before God* by L. Byrne, London, © Lavinia Byrne, 1988 and from *Science and Christian Belief* by J. Polkinghorne, London, © John Polkinghorne,1994.

k. The Tyndale Society: for one quotation by W.R. Cooper from preface to facsimile edition of 2000, published by the British Library, © The Tyndale Society.

l. Penguin Books Ltd.: *Only One Earth,* by B. Wood and R. Dubois, published by Penguin Books in association with Andre Deutsch, © The Report on the Human Environment Inc. Also *The Universe Story,* by B. Swimme and T. Berry, © Brian Swimme, Arkana Penguin Books, © Brian Swimme 1992.

m. *The Encyclopaedia Britannica*: for Para. on the Amish; Reprinted with permission from Encyclopaedia Britannica, © 2003 by Encyclopaedia Britannica, Inc. Also, a definition of the "Enlightenment".

n. The BBC: for quotation from *History of Britain,* Vol. 3, by S. Schama, © Simon Schama, 2002.

o. Random House: quotation from *The Victorians,* by A.N. Wilson, London, 2002

p. Fourth Estate Ltd. permission to quote from *Galileo's Daughter*, D. Sobel, London, © Dava Sobel 1999 (UK rights only)
q. Zondervan (New Christian Classics): for *The Book and the Parchments*, F.F Bruce, © 1984, F.F.Bruce.

DISCLAIMERS:
We have sought permission, but received no reply from the Costello Publishing Company, New York and Dominican Publications, Dublin, 1996 for permission to quote excerpts from V*atican Council II, Constitutions, Decrees, Declarations,* General Editor, Austin Flannery, O.P." ." Nor have I been able to trace the copyright holders of *Documents from Old Testament Times*, edited by D. Winton Thomas, originally published as a Harper Torchbook, Harper & Row, New York, 1958, © 1958, by Thomas Nelson and Sons Ltd.
Nor from the US Rights for Dava Sobel's *Galileo's Daughter*.

I apologise in advance for any omissions with regard to copyright; and will seek to put right wherever I may have inadvertently trespassed on somebody's rights.

Finally, I wish to thank Mr. John Hunt and his staff, Anne O'Rorke, Maria Watson and Donna Wood, for their unfailing patience, helpful advice and encouragement; also Andrew Milne Design who designed the book's layout and improved my illustrations.

Roy Robinson

Bibliography

This list is highly selective. My intention is to list books known to myself which are easily accessible, readable by people without theological training and reliable. I will not list the more specialist and technical books unless they are so outstanding as to be indispensable.

General Introductions to the Bible:
BARTON, John *What is the Bible?* Triangle. SPCK London 1991
COPLEY, Terence *The Bible: the Story of the Book* Bible Society. London 1990
Ed. ROGERSON, John *The Oxford Illustrated History* of the Bible Oxford Oxford.1990

Reference Books:
Ed. METZGER, Bruce & COOGAN, Michael *The Oxford Companion to the Bible* Oxford New York 1993
Ed. RICHARDSON, Alan *A Theological Word Book of the Bible* SCM London 1957
BRUEGGEMANN, Walter: *Reverberations of Faith*, Westminster John Knox Press, Louisville, 2002

Bible Commentaries, one volume:
BROWN, FITZMYER, & MURPHY *The New Jerome Bible Commentary* Geoffrey Chapman London 1990
BARTON & MUDDIMAN *Oxford Bible Commentary* Oxford 2001
BLACK, Matthew & ROWLEY, *H.H. Peake's Commentary on the Bible* Thomas Nelson LondonNew York 1962

Textual Criticism:
METZGER. Bruce *The Text of the New Testament* Oxford Oxford 1964
BRUCE, F.F. *The Books and the Parchments* Pickering & Inglis 4th Edition 1984

Historical Surveys of the Study of the Old Testament:
ROWLEY, Harold *The Old Testament and Modern Study* OUP London 1961
CLEMENTS, Ronald *A Century of Old Testament Study* Lutterworth Press London 1976

Introductions to the Old Testament & History of Israel:
ANDERSON, Bernard *The Living World of the Old Testament* Longman London 2nd Edition 1967
BRIGHT, John *A History of Israel* SCM Press London 3rd Impression 1964
BRUEGGEMANN, Walter *An Introduction to the Old Testament* Westminster John Knox Louisville London 2003
WESTERMANN,Claus *Handbook to the Old Testament* SPCK London 1969

Old Testament Issues:
DAVIDSON, Robert *The Courage to Doubt* SCM & Trinity Press International London Philadelphia 1983
CLEMENTS, Ronald *Wisdom in Theology* Eerdmans Grand Rapids 1992

Introduction to the New Testament:
MOULE, C.F.D. *The Birth of the New Testament* A & C. Black London 1962
NEILL, Stephen & WRIGHT, Tom *The Interpretation of the New Testament, 1861 - 1961* Oxford London 2nd Edition 1988
BROWN, Raymond *An Introduction to the New Testament* Doubleday New York 1997

The Gospels:
BURRIDGE, Richard *Four Gospels, One Jesus?* SPCK London 2nd Impression 1997
STANTON, Graham *The Gospels and Jesus* Oxford New York 1989
STANTON, Graham *Gospel Truth?* Fount, HarperCollins London 1995

Jesus Research:
ALLEN, Charlotte *The Human Christ* Lion, Oxford The Free Press, New York 1998
DUNN, James *The Evidence for Jesus* SCM London 1985
POWELL, Mark *The Jesus Debate* Lion Oxford 1998
SANDERS, E.P. *The Historical Figure of Jesus* Allen Lane London 1993
WRIGHT, Tom & BORG, Marcus *The Meaning of Jesus* SPCK London 1999

Apocryphal Gospels:
PAGELS, Elaine *The Gnostic Gospels* Penguin London 1979
GRANT, Robert & FREEDMAN, David *The Secret Sayings of Jesus* Collins Fontana London 1960

The Dead Sea Scrolls:
CAMPBELL, Jonathan *Deciphering the Dead Sea Scrolls* Fontana London 1996
SHANKS, Hershel *Understanding the Dead Sea Scrolls* SPCK London 1992
VERMES, Geza *The Complete Dead Sea Scrolls in English* Penguin London 1997
VERMES, Geza *The Dead Sea Scrolls: Qumran in Perspective* SCM London 1994

The Apostle Paul:
DUNN, James *The Theology of Paul the Apostle* T.T. Clark Edinburgh 1998
ZIESLER, John *Pauline Christianity* Oxford Oxford 1983
WRIGHT, Tom *What Saint Paul really said* Lion Oxford 1997
BARRETT, C.K. *Paul, an Introduction to his Thought* Continuum London 1994

The Authority of the Bible:
BARR, James *Holy Scripture: Canon, Authority,* Criticism Oxford New York
BARTON, John *People of the Book: the Authority of the Bible in Christianity* SPCK London 1988
GUNTON, Colin *A Brief Theology of Revelation* T.& T. Clark Edinburgh 1995
KUNG, Hans *Infallible?* Collins London 1971

On Fundamentalism:
BARR, James *Escaping from Fundamentalism* SCM London 1984
SPONG, John *Rescuing the Bible from Fundamentalism* Harper Collins San Francisco 1991

On the English Bible:
BRUCE, F.F. *The English Bible* Methuen London 1961
DANIELL, David *The Bible in English* Yale New York 2003
McGRATH, Alister *In the Beginning: Story of the King James Bible* Hodder & Stoughton London 2001

The Reformation and the Bible:
McGRATH, Alister *Reformation Thought: an Introduction* Blackwell Oxford 1993
CALVIN, John *Institutes of the Christian Religion* Westminster John Knox

On the Interpretation of the Bible:
BARTON, John, ed. *The Cambridge Companion to Biblical Interpretation* Cambridge UP Cambridge 1998
MORGAN,R & BARTON, J *Biblical Interpretation* Oxford Oxford 1988
GOMES, Peter *The Good Book* Wm.Morrow New York 1996

Religion and Science
DAVIES, Paul *The Mind of God* Penguin London 1992
GOULD, Stephen *Rocks of Ages* Jonathan Cape London 1999
POLKINGHORNE John *Science and Creation* SPCK London 1988
SOBEL, Dava *Galileo's Daughter* Fourth Estate London 1999

Global Issues:
KUNG, Hans *Global Responsibility* SCM London 1990
REES, Martin *Our Final Century* Heinemann London 2003
SWIMME, Brain & BERRY, Thomas *The Universe Story* Penguin London 1992
WARD, Barbara & DUBOS, Rene *Only One Earth* Pelican London 1972